美国社会与文化新概览

主 编 田 耀

天津大学出版社
TIANJIN UNIVERSITY PRESS

图书在版编目(CIP)数据

美国社会与文化新概览 / 田耀主编. —天津：天津大学出版社，2018.3
ISBN 978-7-5618-5806-6

Ⅰ.①美…　Ⅱ.①田…　Ⅲ.①英语—阅读教学—高等学校—教材②美国—概况　Ⅳ.①H319.37：K

中国版本图书馆CIP数据核字(2017)第075336号

出版发行　天津大学出版社
地　　址　天津市卫津路92号天津大学内(邮编:300072)
电　　话　发行部:022-27403647
网　　址　publish.tju.edu.cn
印　　刷　昌黎县佳印印刷有限公司
经　　销　全国各地新华书店
开　　本　185mm×260mm
印　　张　22.5
字　　数　738千
版　　次　2018年3月第1版
印　　次　2018年3月第1次
定　　价　49.00元

天外“求索”文库编委会

编委会

主　编　田　耀

副主编　王雪莹　田　路　蒋　瑜

参　编　窦　伟　张　婷　巨威莉
王秋燕　张　欣　张瑞晓
苏二萍　刘卫珍　王雅平
于秀玉　张　驰　郭光迪
陈青秋　季光鑫　田增润
申丽娜　裴丽萍　王　鸽
王　倩　王雨奇　田卓妍
罗蓓蓓　王　佳　王　蓓

前　　言

《美国社会与文化新概览》一书共分22章，主要包括美国土地与人口、政府、政治、宗教、教育、体育与娱乐、经济、影响美国社会文化发展的主要历史事件、工农业、外交、媒体、文学及音乐等内容。与目前已出版的同类书籍相比，本书主要体现了一个”新”字，大部分内容涉及2015或2016年的相关话题，力争每一个章节都能涵盖符合21世纪读者需求的新内容，所以本书是一部了解当今美国社会文化发展的全新著作。

有人说20世纪在一定意义上说是美国的世纪，在过去百年中美国在科技和经济上取得了巨大的进步，从一个被殖民的国家摇身一变成为世界强国。究其原因，除了美国拥有优越的天时地利条件，在两次世界大战中不但未伤元气，反而还刺激了经济的发展，掠夺了大量第三世界国家的资源以及美国人民思想较为开放、勇于开拓创新等因素外，还和美国能够不断促进科技、工农业和教育等的发展和改革，培养出大批优秀人才，推动和引导经济与社会的发展密不可分。

俗话说，不了解美国社会文化，就不能全面了解美国，不了解美国就不能够全面了解世界文化。美国作为一个历史不过几百年的国家，却能在经济、工农业、军事、教育等方方面面达到世界领先水平，一定有我们可以借鉴和学习的地方，肯定会对我国的社会主义事业发展有一定的启示作用。我们可以把此书当作一个窗口，通过这个窗口了解美国社会文化的方方面面。读者从中既可以获得美国社会与文化生活方面的新信息和新知识，又可以提高英语水平。

编者

2018.1

Contents

Chapter One

Land and People

Unit 1 A Panoramic View

What people do with their geography is an exciting tale. So does the partnership of land and people in the United States. The United States of America is situated in the central-southern part of the North America, with Canada to the north, Mexico and Gulf of Mexico to the South, the Atlantic Ocean to the east and the Pacific Ocean to the west. With the exception of Alaska, which borders on northwest Canada, and Hawaii, Which lies in the Pacific, all the other states are on the mainland. As a result, one primary characteristic of the American landscape is its insulation(隔绝) from Europe and Asia. It offers itself a haven for those who wish to seek a new life free of restrictions. The immigrants in its early history enjoy a great chance to create a different life.

The United State has a total area of 9,629,091 square kilometers, which makes it the fourth largest country in the world. On a topographic map of the United States, the mountains look like jaded masses, the plains like vast open flat spaces, and the rivers like meandering threads. Much of the geography of the United States was determined from 10,000 to 25,000 years ago. At that time, the great polar ice cap flowed over the North American continent and ground it into a number of major changes.

On the Atlantic shore of the United States, much of the northern coast is rocky and uninviting (令人反感的), but the middle and the southern Atlantic coast rises gently from the sea then becomes rolling coastal lowland. To the west of this coastal lowland lie the Appalachian Mountains, which extend from southwest Maine to central Alabama. These are old mountains, largely eroded away, with rounded contours (轮廓), as forested as a rule to their summits. Few of these raise much above 1,100 meters.

Beyond the Appalachian Mountains are the great Central Lowland and the Great Plains stretching westwards until stopped by **the Rocky Mountains**[1]. The soil here is fertile, the climate is favorable, and the rainfall is moderate. Because of these, it is the most important agricultural area in the United States, known variously as "the Barn (谷仓) of America", "the Corn Belt", and so on.

The Rocky Mountains is regarded as "the backbone of the continent". They are young mountains with high, rough and irregular shape.

The west land of the Rockies appears to be tumbled masses of mountains. Actually, however, it is made up of quite distinct and separate regions. Such facts explain the establishment of the many national parks here—38 in all. The most famous ones include Yellowstone National Park, the Grand Canyon National Park and so on. At the same time, here lies a large area of desert, Death Valley, as well as the most extensive lowland—the Great Valley of California.

Separated from the mainland by Canadian territory, the state of Alaska occupies the extreme northwest portion of the North American continent, while a group of Pacific islands formed by volcanoes rising sharply from the ocean floor compose the state of Hawaii.

The United States enjoys abundant（充裕的）fresh water due to the rivers and lakes flowing on the continent. The Mississippi is one of the world's great continental rivers. It has been called the "**Father of Waters**"[2]. The Mississippi River system consists of the main river itself and more than 40 tributaries（支流）which drain 28 states, for a drainage area of 3,222,000 square kilometers. The Mississippi flows some 6,400 kilometers from its northern sources in the Rocky Mountains to the Gulf of Mexico. Through its upper course, it wanders along, appearing lazy and harmless. But the lower Mississippi area, like Ohio, is subject to great floods, which, nevertheless, spread alluvium（冲积层）over the land and increased its fertility.

Like Mississippi, all the rivers to the east of the Rocky Mountains finally reach the Atlantic; all the waters to the west of the Rocky Mountains finally arrive at the Pacific. Thus, the crests（山峰）of the Rocky Mountains are known as the continental divide.

The two great rivers of the Pacific side are the Columbia River, which rises in drains in the north, and the Colorado River in the south. In the dry western country, both rivers are vital sources of life.

Another important river in the southwestern part of the country is the Rio Grande, about 3,200 kilometers long. It forms a natural boundary between Mexico and the United States and performs as an important irrigation source for both the southwestern United States and northern Mexico.

The most important lakes in America are the Great Lakes. They lie between the United States and Canada, extending for almost 244,106 square kilometers. The lakes were estimated to contain about half of the world's fresh water. The Great Lakes include Lake Michigan, Lake Superior, Lake Huron, Lake Erie and Lake Ontario. Only Lake Michigan is entirely surrounded by American territory, while the other four are shared with Canada.

With its huge range of latitude（纬度）and altitude（海拔）, the USA includes a full range of climate zones. The continental land mass itself has a big effect, with inland areas experiencing much greater extremes of hot and cold. The USA is subject to a range of climate-related calamities（灾难）—**hurricanes**[3] in the Southeast, **tornadoes**[4] on the plains, floods around the main rivers, severe snowstorms in the mountains and northern plains, forest fire in the West and California. Here is a summary of conditions in the main regions.

New England has a cool, temperate climate, with warm summers, cold winters and snow in higher and inland areas. Atlantic Coast states become warmer and milder at more southerly latitudes, with longer summers and fewer snow winters. Florida and the Gulf Coast are warm all year round and can be very wet and humid. Great Lakes states have a continental climate, quite warm in summer and very cold in winter, with the lakes usually frozen for several months. Great Plains states have a more temperate continental climate, with less severe winters further south.

Western Mountain & Plateau Areas are mild（暖和的）in summer and very cold in winter, with heavy snowfall, especially in the north. All the higher-altitude areas get very cold in winters, but the amount of precipitation decreases further south. The extensive desert areas are cold in winter, hot in summer and dry most of the year. The Low Desert areas are even hotter and drier. Pacific Coast is warm year round in the south, becoming cooler in Northern California, Oregon and Washington. Rainfall is high anywhere north of San Francisco.

There is no doubt that the physical environment helps define human opportunities, but it does not in itself determine human activities. In general, the more advanced technology is, the greater leeway（余地）a population has in dealing with the land. In this book, our central interest will be the concerto（协奏曲）between the geography and the human imprint on the landscape.

Notes

1. the Rocky Mountains 落基山脉：位于北美洲西部，从加拿大横越美国西部直到新墨西哥州，绵延超过 4 800 千米。此山脉的最高峰是埃尔伯特峰，位于科罗拉多州境内，高度有 4 401 米。罗布森峰是加拿大境内的最高峰，高度为 3 954 米。整个落基山脉系统是美国地文区的一大部分。

2. Father of Waters 河流之父：指密西西比河（The Mississippi River），是世界第四长河，也是北美洲流程最长、流域面积最广、水量最大的河流。“密西西比”是英文“mississippi”的音译，来源于印第安人阿耳冈昆族语言，“密西”（misi）和“西比”（sipi）分别是“大、老”和“水”的意思，“密西西比”即“大河”或“老人河”。它被印第安人称为“河流之父”。

3. hurricane 飓风：发生在大西洋、墨西哥湾、加勒比海和北太平洋东部的热带气旋称为飓风。飓风通常发生在夏季和早秋，它来临时常常电闪雷鸣。英文 hurricane 一词一说源自加勒比海语言中的恶魔（Hurican），亦有说是玛雅人神话中创世众神的其中一位，即雷暴与旋风之神 Hurakan。

4. tornado 龙卷风：又称“卷风”，是一种相当剧烈的天气现象，由快速旋转的直立中空管状气流形成。龙卷风是大气中最强烈的涡旋现象，常发生于夏季的雷雨天气中，尤以下午至傍晚最为多见，虽然影响范围小，但破坏力极大。

Unit 2 Traditional Cultural Regions in the U.S.

Geographers use regions as a neat system of categorization（分类）, a way of organizing a complex set of facts about places into a more compact, meaningful set of information. As with any categorization, the regions are satisfactory if they identify understandable patterns in the facts or if they help clarify the complex patterns. This scheme has resulted in our division of the United

States into 8 regions, each of which will be discussed in this unit.

A great many of the institutions and the way of life that many people think of as typical of the United States or as typical Americans began in the Northeastern States. Although the United States is a relatively young country, the Northeastern States of Maine, New Hampshire, Vermont, Massachusetts, Rhode Island, Connecticut, New York, New Jersey, Pennsylvania, and Delaware have historical roots that go far into the nation's past.

It was in the Northeast that the **Pilgrims**[1] landed and began a way of life and established a democratic form of government that was to be unique. It was in the Northeast that the struggle for freedom from colonial role began. It was in this region that the young American nation's first great cities — Boston, New York and Philadelphia—grew up. And it was from the Northeast that the country was first governed.

In modern times it has been in this region that the greatest concentration of Americans has lived. The great **megalopolis**[2], the super city that some people feel will one day stretch solidly from Portland, Maine, to Norfolk, Virginia, is located for the most part in the Northeast. Just as the Northeast saw the beginning of the nation, so many people feel it hold the key to the future. As the 2015 United States Census Bureau estimates, the New York metropolitan area remains by a significant margin the most populous in the United States.

The Northeast States have much in common—and much diversity. Perhaps the most important thing they have in common is their access to the Atlantic Ocean. The access to the great waterway has given birth to the country and helped it grow into a modern industrial and trading power. On the other hand, the Northeast is a vast region and diverse cultures have developed within its boundaries because of the different peoples from all parts of the world who have lived here.

The Southeastern States have played a unique and vital role in the history of the United States. They include the Atlantic seaboard states of Maryland, Virginia, North Carolina, South Carolina, Georgia, and Florida as well as the "old west" frontier of colonial times—West Virginia, Kentucky, and Tennessee, carved out of land grants originally held by Virginia, the "mother of states". With terrain varying all the way from tidewater to the highest mountains east of the Rockies, it shows striking contrasts not only between black and white populations, but also between city and country people, coast and hill people.

The Southeastern States are the scene of exploration and discovery, of the beginnings of representative government in the New World, of revolution, of the building of a complex plantation society and of its destruction in the disastrous Civil War. Some of America's worst problems have been faced in the Southeast. The problem of racial discrimination and segregation is a serious issue here. However, some of the best solutions to national problems have been worked out in the Southeast. For instance, many of the most treasured aspects of the unique American system of government were born in the Southeast, and many of the country's first leaders were southeasterners.

The North Central region, also known as the Mid-west, includes 12 states—Ohio, Indiana,

Michigan, Wisconsin, Missouri, Iowa, Minnesota, Kansas, Nebraska, North Dakota, and South Dakota. These 12 states occupy the northern part of the vast region drained by the Mississippi River and its tributaries. This is the heart land—the geographical center of the United States, and is known as the breadbasket of the nation. This region provides the nation with great bulk（大部分）of basic foodstuffs and meat and grain. Over all, the North Central states account for about 43 percent of the total farm income in the United States.

Agricultural production does not end on the farm. Produce has to be processed and shipped to stores and markets all over the country and the world. Food processing had already become a major industry in the Middle West before the Civil War. In addition to all this farm-related manufacturing, the Middle West has its heavy industry as well. Heavy industry is concentrated in the lower Great lakes area, a region that has access to important sources of iron ore, coal, oil, and natural gas.

In many ways, Mid-westerners have made good use of their land, but they have also abused it and exploited it. Hundreds of thousands of acres of rich farmland have been covered over by layers of asphalt（沥青）and concrete, transformed into parking lots, factories, and suburban shopping centers.

The South Central States or the **Deep South**[3]—as this area is often called—is a special, unique world, and if outsider criticizes it that is because of his ignorance. This region includes Alabama, Mississippi, Louisiana, and Arkansas. Outsiders often think only in terms of the stereotyped（模式化的） images of the south: white magnolia（木兰）blossoms, the mile-wide "Old Man River", hound dogs baying after raccoons（浣熊）in the moonlight. Outsiders sometimes see in these same lush terrain images that are close to nightmare. But the southerner, resenting outside criticism, increasingly reminds the northerner of his own problems in urban ghettos.

It is particularly easy for the southerner to keep his feelings of "specialness" because he is far more likely than other Americans to be a native of his home region, with little experience outside it.

In its history, the rich virgin lands of the southern frontier states were far more attractive to cotton planters than the frequently worn-out acres of the eastern seaboard South. There, early over-cultivation of rice, tobacco and cotton had already eroded and exhausted the land. The large planters, merchants and bankers of King Cotton's domain were usually conservative politically.

The conflicting and social beliefs of North and South reached the boiling point after the election of Abraham Lincoln as president of the United States in 1860, and the Civil War broke out. In the first year after the Civil War, when the whole South suffered grinding（极度的）agricultural poverty, many local leaders began to campaign for industrial development. Today, the South Central States, like their neighbors in the rest of the South, have caught up with the rest of the United States in their rate of industrialization.

Mountain States or Rocky Mountain States refer to the immense area between the northward bend of the Missouri River and the central valley of California which can be divided into eight states — Montana, Idaho, Wyoming, Nevada, Utah, Colorado, Arizona, and New Mexico. Although the Spaniards were already skirting the California coast 50 years after Columbus' voyages to the New World, this region remained a mystery for another 3 centuries.

But once the pall（阴影）of ignorance started to lift early in the 19th century, knowledge of the American Far West spread light after sunrise. The names of its monumental natural features—**the Grand Canyon**[4], Great Salt Lake, Yellowstone Park, **Pikes Peak**[5], **Monument Valley**[6], **Grand Teton**[7], and the Garden of the Gods—had become household words in almost every corner of the globe.

Until 1847 the region that become the Mountain States had been regarded as a fine place to trap beaver and a challenge for hardy souls to cross, but few American families dreamed of living here.

The pitfalls（困难）and glories of the Rocky Mountains remain today. The Mountain States area is still poor in water but rich in beauty, in space, in challenges, and in precious metals. Much less has changed.

The Southwest is a region of great semi-arid plains, of old Spanish forts and churches and missions, of Mexican-Americans, of cowboys and Indians, of oil and cattle, and of big money and mushrooming cities. But the Southwest—which includes Texas, Oklahoma, Arizona and New Mexico—is also an immense region.

The Southwest may very well be the fastest changing part of the country. These dynamic people have roots that go deep into the past. The Southwest, in fact, can lay claim to some of the oldest settlement in North America. In general, it is a combination of exuberance（精神焕发）and age that set the region apart. South westerners are something of a contradiction—a fast changing people who are also much taken up with their own past, its traditions and its many colorful frontier figures.

This region is blessed with vast reserves of metallic（金属的）and nonmetallic minerals. The principal ones are gas and oil. Oil has brought untold material wealth to the Southwest. Oil has also brought another kind of wealth to the region. It has played a major role in supporting universities, symphony orchestras, museums, and other cultural, scientific, and business institutions. Thus it is the grit（坚毅）and sweat of the frontier that are today producing a new south westerner, better educated, more cultivated, more sophisticated than his hardworking forebears. A new generation emerging from the universities of the Southwest is bringing a new style to the region.

To many people, everything seems "more so" in the Pacific States of Washington, Oregon and California. There is more money, more outdoor living, more sports and leisure in the sun. People in the Pacific States move more often than people in other parts of the United States. They drive faster and faster along some of the nation's most modern superhighways. Although the Pacific Coast is still a region with large areas of unique wildness beauty, most of the people choose to settle in cities.

One of the things the people of the Pacific Coast share is pride in the scenic beauty and astounding physical variety of their land. Climate and natural resources shaped the life style of the original inhabitants of the Pacific States as well as that of later ones. For the most part, Pacific Indians lived in small villages, many speaking their own language.

Although settlement of such a vast, remote land would normally not be rapid, a stroke of luck was to make the settlement of California unique. The shout of "Gold in California" echoed around the world. It was the signal for the most hectic (繁忙的) mass migrations in history. Beginning in 1849, thousands of people arrived by land and sea. Within a few months New York bank clerks, Illinois farmers, Germans, Frenchmen, Mexicans, South Americans, Chinese, and Australians were all digging away frantically (紧张忙乱地) in the foothills and streams of the Sierra Nevada.

Until recently, the economy of the Pacific States rested primarily upon agriculture and extractive industries. California leads all the states of the nation in the value and variety of its agricultural production. Despite the importance of agriculture, the Pacific Coast has a predominantly urban society. Even as early as 1910, about half of the population of Washington and Oregon lived in cities and towns.

The discerning (有鉴赏力的) visitors will note that the Pacific Coast is in many ways two different societies, divided a little north of San Francisco. The southern section contains the larger, more restless, faster growing population. The Pacific Northwest, including the northern third of California, Oregon, and Washington, is a younger, greener, less hectic world than the area to the south. Its population is increasing at a more moderate rate, and its people are more rooted and less mercurial.

Hawaii is the only one of the 50 states of the United States not located on the North American continent. It is the southernmost and westernmost state, the only island state, and the last state to enter the union. Uniqueness is Hawaii's very essence.

Located as it is in the middle of the Pacific Ocean, about equidistant from North America and Asia, Hawaii has become a meeting ground for Western and Oriental peoples. In Hawaii marriages between people of different races and nationalities have been commonplace.

Whatever the disadvantages of living on an island in the mid-Pacific may be, there is no question that Hawaii is a very beautiful state to visit. The landscape is dominated by steep, emerald-green mountains, some of which rise out of the surf (浪花) itself. Most of Hawaii's coastline is rocky, but nevertheless, Hawaii is famous for its beaches.

An economic boom followed the achievement of statehood in 1959 has opened up new economic opportunities for all Hawaiians. The pattern of concentration of wealth and power in a still large white minority remains. But more and more, Hawaii has come to live up to the description of "a unique example of community that is a successful laboratory in human brotherhood" which was given by Dwight D. Eisenhower, the president of the United States who signed the act that made Hawaii a state.

In 1959, a young giant joined the union: Alaska, the 49th state, nearly one-fifth the size of all other states put together. Tales about the new state also grow tall. Some people think of it as a vast refrigerator, with isolated prospectors and Eskimos shivering in igloos（冰屋）through eternal nights. Others regard it as a place to get rich quickly and easily. Alaska is not that simple. It is a place of variety and contrast, a state with four time zones and many different kinds of weather. Only about a quarter of the state lies above the Arctic Circle, and the Panhandle is no colder than most of the continental United States. As for getting rich, Alaska offers many opportunities, but exploiting them takes hard work, endurance, and imagination.

Statehood heralded（预示）a new day for Alaska. Another influx（大量涌入）of settlers trooped north to seek their fortunes, to homestead, to hunt, and to fish, as Americans discovered Alaska all over again.

To Alaskans the future offers an exciting challenge and the opportunity to play an imaginative role in making this great northern empire the brightest star in the Union. One and all, Alaskans are aware that it is their special destiny to live on America's last frontier.

Thought we have divided the United States into different regions, rigid（严格的）regional boundaries do not fit the landscape of this country. A given portion of the country may be occupied by parts of two or more regions, but the boundaries of many regions may also be fairly broad transitional zones that contain many of a region's characteristics. Regional boundaries and regions themselves are not static. Settlement patterns shift, society develops significant new technological abilities, and political patterns are altered; regions reflecting these patterns may expand, contract, appear, or disappear.

Notes

1. Pilgrims 清教徒的一支：他们要求清除英国天主教残余的改革派，信奉加尔文主义，认为《圣经》是唯一最高权威，任何教会或个人都不能成为传统权威的解释者和维护者。斯克鲁比小镇的清教徒在1608年逃亡到荷兰，因为在那里他们能享有宗教自由。可是，过了一段时间后，荷兰对宗教宽容、不太要求道德的态度令这群清教徒大感不安，于是他们决定离开欧洲，迁往北美洲开创新生活。

2. megalopolis 大都市：1961年，Jean Gottman 出版了他的著作 *Megalopolis: The Urbanized Northeastern Seaboard of the United States*，这位法国地理学家在书中用 Megalopolis 一词描述了美国东北部沿海地带的、从北面的波士顿一直向南、由纽约、费城、巴尔的摩和华盛顿等多个大城市组成的一个超级城市。Gottman 通过多年研究发现，这些原本相互独立的城市区域在20世纪50年代发展形成了整个地区的城市及郊区绵延不绝、相互咬合的状态，而这一地带的土地利用性质和人的生活方式显现出趋同一致的特征。

3. Deep South 美国南部诸州：美国南部有相当特殊的文化和历史背景，包括早期欧洲殖民时期留下的痕迹。由于对州权原则的坚持、早期的奴隶制度以及在美国内战中受到的冲击，美国南部发展出了它独特的传统、文学、音乐形式以及烹饪食物。

4. the Grand Canyon 科罗拉多大峡谷：科罗拉多大峡谷位于美国亚利桑那州（Arizona）西北部，科罗拉多高原西南部。大峡谷全长446千米，平均宽度16千米，最深处2 133米，平均深度超过1 500米，总面积2 724平方千米。1919年，威尔逊总统将大峡谷地区辟为“大峡谷国家公园”(Grand Canyon National Park)。大峡谷是科罗拉多河的杰作,这条河发源于科罗拉多州的落基山,洪流奔泻,经犹他州、亚利桑那州,由加利福尼亚州的加利福尼亚湾入海,全长 2 320 千米。

5. Pikes Peak 皮克峰:美国落基山脉前岭山峰,在科罗拉多州厄尔巴索(El Paso)县,距科罗拉多斯普林斯(Colorado Springs)西 16 千米。虽然在科罗拉多群峰中高度居第 32 位,海拔 4 301 米,但因便于攀登和眺望而远近闻名。

6. Monument Valley 纪念碑山谷:纪念碑山谷位于美国亚利桑那州和犹他州交界的科罗拉多高原(Colorado Plateau)上,横跨亚利桑那和犹他两个州,被称为世界上最著名的地质奇观之一。远古落基山的堆积物沉积于此并转变成沙岩,后来由于地层下的压力不断增加,导致地表断裂隆起并逐渐形成峡谷,加上上百万年的风噬和雨水,才形成了今天这一奇特景观。

7. Grand Teton 大提顿国家公园:大提顿国家公园位于美国怀俄明州西北部壮观的冰川山区,1929 年建立,占地 1 256 平方千米。公园内最高的山峰是大提顿峰,海拔 4 198 米,有存留至今的冰川。分布在该地的冰湖以珍尼湖最为著名。斯内克河上用水坝拦堵形成的杰克森湖为当地最大的水域。高耸入云的山巅覆盖着千年的冰河,山连山,峰连峰,宛如进入人间仙境。公园内有成群的美洲野牛、麋鹿和羚羊,还有许多种其他哺乳动物。

Unit 3 Traditional Culture Regions vs. Voluntary Culture Regions[1]

American movies, television programs, magazines, popular music, fast food, dress, software, along with a host of other goods and services, have been aggressively exported to the rest of the world. Though this country has a trade deficit on the whole, it is still the second largest exporter. In 2015, the export sales have topped 1.5 trillion U.S. dollars. As a result, outsiders view the U.S. as a largely homogeneous country which human activities firmly take control of the natural world. This perception does correspond to a discernible(明显的)trend of greater cultural convergence(趋同)over the last quarter of the 20th century.

What will happen to this seemingly placeless(无固定位置的)cultural convergence when American enters the 21st century? Given the widespread postmodern values, including an enthusiasm for local landscapes, historic preservation and ethnic communities and traditions, cultural critics argue, it makes sense that regional diversity and cultural convergence will in congruously(一致地)exist side by side at different levels of American society. One new approach to American cultural geography is to distinguish traditional from voluntary cultural areas. A traditional culture region is formed over a long period of time in an environment setting by people who come to share a common worldview and a way of life. Such traditional areas are never static: assimilation, interactions with other areas and internal events and inventions are always bringing changes. A voluntary region, on the other hand, is formed by people with similar interests moving to a common destination region. The last unit is about the traditional culture regions. The following is a region-by-region description and interpretation of American voluntary culture regions.

In 1961, a French geographer published a monumental study of the highly urbanized region located in the northeastern United States, extending from southern New Hampshire and Northern Massachusetts to Washington, D.C. Professor Jean Gottmann argued that this was a "very special region", and he named it Megalopolis.

Megalopolis was formed along the northeastern coast of the United States by the gradual coalescence（合并）of large, independent metropolitan areas. As the populations of these cities grew, the effects of growth spilled over into the surrounding rings of smaller places. The outer fringes of the resultant metropolitan regions eventually began to merge with each other to form an extensive urbanized region.

The dominant theme of Megalopolis is "**urban-ness**[2]". In varying degrees, urban services provide for the millions who live in this region, and urban forms are never far away. But Megalopolis also contains many green spaces. Some are parks or other land available for recreation and over 3 million hectares are devoted to farming.

In spite of the mixed character of Megalopolis, it is its massive urban presence that makes this region so important in the United States. This region holds 17 percent of the total U.S. population in only 1.5 percent of the area of the country.

Why has this particular portion of the United States developed as it has? The first aspect of the region considered is usually its location. Occupying a coastal position, islands are scattered along the coast, some large enough to support communities. Megalopolis straddles some of the best natural harbors in America. This portion of North America was also on or near the most direct sea route between Europe and the productive plantations of the Caribbean colonies and southern America, at least on the homeward voyage. Also critical to its growth was the location of the core cities relative to the country's interior.

Throughout Megalopolis, it is the urban forms and urban functions that provide the most significant regional unity to the territory. This kind of characteristics is also found in most large cities around the world. What distinguishes Megalopolis is that the urban characteristics in this region have spread out so far from their core cities that these urban regions have began to merge with one another in a process of metropolitan coalescence. Megalopolis became in this way a kind of gigantic laboratory in which intensively urban patterns and peculiarly urban problems could be observed developing at a very large scale.

Florida is one of the most dramatic tourist magnets in the United States. With long beaches facing both the Atlantic Ocean and the Gulf of Mexico, this state has drawn winter vacationers for decades. The demand for subtropical amenities（舒适）has become so strong that the development of recreation resources has spread well north along the Atlantic margin into coastal Georgia and coastal South and North Carolina.

Not all tourist attractions depend on resources provided by nature. The construction of Disneyworld has brought millions of out-of-state visitors to south-central Florida. Many other new attractions were drawn to this part of the state, especially around Orlando, by the promise of tourist traffic and the possibility of tourist expenditures. This central Florida recreation complex is expected to become the inland link between Florida's east coastal and west coastal urban clusters.

Although the subtropical environment has lead to the boom of tourism and agricultural activity, this environment is not entirely beneficent. Agriculturally, successful vegetable production has encouraged the growers to attempt to produce crops year-round. Thus, when an occasional midwinter frost reaches into southern Florida, considerable crop damage can occur. More erratic, more sporadic, more dramatic, and locally more destructive are the region's hurricanes. Because these storms are an accepted feature of the region, and weather satellites and other forecasting tools are available, preparations to withstand the greatest force of the wind and rain can be made early.

Another factor that helps to distinguish Florida from others is Cuban immigration. In the last few decades, the Latin American population in the state has tripled. The Cuban population was absorbed relatively quickly into financial, commercial, and retail activities. The rapidity with which a large number of people settled in Florida created its own "instant" market. Business in other parts of the United States that wished to expand their activities into Latin American markets began to move at least part of their domestic operations to Florida to employ Spanish-speaking Cubans. The trans-Caribbean business contacts brought with the Cuban refugees were also attractive to Anglo business interests.

California is the home to more than 10 percent of all Americans and a central element in the American cultural fabric. Although two-thirds of native born Americans live in their state of birth, fewer than half of all Californians were born in the states. Rather, California has been an important destination for U.S. internal migration in nearly every decade since 1850.

Perhaps California's greatest disadvantage, at least recently, is its location at the far western periphery（外围）of the United States, some 3,500 kilometers from the most important areas of economic demand and supply in the country. Following U.S. seizure of California in 1846, a great gold strike in the foothills of the central Sierra Nevada in 1848 brought the first significant change in the region's settlement fortunes. The frantic period of the gold rush lasted only a few years, but it succeeded in breaking the state's isolation from the rest of the country. The completion of railroads going west in the 1880s brought a sudden end to the area's quiet existence.

California, by some measures America's most urbanized state, is at the same time its most agricultural state in terms of total farm income. California's agriculture is thanks to the variety of climatic regions and the market demand of its own large population. Vegetables such as artichoke, lettuce, broccoli, and Brussels sprout grow well in the Coastal Range Valleys. The varietal grapes that can produce the best of American wines can be found in the inland Coastal Range Valleys around San Francisco. Navel oranges and lemons are grown almost exclusively along the coast and the interior surrounding the Los Angeles.

Despite California's agricultural importance nationally, its population is overwhelmingly urban and still increasing. Most of the state's population live in one of its two major urban regions, one centered on Los Angeles, the other on San Francisco.

California is known worldwide as the location of Hollywood, the center of America's motion picture industry. Los Angeles remains one of the centers of American filmmaking and television, but today the motion picture industry plays only a small role in the metropolitan area's economy, employing less than 2 percent of its workers.

Its climate and its varied scenery, especially along the coast, early made southern California one of the country's center of outdoor recreation. Today, the natural advantages have been supplemented by some of the country's largest and best-developed recreation facilities.

California is also the major destination of Latin American and Asian migrants entering the United States. Recent migrants especially often settle in ethic neighborhoods. Little Tokyo, a part of the city, has a renewed vibrancy. Monterey Park in the San Gabriel Valley is 50 percent Asian, making it the most heavily Asian city in the mainland United State. A rich diversity of ethnic restaurants, many found within ethnic enclaves, dot the city.

Pacific Northwest is the last area just beginning to emerge as a distinct voluntary culture region. Cold, clear mountain streams tumble down rock-strewn courses. The destination: a ragged, unused coastline where precipitous, fog-enshrouded cliffs rise out of pounding surf. Mountains are visible in the distance — lofty, majestic（庄严的）, and covered with snow. Tall needle-leaf evergreens cover the land between with a mantle of green. Cities, where exist, give the impression that they are new. This is America's North Pacific Coast, or more popularly, the Pacific Northwest — the coastal zone that stretches from northern California through coastal Canada to southern Alaska.

An important element of its regional character is the North Pacific Coast's relative isolation from the rest of America. Less than 3 percent of the American population live there. Populated sections of the region are separated from the other principal population centers by substantial distances of arid or mountainous terrain. Residents of the region often view this isolation as positive, a geographic buffer against the rest of the world. Economically, however, it has been a hindrance. High transportation costs inflate the price of Pacific Northwest products in distant eastern markets and discourage some manufacturers from locating in the region. Dubbed as an "**Ecotopia**[3]", this region has found a balance between economic growth and environmental wellbeing, its extensive rainforests having been well-preserved.

Notes

1. Voluntary Culture Regions 自发形成的文化区域：用以指代拥有相同世界观与生活方式的人们通过定居而形成的特定区域。与传统文化区域相比有着更大的灵活性与发展空间，自发形成的文化区域往往以各自不同的特点著称。

2. urban-ness 城镇化：又称"城市化"或"都市化"，指社会经济关系、人口和生活方式等由农村型向都市型转化的过程和状态。都市化是生产力发展到一定阶段的必然产物，是近代工业化的直接结果。它包括相互关联和相互作用的三个方面：①在社会生产力发展的基础上，产业结构由农业型经济转变为工业型经济；②人口向都市地区集中，农业人口向非农业人口转变，市镇人口占总人口的比重增大；③社会生活向都市型状态转变，都市生活方式扩展到其他领域，人际间的血缘、亲缘关系削弱，业缘关系强化。这三个方面综合的空间形式是都市地域的扩大、市镇数目的增多和都会地区的出现。

3. Ecotopia 生态乌托邦：来源于美国当代著名环保作家欧内斯特·卡伦马赫所著的同名书籍。该书出版于 1975 年，书中通过日记与报纸专栏报道相结合的方式，记述了特派记者阿威在一个虚拟的生态乌托邦国家的所见所闻与所思所想，讲述了人们对自己的命运负责，运用手中已有的工具，创造一种人道的、快乐的、对环境友好的“稳定态”生活方式，成为乐活一族的故事。书中许多设想现在都已变成现实，并促成德国绿党成立。在当前的社会背景下，该书内容积极向上，有助于提高公民的环保意识，采取新的绿色生活方式，营造绿色环境，创建绿色社会。

Unit 4 A Nation of Immigrants

John Kennedy's unfinished task remains sketched in his excellent short book—***A Nation of Immigrants***[1]—in defense of his immigration policy and his belief in the American philosophy of equality in opportunities and freedoms. With the president's word, "Every American who ever lived ... was either an immigrant himself or a descendent of immigrants." we can have a general view of the population of the United States. On a global scale, considering all forms of immigration, the United States ranks 34th with 19,148.45 immigrants per 1 million citizens in 2014. The population growth in the United States has developed in a series of immigrant waves.

The first wave occurred during colonial times when most of the new arrivals in North America came from England, although many other European countries were also represented, including France, Germany, Ireland, Italy, the Netherlands, Sweden and Wales.

The second wave of immigrants began in 1820 and lasted for about 50 years. During this period, nearly 7.5 million immigrants arrived in the United States. Many of them were Irish who came here to escape the rigors（艰苦）of the **Great Famine**[2] in Ireland. They settled in the cities along the eastern seaboard of the United States. The Great Irish Famine—which heavily influenced the number of Irish immigrants coming to the United States—began in 1845 when Ireland's potato crop failed. That year, crops failed across Europe, but in Ireland, it was more devastating since the potato was so important to the Irish, who had exported their grain and millet and were dependant on the potato for sustenance. At the same time, an equal number, approximately one third of the immigrants, were Germans, who settled in the nation's farmlands, especially in the Midwest States.

The third wave of immigrants came between 1881 and 1920 with more than 23 million immigrants arriving here. These new arrivals were largely from eastern and southern Europe. In 1882, German immigration reached its peak and in 1883 came the peak of immigrants from Denmark, Norway, Sweden, Switzerland, Netherlands and China. Immigrant records were set in 1902 with the arrival of people from Italy, Austro-Hungary and Russia.

Immigration slowed between 1920 and 1965. But in the last three and a half decades of the 20th century into the 21st, the fourth wave of immigrant has taken place. As for this time, the origin countries have shifted. Latin Americans now account for about half of the new arrivals while one fourth are Asian-born and one fifth are European. With so many immigrants, America becomes "a teeming（热闹的）nation of nations". An immigrant ancestor is at the end of the genealogical trail of every American citizen. We are told in *A Nation of Immigrants*, "We are the heirs of all time, and with all nations we divide our inheritance."

However, of the unique and successful experience of the building up of the American nation is not so much in the heterogeneous（多种的）blending of immigrants of different backgrounds shaping the style of life, the colorful richness of the language. **The Chinese exclusion acts**[3], the **Ku Klux Klan**[4], the American Protective Association and the national origin system are "without basis in either logic or reason. It neither satisfies a national need nor accomplishes an international purpose. In an age of interdependence among nations such a system is an anachronism, for it discriminates among applicants for admission into the United States on the basis of accident of birth." And this "violates the spirit expressed in the Declaration of Independence that 'all men are created equal'!"

Until today, the nation of immigrants is still divided over the subject of immigration. The concerns expressed in public debate are usually not so much about immigration itself but about illegal immigration. About eleven million or more people are in the United States without permission. Most of them came across the borders with Mexico or Canada illegally. Others came to the United States on a temporary visa and never go back home.

Supporters of stronger immigration laws say illegal immigrants use health care and public education systems without paying their fair share. They say undocumented workers push down wages in some jobs, like in the building industry. Still, they point out that some communities face greater problems than others with crime by illegal immigrants. But others argue that employers have trouble finding Americans to take low-paying jobs so they need immigrants. Further more, illegal immigrants put money into local economies and often have taxes taken out of their wages. Such arguments are nothing new. What is new is that immigrants are moving beyond big states like California, Texas or New York. They are settling all across the country, in big cities as well as small towns. These new residents are bringing cultural changes to many areas. Some of these changes are welcome, others are not.

In short, American immigration history presents a pattern of history repeating itself. Hard times or conflict in other countries lead people to seek a better life in America. When groups of Americans begin to feel threatened, the federal government moves to restrict immigration.

The ethic issue has had a long history ever since the founding of the United States, or even before that time. The first settlers living in Virginia（1607）and Massachusetts（1620）brought to the New World the issue of ethnic groups as they had to first of all make adjustments to their relationship with the native and local Americans. At that time, a prominent factor that posed enduring influence on local society was the successful transplanting of English language and laws, Protestant ethics, social customs, and economic mechanism. Faced with the dominance of English culture, in a sense, all other groups had to adjust themselves with these "indigenous"（本土的）standards although they simultaneously retained their own cultural and social norms to a degree.

There has long been a **Hispanic**[5] or Latino presence in the U.S. southwest. Their number grew significantly from the 1880s onwards when Mexican laborers came to the border states such as Texas and California in search of work. There has been renewed growth in recent years following the liberalization of **immigration laws in 1965**[6]. By 2010， Hispanics represents 15.1% of the whole population, surpassing African American and becomes the largest ethic group. This rise can be attributed to immigration and a relatively high birth rate.

The diverse groups within the Hispanic population share a common predicament as a primary poor, Catholic, Spanish-speaking people in a predominantly affluent, Protestant, English-speaking country. Most Hispanics have relatively low levels of education and income. The significant exception to this pattern is the Cuban population, which consists mostly of middle-class refugees who emigrated from their country in the 1960s and who have since used their skills to build a relatively prosperous community, centered in Miami.

Mexican Americans, or Chicanos have occupied the territories of the Southwest for over four centuries; ancestors of some of the present inhabitants became United States citizens involuntarily in 1848 when parts of the Southwest were ceded to the United States after the Mexican War. Since then, there has been a tendency to think of them as Mexican rather than American as sojourners（旅居者）in the United States who can "go back home" if they are dissatisfied, or as "American on parole". It is only in recent years that the Chicanos have come to be generally recognized as a genuinely American minority. Their ambiguous status has resulted from the fact that, unlike most other immigrant groups, they did not have to desert a homeland and cross an ocean in order to immigrate the United States; and because Chicanos can and do travel easily and frequently between the United States and Mexico, constantly renewing their personal and cultural ties with their country of origin.

For the Native Americans, or "Indians", the westward movement led to the final destruction of tribal societies and their nomadic way of life. Despite occasional victories, Indian resistance was crushed. The tribes were not only outgunned. Mass slaughter led to near extinction of the buffalo herds on which they depended. Today, the remnants of Native American society are able to be found on the reservations. The largest—the Navajo（纳瓦霍人）nation—stretches across parts of Arizona, New Mexico and Utah.

During the 1970s and 1980s, Indians won a series of legal and political victories that bolstered the principle of what the Supreme Court called "unique and limited sovereignty". The federal government recognized tribal sovereignty except where limited by treaty or Congress. But this strengthening of the principle of self-determination had only a limited impact on lives of most

Indians. As Indians experienced the greatest cut in federal funding in 1981, reservations saw a dramatic increase in unemployment and poverty. Some of those living on the reservations have made a living by offering goods and services such as fireworks and gambling that are prohibited elsewhere under state law. In some tribes, reservation casinos prove to be spectacular economic success. Despite these, great numbers of reservation dwellers face severe problems, including economic hardship and unemployment. Until now, about one third of Native Americans live below the poverty level.

African Americans as a group do not share the common defining experience of voluntary immigration to the United States which most of other Americans share; instead, their ancestors were kidnapped or sold into slavery and forced to adapt to a country with established racial hierarchies (等级). This substantial difference still affects race relations as other racial and ethic groups—other assimilated citizens—feel themselves more authentically American because of the original intent of their ancestors to make a new and better life for themselves from the one they were living behind. It is important to remember that the United States had no feudal past and thus no established peasantry. For African Americans, the continent of origin, slavery and its confrontation with America's stated moral vision and the long-standing status as the nation's central minority set them apart. For many African Americans, who believe that each new immigrant group succeeds only at their expense, the recent surge in immigration hampers the effects towards equal citizenship.

After decades of struggle, the Civil Rights Movement of the 1950s and 1960s mobilized the African American community in line with the actions and words of leaders such as Martin Luther King, Jr. and **Malcolm X**[7]. While still facing discrimination by private individuals, in job promotions and by financial institutions, much as changed as blacks have succeeded in wiping away all rule sand regulations that denied equality before the law.

In contemporary United States, 34 million people identity themselves as African Americans. Being African Americans is more than visual as blacks define themselves as much by self choice and social definition as by ancestry. Social definitions count. For example, historian Barbara Fields has explained that American society "considers a white woman capable of giving birth to a black child but denies that a black woman can give birth to a white child".

Asian American community is extremely heterogeneous (各种各样的)—comprised of many ethnicities, new immigrants and persons of all socioeconomic status. This diversity means that the problems facing Asian Americans are themselves' diverse, ranging from issue facing those who are not proficient in English to issues affecting highly educated professionals, such as the existence of invisible barriers that limit opportunities for Asian Americans at the top of their professions.

With a population of about million, Asian Americans today make up about 1% of the United States population. After 40 years of being virtually banned from the United States by immigration laws, people from Asia began to arrive in America in greater numbers starting from 1965. This recent high rates of immigration have resulted in a large proportion of Asian Americans being foreign born.

Asian immigrants are heavily concentrated in certain geographic areas. In the 1980s, about half of the Asian American population settled in the western United States. Three non-Western states also have considerable Asian Americans: New York, Illinois, and Texas. According to the summary statistics, Asian Americans are a better-educated group, more likely to be in high-paying occupations and have higher family incomes than general population. Yet it is wrong to assume that Asian Americans do not face racism or encounter barriers to equal opportunity. The Asian American population is extremely heterogeneous in terms of socioeconomic status. Many Asian Americans do not share in the relatively favorable socioeconomic outcomes enjoyed by the "average" Asian Americans. The newer immigrants groups from Southeast Asian have sharply lower socioeconomic status than other Asian Americans do. There is also considerable difference among the better-off Asian American groups such as Chinese, Asian Indians, and Koreans. There are indications that high levels of family income be an artifact created by Asian Americans' concentration in high cost of living areas and the high education levels of many Asian Americans. Further more, if Asian Americans have larger than average families, high levels of total income may not necessarily translate into high levels of per capita income.

Notes

1. *A Nation of Immigrants*《移民国家》: 美国总统 John F. Kennedy 所著的一本小册子。在书中，肯尼迪总统记述了美国移民史上的重要历史事件，并对美国的移民政策提出了自己的见解。他认为，移民对于美国发展的作用不言而喻，所以宽松而公平的移民政策是促进社会发展的必要条件。

2.Great Famine 爱尔兰大饥荒: 是一场发生于 1845 年至 1852 年间的饥荒。造成饥荒的主要因素是一种被称为 Phytophthora infestans 的卵菌造成马铃薯腐烂。马铃薯是当时的爱尔兰人的主要粮食来源，加上许多社会与经济因素，使得广泛的欠收严重地影响了贫苦农民的生计。在这 7 年的时间内，爱尔兰人口锐减了将近四分之一；这个数目除了饿死、病死者，也包括近两百万因灾荒而移居海外的爱尔兰人。

3. the Chinese exclusion acts 排华法案: 1882 年 5 月 6 日，美国国会通过了美国史上第一个限禁外来移民的法案：《关于执行有关华人条约诸规定的法律》，即通常所谓的"排华法案"。这一法案声称，美国政府认为，华工的到来使得美国境内一些地方的良好秩序受到威胁，规定从任何外国港口将华工带至美国的船只都将被认定为犯罪，美国州法院和联邦法院不得给予华人美国公民身份，与此相悖的法律均被废除。1902 年，该法律被无限期延长。直到 1943 年，为了推动美国战争目标的实现，在罗斯福总统的敦促下，国会撤销了此前的议案，允许中国人成为美国公民。

4.Ku Klux Klan 三 K 党: 三 K 党（缩写为 K.K.K.）是美国历史上和现在的一个奉行白人至上主义运动和基督教恐怖主义的民间仇恨团体，也是美国种族主义的代表性组织。三 K 党是美国最悠久、最庞大的恐怖主义组织。Ku 和 Klux 来源于希腊文 KuKloo，意为"集会”，Klan 是种族。因三个词首字母都是 K，故称“三 K 党”，又称白色联盟和无形帝国。

5. Hispanic 西班牙裔：在美国官方定义里，西班牙裔统指来自墨西哥、波多黎各、古巴及中南美洲其他西班牙语地区的人和他们的后裔。2010 年，西班牙裔的人口在美国市区第一次超过黑人，成为美国最大的少数民族，每六个美国人里，就有一个西班牙裔人。预计到 2050 年，西语裔人口将占美国总人口的四分之一。

6. immigration laws in 1965 1965 年移民法案：林登·约翰逊总统（Lyndon Johnson）于 1965 年 10 月 3 日在自由女神像下签署《1965 年移民法》（*The Immigration Act of 1965*）。法案的签署在一定程度上是由于 20 世纪 60 年代自由主义意识形态的气候。这项新法彻底废除了国籍配额制，取而代之的是东西半球限额：东半球为 17 万名，西半球为 12 万名，任何一国每年的限额为 2 万名。此外，新法扩大了可以不受配额限制入境的家庭成员类别，并为公民的非直系亲属甚至拥有永久居住身份的外国人的家属保留了大部分配额。

7. Malcolm X 马尔克姆·X：马尔克姆·X（1925 年 5 月 19 日—1965 年 2 月 21 日）生于美国内布拉斯加州，是伊斯兰教教士、美国黑人民权运动的领导人之一。批评人士认为他煽动散布暴力、仇恨、黑人优越主义、种族主义、反犹太主义，肯定人士则视他为非裔美国人权利的提倡者以及对于美国白人对黑人罪行的有力批判者。

Unit 5 People in Nowadays

Total Population

The U.S. Census Bureau estimated the country's population to be 323,425,550 as of April 25, 2016, and to add 1 person (net gain) every 13 seconds, or about 6,646 people per day. Despite this apparent precision, population figures from different sources are often wildly inconsistent. A national census is taken every 10 years, but most states, cities and towns update the census with their own estimates. For literally up-to-the-minute population estimates, you can check the **Census Bureau**[1] website.

The population is about 79.96% white, 12.85% black, 4.43% Asian and 0.97% Native American. These figures include 15.1% who are of Hispanic origin, but they are not counted separately in the census. The proportions vary significantly between states and are changing over time, with a higher-than-average birthrate in the black and a high proportion of new immigrants coming from Asia and Latin America.

The rate of natural population increase is low, but continued immigration maintains the overall population growth rate at about 0.9% per year. The number of illegal residents ("undocumented aliens") in the USA is variously estimated at 5 to 11 million, mostly Latino. Historically, America is a nation of immigrants, and currently about 1 million new immigrants arrive annually. Nevertheless, only 9% of the resident population was born outside the USA, which is considerably less than the proportion in Canada (16%) or Australia (20%), and is comparable to that in many western European countries.

The median age of the population is increasing as a result of longer life expectancy and lower birth rate. About 13% of people are over age of 65. This proportion has been steadily rising for years and will continue to be so. Providing services, especially medical care, for a growing aged population is an emerging problem for the country.

Geographically, the Northeastern states have about 53 million people; the Great Lakes States, 63 million; the South, 93 million; and the West, 59 million. In the past two decades, population growth has been above average in the West and the South, while the Northeast and the Great Lakes States have grown more slowly. After the 1980s, populations actually declined in some northern cities like Detroit, Chicago and Philadelphia. Historically, there has been a movement away from the countryside, and 75% of people now live in urban areas, defined as cities or towns with over 2,500 inhabitants.

The United States has grown from a diverse cultural background. African Americans have made important contribution to the national culture. A distinctive cultural region has developed in the Southwest, with an admixture of Hispanic Americans, American Indians, and European Americans. The Chinese contributed to the life of such cities as San Francisco, and New York. This cultural diversity is an important element in the distinctive character of the country.

Although the country is so big and its people have so many different ethic backgrounds, the United States still has a sense of uniformity. The national origins of the people are by now fairly well mixed all over the country, though there are exceptions on small and large scales. The English language is virtually universal in its American form. Some Americans speak rather indistinctly, not pronouncing consonants properly, others show by their speech that English is not their mother tongue, and Irish of Negro accents can often be recognized; but the lack of real regional or class variety in speech or usage is one of the characteristics that tend to make the whole country very obvious one.

Another basic theme about Americans is urbanization. Though some Americans seem to believe that rurality provides the country with a basic national vigor, they can not deny that they have entered the urban epoch. Less than a tenth of the people are engaged in agriculture and forestry, and most of the rest live in or around towns, small and large. City is the best speaker of urbanization. Cities exist for many different reasons. Many of them are characterized by certain dominant functions that were the reasons for their development and much of their early growth, and that today continue to give them their special character.

America's extensive transportation network is an important element in its high level of interaction. Goods and people move freely within and between regions of the country. Regional interdependence is great; it is made possible by these regional flows. Relative isolation is uncommon, but it does exist. Nearly 20 percent of all Americans change their residence in any one year. Although much of this residential migration is local in nature, it does result in substantial interregional population movement. Until the last decade of the 19th century, there was a strong westward population shift toward frontier agricultural lands. However, more recently, the U.S.

economy has entered what some call a post-industrial phase; employment growth is primarily in professions and services rather than primary or secondary sectors.

Notes

1. Census Bureau 美国人口调查局：美国商务部下属的一个机关。它的任务由美国宪法注明：它必须至少每十年进行一次人口普查，相应的美国众议院的成员数由这个调查结果决定。除此之外它还提供美国国家、人民和经济的统计数据。

References

[1] JEANETTE K. The south : a concise history [M]. New York: Pearson, 2001.

[2] KENNEDY J F. A nation of immigrants [M]. New York: Harper Perennial, 2008.

[3] LEVY M I. Native American culture [M]. New York: Britannica Educational Publishing, 2011.

[4] RICE R B. The elusive Eden: a new history of California [M]. Boston: McGraw-Hill Humanities/Social Sciences/Languages, 2011.

[5] KEITER R B. Reclaiming the native home of hope: community, ecology, and the American west [M]. Salt Lake City: University of Utah Press, 1998.

[6] BIRDSALL S S, FLORIN J. Outline of American geography [M]. Hoboken: John Wiley & Sons, Inc., 1992.

[7] ZELINSKY W. The cultural geography of the United States[M]. Upper Saddle River: Prentice Hall, 1992.

[8] 李荣荣 . 美国的社会与个人 : 加州悠然城社会生活的民族志 [M]. 北京：北京大学出版社，2007.

[9] 刘阿兰 . 美国地理环境概述 [M]. 成都：四川大学出版社，2011.

[10] 美国新闻处 . 美国地理述略 [M]. 香港：今日世界出版社，1978.

[11] 梅仁毅 . 美国研究读本 [M]. 北京：外语教学与研究出版社 , 2002.

[12] 尼尔 • R. 彼尔斯，杰里 • 哈格斯特洛姆 . 美国志 [M]. 北京：中国社会科学出版社, 1987.

[13] 聂崇彬 . 行走美国：讲述 ABC 和 CBA 的真实故事 [M]. 上海：上海画报出版社 , 2005.

[14] 王恩铭，吴敏，张颖 . 当代美国社会与文化 [M]. 北京：上海外语教育出版社, 2007.

[15] 美国国务院国际信息局 . 美国地理概况 [M]. 杨俊峰，等，译 . 沈阳：辽宁教育出版社，2003.

[16] 周静琼 . 当代美国概况 [M]. 上海：上海外语教育出版社，2003.

Chapter Two

American Government

Unit 1 The Constitution of the United States of America

Constitutionalism

"What is a constitution?" asked Supreme Court Justice **William Paterson**[1] (1745—1806) two centuries ago. "It is," he answered, "the form of government, delineated by the mighty hand of the people, in which certain first principles of the fundamental laws are established." Like Paterson and his contemporaries, most Americans embrace constitutionalism: the limiting governmental power by a written charter.

American government does not begin with the constitution. Prior to 1787, there were many years of British rules, followed by the turbulence of revolution. After years of struggle and numerous battles, the United States finally succeeded in breaking from the British Empire and became the first colonial possession to achieve independence from the mother country and an experiment with national government was begun under **the *Articles of Confederation***[2].

If the *Declaration of Independence* proclaimed separation from England, it did little knit the former colonies into a nation. Central political control disappeared in 1776. Something would now have to take its place for successful execution of the war and for development of the nation once liberty was won. Only eight days after the adoption of the *Declaration of Independence*, a committee of Congress chaired by John Dickinson placed before the entire body a plan of union. The *Articles of Confederation* became the first American constitution. The Articles created a type of government called a confederation or confederacy. Unlike Great Britain's unitary system of government, wherein all the powers of the government reside in the national government, the national government in a confederation derives all of its powers from the states. Thus, the national government in a confederacy is weaker than the sum of its parts, and the states often consider themselves independent nation-state linked together only for limited purposes such as national defense.

Defects of the *Articles of Condefedreration* soon became apparent. The first was an absence of sufficient power in the central government. The second was the presence of too much power in the hands of the state government. Therefore, in 1785 and 1786, some state governments began to discuss ways to strengthen the national government. Finally, several states jointed together to call for a convention in Philadelphia in 1787. After the ratification and the great compromise, the first written constitution was finally drafted.

The ideas of political philosophers, especially two political philosophers, the French Montesquieu, and the English John Locke, heavily influenced the shape and nature of the government proposed by the framers.

Federalism[3]: The constitution set up a form of government based on the principle of federalism. In a federal system, some powers belong to the national or the federal government, while the others belong to the states. This division of powers was a compromise between two groups of delegates to the Philadelphia convention: those who had strong nationalist views and those who felt that these states should retain most of their rights.

Separation of Powers[4]**:** The framers of the constitution wanted to create a government that would prevent the rise of tyranny—absolute and unlimited power and authority. To do so, they separated the powers of the government. Its three key features are:

a. Three distinct branches of government: the legislative, the executive, and the judicial.

b. Three separately staffed branches of government to exercise these functions.

c. Constitutional equality and independence of each branch.

Checks and Balance: The separation of powers among the three branches of the national government is not complete. According to Montesquieu and the Framers, the powers of each branch could be used to check the powers of the other two branches of government. The power of each branch of government is checked, limited and balanced because the legislative, executive and judicial branches share some authority and no branch has exclusive domain over any single activity. The creation of this system allows the framers to minimize the threat of tyranny（暴政）from any one branch.

Judicial Review[5]**:** Judicial review refers to the power of the courts to decide whether a law or other governmental action violates the Constitution. In cases that come before the U.S. Supreme Court, if the justices find that a federal or state law violates the U.S. Constitution, the law is declared unconstitutional. Such a law no longer has any validity or legitimacy. The Constitution doesn't specifically mention judicial review. Most scholars believe, however, that the Framers meant the federal courts to have that power.

Evidently the judges of the Supreme Court have an interesting power. We cannot say with certainty whether this development fits in with the original intentions of the founders of the Constitution; they had not really thought about the implications of the document which they had worked out.

If it were really possible to find judges who interpret the meaning of the Constitution as absolutely infallible arbiters, by an ineluctable process of reasoning, everything would be satisfactory. But the chief points in the Constitution involve much uncertainty of interpretation. It would not be surprising to find judges interpreting these vague words in such a way as to suit their own concepts and ideas, and even their own political opinions.

Most of the Constitution's twenty-seven amendments were adopted to keep it abreast of changes in political thinking. As a matter of fact, the first ten amendments (**the *Bill of Rights*[6]**) were the price of ratification. They refrained the national government from tampering with fundamental rights and civil liberties and emphasized the limited character of national power.

First Amendment	Prohibits the government from abridging freedom of speech, the press, assembly, petition and from establishing an official religion.
Second Amendment	Guarantees the rights to bear arms.
Third Amendment	Prohibits troops from occupying citizens' homes in peacetime.
Fourth Amendment	Protects against unreasonable searches and seizures.
Fifth Amendment	Requires an indictment by a grant jury for serious crimes; prohibits the government from trying a person twice for the same crime; prohibits the government from taking life liberty or property without due process of law; and prohibits the government from taking private property for public use without fair compensation to the owner.
Sixth Amendment	Guarantees a speedy and public jury trial, the right to confront witnesses in court, and the right to legal counsel for defense.
Seventh Amendment	Protects the right to a jury trial in civil cases.
Eighth Amendment	Prohibits the government from setting excessive bail or fine or inflicting cruel and unusual punishment.
Ninth Amendment	Protects all other unspecified rights of the people.
Tenth Amendment	Reserves to the states or to the people those powers neither granted to the federal government nor prohibited to the states in the Constitution.

The most important of these amendments are the first, fifth and tenth. Under the tenth amendment "the powers not delegated to the United States by the constitution, not prohibited by it to the states, are reserved to the states respectively, or to the people", this statement is extremely important as it specifically lay down that any action by federal authorities which goes beyond the powers granted in the Constitution is amended so as to make it lawful.

The first amendment forbids Congress to make any laws "respecting an establishment of religion or prohibiting the free exercise thereof". It also forbids any laws which might in any way take away freedom of speech or of the press, or the right of the people to assemble peacefully and to petition the government for a redress of grievances. The fifth amendment provides that "no person shall be deprived of life, liberty or property without due process of law; nor shall private property be taken for public use without just compensation".

Two more amendments were adopted in the next seven years, and the thirteenth, fourteenth, and the fifteenth were passed only after the Civil War and as a result of the victory of the North.

There have been more amendments since then, including one which outlawed alcoholic liquor in 1919 and one which allowed it again in 1933.

Like the other national constitution, **the *1787 Constitution***[7] establishes a general framework for organizing and operating a government. After 200 years, the Constitution has been constantly revised and improved so that the United States as the world's most typical western democracies has never had any split with the dictatorship, the United States for long-term stability and development have made indelible contributions to becoming the biggest bright spot in American politics.

Notes

1. William Paterson 威廉·佩特森：新泽西州议会议员，1790—1793年出任新泽西州州长，积极支持联邦宪法，曾任联邦最高法院大法官。

2. the *Articles of Confederation*《邦联条例》：在1776年北美宣布独立后不久，第二届大陆会议就提出并着手起草全国宪法——《邦联和永久联合条例》(*Articles of Confederation and Perpetual Union*)，简称《邦联条例》(*Articles of confederation*)。1777年11月19日，大陆会议通过了《邦联条例》。这部条例是北美殖民地筹建十三个新州统一政府的第一个正式文件。

3. federalism 联邦主义：既是一种观念又是一种制度。作为国家政治组织形式的联邦主义制度是在政治上介于中央集权和松散的邦联之间的一种制度。

4. separation of powers 三权分立：亦称"三权分治"，是西方民主国家的基本政治制度的建制原则。政治上的三权分立指司法权、行政权和立法权相对独立。在美国，行政权属于政府，立法权属于国会的参众议院，司法权属于法院。

5. judicial review 司法审查权：是三权分立相互制衡的很好体现。主要指法院，也就是judiciary可以裁决国会通过的法案是否符合本国宪法。如果最高法院认定不符合宪法，就会宣布这项法案无效。

6. the *Bill of Rights*《权利法案》：指美国宪法中第一至第十条宪法修正案，由詹姆斯·麦迪逊起草。

7. the *1787 Constitution*《1787宪法》：即美国1787年制定并于1789年批准生效的美利坚合众国联邦宪法，也是世界上第一部比较完整的资产阶级成文宪法。它奠定了美国政治制度的法律基础，制定后多年来附有27条修正案，迄今依然有效。

Unit 2 Congress[1]

The U.S. Congress is the "first branch" of government under Article I of the Constitution and is also among the world's most representative bodies. Congress is also the only national representative assembly that can actually be said to govern. According to the U.S. Constitution, Congress' essential function is to make laws, which consists of two houses: **the Senate**[2] and **the House of Representatives**[3]. The two houses are granted with equal powers and all bills have to pass both the Senate and the House of Representative before going to the President for his signature.

Constitutional Powers of Congress: The Constitution specifically gives the Congress its most important power: the authority to make laws. Both houses share the law-making power. For example, no bill can become law without the consent of both houses. Examples of other constitutionally shared powers include the power to declare war, raise an army and navy, coin money, regulate commerce, establish the federal courts and their jurisdiction, establish rules of immigration and naturalization（归化）, and “make all laws which shall be necessary and proper for carrying into execution the foregoing powers”. As interpreted by the U.S. Supreme Court, the necessary and proper clause, found at the end of Article I, section 8, when coupled with one or more of the specific powers enumerated in Article I, section 8 has allowed Congress to increase the scope of its authority, often at the expense of the states and into areas not necessarily envisioned by the Framers.

Congress alone is given formal law-making powers in the Constitution. But it is important to remember that the President issues proclamations and executive orders with the force of law, bureaucrats（官僚）issue quasi-legislative rules, and the Supreme Court and lower federal courts render opinions that generate principles that also has the force of law.

The House of Representatives and the Senate play different roles in the legislative process. In essence, the Senate is more deliberative of the two bodies—the forum in which any and all ideas can receive a thorough public airing. The House of Representatives is more centralized and organized of the two bodies—better equipped to play a routine role in the governmental process.

The Structure of Congress: Congress contains a complex network of party organizations, committees, subcommittees, and supporting agencies. Understanding each part of this network is important to comprehending the whole. Overall, most leadership positions in Congress are governed by the seniority rule.

The House of Representatives: With its 435 members, the House of Representatives is over four times larger than the Senate. Still, it is referred to as the lower chamber of the Congress. **The Speaker**[4] of the House is the presiding officer of the House of Representatives. The position, established by the Constitution（**Article I, Section 2**[5]）, is next in line to succeed the President after the Vice President. Although formally elected by the entire House membership, the Speaker is nominated by the majority party, all of whose members routinely vote for him or her. The majority leader is the Speaker's chief deputy and the second most powerful figure in the majority party. The party whip（党干事）acts as an assistant majority or minority leader. Whips are chosen by the party caucus. Although they have little independent power, they serve their party leadership by encouraging party discipline and floor attendance during important votes.

Term of Office of the Representatives: Members of the House of Representatives are elected for two-year terms. Congressional elections are held in November of even-numbered years, and representatives begin their terms of office on January 3rd following the November election. This means all 435 members must run for reelection at the same time, and the House begins anew following each election.

Qualifications of the Representatives: The Constitution sets forth the qualifications for election to the House of Representatives. Members of the House must be at least twenty-five years of age, citizens of the United States for at least seven years old prior to the election, and legal residents of the state from which they are elected.

Although not required to do so by the Constitution, representatives have traditionally lived in the district they represent. This practice is rooted in the belief that representatives should be familiar with the needs of people they represent in Congress.

The Senate: The Senate is composed of two senators from each state, for a total of one hundred. Wyoming, with 450,000 citizens, is entitled to two senators, just as California, with a population of around 30 million. The Constitution specifies that the presiding officer of the Senate is the Vice President. Because he is not a member of the Senate, he votes only in the case of a tie. The true leader of the Senate is the majority leader, elected to the position by the majority party.

Term of Office of the Senators[6]: Senators serve for six-year term, three times of the length of those for which members of the House are chosen.（Article I, Section 3, Clause 1）Senators may be elected to any number of terms. Senators' terms are staggered. Only a third of them—33 or 34 terms—expire every two year. The Senate is , then a continuous body. That is, all of its seats are never up for election at the same time. The six-year term gives senators a somewhat greater degree of job security than members of the lower house have. Those six years give senators some insulation from the rough-and-tumble of day-to-day politics. The six-year term is also intended to make senators less subject to the pressures of public opinion and less susceptible to（对……敏感）the pleas of special interests than members of the House.

Qualifications of the Senators: A senator must meet a higher level of qualifications than for those the Constitution sets for a member of the House. A senator must be at least 30 years of age, must have been a citizen for at least nine years and must be an inhabitant of the state for which he or she is elected.（Article I, Section 3, Clause 3）Under the inhabitant qualification, a senator need not have lived in the state for any particular period of time. Most often, of course, senators have been long time residents of their states. The Senate, like the House, judges the qualifications of its members, and it may exclude a member by a majority vote.

The Committees[7]: In 1789 the House and Senate each adopted the practice of naming a special committee to consider each bill as it was introduced. By 1794 there were more than 300 committees in each chamber. Each house then began to set up permanent panels（专门小组）, known as standing committees, to which all similar bills could be sent. At times, each house finds need for a select committee. These groups are sometimes called special committees; they are panels set up for some specific purpose and, most often, for a limited time. The Speaker of the House or the President of the Senate appoints the members of these special committees with the advice of the majority and minority leaders. Most selected committees are formed to investigate a current matter. The congressional power to investigate is an essential part of the law-making function. Congress must decide on the needs for new laws and gauge the adequacy of those already on the books. It also must exercise its vital oversight function, to ensure that federal agencies are following the laws it has already passed. At times, too, a committee may conduct an investigation of an issue—for example, the threat of domestic terrorism—in order to focus public attention on that matter.

Permanent Committees of Congress		
House Standing Committees	Jointed Committees of Congress	Senate Standing Committees
Agriculture	Economic	Agriculture, Nutrition, and Forestry
Appropriations	The Library	Appropriations
Armed Services	Printing	Armed Services
Budgets	Taxation	Banking, Housing, and Urban Affairs
Education and the Workforce		Budgets
Energy and Commerce		Commerce, Science, and Transportation
Financial Services		Energy and Natural Resources
Government Reform		Environment and Public Works
House Administration		Finance
International Relations		Foreign Relations
Judiciary		Governmental Affairs
Resources		Indian Affairs
Rules		Judiciary
Science		Labor and Human Resources
Small Business		Rules and Administration
Standards of Official Conduct		Small Business
Transportation and Infrastructure		Veteran Affairs
Veteran Affairs		
Ways and Means		

Function of Congress: The primary duty of Congress is to make laws for the country. However, the law-making process is a very complicated one, like a labyrinth. For any bill to become a law, it must go through that labyrinthine procedure. It is confusing and frustrating. But briefly, its procedures can be summarized as follows.

(1) A bill is introduced. Anyone can draw up a bill—a member of Congress, the President or

a student. Many major bills are either conceived or written elsewhere. Thus, members of Congress spend considerable time processing what has been invented outside the Congress. However, official introduction of a bill can come only from a representative or a senator.

(2) The bill is referred to the committee by leadership in that particular House.

(3) The committee takes action. If the committee approves the bill, it is reported to the full House. In the House of Representatives, the Rules committee issues a rule of resolution to bring it to the floor.

(4) The bill goes on a calendar, which is a traffic-regulating device. In the House, there are five calendars: the union calendar for revenue and appropriations bills, the House calendar for all other public bills, the consent calendar for items having no opposition, the private calendar dealing with private matters such as a veteran's pension, and the discharge calendar for bills brought out of the committee by discharge petition. In the Senate, there are two calendars, one legislative and the other executive, the latter contains treaties and nominations.

(5) The bill goes to the floor. In the House, members who want to express their views on the proposed bills may debate among themselves within the allotted time, and after that, the House resolves itself into formal session and asks its members to cast vote. By contrast, the Senate debates major legislative measures at length, and they often merit being called "great debates".

(6) The bill may be subject to several votes on the floor. Once a bill has been approved at second reading, it is engrossed. This means the bill is printed in its final form. If the bill is approved at third reading the Speaker will sign it. A page—a legislative aide—then carries it to the Senate and places it on the Senate President's desk.

Notes

1. Congress 美国国会：行使立法权，制定影响每一个美国人的法律。立法经常需要在一些有争议的问题上作出决定，例如医疗保险改革、战争、贸易汇率等，法案经过一系列的审议程序后才能成为法律。

2. the Senate 美利坚合众国参议院：简称“美国参议院”，是美国的立法机构——美国国会的两院之一。美国每一个州的参议院中均有两位议员作为代表，与各州人口无关，全院员额为 100 名议员。

3. the House of Representatives 美利坚合众国众议院：简称“美国众议院”，是美国的立法机构——美国国会的两院之一。众议院一般被认为较参议院更具党派色彩。

4. the Speaker 美国众议院议长：是美国众议院的首席主持议会官员。一般美国众议院议长是由众议院成员选举出来的。

5. Article I, Section 2 宪法第一条第二款：美国《1787 年宪法》第一条第二款规定众议院由各州人民每两年选举产生的议员组成，众议院应选举该院议长和其他官员，并独立享有弹劾权。

6. Term of Office of the Senators 参议员任期：时间为六年，相互交错，每隔两年改选约三分之一席。

7. the Committees 委员会：在联邦层次上，两个大党都有自己的全国委员会，功能是筹款，组织宣传活动，尤其是积极准备总统大选。各委员会的成员构成都不同，但都主要由州层次党派的代表、附属组织和其他党派的重要人士组成。

Unit 3 The Presidency

"The presidency has made every man who occupied it, no matter how small, bigger than he was, and no matter how big, not big enough for its demands."

—Lyndon B. Johnson[1]

As President Johnson knew, the responsibilities of the President can be overwhelming. The President not only leads the government and the nation, but also heads a political party. Even before he or she reaches the White House, the long and arduous campaign process tests the president's mettle.

The President's Role: At any given time, of course, only one person is the President of the United States. The office, with all its powers and duties, belongs to that one individual. Whoever that person may be, he must fill a number of different roles, and all of them at the same time. The President is simultaneously (a) chief of state (元首), (b) chief executive(首席行政长官), (c) chief administrator, (d) chief diplomat (首席外交官), (e) **commander in chief[2]**, (f) chief legislator(首席立法者), (g) party chief, and (h) chief citizen.

(a) To begin with, the President is chief of state. This means he is the ceremonial head of the government of the United States, the symbol of all the people of the nation.

(b) The President is the nation's chief executive; he is vested by the Constitution with "the executive power" of the United States. That power is immensely broad in both domestic and foreign affairs. Indeed, the American presidency is often described as "the most powerful office in the world".

(c) The President is also the chief administrator or director of the federal government, heading one of the largest governmental machines the world has known.

(d) The President is also the nation's chief diplomat, the main architect of American foreign policy and the nation's chief spoken person to the rest of the world.

(e) In close connection with the President's role in foreign affairs, the Constitution also makes the President the commander in chief of the nation's armed forces. The one and a half million men and women in uniform and the nation's entire military arsenal are subject to the President's direct and immediate control.

(f) The President is also the nation's chief legislator, the main architect of its public policies. Most often it is the President who sets the overall shape of the congressional agenda. As chief legislator, the President initiates, suggests, requests, insists, and demands that Congress enact much of its major legislation.

These six presidential powers all come directly from the Constitution. Yet they do not complete the list. The President must still fill other vital roles.

(g) The President acts as the chief of party, the acknowledged leader of the political party that controls the executive branch. As you know, parties are not mentioned in the Constitution, yet they play a vital role in the working of the American governmental system. Thus, much of the real power and influence wielded by the President depends on the manner in which he or she plays this critical role.

(h) The office also automatically makes its occupant the nation's chief citizen. The President is expected to be "the representative of all the people". As the chief citizen, the President is expected to represent the public interests against many private interests.

Formal Qualification: The Constitution says that the President must (Article II , Section 1, Clause 5)

(a) Be "a natural born citizen". Under **the doctrine of jus sanguinis**[3] it is apparently possible for a person born abroad as an American citizen to become the President.

(b) Be at least 35 years of age. John F. Kennedy, at 43, was the youngest person ever to be elected President.

(c) Have lived in the United States for at least 14 years.

Given **Herbert Hoover**[4]'s election in 1928 and **Dwight Eisenhower**[5]'s in 1952, the 14-year requirement means any 14 years in a person's life. Both Hoover and Eisenhower spent several years before election outside the United States.

The President's Terms: The Framers considered a number of different limits on the length of the presidential term. Most of their debates centered on a four-year term, with the president eligible for reelection, versus a single six-year or seven-year term. They finally settled on a four-year term. They agreed, as **Alexander Hamilton**[6] wrote in *The Federalist No.71*, those four years was a long enough period for a president to have gained experience, demonstrated his abilities and established stable politics. Franklin D. Roosevelt broke this tradition by seeking and winning a third term in 1940, and then a fourth in 1944. To prevent future presidents from following this precedent, the 22nd Amendment made the unwritten custom limiting presidential terms a part of the written Constitution. This amendment, adopted in 1951, reads in part: "No person shall be elected to the office of the President more than twice, and no person who has held the office of President, or act as President, for more than two years of a term to which some other person was elected President shall be elected to the office of the President more than once."

Presidential Powers: The President heads the largest organization in the nation, a government that has nearly three million civilians and one million military employees. The President is entrusted with carrying out the laws of the land. In addition, the President is the chief architect of the American foreign policies, an increasing difficult task in our rapidly changing world. The President is the head of the world's most powerful military arsenal, the negotiator of treaties with other nations, the chief collector of taxes and the leading speaker for our nation. With a multitude of powers and duties that have increased greatly over time, the President has become ever more powerful and more complex.

Constitutional Power: Article II begins by simply stating that "the Executive Power shall be vested in the President of the United States of America." Article II grants the president broad but vaguely described powers. Because the power is not precisely defined, it can change with differing circumstances.

Section 2 and 3 of Article II go on to list specific presidential powers.

(a) Serve as commander in chief of the armed forces and the state militias.

(b) Appoint heads of executive departments with Senate approval.

(c) Grant reprieves and pardons, except in cases of impeachment.

(d) Make treaties, with the advice and consent of the Senate.

(e) Appoint ambassadors, federal court judges, justices of the Supreme Court, and other top officials with Senate consent.

(f) Deliver the annual State of the Union address to Congress and send other messages to Congress from time to time.

(g) Call either or both chambers of Congress into special session.

(h) Receive ambassadors and other representatives from foreign countries.

(i) Commission all military officers of the United States.

(j) Ensure that all laws passed by Congress are carried out.

Other Presidential Powers

Military Power: Often, a president has exercised military powers that Congress has argued were outside the president's authority. Several presidents have used the armed forces abroad, without a declaration of war by Congress. In fact, most presidents have done so, and on no fewer than 200 occasions.

Executive Powers: An executive order is an order issued by the President to carry out policies described in laws that have been passed by Congress. Executive orders have the force of law. In all, the U.S. presidents have issued about thirteen thousand executive orders for many purposes.

Presidential succession and the Vice President: Presidential succession is the scheme by which a presidential vacancy is filled. If a president dies, resigns, or is removed from office by impeachment, the Vice President succeeds to the office. Originally the Constitution did not provide for the succession of the Vice President. But in practice the Vice President did succeeded to the office when it became vacant. This practice became a part of the Constitution with the adoption of the 25th Amendment in 1967.

"In case of the removal of the President from office or of his death or resignation, the Vice President shall become President."

Vice Presidential Vacancy: The Vice President has been vacant 18 times thus far: nine times by succession to the presidency, twice by resignation, and seven times by death.

John C. Calhoun resigned to become a senator from South Carolina in 1832. Spiro T. Andrew resigned in 1973, after a conviction for income tax evasion and in the face of other charges. The seven who died in office were: George Clinton (1812), Elbridge Gerry (1814), William R. King (1853), Henry Wilson (1875), Thomas A. Hendricks (1885), Garret A. Hobart (1899), and James S. Sherman (1912).

Yet, not until 1967 and the 25th Amendment did the Constitution deal with this matter. The Amendment provides, in part:

"*Whenever there is a vacancy in the office of the Vice President, the President shall nominate a Vice President who shall take office upon confirmation by a majority vote of both House of Congress.*"

The Cabinet[7] : The Cabinet is an advisory group chosen by the President to help accomplish the work of the executive branch. Today, the cabinet is made up of the heads of the fourteen executive departments, the Vice President, and other key officials chosen by the President. The fourteen departments of the executive branches are:

- State
- Treasury
- Defense
- Commerce
- Labor
- Health and Human Services
- Housing and Urban Development
- Justice
- Interior
- Agriculture
- Education
- Energy
- Transportation
- Veteran Affairs

The Cabinet members play two major and sometimes conflicting roles. First, as Cabinet members, they are appointed by the President and serve as advisers to the President. The extent to which a president uses the Cabinet for advice depends on the President's view of the Cabinet. The second role is as the administrative heads of their executive departments. By custom, the Cabinet members resign after a new President is elected. In this way, the new President can create a new Cabinet.

The Executive Office of the President

White House Office: Of all the executive staff agencies in the EOP, the White House Office has the most direct contact with the President. The White House Office consists of the President's key aides, whom the President sees daily, as well as several hundred professional and clerical staff members.

Office of Management and Budget: The Office of Management and Budget（OMB）has become an important and influential unit of the executive office. The main function of the OMB is to assist the President in preparing the proposed annual budget, which the President must summit to Congress each year.

National Security Council: The National Security Council（NSC）was created to provide advice on and managerial assistance with matters concerning American military and foreign policies, as well as national security.

Office of National Drug Control Policy: The Office of National Drug Control Policy was created in 1989. Its existence dramatizes the nation's concern over drugs. The office is headed by a director who is appointed by the President, subject to the Senate's approval.

Council of Economic Advisers: The Council of Economic Advisers（CEA）was created by Congress in 1946 to advise the President on economic matters. It analyzes the national economy, advises the President on how the economy is doing and recommends measures to maintain economic stability in the nation.

Notes

1. Lyndon B. Johnson 林登·贝恩斯·约翰逊: 林登·贝恩斯·约翰逊(1908年8月27日—1973年1月22日)是美国第36任总统。约翰逊从年轻时就开始从政，29岁即当选为国会议员，是罗斯福总统“新政”的积极支持者。第二次世界大战后，不论是民主党执政，还是共和党掌权，他都紧跟执政者，因而官运亨通，步步高升。肯尼迪被刺后他入主白宫，任内在外交上无甚建树，内政方面提出过不少有关社会福利和民权的法案，以推行其“伟大的社会”施政计划。他一手扩大越南战争，使侵越美军从他出任总统时的1万余人激增至卸任前的50多万人。在战事失利后，美国国内出现反战浪潮，同时种族暴乱频仍，民主党党内矛盾重重，陷于分裂。他做出了不参加下届总统竞选的决定，从此退出政坛。

2. commander in chief 三军统帅: 美国武装部队总司令。在战争和紧急情况下，经国会授权，总统还可以拥有更大的权力。

3. the doctrine of jus sanguinis 血统主义: 根据血统决定国籍。

4. Herbert Hoover 赫伯特·胡佛: 美国第31任总统，全名赫伯特·克拉克·胡佛，生于艾奥瓦州，毕业于斯坦福大学，曾是一名采矿工程师。1897年，胡佛与罗·亨利结婚。亨利受过良好的教育，婚后成为胡佛的贤内助，他们有两个儿子。胡佛为一家公司所雇用去了澳大利亚，后来到中国，在一家私人企业公司工作，担任主要的工程师。他在1953年被任命为艾森豪威尔总统的委托主席。1964年10月20日，胡佛逝世于纽约。24岁的胡佛曾作为美国白领被派往中国河北唐山的开滦煤矿打工。

5. Dwight Eisenhower 德怀特·艾森豪威尔: 美国第34任总统(1953—1961年)。1890年，艾森豪威尔出生于美国得克萨斯州丹尼森的一个基督徒家庭。1915年毕业于西点军校，毕业时在班上排在第61名，只得到军士长的军衔。后来在得克萨斯州圣安东尼第19步兵师服役，获得少尉军衔。第二次世界大战期间，他担任盟军在欧洲的最高指挥官，1944 至 1945 年负责计划和执行监督进攻维希法国和纳粹德国的行动。1948 年 2 月退役，任哥伦比亚大学校长至 1953 年（但从 1950 年起一直担任北约总司令）。1952 年作为共和党总统候选人参加竞选总统并获胜，成为美国第 34 任总统，1956 年再次竞选获胜，蝉联总统。1969 年 3 月 28 日在华盛顿因心脏病逝世。

6. Alexander Hamilton 亚历山大・汉密尔顿： 亚历山大・汉密尔顿（1757 年 1 月 11 日—1804 年 7 月 12 日）是美国的开国元勋之一、宪法的起草人之一、财经专家、美国第一任财政部长。他是美国政党制度的创建者，在美国金融、财政和工业发展史上占有重要地位，最终因政党相争而丧生。2006 年，汉密尔顿被美国的权威期刊《大西洋月刊》评为影响美国的 100 位人物第 5 名。

7. The Cabinet 内阁： 内阁是美国联邦行政部门，总统有权提名，并于取得参议院的意见和同意后，任命大使、公使及领事、最高法院的法官以及一切其他在宪法中未经明定、但以后将依法律的规定而设置之合众国官员。

Unit 4 The Judiciary and the Supreme Court

Sources of American Law: The body of American law includes the federal and state constitutions, statues passed by legislative bodies, administrative law and case law the legal principles expressed in court decisions.

The Federal Court System: The United States has a dual court system. There are state courts and federal courts. Each of the fifty states, as well as the District of Columbia, has its own fully developed, independent system of courts. The only federal court that the Constitution requires is the Supreme Court, as specified in Article III. All other federal courts and their jurisdictions are creation of Congress.

Congress has created two kinds of lower federal courts to handle cases that need not be decided by the Supreme Court: constitutional and legislative courts. A constitutional court is one exercising the judicial powers found in Article III of the Constitution, and therefore its judges are given constitutional protection: they are not to be fired nor may their salaries be reduced while they are in office. The most important things of the constitutional courts are the district courts and the courts of appeals. A legislative court is set up by Congress for some specialized purpose and staffed with people who have fixed terms of office and can be removed or have their salaries reduced. Legislative courts include the Court of Military and the territorial courts.

Jurisdiction of the Federal Court: In Latin, juris means "law", and diction means "to speak". Thus, jurisdiction literally refers to the power "to speak the law". In other words, jurisdiction is the authority of a court to decide a certain case. Before any court can hear a case, it must have jurisdiction over the persons, property or subject matter of the dispute. A court has original jurisdiction when it can hear the case for the first time. Because the national government is a government of limited powers, the jurisdiction of the federal courts is also limited. Basically, the federal courts can only decide cases involving federal questions or diversity of citizenship.

The Supreme Court: The U.S. Supreme Court is the highest level of the three-tiered（三层式）federal court system. The Supreme Court consists of nine justices, who are nominated by the President and confirmed by the Senate. The Constitution is silent on the qualifications for the appointment to the Supreme Court. The Framers quite purposely placed the Court on an equal plane with the President and Congress. As the highest court in the land, the Supreme Court stands as the court of last resort in all questions of federal laws. That is, it is the final authority in any case involving any question arising under the Constitution, an act of Congress, or a treaty of the United States.

Factors bearing on a decision include whether a legal question has been decided differently by various lower courts and need resolution by the highest court, whether a lower court's decision conflicts with an existing Supreme Court ruling and whether the issue could have significance beyond the parties to the dispute. Another factor is whether the solicitor general is pressuring the Court to take a case.

If the Court decided to grant a petition for review, it will issue a **writ（令状）of certiorari**[1]. The writ orders a lower court to send the Supreme Court a record of the case for review. More than 90 percent of the petitions for writs of certiorari are denied. A deny is not a decision on the merits of a case, nor does it indicate agreement with the lower court's opinion. Therefore, denial of the writ has no value as a precedent. The Court will not issue a writ unless four justices approve it. This is called **the rule of four**[2]**.**

Once the Supreme Court grants certiorari in a particular case, the justices do extensive research on the legal issues and facts involved in the case. Each justice is entitled to four law clerks, who undertake much of the research and preliminary drafting necessary for the justice to form an opinion.

The Court normally does not hear any evidence, as is true with all appeal courts. The Court's consideration of a case is based on the abstracts, the record and the briefs. The attorneys are permitted to present oral arguments. The Court hears oral argument on Monday, Tuesday, Wednesday and sometimes Thursday usually for seven two-week sessions scattered from the first week in October to the end of April or the first week of May. All statements and the justices' questions are tape-recorded during these sections. Unlike the practice in most courts, lawyers addressing the Supreme Court can be questioned by the justices at any time during oral argument.

When the Court has reached a decision, its opinion is written. The opinion contains the Court's ruling on the issues or issues presented the reasons for its decision, the rules of law that apply and other information. In many cases, the decision of the lower court is affirmed, resulting in the enforcement of that Court's judgment or decree. If the Supreme Court feels that a reversible error is committed during the trial or that the jury is instructed improperly, the decision will be reversed.

Shortly after the opinion was written, the Supreme Court announces its decision from the bench. At that time, the opinion is made available to the public at the office of the clerks of the Court. The clerks also release the opinion for online publication. Ultimately, the opinion is published in the United States Reports, which is the official printed record of the Court's decisions.

Most courts in this country, both federal and state, may exercise the critically important power of judicial review. They have the extraordinary power to decide the constitutionality of an act of government, whether executive, legislative or judicial. The ultimate exercise of that power rests with the Supreme Court of the United States. That single fact makes the Supreme Court the final authority on the meaning of the Constitution. The power of judicial review is not mentioned in the Constitution. Rather, it was established by the United States Supreme Court's decision in **Marbury v. Madison**[3] in 1803. The impact of the Court's decision goes far beyond the fate of an obscure individual named William Marbury. In this decision, **Chief Justice Marshall**[4] claimed for the Supreme Court the right to declare acts of Congress unconstitutional, and so laid the foundation for the judicial branch's key role in the development of the American system of government. The Court has used its power of judicial review in thousands of cases since 1803. Usually it has upheld the constitutionality of federal and state actions. The dramatic and often far-reaching effects of the Supreme Court's exercise of the power of judicial review tend to overshadow much of its other work. Each year, it has dozens of cases in which questions of constitutionality are not raised, but in which federal laws are interpreted and applied. In interpreting those laws and applying them to special situations, the Court has had a real impact on both their meaning and their effect.

Checks on Judicial Power: No institution of government, including the Court, operates without restraints. The fact that judges are not elected does not make them immune to public opinion or to the views of the other branches of government. The importance of these restraints varies from case to case, but in the broad course of history they have been significant.

Congress and the Courts: Congress has a number of ways of checking the power of judiciary. It can gradually alter the composition of the judiciary by kinds of appointments the Senate is willing to confirm or it can impeach judges it does not like. In practice, however, **impeachment**[5] can rarely be used to make much of an impact on the federal courts because simple policy disagreements are not generally regarded as adequate grounds for trying to impeach（弹劾）a judge, and most judicial appointments are not challenged.

Notes

1. writ of certiorari 调卷令：指上级法院向下级法院 / 准司法机构调取案卷的令状。

2. the rule of four 四人规则：美国最高法院程序要求在审理案件之前必须获得四个肯定票才允许听审。

3. Marbury v. Madison 马布里诉麦迪逊案：美国宪法中最著名的案例之一，此案奠定了美国宪法中司法审查权的先例，从司法角度来看，本案堪称法律史上最伟大的判例之一。

4. Chief Justice Marshall 最高法院首席法官马歇尔：任美国最高法院首席法官长达 34

年，创造了许多司法惯例。

5. impeachment 弹劾：凡对行政或司法官员有失职或违法行为所提出的处分与惩戒的请求叫作弹劾，在三权分立的国家，此权多属于议会。

Unit 5 State and Local Government

"The powers reserved to the several States will extend to all the objects which, in the ordinary course of affairs, concern lives, liberties and properties of the people, and the internal order, improvement, and prosperity of the State."

— *Federalist No.*45

Federalism divided sovereignty between the states and the national government. Its existence in the United States in the result of a compromise between Constitutional Convention delegates who believed that a strong national government was necessary to preserve stability, and those who feared that centralized power would lead to tyranny.

Because the federal structure was a compromise, the Constitution does not clearly define the powers of federal and state government. And the power of the states was further eroded with the election of **Franklin D. Roosevelt**[1] and the enactment of **New Deal**[2] legislation. Despite the expansion of federal power, state and local governments remain vital components of the federal system. Nearly half the domestic expenditures of the government are paid for with state and local tax dollars.

State Government: When the Constitution is written, the design of the federal government was adapted from that which existed in many states. Thus, it is not surprising that the basic organization of most state government bear a strong resemblance to that of the national government. Just as Congress has Senate and the House of Representatives, the legislatures of all states except Nebraska have an upper and lower chamber of the federal system. And every state has an independently elected governor, the state chief executive whose responsibilities roughly parallel those of the president.

State governments vary in many important ways, however. State legislatures vary greatly in size. Lower houses have around 100 representatives, but in **Alaska**[3], Delaware, and Nevada they have as few as 40 members each, whereas in New Hampshire, with a similarly small population, the lower house has 400 legislators. Some state government holds their elections in even-numbered year, in conjunction with federal races. In some states, state administrative officers from the secretary of state to the attorney general are elected, whereas in other states, the governor appoints these officials. State government can play key roles in economic development, and governors are often well positioned to seek the presidency.

State Elections: Despite policies differences among the states, state elections bear a strong resemblance to national elections. The same two political parties—Republic And Democratic—are the dominant competitors in nearly all state elections. For many decades following **the Civil**

War[4], the Republicans dominated the North, whereas the South was solidly Democratic. These regional patterns of party dominance have broken down in recent years as a result of the civil right movement and population shifts. Republicans now often win as many southern elections as Democrats do. A new trend towards competitive politics and divided government has developed in most states. Democrats have had the advantage in state legislative races; Republicans have more often elected governors.

Local Government: State and local governments now play a more prominent role in the federal system. In sheer number, local government constitutes an overwhelming and growing presence—there were over 74,000 in 2002, up from about 46,000 in 1942. There were several major types of local governments, each of which has responsibilities that vary from state to state. Though the basic unit in most states is the county, not all counties are alike. Many counties are divided into townships—there are 16,500 of them nationwide—whose duties generally include local road maintenance and other small-scale activities.

As the population has become concentrated in urban areas, the total number of municipalities—cities, suburbs, and towns—has increased to nearly 20,000. In most states, these municipal governments have assumed many of the responsibilities once performed by counties.

States, counties, and municipalities have also created an extraordinary array of special districts—over 35,000 in all. Each special district has responsibility for only one or a few special governmental functions. Such governments are unique in that they overlap the boundaries of other governments, sometimes spanning many different municipal jurisdictions.

Local Elections: Most local governments are run by elected officials, although special district heads are sometimes appointed by other local governments. In the United States as a whole, the total number of elected local officials approaches half-a-million people. But despite the large number of local elections, actual rates of citizen participation in them are surprising low.

Notes

1. Franklin D. Roosevelt 富兰克林·德拉诺·罗斯福: 富兰克林·德拉诺·罗斯福（1882年1月30日—1945年4月12日），美国第32任总统，美国历史上唯一连任超过两届（连任四届，病逝于第四届任期中）的总统，美国迄今为止在任时间最长的总统。罗斯福家族在美国有近300年的历史，美国第26任总统西奥多·罗斯福是富兰克林·罗斯福的堂叔。在20世纪30年代经济大萧条时期，罗斯福推行新政以提供失业救济与复苏经济，并成立众多机构来改革经济和银行体系，从经济危机的深渊中挽救了美国，他所发起的一些计划至今仍在国家的商贸中扮演着重要角色。除此之外，在其任内设立的一些制度仍然保留至今。罗斯福曾促成了政党重组，他与其妻埃莉诺·罗斯福至今仍是美国现代自由主义的典范。罗斯福是第二次世界大战期间同盟国阵营的重要领导人之一。1941年珍珠港事件发生后，罗斯福力主对日本宣战，并引进了价格管制和配给。罗斯福以租借法案使美国转变为“民主国家的兵工厂”，使美国成为同盟国主要的军火供应商和融资者，也使得美国国内产业大幅扩张，实现充分就业。二战后期同盟国逐渐扭转形势后，罗斯福对塑造战后世界秩序发挥了关键作用，其影响力在雅尔塔会议及联合国的成立中尤其明显。后来，在美国的协助下，盟军击败德国、意大利和日本。

2. New Deal 新政：美国罗斯福政府于 1933 年 3 月至 1939 年年间为克服 1929—1933 年经济危机采取了一系列政策措施，1932 年 7 月 2 日，罗斯福在接受总统候选人提名演说中第一次使用这个名词。一般来说，新政的目的在于在保存资产阶级民主的前提下挽救资本主义制度，防止法西斯主义。它大体有三个方面的内容：①恢复陷入大萧条的经济；②救济大规模失业者和贫民；③限制垄断资本的某些弊端。为实现这些目标，罗斯福大力加强国家对社会经济生活的干预。新政大体可分为两个阶段：1935 年以前和 1935—1939 年。第一阶段着重调整与恢复，第二阶段着重改革，救济则贯彻始终。

3. Alaska 阿拉斯加州：位于北美大陆西北端，东与加拿大接壤，另三面环北冰洋、白令海和北太平洋。该州拥有全美 20 座最高山脉中的 17 座，6 194 米的麦金利峰是北美最高峰。世界上大多数活动冰川在此州境内，其中最大的马拉斯皮纳冰川流域面积为 5 703 平方千米。全州面积 1 717 854 平方千米，占全国面积的五分之一，是美国面积最大的州。东南部与中南部为温带气候，全年气温约 0~15 ℃；内陆为大陆型气候，夏季极昼时可达 26 ℃，冬季极夜时可达 –15 ℃。西部与西南部受海洋影响，寒冷风大。北极圈内为极地气候，气温常年处于零度以下。

4. the Civil War 南北战争：又称“美国内战”（American Civil War），是美国历史上一场大规模的内战，参战双方为美利坚合众国（简称“联邦”）和美利坚联盟国（简称“邦联”）。这场战争的起因为美国南部 11 州以亚伯拉罕・林肯于 1861 年就任总统为由而陆续退出联邦，另成立以杰斐逊・戴维斯为“总统”的政府，并驱逐驻扎南方的联邦军，而林肯下令攻打“叛乱”州。1865 年 4 月 3 日，联邦军攻克里士满；4 月 9 日，同盟军总司令罗伯特・李将军率部 2.8 万人向联邦军投降，美国南北战争以北方的胜利而告终，美国恢复统一。

References

[1] FIORINA M P, PETERSON P E. The new American democracy [M]. Boston: Allyn and Bacon, 1998.

[2] O'CONNOR K, Sabato L J, Yanus A B. American government [M]. New York: Pearson longman, 2006.

[3] MCCLENAGHAN W M. Magruder's American Government 2001 [M]. Upper Saddle River: Prentice Hall, 2001.

[4] WILSON J Q. American government: brief version [M]. Boston: Cengage Learning, 2013.

[5] SCHMIDT S W, SHELLEY M C, BARDES B A. American government and politics today (2013-2014) [M]. Boston: Cengage Learning, 2013.

Chapter Three

American Politics

Unit 1 American Democracy

Democracy, which derives from the Greek word "demos" or "people", is defined, basically, as government in which the supreme power is vested in the people. In some forms, democracy can be exercised directly by the people; in large societies, it is by the people through their elected agents. Or, in the memorable phrase of President Abraham Lincoln, democracy is **government "of the people, by the people, and for the people"** [1].

Most Americans have rooted beliefs that liberty and equality are the nation's founding principles and people should have civil rights to protect themselves from any forms of governmental oppressions. Though democracy remains a central feature of the American political system in principle, in practice debates and conflicts over how to deal with the power of government and how to protect most people's benefits have never ceased in the political arena. The *Declaration of Independence* set forth some of the principles of American democracy besides declaring the colonies to be a new nation. The document says that all people are created equal, that all have the right to "life, liberty, and the pursuit of happiness" and that governments obtain their powers from "the consent of the governed". The Declaration, and the Constitution after it, combined America's colonial experience with reflection upon the thought of political philosophers such as **John Locke**[2] to produce the new concept of a democracy governed by the people's representatives for the purpose of protecting the rights of individuals. To better understand American democracy, we need to, first of all, get acquainted with the key principles embedded in it.

Rule by Law

For much of human history, rulers and law were synonymous (同义词的)—law was simply the will of the ruler. A first step away from such tyranny was the notion of rule by law, including the notion that even a ruler is under the law and should rule by virtue of legal means. Democracies went further by establishing the rule of law. Although no society or government system is problem-free, rule of law protects fundamental political, social and economic rights and reminds us that tyranny and lawlessness are not the only alternative.

Popular Consent

Popular consent, the idea that governments must draw their powers from the consent of the governed, is one distinguishing characteristic of American democracy. Derived from Locke's social contract theory, the notion of popular consent was central to the *Declaration of Independence*. A citizen's willingness to vote represents his or her consent to be governed and is thus an essential premise of democracy. Growing numbers of nonvoters can threaten the operation and legitimacy of a truly democratic system. So, too, can voting systems that appear to disregard people's election choices.

Popular Sovereignty

Sovereignty, by definition, means the greatest authority and power to command all others. Every nation-state in the modern world has sovereignty. It may reside in a king, in a parliament, or in the state. In the case of the United States, popular sovereignty means that people are sovereign, because they, by consent, "do ordain and establish this Constitution for the United States of America". By resting sovereignty in the people, the notion suggests, in theory at least, that a government can always be changed, preferably by majority rules, and, if necessary, by revolution. However, this concept is ambiguous, because it does not say clearly who are these "people" in whom sovereignty rests. Obviously, the Founding Fathers did not include women, blacks, Indians, and youths under eighteen in the "people". At its best, it is hoped, now and then, that it means an ever-improving democracy that seeks to draw more and more of the citizenry in the bloodstream of political decision making.

Individualism

Tremendous value is placed on the individual in American democracy and culture. All individuals are deemed rational and fair, and endowed, as Thomas Jefferson proclaimed in the *Declaration of Independence*, "with certain unalienable rights". Individualism, which holds that the primary function of government is to enable the individual to achieve his or her highest level of development, makes the interests of the individual more important than those of the state and at the heart of the capitalistic system. It is also a concept whose meaning has changed over time. The rugged individualism of the western frontier, for example, was altered as more citizens moved westward, cities developed, and demands for government services increased. This does not mean, however, that Americans aren't concerned with others.

Personal Liberty

Personal liberty is perhaps the single most important characteristic of American democracy. The Constitution itself was written to assure "life" and "liberty". The Framers intended Americans to be free from governmental infringements（侵犯）on freedom of religion and speech, from unreasonable search and seizure, and so on. The *Bill of Rights* contains the most sweeping and substantive protection for personal liberty in the United States. The addition of **the Fourteenth Amendment to the Constitution**[3] and its emphasis on equal protection of the laws and subsequent passage of laws guarantee civil rights.

American Political Culture: Conflict and Consensus

Underlying and framing political struggles in the United States are agreements and disagreements over basic political values and philosophies. Philosophical positions and values shape citizens' view of the world and define their sense of what is right and wrong. Philosophical principles or values can help people communicate and agree upon a common system of government and politics. However, sharing broad values does not guarantee political consensus. American history is a story of success in which the American consensus around a set of basic political ideals provides the framework for the political inclusion of all groups. But today this story of progress is questioned from different sides, highlighting the continuing significance of conflict. For example, Americans have disagreed over the meaning of equality, but they still agree on the importance of this ideal.

Notes

1. government "of the people, by the people, and for the people" "民有、民治、民享"之政府：这一纲领性口号出自林肯的《葛底斯堡演说》，它描绘了一个理想的政府，道出了民主的真谛。

2. John Locke 约翰·洛克：约翰·洛克（1632—1704）是英国伟大的思想家、哲学家和著述家。他的思想对于后代政治哲学的发展产生巨大影响，他的著作也大大影响了伏尔泰和卢梭以及许多苏格兰启蒙运动的思想家和美国开国元勋。他的理论体现在美国的《独立宣言》上。

3. the Fourteenth Amendment to the Constitution 美国宪法第十四条修正案：这一修正案涉及公民权利和平等法律保护，最初提出是为了解决南北战争后昔日奴隶的相关问题。第十四条修正案对美国历史产生了深远的影响，有"第二次制宪"之称，之后的大量司法案件均是以此为基础的。

Unit 2 Federalism[1]

Federalism is a rather unusual system for governing, with particular consequences for those who live within it. This section explains the federal system and how it affects Americans living in such a system.

What Is Federalism?

Federalism is a way of organizing a nation so that two or more levels of government have formal authority over the same areas and people. It is a system of shared power between units of government. In a federal system, authority is divided, usually by a written constitution, between a central government and regional governments. The central government and the constituent governments both act directly on the people through laws and through the actions of elected and appointed governmental officials. For example, the state of California has formal authority over its inhabitants, but the national government can also pass laws and establish policies that affect Californians.

The Roots of the Federalism

The relationship between the national and state governments, and their intertwined powers, are the heart of federalism, the philosophy that defines the allocation of power between the national government and the states. Federalist supporters of the new Constitution articulated three major arguments for federalism: (a) the prevention of tyranny; (b) the provision for increased participation in politics; and, (c) the use of the states as testing grounds or laboratories for new policies and programs.

The historical basis of the federal system was laid down in Philadelphia at the Constitutional Convention, where strong national government advocates opposed equally strong states' rights advocates. This dichotomy (观点分歧) continued through to the ratifying conventions in the several states. The resulting federal system was a compromise. The appeal of federalism was that it retained state traditions and local power while establishing a strong national government capable of handling common problems.

The Powers of Government in the Federal System

No mention of the designation "federal system" can be found in the U.S. Constitution. Nor is it possible to find a systematic division of governmental authority between the national and state governments in that document. Rather, the Constitution sets out different types of powers—the powers of the national government, the powers of the states, and prohibited powers. The Constitution also makes it clear that if a state or local law conflicts with a national law, the national law will prevail.

Powers of the National Government

Three types of powers are delegated to the national government by the Constitution: expressed (or enumerated) powers, implied powers and inherent powers.

Most of the powers explicitly delegated to the national government are enumerated—that is, specifically listed—in Article I, Section 8. These are called expressed powers, or **enumerated powers**[2], which include:

- Coining money.
- Regulating interstate commerce.

• Levying and collecting taxes.
• Declaring war.
• Establishing post offices.

Some of the amendments to the Constitution give expressed powers, too. The Sixteenth Amendment, for example, gives Congress the power to impose a federal income tax.

The national government has certain powers that are not expressly given to it in the Constitution but are reasonably implied by the expressed powers. These powers are called **implied powers**[3]. Their constitutional basis is found in Article I, Section 8, and Clause 18. This clause states that Congress shall have the power "to make all Laws which shall be necessary and proper for carrying into Execution the foregoing Powers, and all other Powers vested by this Constitution in the Government of the United States, or in any Department or Officer thereof". This clause is sometimes called the elastic clause, or the necessary and proper clause, because it provides flexibility to the constitutional system.

The final category of powers, is known as **inherent powers**[4], and these are powers that the national government has simply to ensure the nation's integrity and survival as a political unit. The inherent powers are few but important. Each nation's government must clearly have the ability to act in its own interest within the community of nations. Therefore, each national government must have the ability to make treaties, to regulate immigration, to acquire territory, to wage war, and to declare peace.

Powers of the State Governments

The Tenth Amendment states that the powers not delegated to the United States by the Constitution, nor prohibited by it to the states, are reserved to the states, or to the people. These are the **reserved powers**[5] that the national government cannot deny to the states. One reserved power is each state's right to regulate commerce within its borders. Another is the right to provide for a state militia. In essence, states have the authority over all their internal affairs and over the health, safety, and welfare of their people. These are called **police powers**[6] which enable states to pass laws governing such activities as crimes, marriage, contracts, education, intrastate transportation, and land use.

Notes

1. federalism 联邦制：美国实行的是联邦制，即由中央联邦政府和州政府共同分享政治权力，但联邦宪法高于各州宪法，联邦法律高于各州法律。因此，美国公民都在两种法律下生活，他们既要遵守联邦法，又要遵守各自所在州的法律。

2. enumerated powers 列举权力：指宪法明确授权由联邦享有的权力。例如，组织和供养陆军和海军的权力。

3. implied powers 默示权力：美国联邦政府除依宪法明文规定所享有的各项权力外，还拥有依宪法第 1 条第 8 项第 18 款引申出来的其他权力，只要与宪法的条文和精神相一致，就都是符合宪法的。

4. inherent powers 固有权力：国家政府代表国家处理与他国关系的自然权力。

5. reserved powers 保留权力：宪法未提供给联邦政府或禁止州政府执行的权力称为保留权力。

6. police powers 治安权：各州政府行使治安权，管理内部事务，维护社会治安、公民健康、道德规范、安全及福利。

Unit 3 Political Parties and Interest Groups

There is one more important part of the American political scene which is not part of any formal written document: the political party system. Parties began to form shortly after the Constitution went into effect; parties proved to be an effective way within a system of checks and balances for people with similar views to band together to achieve national goals.

What Is a Political Party?

A political party is an organization where a group of people who, sharing political beliefs, ideals and values, get themselves organized for common interests to seek political power by trying to elect their own people to political positions. Political parties are not mentioned in the U.S. Constitution. The framers believed the government would work better without parties, because parties represent narrow interests instead of the general interests of the public. Yet, parties began to form shortly afterwards, and have since played a central role in American political history. Political parties in the United States engage in a wide variety of activities, through which, parties perform a number of functions for the political system. These functions include the following:

Recruiting Candidates for Public Office: Because it is the goal of parties to gain control of government, they must work to recruit candidates for all elective offices.

Organizing and Running Elections: Although elections are a government activity, political parties actually organize the voter-registration drives; recruit the volunteers to work at the polls, and work to increase voter participation.

Presenting Alternative Policies to the Electorate: In contrast to factions, which are often centered on individual politicians, parties are focused on a set of political positions.

Accepting Responsibility for Operating the Government: When a party elects the president or governor and members of the legislature, it accepts the responsibility for running the government.

Acting as the Organized Opposition to the Party in Power: The "out" party, or the one that does not control the government, is expected to articulate its own policies and oppose the winning party when appropriate.

The Two-Party System[1]

In the United States, the two-party system has become the dominant feature in the political landscape. When one says that Americans have a two-party system, it doesn't mean that there are only two parties in the United States. Usually about a dozen parties nominate candidates in the presidential election. We call it a two-party system because there are two major parties—the Democratic Party and the Republican Party—and a number of third parties. Although third parties havc often appeared in presidential elections, no third-party candidate has ever won. And very few third-party candidates have won seats in Congress.

The Democratic Party, which evolved out of Thomas Jefferson's party, formed before 1800. The symbol of the party is the donkey. The Republican Party, also known as the GOP, **Grand Old Party[2]**, was formed in the 1850s by people in the states of the North and West, such as Abraham Lincoln, who wanted the government to prevent the expansion of slavery into new states then being admitted to the union. The symbol of the Republican Party is the elephant.

Most Americans today consider the Democratic Party the more liberal party. The Democrats believe in a strong role for government. They propose higher taxes to pay for social and economic programs for those who need them. The Democrats earned that reputation in the 1930s when there was a worldwide economic depression. Under President Franklin Roosevelt's "New Deal" plan, Democrats set up government programs that provided paid employment for people building dams, roads and public buildings. Regarded as "the party of the people", the Democratic Party now has particular appeal to ethnic minorities and women.

Considered to be more socially conservative than the Democrats, the Republican Party favors state rights and strengthening the armed forces. They believe that many social programs are too costly to the taxpayers and that when taxes are raised to pay for programs, everyone is hurt. They place more emphasis on private enterprise and often accuse the Democrats of making the government too expensive and of creating too many laws that harm individual initiative. Republicans count a strong following among the middle class, business interests, and the farming community.

Why Has the Two-Party System Endured?

There are several reasons why two major parties have dominated the political landscape in the United States for almost two centuries.

1.The Historical Foundations of the Two-Party System

As we have seen, at many times in American history there has been one preeminent issue or dispute that divided the nation politically. In the beginning, Americans were at odds（争执，不合） over ratifying the Constitution. After the Constitution went into effect, the power of the federal government became the major national issue. Thereafter, the dispute over slavery divided the nation by section, North versus South. When politics is based on an argument between two opposing points of view, advocates of each viewpoint can mobilize most effectively by forming a single, unified party. Also, when a two-party system has been in existence for almost two centuries, it becomes difficult to imagine an alternative.

2.Political Socialization and Practical Considerations

Given that the majority of Americans identify with one of the two major political parties, it is not surprising that most children learn at a fairly young age to think of themselves as either Democrats or Republicans. This generates a built-in mechanism to perpetuate（使永久存在）a two-party system. Also, many politically oriented people who aspire to work for social change consider that the only realistic way to capture political power in this country is to be either a Republican or a Democrat.

3.The Winner-Takes-All[3] Electoral System

At virtually every level of government in the United States, the outcome of elections is based on the plurality, winner-takes-all principle. A plurality system is onc in which the winner is the person who obtains the most votes, even if a majority（over 50 percent of the votes）is not obtained. Minor parties have a difficult time competing under such a system, even though they may influence the final outcome of the election. Because voters know that minor parties cannot succeed, they often will not vote for minor-party candidates.

4.State and Federal Laws Favoring the Two Parties

Many state and federal election laws offer a clear advantage to the two major parties. In some states, the established major parties need to gather fewer signatures to place their candidates on the ballot than minor parties or independent candidates do. The criterion for determining how many signatures will be required is often based on the total party vote in the last general election, thus penalizing a new political party that did not compete in that election. At the national level, minor parties face different obstacles. All of the rules and procedures of both houses of Congress divide committee seats, staff members, and other privileges on the basis of party membership.

What Is an Interest Group[4]?

All of us have interests that we want represented in government. Farmers want higher prices for their products. Young people want good educational and job opportunities. Environmentalists want clear air and water. Homeless people want programs for food and shelter. Throughout American history, organizing to promote and protect such interests has been a natural part of democracy. Defining the term interest group seems simple enough. Interest in this sense refers to objectives and policy goals. A group is an accumulation of people with something in common. An interest group is an organization made up of people who share common objectives and who actively attempt to influence government policymakers through direct and indirect methods. Interest groups are often criticized in the United States, but they do serve several purposes in American politics:

• Interest groups help bridge the gap between citizens and government and enable citizens to explain their views on policies to public officials.

- Interest groups help raise public awareness and inspire action on various issues.
- Interest groups often give specialized and detailed information to public officials that might be difficult to obtain otherwise. This information may be useful in making public policy choices.
- Interest groups serve as another check on public officials to make sure that they are carrying out their duties responsibly.

Interest Group Strategies

Interest groups employ a wide range of techniques and strategies to promote their policy goals. The techniques used by interest groups can be divided into direct and indirect techniques. With direct techniques, the interest group and its lobbyists（院外活动集团成员，说客）approach the officials personally to present their case. With indirect techniques, in contrast, the interest group uses the general public or individual constituents to influence the government on behalf of the interest group.

1.Direct Techniques

Lobbying: Today, lobbying refers to all attempts by organizations or individuals to influence the passage, defeat, or contents of legislation and the administrative decisions of government. Most of the larger interest groups have lobbyists in Washington, D.C. These lobbyists often include former members of the Congress or former employees of executive bureaucracies who are experienced in the methods of political influence and who "know people".

Providing Election Support: Interest groups often become directly involved in the election process. Many interest group members join and work within political parties in order to influence party platforms and the nomination of candidates. Today, interest groups often provide money to campaigns through political action committees, which are groups organized to collect money and provide financial support for political candidates.

2.Indirect Techniques

Shaping Public Opinion: Public opinion ultimately puts pressure on policymakers, so interest groups pay careful attention to their public images. If public opinion favors a certain group's interests, then public officials will be more likely to listen to that group and more willing to pass legislation favoring its interests.

Mobilizing Constituents: Interest groups also use constituents to lobby for the group's goal. They sometimes urge members and others to write letters or call government officials to show their support for or opposition to certain policies. Large interest groups can generate hundreds of thousands of letters, calls, and e-mail messages.

Bringing Lawsuits: Achieving policy goals through the legal system offers another avenue for influencing the political process. Civil rights groups paved the way for using lawsuits to achieve policy goals with major victories in cases concerning equal housing, school desegregation, and labor market equality in the 1950s and 1960s.

Notes

1. the two-party system 两党制：所谓“两党制”，是指在一个资本主义国家中，由两个势均力敌的政党通过竞选取得议会多数席位，或者赢得总统选举的胜利而轮流执掌政权的政党制度。是指一国内两大政党轮流执政的政治制度，并不是说实行两党制的国家内只存在两个执政党。

2. Grand Old Party 共和党：简称“GOP”，又称“Republican Party”，是美国当代两大主要政党之一，另一个是民主党，两党都是起源于1792年成立的民主共和党。1854年创党以来，从共和党首位总统林肯至今，29任美国总统有19位都是共和党人。共和党创立时期，结合了当时反对奴隶制度扩张的政治势力，并且将党的价值奠基于“个人自由”和“国家团结”之上。而在当代政治中，共和党则被视为是社会保守主义（包括维护“家庭价值”）、经济古典自由主义（包括支持“保守财政政策”）以及在外交、国防问题上采取强硬态度（支持反恐战争）的右派政党。

3. winner-takes-all 胜者全拿的选举制度：在美国大选中，如果某一政党候选人在该州获得的票数高于对手，即可获得该州所有的选举人票。此制度的正式名称为“General Ticket System”。

4. Interest Group 利益集团：西方国家中基于共同利益要求而组成的社会团体。利益集团是使用各种途径和方法向政府施加影响，进行非选举性的鼓动和宣传，用以促进或阻止某方面公共政策的改变，以便在公共政策的决策中体现自己的利益主张的松散或严密的组织。

Unit 4 Campaigns and Elections

At the heart of American government is the electoral system. While the base of suffrage（选举权）in the United States has gradually been broadened to include more and more citizens, a free and unfettered suffrage has always been a basic cornerstone of American political system. Government in the United States rests upon, in theory at least, the consent of the governed and that consent is gained through the ballot box. Since the creation of the nation, Americans have never failed to hold an election—national, state, or local—on schedule. Today, the United States of America is a democrat's paradise in many respects because it probably conducts more elections for more offices more frequently than any nation on earth. This record of electoral stability is unparalleled.

Presidential Election

There are many kinds of elections in the United States, but the most important and eye-catching is the presidential election. The general election is normally divided into three steps: **primary election**[1], **party conventions**[2], and the campaign for the general election. From February to June in the election year, the parties choose all their respective candidates for election, except for the president. All the aspirants for the nomination begin their personal campaigns within the party. These "primaries" choose delegates to represent the state at the national party conventions. The more supporters they have, the greater the chance for them to be nominated for the candidacy.

The second step is for political parties to hold their national conventions, which are attended by delegates elected in the primary election. Normally, each party begins its national convention with the work of writing the party's platform（纲领）, a statement of the party's general policy for the next few years. After approving the platform of the party, the convention starts the election of the party's presidential candidate. The final choice is made when one candidate has received more than half of the votes. After the convention, the whole party will help its candidate run for election all over the country.

The third step consists of candidates' nation-wide campaign and balloting. This is a very important stage. By the early fall of the election year, the presidential race is on. Candidates use various means for winning votes—television, radio, newspapers, telephone calls, door-to-door visits, public speeches, and other kinds of propaganda appeals.

The general election is always held on the first Tuesday after the first Monday in November, called Election Day. This stage is to choose a slate of presidential electors in their state who make up the **Electoral College**[3]. The number of members to the Electoral College in each state is equal to that of its senators and representatives in Congress. There are now 538 presidential electors, 535 from 50 states and 3 from Washington D.C. The candidate that wins most votes in a state wins all the electoral votes for the state and the defeated candidate gets none. This is known as the "winner-takes-all" principle.

The continued use of the Electoral College is a controversial issue every four years. The College was first instituted 200 years ago when the founding fathers of the nation were not confident that the average citizen knew enough about the candidates and the issues to vote intelligently. Many people argue that with modern media, the average citizen today is much better informed, and that presidential elections should be decided by the direct vote of the people; others disagree.

When the presidential electors in each state are chosen, people already know the result of the general election. But the electors cast their votes for the President in December, and they can only vote for their parties' presidential candidates. The candidate who wins the majority（270）of the Electoral College votes will be the president of the next term. The elected president is sworn into office on January 20th. The president's four-year term begins on this date.

The United States presidential election of 2016, scheduled for Tuesday, November 8th, 2016, will be the 58th quadrennial（每四年一次的）U.S. Presidential election. The term limit established in the Twenty-second Amendment to the United States Constitution prevents the incumbent President, Barack Obama, of the Democratic Party, from being elected to a third term. Former Secretary of State Hillary Clinton and real estate mogul **Donald Trump**[4] clinched major victories in northeastern primaries of the U.S. presidential election, marching closer to claiming the nominations for the Democratic and Republican parties respectively. The U.S. presidential election of 2016 is more unpredictable than ever, as Trump's popularity among Republican voters stirs deep worries from the rest of U.S. society.

Who Votes and How?

One noted political scientist said, "Americans like elections, but we don't like to vote." This ironic statement appears justified in view of what has happened to voter turnout（投票率）—the number of eligible voters who actually vote. In the 1960 presidential election 62.8 percent of the eligible voters cast ballots; in 1992 the figure was 55 percent. Still, an overall general decline persists despite major efforts by both political parties to register new voters. There is no getting around the fact that the United States has one of the lowest voter participation rates of any nation in the industrialized world. Several explanations have been offered as to why Americans often opt not to vote.

Difficulty of Registration: The cost（in terms of time and effort）of registering to vote is higher in the United States than it is in other industrialized democracies.

Difficulty of Voting: Not every prospective voter can get to the polls on Election Day. Stringent（严格的）absentee ballot laws are another factor in the United States' low voter turnout.

Number of Elections: Another explanation for low voter turnout in this country is the sheer number and frequency of elections.

The Effect of Low Voter Turnout

There are two schools of thought concerning low voter turnout. Some view low voter participation as a threat to representative democratic government. Too few individuals are deciding who wields political powers in society. In addition, low voter participation presumably signals apathy about the political system in general. It also may signal that potential voters simply do not want to take the time to learn about the issues.

Others are less concerned about low voter participation. They believe that low voter participation simply indicates more satisfaction with the status quo（现状）. Also, they believe that representative democracy is a reality even if a very small percentage of eligible voters vote. If everyone who does not vote believes that the outcome of the election will accord with his or her own desires, then representative democracy is working.

Notes

1. primary election 初选：党员在大选之前选择本党候选人的选举称为"初选"。初选的目的并不是确定总统候选人，而是推选代表本党参加党代表大会的代表的人选。初选是美国总统选举的第一阶段。通常大选年 2 月到 6 月为初选阶段。

2. party conventions 各党全国代表大会：初选结束后，两党通常将分别在 7、8 月份召开全国代表大会。会议的主要任务是最终确定本党总统、副总统候选人，并讨论通过总统竞选纲领。

3. Electoral College 总统选举人团：美国总统选举实行选举人团制度，各州选民根据本州各党提出的总统选举人名单进行投票，获选的各州选举人组成“选举人”，于 12 月正式选举总统。换言之，选举人受选民委托到首都华盛顿投票，但投票意向由选民事先决定，选举人团投票表决只是例行公事。各州选举人票多寡取决于各州的人口。

4. Donald Trump **唐纳德·特朗普：**1946 年 6 月 14 日生于美国纽约，政治家、商人、作家，主持人。曾经是美国最具知名度的房地产商之一，人称“地产之王”。依靠房地产和股市，特朗普拥有纽约、新泽西州、佛罗里达州等地黄金地段的房地产，并且创建“特朗普梭运航空”，也是新泽西州“将军”职业足球队老板。他在风景怡人的城镇兴建数幢豪华大厦与别墅，还购买价值一亿美元的豪华游艇，此外还拥有私人飞机。2015 年 12 月 7 日，入围美国知名新闻周刊《时代》2015 年度人物的候选名单。2016 年 5 月 26 日，特朗普在共和党内的代表支持数达到 1 238，正式锁定共和党总统候选人提名。2016 年 11 月 9 日，当选美国第 45 任总统。

References

[1] BARDES B A, CRAIN E, MAXWELL W E, SCHMIDT S W, SHELLEY S W. American government and politics today（2007-2008 Texas edition）[M]. Belmont: Thomson Higher Education, 2008.

[2] HOLMES J E, ENGELHARDT M J, ELDER R E. American government: essentials and perspectives [M]. Boston: McGraw-Hill, Inc., 1994.

[3] MILLER R L. American government [M]. Chicago: National Textbook Company, 2002.

[4] O’CONNER K, SABATO L J. The essentials of American government: continuity and change [M]. New York: Pearson Longman, 2006.

[5] 江宁康 . 美国概况——美国社会、历史与文化 [M]. 南京：东南大学出版社 , 2013.

[6] TEAGUE G. 文化之旅・美国 [M]. 张荣婕，注 . 北京：外语教学与研究出版社，2009.

[7] 田耀 . 美国文化点滴 [M]. 天津：天津大学出版社, 2009.

[8] 王恩铭 . 美国文化与社会 [M]. 上海：上海外语教育出版社, 2005.

Chapter Four

American Economy

The United States, as the only super power in the world, dominates world affairs in various aspects—economy is just one epitome. Nowadays, economy instead of ideology has become a theme of world affairs. The achievements of American economy deserve researches and learning. It is quite hard for nonprofessionals (非专业人士) to analyze the national economy of the United States from the perspective of economics. Across the American history of economic development, the United States took every precious opportunity the train of economic development. In the colonial period, the United States was at the mercy of the Great Britain. Colonial economy had no autonomous power and had no independent rights. In order to acquire independence economically and politically, the Revolutionary War was a must. After the independence, the United States as a nation took a large number of measures to establish their independent economic system. Gradually, slavery plantation dominated South and capitalism dominated North conflicted with each other. Eventually, the aforementioned ideological conflicts between the North and the South evolved into a war—the Civil War. The North won the war and the slavery economy of the South was totally destroyed. However, the Civil War swept all barriers so that the United States had the chance to develop free market economy. After the Civil War, the process of industrialization and urbanization went quickly, and American economy acquired big success. Two world wars stimulated economic development of the United States. Although the Great Recession in the late 1920s and early 1930s almost destroyed the economy of the United States, it successfully solved the crisis. From 1945 until now, economy of the United States played an unswerving role in the world. This chapter aims to analyze the characteristics of American economy during different development periods.

Unit 1 The Colonial Period (1607—1776)

During the colonial period, the United States was an agrarian society (农业社会). Agriculture played a dominant role in American economy. At the end of the 18th century, approximately 90 percent of the American people earned a major portion of their living by farming (compared with about 3 percent today). Due to the favorable natural conditions, agriculture in many southern states developed fast. And tobacco, rice and indigo (槐蓝) had become major cash crops in the southern states. In the colonial period, there was enough land for colonists to settle down and explore. However, the labor shortage was a huge challenge. Under the condition of labor shortage, slavery trade came into stage. Large quantities of slaves were brought to colonial America by shred businessmen. African slaves supplied enough labors for colonies to develop large scale agriculture. Slaves alleviated labor shortage to some degree. The southern states formed systematic plantation slavery depending on slaves. And until the antebellum（南北战争前）years, slavery plantation had always dominated the southern states.

In the North, especially **New England**[1], because of limited natural conditions, agriculture was not suitable for the development of New England. New England had never emphasized agriculture as many southern states. Gary and Rockoff asserted that poor soil, uneven terrain, and a severe climate led to typical "subsistence"（温饱型）farming, the growth of only those crops necessary for family maintenance. Therefore, New England had to resort other measures to developing its economy. Due partly to climate and partly to the protection from wild predators that national barriers furnished, some part of New England became a cattle- and sheep- raising center. Natural resources except soil are abundant. Forests, minerals and seas are all beneficial for the development of the economy in New England. As a result, furs trade, forests and other industries had undergone quick development in New England. Meanwhile, sea products were rich in this region. The manufacturing industries deserved our mention. The industries of mills and shipbuilding aroused people's attention. At last, merchant marine was s sector which people could not turn their backs on. Marine trade was very important for the development of the colonial economy.

In the colonial period, waterway was the only connection between Europe and its colonies. Many African slaves were transported to colonies by sea. Therefore, in colonial period, southern states focused on agriculture while New England paid its attention on industries. As time went by, the conflicts between the North and the South were inevitable. With the development and capitalism and technology, the North aimed to develop large scale industry. On the contrary, the South did not plan to give up slavery plantation economy. During the colonial period, colonial economy was under the control of the Great Britain. The Great Britain exploited colonial people and made fortune for them. Colonial settlers wanted to get rid of British control and form their own economy. Consequently, the **revolutionary war**[2] was unavoidable.

Notes

1. New England 新英格兰：位于美国大陆东北角、濒临大西洋、毗邻加拿大。新英格兰地区包括美国的6个州，由北至南分别为缅因州、新罕布什尔州、佛蒙特州、马萨诸塞州、罗得岛州、康涅狄格州。

2. revolutionary war 美国革命战争：又称"美国独立战争"（1775—1783），是大英帝国和其北美十三州殖民地的革命者以及几个欧洲强国之间的一场战争。由于英国对殖民地的剥削严重阻碍了资本主义的发展，为了对抗英国的经济政策，北美人民开始了抗争。独立战争始于1775年4月的莱克星顿枪声，1776年7月4日大陆会议通过了由托马斯·杰斐逊执笔起草的《独立宣言》，宣告了美国的诞生。经过北美人民的艰苦抗争，终于在1783年迫使英国承认美国独立。独立战争结束了英国的殖民统治，实现了美国的独立，确立了比较民主的资产阶级民主体制，有利于资本主义的发展。

Unit 2 The National Period (1776—1861)

During the colonial period, American economy was under the control of the Great Britain. As part of the British Empire, these colonies had to supply Britain with raw materials and depend on it for manufactured products. Therefore, colonial America descended to the place of raw materials. Great Britain made a great fortune depending on its powerful manufacture industry. The colonial America was not satisfied with the above result. They wanted to establish their own independent economy and developed their own free market and economy. After the American Revolutionary War, America acquired independence and set to develop their own economy and made policies for its infant industries and established banking and financial system without the control of the Great Britain. The colonial economy became considerably more self-sufficient. It was a good start for the development of American economy.

After the Independence, American began to extend its territory. In the early 1800s, the United States started a series of new land acquisition such as the famous **Louisiana Purchase**[1] of 1803 and Texas Annexation（吞并得克萨斯州）of 1845. The new acquired land needed to be explored and settled. Naturally, new territory and land aroused people to settle down and to explore. Furthermore, the exploration stimulated the development of transportation. Rapid economic development and transportation promoted reciprocal advancement and progress. At the same time, specialization and divisions of labor began to take on stage. Due to the favorable natural environment and slavery system, the southern states began to emerge relying on the slavery plantation. Specialization in cotton in southern states had become a trend rather than an illusion. On the contrary, the north paid more attention to manufactured industries. Specialization in cotton, industrial development in northern states and the later **Westward Movement**[2] laid the foundation for the industrialization of the United States.

The northern states wanted to develop capitalist economy and promote industrial development. However, the southern states did not plan to give up their traditional slavery plantation or made compromise with the North. Because of complicated economic reasons and other causes, the Civil War broke out. In 1965, the Civil War came to an end with the victory of the North. The war totally destroyed slavery plantation in the South.

Notes

1. Louisiana Purchase 路易斯安那购地案：美国于 1803 年以大约每英亩 3 美分向法国购买超过 529 911 680 英亩（约 2 144 476 平方千米）土地的交易案，该交易的总价为 1 500 万美元或相当于 8 000 万法郎（如以国内生产总值相对比例计算，此数在 2004 年相当于 4 178 亿美元）。购地所涉土地面积是今日美国国土的 22.3%，与当时美国原有国土面积大致相当。

2. Westward Movement 西进运动：美国东部居民向西部地区迁移和进行开发的群众性运动，始于 18 世纪末，终于 19 世纪末 20 世纪初。西进运动大大促进了美国经济的发展，但是，随着西进运动的进行，大批印第安人遭到屠杀，幸存者被强行赶到更为荒凉的"保留地"。印第安人被迫迁徙之路也被称为印第安人的"血泪之路"。

Unit3 Civil War and Post-Civil War Period (1861—1914)

With the end of the Civil War, slavery in the South came to an end. The war swept away slavery which restricted the development of capitalism. However, plantation economy which has dominated the southern economy for over a hundred years was totally destroyed. An older generation of historians saw in the Civil War itself the origin of the great wave of industrialization. The whole atmosphere in the United States was beneficial for the development of American capitalism. And the war stimulated military industries and manufactured industries.

After the Civil War, the American economy transferred from southern agriculture to northern industrial capitalism. Industrialization was a trend and necessity which had no way to avoid. Technological revolution was a major factor which promoted the advancement of American economy and capitalism. Furthermore, technological revolution also promotes the transfer of America from an agrarian society to an industrialized country. It is argued that spurred by industrialization and technological revolution in the late 19th and early 20th centuries, the United States transformed itself from an agricultural society to an industrialized country. During this period, economy of the United States had undergone rapid growth. The fleeing of 4 million slaves provided enough free labors for industrialization and capitalism. During the process of industrialization, the Westward Movement preluded（拉开了序幕）. Western territories were explored and settled, which, on the contrary, stimulated the development of economy. The result is that the U.S. Census Bureau declared that the frontier had virtually disappeared in 1890. Industrial development achieved big success during this period. Between 1880 and 1920, the United States became the leading manufacturer in the world in terms of total production and output per worker.

Due to frontier exploration and industrial development, transportation has played a more and more important role in the United States. The construction of interstate roads（州际公路）, national railway and canals all stimulated American economy. What's more, infrastructure developed very quickly. Until now, the advanced transportation networks deserved other countries to borrow ideas from the United States. Urbanization also came into stage with the process of industrialization. High urbanization is a characteristic of industrialized country. The United Stated is highly urbanized and citizens in the U.S. enjoy high-standard living. Economic development promotes advancement of other fields such as politics, culture, education and entertainment. Economic power is a major factor to evaluate the comprehensive power of a nation. During this time, a crowd of economy elites came into stage such as **Rockefeller**[1] and **Carnegie**[2]. Their business

Standard Oil Company[3] and Carnegie Steel Company had monopolized national oil and national steel industry. As usual, monopoly often brought unfair competition. The public hoped that the federal government took measures to regulate and restrict such economic giants in order to provide fair competition and avoid monopoly. In response to this, Presidents Theodore Roosevelt and Woodrow Wilson tried to provide some regulations over the trusts and checked the growth. In addition to the aforementioned monopoly problem, crowded housing, poor ghettos, polluted environment and prevalent illness also forced the United States to worry about.

Notes

1. Rockefeller 洛克菲勒：约翰·洛克菲勒（1839—1937），美国实业家、慈善家，以改革了石油工业与塑造现代慈善的企业化结构而闻名。1870 年他创立了标准石油公司，在全盛期他垄断了全美 90% 的石油市场，成为美国第一位十亿富豪与全球首富。

2. Carnegie 安德鲁·卡内基：安德鲁·卡内基（1835—1919）被称为美国"钢铁大王"，在美国工业史上写下了永难磨灭的一页。他征服钢铁世界，成为美国最大钢铁制造商，衣锦还乡，跃居世界首富。而在功成名就后，他又将几乎全部的财富捐献给社会，成为美国人民心目中永远的英雄和个人奋斗的楷模。

3. Standard Oil Company 标准石油公司：19 世纪 70 年代，从洛克菲勒在俄亥俄州创建了股份制的标准石油公司开始，石油公司的发展进入了一个新的时代。 标准石油公司的标准一名，来源于其标榜自己出产的石油是顾客可以信赖的符合标准的产品，也意味着给石油行业带来了秩序上的标准。后来标准石油公司逐渐发展为托拉斯垄断石油公司，控制了美国石油业。

Unit 4 Economy from WWI[1] to WWII (1914—1945)

With the outbreak of WWI, major capitalist countries in Europe were involved in the war. At the beginning of WWI, isolation and non-intervention were the main trends of foreign policy of the United States. Consequently, the United States announced that it would keep neutral in the war. Due to the benefits of neutrality, the United States made a great fortune by selling weapons to both sides—the **Entente Countries**[2] and the **Allied Nations**[3] involved in the war. Before WWI, the United States was debtor country（债务国）; after the war, creditor country（债权国）. Powerful economy improved the status of the United States to a great degree. The economies of the old western capitalist countries were bogged（陷入泥潭）down by WWI. However, the United States took the opportunity to emerge as a super power both economically and militarily. Military industry got a rapid development. Therefore, powerful military industry promotes the economic development of the United States. During this period, government intervention played an indispensable role in domestic and foreign affairs.

In the late 1920s and early 1930s, the golden age of American economy came to an end. This period observed the worst economic crisis which had never occurred in human history. After

WWI, American pubic hoped for a "return to normalcy" (回归常态). The aforementioned "return to normalcy" means that the economy in the United States should depend on market force rather than government intervention. In the former years of 1920s, market force indeed promoted the economic growth. Therefore, people all over the country were optimistic about the economy. However, the sudden outbreak of the 1929 Economic Crisis caused the country into frustration and disaster. The crisis proved that only market force can not deal with all economic problems without government intervention. In order to save the national economy, the U.S. government took a lot of measures among which the most famous was the "New Deal" provided by President **FDR**[4].

The "New Deal" symbolized that the federal government has more power to deal with domestic affairs, which means that the power of the federal government was enlarged to a great extent. Although the "New Deal" had some positive influences on U.S. economy, it did not save the national economy of the United States. It was the Second World War that saved U.S. economy. Just as WWI, the United States was not directly involved in the war. As a result, the United States took the chance to sell weapons to countries in the war. The rapid development of defense industry stimulated economic growth and promoted employment. After **Pearl Harbor Incident**[5], the United States announced war with Japan. Since then, the United States directly took part in WWII. In order to win the war, the United States must develop advanced technology and military weapons. Because of economic development in the war time, after the war, U.S. economy gained great success and dominated world economy in various fields, such as the total output of industry, gold reserve and total export.

Notes

1. WWI 第一次世界大战：第一次世界大战（1914—1918）是在19世纪末20世纪初，资本主义世界向垄断资本主义即帝国主义时期过度、亚非拉殖民地基本上被列强瓜分完毕、新老殖民主义矛盾激化、各帝国主义经济发展不平衡的背景下，为重新瓜分世界爆发的一场帝国主义战争。

2. Entente Countries 协约国：在第一次世界大战中以英国、法国、沙皇俄国为主的国家联盟，还包括南斯拉夫等弱小的欧洲国家。它与以德国、奥匈帝国为中心的同盟国集团形成了第一次世界大战的对立双方。值得注意的是，意大利虽然是同盟国国家，但却和协约国一起攻打同盟国。一战中后期，美国、日本等一些国家也先后加入协约国集团，而俄国在十月革命爆发后退出了战争。最终，协约国赢得了第一次世界大战的胜利。

3. Allied Nations 同盟国：第一次世界大战时期建立了同盟国，参与该联盟的国家主要有德意志第二帝国、奥匈帝国、奥斯曼帝国、保加利亚王国等，战争以德国的失败和第二帝国的瓦解而告终，同时也导致德国第一次建立了联邦共和国。

4. FDR 富兰克林·德拉诺·罗斯福：美国第32任总统，是美国历史上唯一蝉联四届的总统，美国迄今为止在任时间最长的总统。

5. Pearl Harbor Incident 珍珠港事件：1941年12月7日清晨，日本海军的航空母舰舰载飞机和微型潜艇突然袭击美国海军太平洋舰队在夏威夷的基地珍珠港以及美国陆军和海军在瓦胡岛上的飞机场，太平洋战争由此爆发。这次袭击最终将美国卷入第二次世界大战，它是继 19 世纪墨西哥战争后第一次由另一个国家对美国领土发起的攻击。

Unit 5 Modern Economy (1945—Present)

In this unit, we will pay attention to American Economy after **WWII**[1]. With WWII coming to an end, the United States began to focus on domestic development instead of international affairs. After the war, the government of the United States faced to several thorny problems. The aforementioned problems include the reemployment of the veterans, high unemployment and inflation, severe strikes and shortage of housing and basic essentials. After WWII, the United States enjoys a short period of development and prosperity. The United States government took a series of measures to stimulate economic development. Take several measures for example. The government passed **G.I. Bill**[2] which helps veterans to get further education and employment training, buy farms and housing and so on and so forth. Furthermore, the government made efforts to reduce defense expenditure and national infrastructure investment. Due to the efforts of the government, economic recession did not appear as some economists have estimated. People in the United States enjoyed prosperity and peace during several years from 1945 to 1950 after WWII.

With the end of WWII, the international atmosphere is comparatively peaceful. However, district turbulence is here and there due to ideological conflicts or other reasons. In 1950, the **Korean War**[3] broke out. The United States was totally involved in the hot war. Just as WWII, the Korean War was the occasion for a renewed surge of U.S. economic expansion. From Eisenhower to John F. Kennedy, the United States government made endeavors to promote the economic development. JFK began the New Frontier which combines monetary and fiscal policy with tax and expenditure with the purpose of stimulating stable economic growth. However, in the following years, the United States was involved in another war—the **Vietnam War**[4], which was a disaster for economy. With the involvement of U.S. in the Vietnam War, the short period of development and prosperity after WWII ended.

From 1970 to 1990, the United States observed "stagflation"（停滞性通货膨胀）and **the economic policy of Reagan**[5]. "Stagflation" means that economic recession has the features of low productivity, high employment and severe inflation. President Reagan proposed the economic recovery plan to the Congress. The tight monetary policy of Reagan administration contributed a lot to restricting the inflation and stimulating the economy. But it has some side-effects, too. Due to Reagan's policy, the financial deficits were very high and the rich gap was enlarged. For many Americans, Reagan administration was a very special period. During this period, Americans were full of pride and confidence. In political area, Reagan administration turned people's attention to arms race between the United States and the Soviet Union. With abundant passion, Reagan proposed the space war plan and fought against communist Soviet Union. The military affairs underwent great development. Therefore, defense expenditure can partly explain the high deficits of government.

Since 1960s, the United States has entered post-industrial society. Industrialization, modernization and urbanization are the characteristics of American society. Traditional sectors, such as agriculture and industry, play a less and less important role in the economic development. The economic sectors are divided into three parts: namely, primary (agriculture), secondary (industry) and tertiary (service) sectors. Third industry instead of traditional sectors has dominated the economic area of the United States.

In the 1990s, the so-called "**new economy**[6]" came into being. High-tech industry has become the main factor to promote national economy. High-tech, combined with other factors, was beneficial for maintaining the United States as the economic leader. In the 1990s, there has been a market shift from goods-based production to high-skill, high-technology, service-based growth. And further, the main feature of post-industrial society is that service industry develops quickly.

E-commerce leads to intensified price competition, as it increases consumers' ability to gather information about products and prices. E-commerce is recognized for its ability to allow business to communicate and to form transaction anytime and anyplace. The power of e-commerce allows geophysical barriers to disappear, making all consumers and businesses on earth potential customers and suppliers. For traditional businesses, information technology and cross-border e-commerce is a good opportunity for the rapid development and growth of enterprises. Many companies have invested enormous volume of investment in mobile applications. E-commerce has huge impact on the economy and society.

First, e-commerce has emerged as the fastest growing sector of the U.S. market place. There are some economic factors that have contributed to the rapid growth of e-commerce. For sellers, e-commerce provides several advantages over conventional ways of selling products, such as lower transaction costs, more efficient distribution, and greater market access. The primary benefits for buyers are that goods and services can be purchased easier, quicker, and often cheaper via e-commerce.

The rapid growth of e-commerce is due in part to a significant cost advantage it provides e-firms due to its advanced use of information technology. In addition to reducing transaction costs, e-commerce also can reduce delivery costs. By conducting transactions via e-commerce, e-firms are also able to achieve cost savings through better management of supply chains. Second, productivity and inflation are two areas of economic activity that are likely to be affected by e-commerce. The cost savings achieved by e-firms has led to higher productivity, and productivity growth will continue with new innovations. The emergence of e-commerce has also made the marketplace more competitive, leading many firms to charge lower prices and creating downward pressure on inflation.

E-commerce is not a kind of new industry, but it is creating a new economic model. As a type of business active procedure, the e-commerce is going to lead an unprecedented revolution in the world. In the areas of law, education, culture and also policy, the e-commerce will continue that rise in impact. The e-commerce is truly to take human beings into the information society.

21st century is an age of challenges and opportunities with the cold war coming to an end. Ideological conflicts in international atmosphere have become less vital. Instead, connection and communication among states have become closer and closer. Globalization has become a reality rather than a dream. Economy instead of ideology has become the priority in the international relations. National economy of the United States is just a part of the world link. The strong economic power of the United States still leads world economy.

After entering 21st century, American economy began to undergo recession again. In 2008, a worldwide economic recession stirred up by the United States spread all over the world. American economy was trapped in the economic crisis. The incumbent President（现任总统）Barack Obama took the task of solving economic problems. Obama administration paid more attention to develop clean energy and increase domestic employment. The 2008 economic crisis was a lesson from which politicians must learn. The position of real economy can not be replaced. Although the United States has undergone periodic recession and recovery, its economic hegemony and power are still incomparable. In the long run, as the economy of the United States concerned, the United States will still be at the top of the world's economy list.

A 2012 study concluded that the U.S. financial sector has grown so large that it is slowing economic growth. In 2012, U.S. gross domestic product（GDP）growth was 2.8%. New York University economist Thomas Philippon supported those findings, estimating that the U.S. spends $300 billion too much on financial services per year, and that the sector needs to shrink by 20%. United States employment as estimated in 2012 is divided into 79.7% in the service sector, 19.2% in the manufacturing sector and 1.1% in the agriculture sector.

In 2013, its growth slowed to just 1.9%. U.S. exports goods and services amounted to $2.27 trillion and imports goods and services amounted to $2.74 trillion, with a trade deficit was $450.3 billion.As of year 2013, the unemployment rate in the United States was 7.7% or 12.0 million people. Total household net worth in the United States was $80.664 trillion, an increase of $9.8 trillion from 2012. Employee compensation amounted to $8.969 trillion, while gross private investment totaled $2.781 trillion. The mean net worth of U.S. adults increased to $301,140 in 2013, with the majority being held in financial assets, due to higher activity by shareholders and more private investment.

The United States is the world's second largest manufacturer, with a 2013 industrial output of the U.S. being $2.4 trillion. The gap in income between rich and poor is greater in the United States than in any other developed country. In 2013, child poverty reached record high levels, with 16.7 million children living in food insecure households, about 35% more than 2007 levels. Harvard University and University of Chicago economists agreed, calculating in 2014 that workers in research and development added $5 to the GDP for each dollar they earned, but finance industry workers caused the GDP to shrink by $0.60 for every dollar they were paid.

In December 2014, public debt was slightly more than 100% of GDP. Domestic financial assets totaled $131 trillion and domestic financial liabilities totaled $106 trillion. Feeding America reported in 2014 that 49 million Americans are "food insecure". The overall financial position of the United States as of 2014 includes $269.6 trillion of assets owned by households, businesses and governments within its borders, representing more than 15.7 times the annual gross domestic product of the United States. Debts owed during this same period amounted to $145.8 trillion, about 8.5 times the annual gross domestic product. The study reached similar conclusions, saying the finance industry impedes economic growth and research and development based industries. Because of the influential role that the U.S. stock market plays in international finance, a New York University study in late 2014 interpreted that in the short run, shocks that affect the willingness（不情愿）to bear risk independently of macroeconomic fundamentals explain most of the variation in the U.S. stock market. In the long run, the U.S. stock market is profoundly affected by shocks that reallocate the rewards of a given level of production between workers and shareholders. Productivity shocks however play a small role in historical stock market fluctuations at all horizons in the U.S. stock market.

In November 2015, the economy began to recover. Unemployment had declined from a high of 10% to 5%. The U.S. economy showed further signs of a slowdown as the U.S. Department of Labor announced just 160,000 new jobs had been created in April, 40,000 fewer than had been expected.In 2016 the U.S. unemployment rate remained steady at 5%. Economists surveyed by Reuters had expected the economy to add 202,000 jobs. February and March of 2016 job gains were revised down, with the U.S. economy now estimated to have added 19,000 jobs fewer than originally thought. Over the last 12 months, employment growth averaged 232,000 jobs per month. April's job gains were the lowest in seven months.

The U.S. labor market in year of 2016 is at or possibly well beyond reasonable conceptions of full employment. Full employment is when the labor market no longer shows signs of cyclical weakness and most people who are willing and looking for work are able to find a job.

At the start of 2016 as consumer spending slowed, business investment plunged and exports declined further, The U.S. gross domestic product grew by just 0.5% in the first quarter, down from 1.4% in the fourth quarter of 2015. The news of disappointing GDP growth from January to March came as Barack Obama defended his economic legacy. "I actually compare our economic performance to how, historically, countries that have wrenching financial crises perform," Obama told the New York Times magazine. "By that measure, we probably managed this better than any large economy on Earth in modern history," he said. Each month, even as the unemployment rate has dropped below 5%, officials at the U.S. Department of Labor note that wages remain the "unfinished business"（未尽事宜）of the U.S. recovery. U.S. wages have remained largely stagnant as, on average, Americans are still earning the same wages they were in 1997 and 46.7 million of them are still living in poverty. Over the years, Obama has called on U.S. lawmakers to increase the national minimum wage and pass an infrastructure bill, which was finally signed into law earlier this year of 2016. "In the detail, all main parts of the economy slowed with the exception of the housing market, the latter probably reflecting low mortgage rates," said Chris Williamson, chief economist. Economists expected the GDP to grow by 0.7% in the first quarter. Since typically GDP growth is weaker in the beginning of the year but rebounds by spring, economists predict second quarter growth to be around 2%. Stock market may give it the strength to set a new record in 2016. It may trade sideways for the first six months of 2016 before moving higher again by the end of the year.

It is obvious that periodic crisis bothered the United States ceaselessly. In the long run, the United States will still dominate world economy in many aspects. Until now, the economy of the United States still dominated world economy.

Notes

1. WWII 第二次世界大战：继第一次世界大战之后人类历史上发生的最大规模的战争。1939 年 9 月 1 日至 1945 年 8 月 15 日，德国、意大利、日本法西斯等组成的轴心国，与中国、美国、英国、苏联等反法西斯同盟和全世界反法西斯力量组成的同盟国进行的第二次全球规模的战争。从欧洲到亚洲，从大西洋到太平洋，先后有 61 个国家和地区、20 亿以上的人口被卷入战争，作战区域面积 2 200 万平方千米。第二次世界大战最终以美国、苏联、中国、英国、法国等反法西斯国家和人民战胜法西斯侵略者赢得世界和平而告终。

2.G.I. Bill 军人安置法案: G.I. 全称"Government Issue"，正式名称是"Servicemen's Readjustment Act of 1944"。该法案最先于二战末期起草生效，给退伍美军军人提供免费的大学或者技校教育以及一年的失业补偿。美国国会于 1944 年颁布，旨在帮助退伍军人在二战后更好地适应平民生活。法案的基本内容有：美国国会授权联邦政府，对在二战中服兵役超过 90 天的美国公民提供医疗、卫生、住房等方面的优惠政策，对因战争中断深造机会的美国公民提供资助，让他们有机会接受适当的教育或训练。该法案的颁布实施，使数百万美国退伍军人受惠，对美国迅速从战时经济向民用经济转变提供了智力支持和人才保障。

3. Korean War 朝鲜战争：原是朝鲜半岛上的朝韩之间的民族内战，后分别支持朝韩双方的美国、苏联等多个国家不同程度地卷入这场战争。1950 年 6 月 25 日，朝鲜进攻韩国，历时三年的朝鲜战争爆发。7 月 7 日，联合国安理会通过第 84 号决议，派遣联合国军支援韩国抵御朝鲜的进攻。8 月中旬，朝鲜人民军将韩军驱至釜山一隅，攻占了韩国 90% 的土地。9 月 15 日，以美军为主的联合国军在仁川登陆，开始大规模反攻。10 月 25 日，中国人民志愿军应朝鲜请求赴朝，与朝鲜并肩作战，经过历次战役最终将战线稳定在北纬 38 度一带。1951 年 7 月 10 日，中国和朝鲜方面与美国代表开始停战谈判，经过多次谈判后，终于在 1953 年 7 月 27 日签署《朝鲜停战协定》。

4. Vietnam War 越南战争：越南战争（1955—1975），简称"越战"，又称"第二次印度支那战争"，为受美国等反共阵营国家支持的南越（越南共和国）对抗受中国等共产主义阵营国家支持的北越（越南民主共和国）和"越南南方民族解放阵线"的一场战争。

5. the economic policy of Reagan 里根政府的经济政策：在 1981—1984 年间实施的取消扩张性货币政策和财政政策。具体来讲，是控制货币发行量、减税、减少政府支出（投资、购买、社会福利）。该政策使物价上涨被控制住，经济增长率提高，失业率下降。美中不足的是，由于社会福利的减少使广大普通百姓利益受损，考虑到政党的支持率，没有减少太多的福利，这使得政府的赤字连创新高，政府通过发行公债来维持运转，美国逐渐变为世界上最大的债务国。

6. new economy 新经济：该词最初出现在 1996 年美国著名刊物《商业周刊》发表的一篇文章上。该文分析了 20 世纪 90 年代以来美国经济发展的轨迹，发现了与 20 世纪七八十年代经济不同的特点，提出美国出现了新经济的观点。主要涉及三个方面：经济结构的调整、经济的全球化浪潮、美国政府的有效调控机制。

References

[1] HUGHES J R, CAIN L P. American economic history [M]. New York: Harper Collins College Publishers, 1994.

[2] WALTON G M, ROCKOFF H. History of the American economy [M]. Boston: Cengage Learning, 2013.

[3] 梅仁毅 . 美国 [M]. 重庆：重庆出版社 .2004.

[4] 梅仁毅 . 美国研究读本 [M]. 北京：外语教学与研究出版社，2002.

[5] 王恩铭 . 美国文化与社会 [M]. 上海：上海外语教育出版社，2005.

[6] 王恩铭，吴敏，张颖 . 当代美国社会与文化 [M]. 上海：上海外语教育出版社，2003.

Chapter Five

American Industry

Unit 1 The Beginning of American Industrialization

Although the British **mercantilist policy**[1] restricted the development of a domestic colonial manufacturing sector, the colonists developed several successful industries. Flours mills, lumber mills, leather tanneries, and the like were ubiquitous. The domestic industry expanded rapidly.

The new manufactures that emerged were different from those which had existed earlier. They involved new products, new technologies, new forms of organization, made new demands upon traditional sources of power, and required new levels of labor commitment.

Early Industrialization in New England

Industrialization began in New England. In New England good and fertile land was limited in supply and agriculture was high for those fortunate enough to have good land in good location but declined sharply as the additional labor was forced to work on less and less productive and more remote land. The expansion of settlement into the Middle West with its fertile soils and the development of transportation routes to the East—initially the Great Lakes and **Erie Canal**[2] and later railroads—had devastating impact upon New England's agriculture. The flood of western farm products onto East coast markets drove down prices, reducing the value of the marginal product of labor in eastern agriculture. Instead of heading west toward the frontier and reestablishing themselves as Midwestern farmers, though, some of the disillusioned eastern agricultural labor sought alternative employment in manufacturing.

In 1820 Agricultural workers accounted for 58 percent of the Massachusetts labor force. By 1850, the share of labor in agriculture had fallen to 15 percent of the labor force. This precipitous decline coincided with the opening of rail links to the west. The successful England farmers switched to more intensive animal husbandry, especially dairying. The pull from manufacturing intensified as a result of rapid and widespread productive growth in the manufacturing sector.

In fact, industrialization in New England was well under way before transportation improvements opened eastern markets to western farm products. The labor was supplied primarily by women and children. Most early manufacturing followed this pattern. The pace of industrialization accelerated when the embargo increased the demand for domestically produced goods and forced mercantile capital to seek new outlets.

Lowell[3]'s Boston Manufacturing Company revolutionized the role of factories. The textile industry, which had previously relied upon labor-intensive production methods, was also rife with potential for mechanization. In the late 18th century, the English textile industry had adopted the spinning jenny（多轴纺纱机）, water frame and spinning mule（纺棉机）which greatly improved the efficiency and quality of textile manufacture, but were closely guarded by the British government which forbade their export or the emigration of those who were familiar with the technology. The 1787 Beverly Cotton Manufactory was the first cotton mill in the United States, but it relied on horse power. **Samuel Slater**[4], an apprentice in one of the largest textile factories in England, immigrated to the United States in 1789 upon learning that American states were paying bounties to British expatriates with knowledge of textile machinery. With the help of Moses Brown of Providence, Slater established America's oldest currently existing cotton-spinning mill with a fully mechanized water power system at the Slater Mill in Pawtucket, Rhode Island in 1793. Slater went on to build several more cotton and wool mills throughout New England, but when faced with a labor shortage, resorted to building housing, shops, and churches for the workers and their families adjacent to his factories.

Slater's Mill was established in the Blackstone Valley, which extended into neighboring Massachusetts, and became one of the earliest industrialized regions in the United States, second to the North Shore of Massachusetts. Slater's business model of independent mills and mill villages began to be replaced by the 1820s by a more efficient system based upon Francis Cabot Lowell's replications of British power looms. The first power looms for woolens were installed in 1820, at Uxbridge, Massachusetts, by John Capron, of Cumberland, Rhode Island. These added automated weaving under the same roof, a step which Slater's system outsourced to local farms. Lowell looms were managed by specialized employees, employed with unmarried young women, and owned by a corporation. Unlike the previous forms of labor, the Lowell system popularized the concept of wage laborer who sells his labor to an employer under contract—a socio-economic system which persists in many modern countries and industries. Lowell's Boston Manufacturing Company revolutionized the role of factories.

Northern manufacturing was male-intensive than the southern, while northern manufacturing was more female-intensive than southern manufacturing. Women and children had low productivity in agriculture in the North at the start of the 19th century. By about 1850 the female wage was 50 percent of the male wage. Labor force participation rates in manufacturing among the women under 30 in New England show a marked rise from virtually zero at the start of the century to at least 10 percent by 1832 and at least 20 percent by 1850.

Despite the sharp rise in female labor force participation rates, women were a declining fraction of the labor force throughout the 19th century as industrialization proceeded rapidly. This may reflect the slowdown in the growth of such female-intensive industries as textiles and clothing, technological change and the rise in female wages relative to male.

The textile industry, which had previously relied upon labor-intensive production methods, was also rife with potential for mechanization.

On the eve of the Civil War the cotton manufacturing industry employed 115,000 workers, producing 7 percent of manufacturing income and more than 2 percent of total commodity production. Cotton textiles were not the only industry to grow in this period. Technological change in cotton textiles is a symbol of the critical role technology can play in growth. Innovations in textile production, embodied in new machinery changed the landscapes of New England in the early nineteenth century.

The huge increases in cotton textile production came at the same time that the factory system had sharply reduced the cost of making cloth. It seems reasonable to assume that the cost reductions were the cause of the increased sales. Productivity change assumes an enormous independent role in economic development by shifting the supply curve and driving the growth of the largest industry in the nation's young industrial sector.

The Spread of Industrialization

By most measures—capital invested, employment, and output—manufacturing in America was developing rapidly across a broad industrial and geographic front during the antebellum years. Census data indicate that this growth was both extensive and intensive but there were substantial regional variations in industry mix, firm size, and extent of manufacturing development.

In the Middle Atlantic States the number of manufacturing firms declined slightly between 1850 and 1860, while average firm size increased. In the South and Midwest: firm size increased at the same time that the number of firms increased sharply. Textile mills were among the industrial giants of the time with an average of ninety-one employees per mill. 178 of the 404 iron furnaces in the United States in 1850 were in Pennsylvania. They were large-scale integrated joint-stock or corporate enterprises, dependent on inanimate（单调）power to drive their machinery, employing a diversified labor force. American major industries in the 19th Century were Lumber mill, Flour mill, Boot-and shoemaker and Blacksmith.

Many historians and economists said that industry before the Civil War must have been competitive, with conditions approaching the economists' notion of **perfect competition**[5]. Others argued that these thousands of small businesses existed solely to meet the needs local markets isolated from one another by the high costs of transportation. Their numbers and scale of operation reflected the multiplicity and proliferation of markets, not the evolution of a competitive marketplace.

The Changing Nature & Organization of Industrial Work

There is growing evidence that changes in the organization of production played a major role in the course and pattern of industrialization by rising efficiency. Increased efficiency, like scale economies, raised labor productivity, lowered costs, and made American industry more able to compete with foreign businesses. There was strong debate over the origin of the productivity difference. One theory favors the increased division of labor in large firms. The other attributes the productivity gain to the intensification of work effort. Both are consistent with the findings. In the decades leading up to the Civil War, total factor productivity in manufacturing seems to have grown rapidly. It was the dominant factor underlying labor productivity growth in American industry. Growth was rapid in the textiles, glass, paper and woodworking industries. Growth was the slowest in traditional industries.

The mechanization of production increased demands upon the sources of power in mills and workshops. As a result, human muscle or animal power was increasingly supplemented or replaced by inanimate sources of power—water or steam. Waterpower powered the majority of the nation's flour and lumber mills at the start of the 19th century. Many of the earliest water wheels were inefficient, capable of capturing only 10 to 15 percent of the potential power. This mattered little so long as power needs were limited and water was plentiful, but increased demands from growing industrial sector and increasingly energy-intensive production processes gradually placed a premium on efficiency. Increased hydraulic(水力的)efficiency temporarily relieved the most serious constraint upon more extensive waterpower use. Waterpower was able to remain competitive with steam power at many locations, especially in New England, until well into the 20th century, when it was replaced by electric, not steam. The limited number of waterpower sites, especially in much of the Midwest, the plains, and the southeastern seaboard meant that spreading industry was increasingly forced to rely upon steam for power.

Steam power gave the mill owner the freedom to locate near low-cost transportation. But transportation bills might be large nonetheless, because fuel would still have to be brought to the factory to feed the boilers. The adoption of steam did reduce the seasonality inherent in waterpower and played a role in the emergency of modern year-round work habits. The cotton mills in Massachusetts, took advantage of the exceedingly good water sites. Along the Atlantic coast, however, mills were driven by steam and fed by coal hauled at relatively low cost from Pennsylvania.

In the mid-1780s, **Oliver Evans**[6] invented an automated flour mill that included a grain elevator and hopper boy. Evans' design eventually displaced the traditional gristmills(磨坊). By the turn of the century, Evans also developed one of the first high-pressure steam engines and began establishing a network of machine workshops to manufacture and repair these popular inventions. High-pressure engines proved uniquely adaptable and were as at home in American factories of all sizes as in American steamboats on the western rivers. The adoption of the high-pressure engine also had an important impact upon American machine technology. American machines tended to be driven at higher speeds with consequently greater wear(耐用)than European. This caused American industry to be closer to the technological frontier at any moment. High operating speeds also led to an exhaustive search for better lubricants(润滑剂), met first by whaling and then by the petroleum industry. Although American hydraulic engineering adapted and improved upon European, American steam technology developed its own unique character in large part because the American Revolution temporarily interrupted the export of technology from Britain at a critical juncture in steam power development.

In 1789, the widow of **Nathanael Greene**[7] recruited **Eli Whitney**[8] to develop a machine to separate the seeds of short fibered cotton from the fibers. The resulting cotton gin could be made with basic carpentry skills but reduced the necessary labor by a factor of 50 and generated huge profits for cotton growers in the South. The invention of the Cotton Gin（轧棉机）made cotton potentially a cheap and readily available resource in the United States for use in the new textile industry.

An American display at the Crystal Palace Exhibition in London in 1851 demonstrated what came to be known as the American System—the technique of interchangeable parts first adopted in firearm construction. The American System eliminated the need for individual parts to be fitted to one another before the finished product would work properly. While Whitney did not realize financial success from his invention, he moved on to manufacturing rifles and other armaments under government contract that could be made with "expedition, uniformity, and exactness"—the foundational ideas for interchangeable parts. However, Whitney's vision of interchangeable parts would not be achieved for over two decades with firearms and even longer for other devices. Interchangeable parts have been widely accepted that American inventors pioneered extensive mechanization as the means to achieve interchangeable parts and mass production. True interchangeability of parts demands careful monitoring of the tolerances produced by each machine and was probably not achieved in most consumer goods and producer goods before the 1870s. Americans also took an early lead in what is now called the machine to industry—the production of machine for manufacturing. This specialization of function, in which separate businesses made tools for other industries, allowed for enormous economies in the creation and diffusion of new technology. Between 1800 and 1820, new industrial tools that rapidly increased the quality and efficiency of manufacturing emerged.

Profitability is the ultimate measure of economic success in a capitalist system. By this measure, the average antebellum manufacturing firm seems to have been a success. Industrial firms earned, on average, high rates of profits-high, at least by comparison with the return on bonds, the rate of return on agriculture, or an assumed competitive return between 6 and 12 percent. The nationwide manufacturing profit rates averaged 18.4 percent on capital in 1850. Within each industry, however, there was a wide dispersion of **rates of return**[9]. This variance might be viewed as a proxy（代理人）for the risk each firm in an industry faced. One rationalization for the relatively high average returns is that they were a compensating payment for the high risks. Rates of return were generally higher in the South and West than in the Northeast, but the differential was probably not great enough to encourage extensive direct investment by northeasterners in southern and Midwestern manufacturing.

By the middle of the 19th century American manufacturing had been transformed from relatively simple processing of raw materials using traditional methods into complex, machine-intensive processes that produced ever more supplicated goods and increasingly minute division of labor and specialization. No longer was industry a mere adjunct（附属）to the agriculture, a secondary source of employment. A growing fraction of the nation's labor force was solely dependent upon industry for its livelihood. An industrial labor force has emerged. Industry moved from the countryside, becoming increasingly concentrated in urban areas. The towns and the cities offered large pools of nearby labor with transferable skills, schooled in the need for industrial discipline. They provided a potential market just beyond the factory gate. And as nodes（节点）in the emerging transportation network the industrial cities provided firms with easier and cheaper access to more distant markets and sources of raw materials. Increasing volumes of trade in turn generated valuable flows of commercial and financial information that lowered transportations cost. Because trade was cheaper, trade expanded. Urban agglomerations（凝聚）were both a cause and a consequence of growing specialization, and they bought with them all problems that we associate with cities today: crime, pollution, congestion（拥堵）, disease, corruption—every that **Thomas Jefferson**[10] had feared from industrialization. America was to remain a predominantly agrarian economy. Industry would not triumph until after the Civil War.

Notes

1. **mercantilist policy 重商主义政策**：重商主义是18世纪在欧洲大受欢迎的政治经济体制。它建立在这样的信念上：一国的国力基于通过贸易的顺差，即出口额大于进口额所能获得的财富。是封建主义解体之后的16至17世纪西欧资本原始积累时期的一种经济理论或经济体系，反映资本原始积累时期商业资产阶级利益的经济理论和政策体系。

2. **Erie Canal 伊利运河**：全长为584千米（363英里），整条运河为12米（39英尺）宽、1.2米（4英尺）深。整条运河总共有83个水闸，每个水闸长27米、宽4.5米（90英尺乘15英尺），最高可以行驶排水量68公吨（75吨）的平底驳船。伊利运河是第一条提供美国东海岸与西部内陆的快速运输工具的河流，这比当时最常用的以动物拉动的拖车还快许多。伊利运河不只加快了运输的速度，也将沿岸地区与内陆地区的运输成本减少了95%。快捷的运河交通使得纽约州西部更便于到达，因此也造成中西部的人口快速增长。

3. **Lowell 罗威尔**：位于美国马塞诸塞州波士顿周围，是美国工业的起源地之一，当时主要以纺织业著称，向美国各地供给大量纺织制成品。

4. **Samuel Slater 塞缪尔·斯莱特**：塞缪尔·斯莱特（1768年6月9日—1835年4月21日），美国早期的一名工业家，人们称他为"美国工业革命的奠基者"。在英国学会棉纺织工艺。在熟记机器详图后秘密移居美国，复制了纺纱机。1793年在罗得岛建立美国第一座棉纺织厂。1817年开始毛纺生产。

5. **perfect competition 完全竞争市场**：指竞争充分而不受任何阻碍和干扰的一种市场结构。在这种市场类型中，买卖人数众多，买者和卖者是价格的接受者，资源可自由流动，信息具有完全性。

6. **Oliver Evans 奥利弗·埃文斯**：美国蒸汽时代的创新英雄，大发明家。他发明并安装了世界第一条自动生产线，制造了第一辆有轮子并且依靠自身驱动的汽车开上公路，制造了第一台水陆两用汽车，制造了第一条用于工厂生产和蒸汽船航行的高效高压蒸汽机。

7. Nathanael Greene 纳瑟内尔 • 格林：纳瑟内尔 • 格林（1742—1786），美国独立战争中著名将领，1780 年 12 月由华盛顿提名接替盖茨，并改组其军队。

8. Eli Whitney 伊莱 • 惠特尼：生于马萨诸塞州韦斯特博罗。1780 至 1782 年在父亲开设的商店工作，制造、修理小提琴和各种五金零件。后到纳撒内尔 • 格林夫人经办的种植园工作。1793 年设计制造出轧棉机，一人操作机器每天可轧棉五十多磅。1794 年获轧棉机美国专利，与人合伙开办轧棉机制造厂，后因侵权事件及长期诉讼，亏损倒闭。1798 年，惠特尼接受美国政府制造 10 000 支滑膛枪合同，在纽黑文附近开办专门工厂，生产军火武器。惠特尼是实行标准化生产的创始者。最初在制锁中采用标准化零件，保证零件可互换，后推广到枪械生产中。实现产品标准化大大提高生产效率，方便了产品在使用过程中的维修，是工业走向成批生产的重要一步。惠特尼曾设计制造出第一台卧式铣床，在自己管理的工厂中实行工人之间劳动分工，对生产发展起了重要作用。1900 年，惠特尼的名字和事迹被选入美国名人纪念馆。

9. rates of return 回报率：一般而言回报率是指投入成本后所得到的收益比上之前的成本所得结果。债券分期支付的利息与债券当前的市场价格叫作资本回报率（ROIC）。资本回报率是用来评估一个公司或其事业部门历史绩效的指标。

10. Thomas Jefferson 托马斯 • 杰斐逊：托马斯 • 杰斐逊（1743 年 4 月 13 日—1826 年 7 月 4 日），美利坚合众国第三任总统（1801—1809），同时也是《美国独立宣言》主要起草人，美国开国元勋中最具影响力者之一。除了政治事业外，杰斐逊同时也是农业学、园艺学、建筑学、词源学、考古学、数学、密码学、测量学与古生物学等学科的专家；又身兼作家、律师与小提琴手；也是弗吉尼亚大学的创办人。许多人认为他是历任美国总统中智慧最高者。他在任期间保护农业，发展民族资本主义工业，从法国手中购买路易斯安那州，使美国领土近乎增加了一倍。

Unit 2 The Changing Structure of American Industry

From the 19th century to 20th century, America was changing dramatically in the economy as well as in its landscape. The transformation of American economy was from an agrarian to an industrial one.

The employment statistics for the 19th and 20th centuries provides a window to study the economic transformation in the USA. In 1810, only 0.96% people worked in industry. Four decades later, the rate increased to 17.9%. Over the next five decades, the rate of employment was climbing up until the WWI when the rate reached about 27% of labor force working in the industry. However, hit by the crisis of the Great Depression, the rate slipped to only about 20% of the labor force. From the WWII to the 1950s, this rate rose but then fell again, as the labor force had shifted more into service occupation.

American industry outweighed agriculture and became the new center of the economy. It not only boomed the domestic economy, but also provided a model for the rest of the world. Various companies had expanded overseas, playing a significant role in shaping industrial development in other countries. Some of them are still famous today such as Coca-Cola, Ford, General Electric and Standard Oil.

The Changing Nature of Production: The Transition from Workshop to Factory

At the mid of 19th century, both workshop and factory played an important role in the economy. Many people worked in small workshops that employed only one or two worker, and other worked in large factories, some of which had thousands of employees. Workshops were widely dispersed(分散的)and it was estimated that twenty thousand sawmills, fourteen thousand flour mills and seventy-five hundred blacksmiths dotted the nation at the mid of 19th century. Most firms without much capital were usually unincorporated organized instead as sole proprietor—ships or partnerships. In addition, the labor forces were small.

Even though these small workshops were easily shutdown as the low volume of demand and the lack of raw materials, year-round transportation and labor, they not only survived, but prospered, and new small firms continued to be established, because they had a tactic in common—the location. They preferred to locate at some physical distance from their larger, more efficient competitors, surviving by virtue of the measure of protection afforded inefficient operations by positive transport cost.

As the small workshops were struggling to survive, several very large mills took off, such as Haxell Mills and Pacific Mills. They were already quite heavily industrialized, and most of them located in the North. Only one southern city Richmond, Virginia had more than five thousand residents engaged in manufacturing activities in 1860. Massachusetts and New York, on the other hand, each had five such cities. Accordingly, it is generally held that, by 1860, industrialization in the South was far below its apparent potential compared to such achievements in the North. During this time, manufacturing in the South's major industries such as cotton textile production, boots and shoes, clothing, and flour and milling came to only about 20% of the national total.

Nevertheless, several very large factories were flourishing throughout the nation during this transitional period. Each of them shared common characteristic, urban, big-scale and profitable. Most of these firms preferred to locate at urban area in order to collect labor forces. Pacific Mill in New England employed eighteen hundred workers and produced more than 8 million worth of cloth. What's more, these enterprises were capitalized at millions of dollars exceeding the financial resources of an individual or small group. In 1860 forty-seven different manufacturing company stocks were being traded on the Boston Stock Market. Moreover, new tactics optimized the firm. In order to lower the risk and keep profitable, these firms attach itself to not only the location, but also new methods. They constructed elaborate systems of storage reservoir and supplied canals to ensure adequate water power, and instituted work rules to guide workers' performance.

Both the workshop and the factory still show its close association with agriculture and the forest. The top 10 industries in term of the value added in 1860 were cotton goods, lumber, boots and shoes, flour and meal, men's clothing, iron, machinery, woolen goods, carriages and wagons, and leather goods. These ten industries provided 1,474,000 jobs, compared a total manufacturing labor force of 1,530,000. The machinery production industry became more specialized, developed into the machine tool industry, where machines were designed to make machine. After the Civil War, it was these larger industries that played a significant role in the nation's manufacturing output, as they relied upon inanimate source of power to drive increasing specialized machinery. The top 10 in terms of value added were machinery, lumber, printing and publishing, iron and steel, malt liquors, men's clothing, cotton goods, tobacco products, railroad cars and boots and shoes.

Industrialization altered forever the business system in the USA. During this period of time, more and more American industrial companies became corporations under state incorporation laws. They were extremely large and profitable. The corporate form of organization, with its promise of limited liability for investors proved especially attractive to would be industrialists. Another advantage of the corporation was that, unlike a partnership, it did not have to be reorganized every time an investor left the business. By 1904, corporation accounted for three-quarters of the United States' industrial output. In 1901, the newly formed the United States Steel Corporation under the Carnegie management was capitalized at 1.4 billion dollars and became the world's first billion-dollar company. It employed over 100,000 workers.

What's more, monopoly was another characteristic during this period. As firm size grew the decisions of business owners and managers in some industries, that is, largely raw materials and setting prices for finished goods. For example, Rockefeller's Standard Oil controlled about 90% of the kerosene refining in the United States by the early 1890s, and the decisions of the firm's leaders largely set the parameters within which much of the United States' oil industry operated.

From the mid of 19th century to the early 20th century, big business was gradually taking over the economy and facilitated the American transitional progress from an agricultural to an industrial society. The small workshop could not complete with these large companies, as the industrialized companies could produce more goods at much lower price.

Unit 3 Manufacturing, Marketing and Industrial Productivity

The Relative Decline of Manufacturing

Although manufacturing has been and continues to be a major force in the U.S. economy, there were some ups and downs of it from the Great Depression to the 1990s. Manufacturing output very nearly doubled between the 1921 recession and the 1929 crash. Then it began to decline. Between 1929 and 1932, manufacturing output fell by half.

And after the World War II, there was a relative decline of manufacturing in the following three aspects. First, total manufacturing employment declined from 24.5 percent of the labor force in 1950 to 14.3 percent in 1992. Second, the share of manufacturing employment in total employment fell dramatically from 24 percent in 1970 to 13.7 percent in 1999. Third, the share of value of the output of manufacturing industries in total GNP also fell dramatically.

The decline in manufacturing employment was a result of the faster growth in the demand for services, the increasing ability of consumers to purchase manufactured goods more cheaply from abroad, and the increasing productivity in the manufacturing sector. Over the last one hundred years, however, the service sector has shown the greatest expansion. In 1870 it accounted for 21 percent of the work force; by 1920 its share had jump to 42 percent; and by 1980 the service sector claimed the majority of workers, over 60 percent. In the 1960s, Japanese and European firms began to penetrate the American market for such products as automobiles, cameras, television sets, textiles, shoes, and others. American technology, which had led the world for most of the twentieth century, was faced with a serious challenge form overseas. Meanwhile, in an effort to cut costs, manufacturing firms often turned to automation, substituting machines for workers, which means that productivity increased.

The relative decline in manufacturing ignited demands for government programs to protect and encourage this sector. In the late 1970s and early 1980s, liberal economists and policymakers advocated a "national industrial policy" to reverse the long-term relative decline. The proposals that fell under this heading included: (a) national development banks to subsidize crucial industries; (b) government spending to train workers for new industrial jobs; (c) tariffs and quotas to protect American industry from foreign competition; (d) legislation to create an "industrial democracy" providing channels through which workers, residents of nearby communities, and government could influence business decisions on investment and plant closings; and (e) controls on merges and acquisitions.

The impact of science on the workplace, particularly through the development of computer, has been so great that commentators began to speak of a "new technology" and a "second Industrial Revolution".

The Fear of Automation

Whenever unemployment rises, demands to limit technological unemployment are sure to follow. During the 1920s and 1930s, there was much talk about "technological unemployment" with the development of mechanization on industry. In 1962, President Kennedy remarked that the "major domestic challenge of the sixties is to maintain full employment at a time when automation is replacing men". The number of employees of telephone companies dropped from 742,000 in 1984 to 648,000 in 1990. This increase in productivity was made possible by rapid advances in computer-based technologies.

The reactions to technological unemployment involve two groups. One group of economists argues that for the economy as a whole, technology progress need not lead, and has not led to long-term unemployment and aggregate unemployment is a short-term phenomenon, frequently exacerbated by mistakes in monetary and fiscal policy. For example, the jobs lost in the telephone industry will be more than made up by new jobs arising elsewhere in the economy with technological innovations.

A second group does not believe that there is anything inherent in economic laws or in technological change that will bring about the solution to our unemployment problem. The hope that technological change will automatically result in more jobs in the long run does not hold true. The machine reduces jobs more quickly than it increases sales and automation changes the nature of the demand for workers—there is a need for more highly skilled and getter educated employees and less need for the unskilled, semiskilled and less educated. Technological change is making the unskilled workers and undereducated employees obsolete.

Productivity Growth

The aggregate productivity must have risen rapidly in the postwar period, but after about 1970, productivity growth slowed due to the shift of production from manufacturing to the service sector, changes in the structure of the labor force, the decline of capital per unit of labor input, the inflation in the 1970s, the high cost of complying with new government regulations stemming from legislation passed in the 1960s and even more in the 1970s and the sharp rise of oil prices in the 1970s. Many producers replaced older equipment with more energy-efficient equipment, but these machines had the same output per labor hour. And producers' prior choices of technology were more directed to saving on energy costs rather than increasing productivity.

The energy crisis in 1973[1] led to greater interest in renewable energy, nuclear power and domestic fossil fuels. Before the energy crisis, large, heavy and powerful cars were popular, but the crisis reduced the demand for large cars for energy serving. That sent a signal to the auto industry globally, which changed many aspects of production and usage for decades to come.

Imports of oil to the U.S. dropped from 6 million in September 1973 to 5 million in subsequent months. By December 1973, the price per barrel rose 130%. The price of crude oil in 1980 was 6.75 times as high as it was in 1970, while the real price of oil increased by 2.45 times. The price of all forms of energy also rose by a small proportion, because of the increased demand on oil substitutes. The fall of the amount of energy used by per dollar of real GDP showed that the number of adjustment that American could take was limited.

By the end of the embargo in March 1974, the price of oil had risen from $3 per barrel to nearly $12 globally. U.S. prices were significantly higher. The embargo, which caused an oil crisis, or "shock", with many short- and long-term effects on global politics and the global economy, was later called the "first oil shock", along with the 1973-1974 stock market crash, has been regarded as the first event since the Great Depression to have a persistent economic effect, followed by the 1979 oil crisis, termed the "second oil shock".

Toward the end of the 20th century, productivity growth began to rise. The computer revolution, adjustment to higher energy prices and corporate restructuring all contributed to a rise in productivity growth.

Marketing and Consumers

In the late nineteenth century, manufacturers began to bypass the wholesaler and to sell directly to retail outlets. The "general merchandise" wholesaler, with a warehouse of heterogeneous(各种各样的)goods, declined rapidly before the World War I. However, the Manufacturing, Marketing, and Industrial Productivity full-service, full-line wholesale house that furnished goods to retailers in one particular line over great regions or even nationally was still an important force. This position was maintained primarily in industries where production remained small-scale. Perhaps the major trend in wholesaling over the past seventy to seventy-five years has been the lessening relative importance of these great houses and the increasing importance of the specialty wholesaler, or "short line" distributor. To a significant extent, this change has been caused by shifting markets.

Advertising

The successful differentiation of a product sold in the nationwide market typically requires large advertising outlays. As early as 1910, the annual volume of advertising expenditure reached $1 billion (about 2.8 percent of GNP). By 1929 the estimated outlay had reached $3.4 billion (3.3 percent of GNP). Advertising declined greatly during the 1930s. And although expenditures recovered in the late 1930s and 1940s, the share of advertising in GNP never recovered the level apparently reached in 1929. Advertising during the end of the 20th century has averaged about 85 percent of total spending on research and development and about 150 percent of the amount spent on research and development by the private sector.

Changes in the Organization of Industry

Mergers and acquisitions[2] (M&A) are among the main ways that firms try to increase their productivity and profitability. Mergers and acquisitions, both horizontal and vertical, allow the combined firms to achieve economies of scale and scope and even to get more profitable. Over the twentieth century, several distinct waves of mergers have made and remade the structure of American industry.

These waves produced a public backlash motivated by the fear that giant corporations were taking over the economy. This backlash was strengthened by the belief that the existence of widespread monopoly had contributed to the Great Depression.

In fact, there was a noticeable difference in character between the mergers and those at the turn of the century. Typically, mergers of the earlier waves produced a high degree of control of the industry's output, usually in excess of 50 percent. In the 1920s, mergers continued to be predominantly horizontal—about 76 percent of all mergers between 1926 and 1930 were horizontal mergers—but most of the merged firms usually took place among companies that were smaller than the dominant company in the industry. Some industries that had been composed of large numbers of firms did become **oligopolies**[3] during 1920s. Dairy products and packaged foods were the outstanding examples of this kind of rapid change in market structure. The postwar period witnessed three waves of mergers: (a) a wave of conglomerate mergers that was particularly marked during 1966 to 1969; (b) a wave of hostile takeovers that marked during 1977 to 1989; (c) a wave of mergers to achieve economies of scale that began in the early 1990s and is still in process.

Conglomerate Mergers[4]

In the first post-World War II wave of mergers, the dominant form was the conglomerate. It is the combination of firms in different industries or firms operating in different geographic areas. Between 1964 and 1972, the peak of the wave, about 80 percent of all mergers was conglomeration. Operating managers were usually given wide latitude in managing their subsidiaries. The fundamental purposes of conglomerate mergers were to reduce the adverse effects of the business cycle or unexpected shocks in individual markets by diversifying the activities the company undertook. It can serve various purposes, including extending corporate territories and extending a product range.

Conglomerate mergers created much of the glamour and fast-paced financial action that characterized the first merger of the wave in post-World War II period. This wave peaked in 1969. During 1970s, many of the conglomerate mergers failed to perform as expected. Diversification also failed to isolate the conglomerates from the troubles experienced by more conventional companies. Moreover, a conglomerate merger is one between two strategically unrelated firms; it is unlikely that the economic benefits will be generated for the target or the bidder. As such, conglomerate mergers seldom occur today.

The third wave of postwar mergers began in the early 1990s. This time companies sought to achieve economies of scale by merging with or acquiring companies that filled out their "core competencies". Companies sought economies of scale through consumer market and marketing. Both the roaring stock market and a relatively indulgent regulatory environment facilitate the rise of the third wave. Many of these mergers, however, soon showed signs of inefficiency. In 2001, the number of U.S. mergers and acquisitions dropped 16.4 per cent, the largest year-over-year drop in volume since 1987.

The Emergence of the Modern Business Enterprise

Although manufacturing industry grew more slowly after 1860 than before, two forces—mass distribution and mass production—fundamentally altered industrial structure and redefined the nature of the firm in the post-Civil War period. The transformation took place first and most swiftly in the distribution system.

Modern transportation—the railroad—and modern communications—the telegraph—assisted by the Great Lakes and ocean steamship and revamped postal system, provided the means for coordinated buying and selling. New transportation and communications systems generated almost instantaneous flows of information, increased the speed and regularity of the flow of goods, and reduced the number of transactions involved in the transfer of goods. The costs of distribution fell, and productivity rose.

The railroad not only assured cheaper and more rapid shipment to market but also facilitated the growth of terminal facilities, such as grain elevators and warehouses. Scholars have crowned the railroad as the most important innovation of the last two-thirds of the nineteenth century.

Institutional changes and the advent of the telegraph stimulated the establishment of centralized markets. New means of transportation and communication also revolutionized the distribution of manufactured goods. The period between 1900-1930 is identified as a key point when two new demand-side consumer technologies, the automobile and radio, fueled the beginnings of a retail revolution. Stores began to offer a selection of products unheard of at the turn of the century. Not only did they offer more brands of each product, but they also broadened the selection of different products. Corporate-owned chain stores started to supplant the independent retailer. Finally, retail workers became more specialized, and a smaller share of the workforce directly interacted with the customer.

The railroad and the telegraph provided the means for market coordination. For the first time, manufacturers were assured of a smooth and continual inflow of raw materials at the back door and outflow of finished goods through the front gate with almost instantaneous updates on demand conditions.

Production processes were made continuous, as in the manufacture of tobacco products, flour, canned goods, soap, and animal and vegetable fats, the refining of oil or the open-hearth process of steel manufacture. As a result, the need for coordination and management increased. Manufacturing processes also became integrated. This integration also demanded increased coordination of the flow of production within the factory and the establishment of testing procedures to monitor product quality. The result was mass production that incorporated economies of speed and economies of scale.

The integration of mass production with mass distribution allowed manufacturers to lower costs and increase productivity largely through the more effective management and coordination of production and distribution. In these firms the level of economic activity was such that administrative coordination within the firm was more efficient and profitable than coordination through the market.

Late-Nineteenth-Century Technical Change

The modern business enterprises employed capital-intensive, energy-consuming, continuous, or large batch production methods. Their emergence and rise to dominate in the United States as well as in the rest of the world are consistent with the perception that technological change in

America was faster than elsewhere and fundamentally different. One distinguishing characteristic of American industrialization was the prominent role played by its natural resources. It is claimed that this characteristic has biased American manufacturing toward relatively capital-intensive production techniques and led, ultimately, to faster and more laborsaving technical change.

Historians have referred to the period from 1880 to 1920 as the "rise of big business" or the "combination movement" or "merger movement". Business firms were largely beyond the reach of federal government control.

More capital-intensive production methods increased firm size and the minimum efficient scale of operation. The high-speed throughput of the modern enterprise and the adoption of continuous or large-scale batch production technologies generated a sharp increase in the size of America's manufacturing plants. Larger establishments were more productive because they practiced division of labor and used powered machinery. The shift towards large scale production had several causes. First of all, a changing legal and institutional environment made the corporate organization form more broadly accessible, which facilitated the financing associated with larger establishments. Secondly, the "transportation revolution", canals, inland waterways and especially railroads, played a role. Thirdly, technological advances in inanimate power sources, steam power first and then electrical power, were important. These advances raised labor productivity and associated levels of capital intensity and facilitated a more intricate division of labor.

The Emergence of Antitrust

In 1890, the U.S. government passed the **Sherman Antitrust Act**[5], setting rules against trust and monopoly. But the Act did little to hinder the dramatic wave of consolidations that took place around the turn of the century. The Act was a compromise written in ambiguous language that provided no guidance as to practical application. Nor were the courts particularly sympathetic to the government. ***United States v. E. C. Knight Company & the Other***[6] in 1895 was a loss for the government. As a result, the merger wave of the late 1890s went ahead unimpeded by any judicial restraint.

However, judicial sentiment began to change. In 1899 the Supreme Court declared the cast-iron pipe pool illegal in the case of ***Addyston Pipe and Steel Company v. United States***[7]. In 1904 the Court ordered **the Northern Securities Company**[8]—the holding company for the Northern Pacific Railway and the Great Northern Railway—dissolved as combination in restraint of trade. And most significant of all, in 1909, the U.S. circuit court held that the Standard Oil Company was a combination in restraint of trade and a monopoly in violation of the Sherman Antitrust Act. In 1911, Standard Oil was ordered dissolved into separate, smaller companies. The U.S. Congress passed **the Clayton Antitrust Act of 1914**[9] at the urging of President Wilson. The Clayton Act extended the Sherman Antitrust Act of 1890, gave the Federal Government even greater authority to act against the trusts. It specifically outlawed tying together multiple products, price discrimination, corporate mergers, and interlocking boards of directors. The Clayton Act also mandated the creation of the Federal Trade Commission. The FTC's original job was to control corporate wrongdoing, and it still carries that mission.

Notes

1. the energy Crisis in 1973 1973 年石油危机：第一次石油危机从 1973 年延续至 1974 年，又称作“1973 年石油危机”。由于 1973 年 10 月第四次中东战争爆发，石油输出国组织（OPEC）为了打击对手以色列及支持以色列的国家，宣布石油禁运，暂停出口，造成油价上涨。

2. mergers and acquisitions 企业并购：简称“M&A”，包括兼并和收购两层含义、两种方式。国际上习惯将兼并和收购合在一起使用，统称为 M&A，即企业之间的兼并与收购行为，是企业法人在平等自愿、等价有偿基础上，以一定的经济方式取得其他法人产权的行为，是企业进行资本运作和经营的一种主要形式。企业并购主要包括公司合并、资产收购、股权收购三种形式。

3. oligopoly 寡头垄断：一种由少数卖方（寡头）主导市场的市场状态。英语中这个词来源于希腊语中“很少的卖者”。在这种市场状态下，每个寡头都关注其他寡头的行为。寡头垄断下的市场一个显著的特征就是寡头们相互影响。一个寡头厂商作出的决策影响其它寡头厂商，也被其它厂商的决策所影响。所以在作战略规划时，它要考虑其它市场参与者会对此决策可能作出的回应。这就是一个典型的博弈状况。

4. conglomerate mergers 混合合并：亦称“多种经营合并”，系没有内在联系的多种产品生产和劳务供应企业之间的合并。混合合并是指从事不相关业务类型的企业间的合并。如机械制造企业合并房地产开发企业，或报业集团兼并旅馆等。美国纳比斯科仪器公司被克拉维斯·罗伯兹投资公司以 250 亿美元收购，就属混合合并。

5. Sherman Antitrust Act 休曼法案：1890 年 7 月 2 日通过，美国联邦的反托拉斯法，要求美国联邦政府有责任去调查并且起诉有托拉斯行为的公司与组织。 它是美国第一个针对独占与卡特尔的法律，由俄亥俄州参议院议员、参议院财政委员会主席约翰·休曼在 1890 年提出。

6. *United States v. E. C. Knight Co. & the Other* 美国诉奈特公司与其同伙案：1892 年，美国糖业公司（American Sugar Refining Company）先后以股权置换的方式收购了包括奈特公司在内的四家位于费城的制糖企业，从而控制了美国国内 98% 的糖品生产。联邦政府认为该项合并已经构成垄断，并企图对美国的糖业贸易进行起诉。但该案的法官认为在宾夕法尼亚州内进行的糖业托拉斯合并，没有涉及州际商务，故不属于联邦政府管辖。至于这家大托拉斯是否只在宾州内销售它的产品，则不关最高法院的事，这项判决使得后来的公司合并缺少了法律根据。

7. *Addyston Pipe and Steel Co. v. United States* 阿迪斯顿钢管钢材公司诉美国：是美国最高法院审理的一个典型案例。法院经审理该案认为，国家对于垄断贸易的限制是合法的。

8. the Northern Securities Company 北方证券公司：一个“短命” 的美国铁路公司，该公司成立于 1901 年，由 E. H. Harriman, James J. Hill, J. P. Morgan, J. D. Rockefelle 共同投资组成。该公司控制着北太平洋铁路公司，大西北铁路公司等所管沿线业务。根据 1890 年

《谢尔曼反托拉斯法》,该公司于 1902 年遭到西奥多·罗斯福总统领导下的司法部起诉。这是美国史上首例公司遭起诉的案列之一。政府胜诉,致使该公司解散。

9. the Clayton Antitrust Act of 1914 1914 年克莱顿反托拉斯法: 是美国国会制定的第二部重要的反托拉斯立法,是对《谢尔曼反托拉斯法》的补充。该法明确规定了 17 种非法垄断行为,其中包括价格歧视、搭卖合同等。其主要目的是制止反竞争性的企业兼并以及资本和经济力量的集中。关于非法兼并和合法兼并的确认原则是在该法实施过程中不断完善的。此外,由于工人运动的发展,它规定工会及农民组织不受《谢尔曼反托拉斯法》的限制。

Unit 4 American Computer and Internet Industry

As technologies developed in earlier ages liberated people from physical toil, computers have liberated people from the more tedious kinds of mental toil—and have revolutionized the transfer of information. The electronic digital computer is the herald of the Information Age.

Two factors spurred development of computers in the mid-twentieth century. One was the war effort, which needed quick calculation of ballistic paths. The other was electronics, which made it possible to use wires and vacuum tubes to simulate logical operations. During the World War II the U.S. Army funded development of a digital computer, planning to use it for military calculations. On 14 February 1946 the first electronic digital computer unveiled at the University of Pennsylvania. They called their machine the Electronic Numerical Integrator and Computer, which is the "Giant Brain". It performed a then-impressive 5,000 additions and 360 multiplications per second. Later computers experience the change from Giant brain to minicomputer. In succession, the invention of transistors and silicon ships, not much bigger than a postage stamp, could contain more than 20 million transistors, make minicomputers become smaller and more affordable.

In 1974, the first commercially available personal computer, the Altair, announced. In 1977 Steven P. Jobs and Stephen G. Wozniak founded Apple Computer, which produced a more successful product, the Apple II. Unlike the Altair, the Apple II included a keyboard and a monitor, came assembled, and could do useful work.

It is important to point out that the United States led the field in the electronic information technology—in the 1950s, the US government began to use a semiconductor in production, and promoted the development and application of computer technology. Since the beginning of the new era of microelectronics industry, the development of American computer technology had grown very rapidly. The United States had produced computers in batch and in 1958 it began to put transistor computer into mass production. In the era of integrated circuits from 1956 to 1970, the United States in 1970 began large-scale production in integrated circuits computers.

The Internet is originally sponsored by **the Department of Defense**[1] in the late 1960s as the **ARPANET**[2]. The purpose of this system was to enable military communication after a nuclear attack. In early 1983, the US military officially connected each subnet of all bases to the

ARPANET, and all use TCP/IP protocol, which marked the official birth of the Internet. In the 1990s, World Wide Web, WWW unveiled in European High-Energy Particle Physical Lab, is the fastest growing, most widely used service. In the 1990s the World Wide Web was launched to share information not just between government agencies, but also universities, nonprofit organizations, and private companies, among others. As a "hypertext" system, the Web supported links functioning as automated cross-references. The Internet provided the infrastructure for the World Wide Web, as well as for sending and receiving E-mail and for downloading files. With the explosion of the World Wide Web, the Internet became the information superhighway.

When Bill Clinton came to power he officially presented the construction of the "information superhighway". After that, the Clinton administration has supported the development of information industry, especially committed to the improvement and popularization of the Internet. In turn, it is the Information Superhighway that led the rapid development of the Internet into a new stage.

Also in the 1990s, commercial organizations involved in the Internet, such as MERIT, MCI, IBM and other commercial companies, on the one hand, received the backbone originally operated by the government funding agencies such as the National Science Foundation Network (NSF-NET), etc., on the other hand began to run and make it their own business networks connected to the backbone network. Commercialization brings a new leap in the Internet.

Computers and Internet as the herald of IT industry originated in the United States have access to all the country's economy and life in many ways. 5% of the world's population in the United States provided 75 percent of the world's technology. U.S. information industry since the 1950s, experienced rapid development from small to large, and successively became the leading industry in America, contributing to the United States' roles as the economic growth locomotive in the world.

Google[3] is an American multinational technology company specializing in Internet-related services and products. The company was founded by Larry Page and Sergey Brin while they were Ph.D. students at Stanford University. Together, they own about 14 percent of its shares and control 56 percent of the stockholder voting power through super voting stock. They incorporated Google as a privately held company on September 4, 1998. An initial public offering followed on August 19, 2004. Its mission statement from the outset was "to organize the world's information and make it universally accessible and useful", and its unofficial slogan was "Don't be evil". In August 2015, Google announced plans to reorganize its interests as a holding company called Alphabet Inc. When this restructuring took place on October 2, 2015, Google became Alphabet's leading subsidiary, as well as the parent for Google's Internet interests.

Rapid growth since incorporation has triggered a chain of products, acquisitions and partnerships beyond Google's core search engine. It offers online productivity software including email, a cloud storage service and a social networking service. Desktop products include applications for web browsing, organizing and editing photos, and instant messaging and video chat. The company leads the development of the Android mobile operating system and the browser-only Chrome OS for a class of netbooks. Google has moved increasingly into communications hardware, partnering with major electronics manufacturers in the production of its "high-quality, low-cost" Nexus devices.

Cisco[4] Systems, Inc. is an American multinational technology company headquartered in San Jose, California, that designs, manufactures and sells networking equipment. It is considered to be the largest networking company in the world. The stock was added to the Dow Jones Industrial Average on June 8, 2009, and is also included in the S&P 500 Index, the Russell 1000 Index, NASDAQ-100 Index and the Russell 1000 Growth Stock Index.

Cisco Systems was founded in December 1984 by Leonard Bosack, who was in charge of the Stanford University computer science department's computers.

Cisco was the 2002–2003 recipient of the Ron Brown Award—a U.S. presidential honor to recognize companies "for the exemplary quality of their relationships with employees and communities". Cisco commonly stays on top of ***Fortune***[5] "100 Best Companies to work for", with position No. 20 in 2011.

Cisco is one of the leading recipients of network security-related patents with the largest portfolio within other companies. Cisco's products and services focus upon three market segments—enterprise and service provider, small business and the home.

Microsoft Corporation[6] is an American multinational technology company headquartered in Redmond, Washington, that develops, manufactures, licenses, supports and sells computer software, consumer electronics and personal computers and services. Its best-known software products are the Microsoft Windows line of operating systems, Microsoft Office suite, and Internet Explorer and Edge web browsers. Its flagship hardware products are the **Xbox**[7] game consoles and the Microsoft Surface tablet lineup. It is the world's largest software maker by revenue, and one of the world's most valuable companies.

Microsoft was founded by Paul Allen and Bill Gates on April 4, 1975, to develop and sell BASIC interpreters for **Altair 8800**[8]. It rose to dominate the personal computer operating system market with MS-DOS in the mid-1980s, followed by Microsoft Windows. The company's 1986 initial public offering, and subsequent rise in its share price, created three billionaires and an estimated 12,000 millionaires among Microsoft employees. Since the 1990s, it has increasingly diversified from the operating system market and has made a number of corporate acquisitions. In May 2011, Microsoft acquired Skype Technologies for $8.5 billion in its largest acquisition to date.

As of 2015, Microsoft is market dominant in both the IBM PC-compatible operating system and office software suite markets. The company also produces a wide range of other software for desktops and servers, and is active in areas including Internet search, the video game industry, the digital services market, and mobile phones. In June 2012, Microsoft entered the personal computer production market for the first time, with the launch of the Microsoft Surface, a line of tablet computers.

Facebook[9] is a corporation and an online social networking service headquartered in Menlo Park, California, in the United States. Its website was launched on February 4, 2004 by Mark Zuckerberg with his Harvard College roommates and fellow students Eduardo Saverin, Andrew McCollum, Dustin Moskovitz, and Chris Hughes. The founders had initially limited the website's membership to Harvard students, but later expanded it to colleges in the Boston area, the Ivy League, and Stanford University. It gradually added support for students at various other universities and later to high school students. Since 2006, anyone in general aged 13 and older has been allowed to become a registered user of the website, though variations exist in the minimum age requirement, depending on applicable local laws. Its name comes from the face book directories often given to American university students.

After registering to use the site, users can create a user profile, add other users as "friends", exchange messages, post status updates and photos, share videos, use various apps, and receive notifications when others update their profiles. Additionally, users may join common-interest user groups organized by workplace, school, or other characteristics, and categorize their friends into lists such as "People from Work" or "Close Friends". Also, users can complain or block unpleasant people. Facebook had over 1.59 billion monthly active users as of August 2015. Because of the large volume of data that users submit to the service, Facebook has come under scrutiny for their privacy policies. Facebook, Inc. held its initial public offering in February 2012 and began selling stock to the public three months later, reaching an original peak market capitalization of $104 billion. On July 13, 2015, Facebook became the fastest company in **the Standard & Poor's 500 Index**[10] to reach a market cap of $250 billion. Following its Q3 earnings call in 2015, Facebook's market cap exceeded $300 billion.

Apple Inc.[11] is an American multinational technology company headquartered in Cupertino, California, that designs, develops, and sells consumer electronics, computer software, and online services.

Apple was founded by Steve Jobs, Steve Wozniak, and Ronald Wayne on April 1, 1976, to develop and sell personal computers. It was incorporated as Apple Computer, Inc. on January 3, 1977, and was renamed as Apple Inc. on January 9, 2007, to reflect its shifted focus toward consumer electronics. Apple joined the Dow Jones Industrial Average on March 19, 2015.

Apple is the world's largest information technology company by revenue, the world's largest technology company by total assets, and the world's second-largest mobile phone manufacturer. In November 2014, in addition to being the largest publicly traded corporation in the world by market capitalization, Apple became the first U.S. company to be valued at over $700 billion. The company employs 115,000 permanent full-time employees as of July 2015 and maintains 475 retail stores in seventeen countries as of March 2016. It operates the online Apple Store and iTunes Store, the latter of which is the world's largest music retailer. There are over one billion actively Apple products users worldwide as of March 2016.

Apple's worldwide annual revenue totaled $233 billion for the fiscal year ending in September 2015. To put this into perspective this revenue generation accounts for approximately 1.25% of the total United States GDP. The company enjoys a high level of brand loyalty and, according to the 2014 edition of the Interbrand Best Global Brands report, is the world's most valuable brand with a valuation of $118.9 billion. By the end of 2014, the corporation continued to receive significant criticism regarding the labor practices of its contractors and its environmental and business practices, including the origins of source materials.

Intel Corporation[12] is an American multinational technology company headquartered in Santa Clara, California. Intel is one of the world's largest and highest valued semiconductor chip makers, based on revenue. It is the inventor of the x86 series of microprocessors, the processors found in most personal computers. Intel supplies processors for computer system manufacturers such as Apple, Samsung, HP and Dell.

Intel Corporation was founded on July 18, 1968 by semiconductor pioneers Robert Noyce and Gordon Moore and widely associated with the executive leadership and vision of Andrew Grove, Intel combines advanced chip design capability with a leading-edge manufacturing capability. Intel was an early developer of **SRAM**[13] and **DRAM**[14] memory chips, which represented the majority of its business until 1981. Although Intel created the world's first commercial microprocessor chip in 1971, it was not until the success of the personal computer (PC) that this became its primary business. During the 1990s, Intel invested heavily in new microprocessor designs fostering the rapid growth of the computer industry. During this period Intel became the dominant supplier of microprocessors for PCs, and was known for aggressive and anti-competitive tactics in defense of its market position, particularly against Advanced Micro Devices, as well as a struggle with Microsoft for control over the direction of the PC industry.

Intel was ranked 56 on the 2015 rankings of the world's most valuable brands published by **Millward Brown Optimor**[15]. The name "Intel" was conceived as portmanteau of the words integrated and electronics. The fact that "intel" is the term for intelligence information also made the name appropriate.

Cray[16] Inc. is an American supercomputer manufacturer headquartered in Seattle, Washington. It also manufactures systems for data storage and analytics. Cray manufactures its products in Chippewa Falls, Wisconsin, where its founder, Seymour Cray, was born and raised. The company also has offices in St. Paul, Minnesota and numerous other sales, service, engineering, and R&D locations around the world.

Several Cray supercomputer systems are listed in the TOP500, which ranks the most powerful supercomputers in the world. The number of Cray systems on the list varies from year to year. The company's predecessor, Cray Research, Inc. (CRI), was founded in 1972 by computer designer Seymour Cray. Seymour Cray went on to form the spin-off Cray Computer Corporation in 1989, which went bankrupt in 1995, while Cray Research was bought by SGI the next year. Cray Inc. was formed in 2000 when Tera Computer Company purchased the Cray Research Inc.

business from SGI and adopted the name of its acquisition.

In April 2012, Cray Inc. announced the sale of its interconnect hardware development program and related intellectual property to Intel Corporation for $140 million USD. On November 1, 2013 Cray announced the acquisition of the Gnodal IP and team in Europe.

Amazon.com, Inc. , often referred to as simply Amazon, is an American electronic commerce and cloud computing company with headquarters in Seattle, Washington. It is the largest Internet-based retailer in the United States. Amazon has separate retail websites for United States, United Kingdom and Ireland, France, Canada, Germany, Italy, Spain, Netherlands, Australia, Brazil, Japan, China, India and Mexico. Amazon also offers international shipping to certain other countries for some of its products. In 2011, it professed an intention to launch its websites in Poland and Sweden.

In 2015, Amazon surpassed Walmart as the most valuable retailer in the United States by market capitalization.

The company was founded in 1994 when Bezos left his employment as vice-president of D. E. Shaw & Co., a Wall Street firm, and moved to Seattle. He began to work on a business plan for what would eventually become Amazon.com.

Amazon product lines include several media, apparel, baby products, consumer electronics, beauty products, gourmet food, groceries, health and personal-care items, industrial & scientific supplies, kitchen items, jewelry and watches, lawn and garden items, musical instruments, sporting goods, tools, automotive items and toys & games.

Notes

1. the Department of Defense 美国国防部：简称“DOD” 或“DoD”，是关于美国军队的部门，它的中心是五角大楼。国防部的领导是美国国防部长。按照美国法律，部长须为文官。美国国防部成立于 1947 年 9 月 18 日，前身为美国战争部。

2.ARPANET 阿帕网：全称为“美国国防部高级研究计划局组建的计算机网（Advanced Research Projects Agency Network），又称“ARPA 网”。现在的 Internet 是在 APRA 的基础上建立起来的。

3. Google 谷歌公司：谷歌公司是一家美国的跨国科技企业，致力于互联网搜索、云计算、广告技术等领域，开发并提供大量基于互联网的产品与服务，其主要利润来自于 AdWords 等广告服务。Google 由当时在斯坦福大学攻读理工博士的拉里・佩奇（Larry Page）和谢尔盖・布卢姆（Sergey Brin）共同创建，因此他们也被称为“Google Guys”。1998 年 9 月 4 日，Google 以私营公司的形式创立，设计并管理一个互联网搜索引擎”Google 搜索”，Google 网站则于 1999 年下半年启用。Google 的使命是整合全球信息，使人人皆可访问并从中受益。Google 是第一个被公认为全球最大的搜索引擎，在全球范围内拥有无数的用户。2015 年 8 月，谷歌宣布重大重组，成为 Alphabet 子公司。

4. Cisco 思科公司：思科公司是全球领先的网络解决方案供应商。Cisco 的名字取自 San Francisco，那里有闻名世界的金门大桥。可以说，依靠自身的技术和对网络经济模式的深刻理解，思科成为了网络应用的成功实践者之一。与此同时思科正在致力于为无数的企业构筑网络间畅通无阻的“桥梁”，并用自己敏锐的洞察力、丰富的行业经验、先进的技术，帮助企业把网络应用转化为战略性的资产，充分挖掘网络的能量，获得竞争的优势。

5. *Fortune*《财富》：是一本由美国人亨利 • 鲁斯于 1930 年创办，主要刊登经济问题研究文章的杂志。现隶属时代华纳集团旗下的时代公司。《财富》杂志自 1954 年推出全球 500 强排行榜，历来都成为经济界关注的焦点，影响巨大。《财富》杂志举办了一系列引人注目的财经论坛，如著名的《财富》全球论坛，即世界 500 强年会便是其中之一。《财富》全球论坛开始于 1995 年，其中 1999、2001、2005 年的年会分别在中国上海、香港和北京举办。

6. Microsoft Corporation 微软公司：简称“MS”，是美国一家跨国电脑科技公司。以研发、制造、授权和提供广泛的电脑软件服务业务为主。总部位于美国华盛顿州的雷德蒙德，最为著名和畅销的产品为 Microsoft Windows 操作系统和 Microsoft Office 系列软件。

7. Xbox 游戏机：由美国微软公司开发并于 2001 年发售的一款家用电视游戏机。微软的 Xbox 和索尼的 PS2 以及任天堂公司的 NGC 形成了三国鼎立局面。内装英特尔公司制造的 Pentium III 基本中央处理器，内建 8GB 容量的硬盘与 DVD-ROM 光驱、以太网路连接埠，支持连接网络，与个人电脑架构相似。控制器端口形状与 USB 规格不相同。从硬件性能指标上，Xbox 属于当时的”三大主机”。Xbox Live 是 Xbox 及其后的第二代占据现在市场主流的 Xbox 360 专用的多用户在线对战平台。

8. Altair 8800 牛郎星：第一台微型计算机“牛郎星”由美国计算机爱好者爱德华 • 罗伯茨（E.Roberts）发明。由一个 Intel 8080 微处理器，256 字节的储存器（后来增加到 4KB），一个电源，一个机箱以及包含若干显示灯与开关的面板组成，对后来微型计算机的发展有指导意义。

9. Facebook 脸书：知名社交服务网站，于美国时间 2004 年 2 月 4 日 15 时上线。互联网用户凡年龄达 13 岁，即可注册成为 Facebook 用户，并享有站内所有免费功能。2012 年 5 月 18 日，Facebook 正式在美国纳斯达克证券交易所上市。2012 年 6 月，Facebook 涉足在线支付领域。根据 Facebook 官方统计，截至 2012 年 9 月，站内已逾十余亿名的活跃用户，上传相片数量逾 2190 余亿张。2014 年 2 月 19 日，Facebook 对外宣布，将以现金和股票方式，斥资 190 亿美元收购即时通讯应用初创企业 WhatsApp，希望借此提高人气。

10. the Standard & Poor’s 500 Index 标准普尔 500 指数：简称“S&P 500 Index”，是记录美国 500 家上市公司的一个股票指数。这个股票指数由标准普尔公司创建并维护。标准普尔 500 指数覆盖的所有公司，都是在美国主要交易所，如纽约证券交易所、Nasdaq 交易所的上市公司。与道琼斯指数相比，标准普尔 500 指数包含的公司更多，因此风险更为分散，能够反映更广泛的市场变化。

11. Apple Inc. 苹果公司：美国的一家高科技公司，2007 年由苹果电脑公司（Apple Computer, Inc.）更名而来，核心业务为电子科技产品，总部位于加利福尼亚州的库比蒂诺。苹果公司由史蒂夫 • 乔布斯、斯蒂夫 • 沃兹尼亚克和罗恩•韦恩在 1976 年 4 月 1 日创立，在高科技企业中以创新而闻名，知名的产品有 Apple II、Macintosh（电脑）、Macbook（笔记本电脑）、iPod（音乐播放器）、iTunes（商店）、iMac（一体机）、iPhone（手机）和 iPad（平板电脑）等。它在高科技企业中以创新而闻名。

12. Intel Corporation 英特尔公司：世界上最大的半导体公司，也是第一家推出 x86 架构处理器的公司，总部位于美国加利福尼亚州圣克拉拉。由罗伯特·诺伊斯、高登·摩尔、安迪·葛洛夫，以“集成电子”（Integrated Electronics）之名在 1968 年 7 月 18 日共同创办公司，将高级芯片设计能力与领导业界的制造能力结合在一起。英特尔也开发主板芯片组、网卡、闪存、绘图芯片、嵌入式处理器以及与通信和运算相关的产品等。

13. SRAM 即静态随机存储器：SRAM 是英文 Static Random Access Memory 的缩写，是一种具有静止存取功能的内存，不需要刷新电路即能保存它内部存储的数据。

14. DRAM 动态随机存取存储器：“DRAM”是英文“Dynamic Random Access Memory”的缩写，即最为常见的系统内存。DRAM 只能将数据保持很短的时间。为了保持数据，DRAM 使用电容存储，所以必须隔一段时间刷新（refresh）一次，如果存储单元没有被刷新，存储的信息就会丢失（关机就会丢失数据）。

15. Millward Brown Optimor 明略行咨询公司：一家世界领先且不断创新的全球化市场调研公司，特别是在帮助客户最大化他们的品牌资产、品牌绩效和品牌健康方面表现卓越，并且擅长帮助客户优化他们的媒体，广告，公关和其他方面的品牌沟通。

16. Cray 超级计算机之父： Seymour Cray 在 1972 年创建自己的公司 Cray Research Inc. 之后，这家公司第一个产品 Cray-1 超级计算机诞生，成为当时速度最快的计算机。这一产品的后续衍生品有 Cray-2 和 Cray-3。同时他们还在陈世卿（Steve Chen）的引领下开始一个并行的项目 Cray X-MP，直到 1987 年陈世卿离开。

References

[1] HUGHES J R, CAIN L P. American economic history [M]. 5ed. Boston: Addison-Wesley Longman, 1998.

[2] PERKINS E J, WALTION G M. A prosperous people: the growth of the American economy [M]. Upper Saddle River: Prentice Hall, 1984.

[3] FRECH M. U.S. economic history since 1945 [M]. Manchester: Manchester University Press, 1997.

[4] DOWNING D A, et al. Dictionary of computer and internet terms [M]. 7ed. New York: Barron's, 2000.

[5] SEGALLER S. Nerds 2.0.1: a brief history of the Internet [M]. New York: TV Books, 1998.

[6] ATTACK J, PASSELL P. A new economic view of American history [M]. 2ed. New York: W.W. Norton & Company, Inc., 1994.

[7] 陈宝森 . 剖析美国“新经济”[M]. 北京：社会科学文献出版社，2007.

Chapter Six

American Agriculture

Unit 1 An Overview of American Agriculture

Geographical Features of the U.S.

The United States is bounded on the east by the Atlantic Ocean, on the south by the Gulf of Mexico, and on the west by the Pacific Ocean. Canada lies to the north and Mexico to the south.

Down the east coast of the U.S. is a range of mountains, **the Appalachians**[1]. In the northeast, the plain between the mountains and the sea coast is only fifty miles wide, but in the south the coastal plain widens to 200 miles. The Appalachians run through thirteen states, which are rich in coal and hydroelectric potential.

The Five Great Lakes[2] on the border between Canada and the U.S. moderate the climate in that part of the country. Niagara Falls, one of the two largest falls in the world, lies between the smaller eastern lakes, L. Eire and L. Ontario. This waterfall is an important source of hydroelectric power for the eastern industrial states. There are rich iron mines around the largest lake, L. Superior in the west. The lakes provide cheap water transportation, shipping the iron ore to ports on Lake Eire, near Niagara electricity and Appalachian coal. So the south area of lakes has become a center of heavy industry.

The Mississippi River is a major river in the U.S. It rises in the north near Lake Superior, and empties into the Gulf of Mexico at New Orleans. With its tributaries, it drains the entire central U.S., from the Appalachian Mountains on the east to the Rocky Mountains on the west. It is navigable for most of its length, north to Minneapolis. The main tributary of the Mississippi River on the east is the Ohio River. There are several tributaries on the west, but the greatest is the Missouri River, which flows into the Mississippi as St. Louis. Known as "**Big Muddy River**[3]（大泥河）". The Missouri and its tributaries drain ten states in the **Great Plains**[4]. The flow is seasonal, and only the lower course of the Missouri river is navigable. West of the Mississippi River valley, the Great Plains begin.

If you look at the map, the U.S. seems to be cut into three parts by the Mississippi River and the Rocky Mountains. The Rocky Mountains arise in northwest Canada and run southeastward through the U.S. down to the Mexico. West of the Rockies is an area of high plateaus and basins. An interesting natural feature of this area is the Great Salt Lake, fourteen miles across, which is surrounded by mountains so that it has no outlet. Through hundreds of thousands of years it has become so salty that salt crusts float upon it like ice. Another feature is the Grand Canyon（大峡谷）on the Colorado River. Through more than 300, 000 years, the river has worn down through the rock of the highlands so that the canyon is a mile deep, with the rushing river at the bottom. The Colorado River rises in the Rockies and flows southeast into the Gulf of California. A series of dams, reservoirs and canals provide electricity and water for southeastern U.S. and northwest Mexico.

On the west of the highlands are two mountain ranges. The range of south, the Sierra Nevada, forms the eastern border of the state of California. The Cascade Range, to the north, is made up of volcanoes. One of these volcanoes, Mount St. Helens, erupted only recently in May, 1980. The Columbia River flows through the Pacific Northwest. A staircase of the reservoirs starts from Canada to its mouth at the Portland Oregon, and the river and its tributaries represent a third of the potential hydroelectric（水力发电的）power of the United States.

Farming Regions in the U.S.

There are 10 major farm production regions in the United States. These farming regions differ in soil, slope of land, climate, distance to market, and storage and marketing facilities. Together they form the agricultural face of the nation.

The Northeastern States and the Lake States are the nation's principal milk-producing areas. Climate and soil in these regions are suited to raising grains and forage for cattle and for providing pastureland for grazing.

Broiler farming is important in Maine, Delaware, and Maryland. Fruit and vegetables are also important to the region. The Appalachian region is the major tobacco-producing area in the nation. Peanuts, cattle, hog, and dairy production are also important there.

In the Southeast region, beef and broilers are important livestock products. Fruits, vegetables, and peanuts are grown in this region. Big citrus groves, winter vegetable, and sugarcane production areas in Florida are major suppliers of agricultural goods. Cotton production is making a comeback.

In the Delta States, the principal cash crops are soybeans and cotton. Rice, corn, and sugarcane are also grown. With improved pastures, livestock production has gained in importance. This is a major broiler-producing region. The **Corn Belt**[5] has rich soil and good climate for excellent farming. Corn, soybeans, cattle, hogs and dairy products are the major outputs of farms in the region. Other feed grains（饲料谷物）and wheat are also important.

Agriculture in the Northern and Southern Plains, which extend north and south from Canada to Mexico, is restricted by rainfall in the western portion and by cold winters and short growing seasons in the northern part. About three-fifths of the nation's winter and spring wheat is produced in this region. Other small grains, grain sorghum, hay, forage crops（饲草作物）, and pastures from the basis for raising cattle and for milk production. In the southern part, cotton is also a major crop.

The Mountain States provide a still different terrain. Vast areas of this region are suited to raising cattle and sheep. Wheat is important in the northern parts. Irrigation in the valleys provides water for such crops as hay, sugar beets, potatoes, fruits, and vegetables.

The Pacific region includes the three Pacific Coast States plus Alaska and Hawaii. Farmers in Washington and Oregon specialize in raising wheat, fruit, and potatoes. Vegetables, fruit, and cotton are important in California. Cattle are raised throughout the region, and California leads the nation in milk production. In Hawaii, sugarcane and pineapples are the major crops. Greenhouse and dairy products are Alaska's top-ranking commodities.

The weather as a major factor too has a great impact on these farming regions. General movement of the weather in the northern hemisphere is in spiral from northwest toward the southeast. The air picks up moisture from the polar ice cap and bodies of water it may pass over. Then it deposits the moisture as rain and snow along its way. In the U.S., the moisture precipitates on the western slopes of the mountain ranges in California and the Pacific Northwest. East of the line formed by the Cascade and Sierra Nevada ranges begins an area of desert and desert shrub (灌木丛). This desert area extends into southwest Texas and Mexico. In the north, winters are quite severe, and some snow comes out of Canada. But farther south one enters the "**sun belt**[6]", a dry, temperate climate.

East of the Rockies, winds come down from northern Canada, bringing some more moisture. This is increased in the south by winds off the Gulf of Mexico. Historically, the 100th meridian is the dividing line between "wet" and "dry" U.S. There is more precipitation east of this line, and the country changes from short grass steppe to long grass prairie. From the Mississippi valley to the Atlantic coast, rainfall is plentiful.

The eastern U.S. can be divided by the Ohio River. South of this river, winter is mild and summer is hot and long. In the northern part, winters are quite severe. Winds coming over Hudson Bay and the Lakes in the north, the Atlantic Ocean in the east and the Gulf of Mexico in the south generally provide plentiful rainfall.

Corn is the largest crop in area and production. About one-fourth of the total agricultural land in America is devoted to corn production, but the major producer is the north and middle Corn Belt (the most productive corn district in the world). This region includes 8 states near the Great Lakes, from Ohio and Michigan in the east, to Minnesota in the northwest, stretching to the south-west Missouri.

Wheat is another main food crop, whose production is second to corn, and the Great Plains is mainly the **wheat district**[7]. It is located in the middle and north part, altogether nine states, including North and South Dakota, Montana, Oklahoma and north part of Texas. The spring wheat belt is in the North, extending from the Middle Mississippi northwest to the Canadian border.

The famous **Cotton Belt**[8] is from east along the Atlantic coast to the west in Texas. The

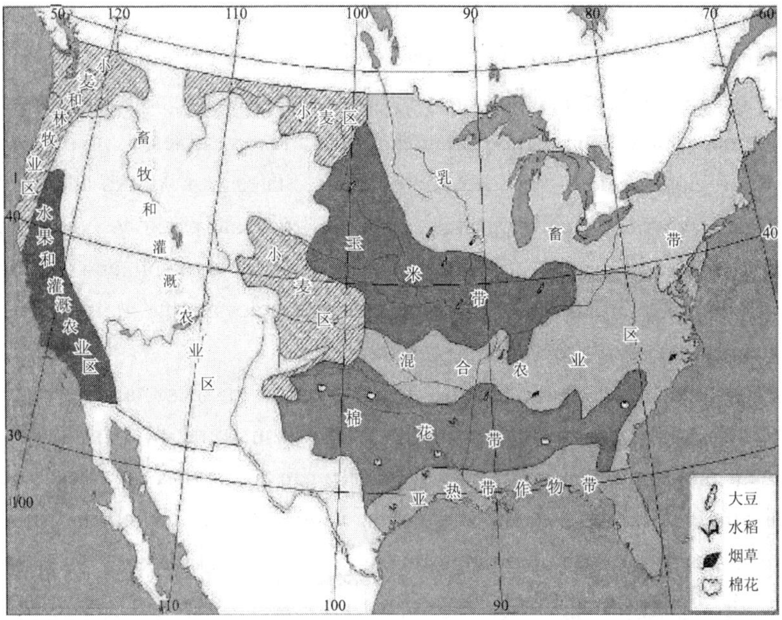

Agricultural Belts in the U.S.

cotton farm here takes one third of the national area of the U.S., estimated 145 hectares, taking 72% of the national volume. Cotton has been an important cash crop for over one hundred years. In recent years, cotton growing areas have moved to the western states of Texas, New Mexico, Arizona and California.

The United States produces half of the world's supply of soybeans, and its production is concentrated heavily in Iowa and Illinois. The United States is also a large exporter of rice, only next to Thailand, and the principal rice growing area lies in the coastal lowlands bordering the Gulf of Mexico.

California is another big "crop basket"(作物之乡), which provides 51% of the national production of fruit and nuts, and almost 31% of the vegetables for the nation. California is most famous for its large variety and huge quantity of fruit. Washington and Oregon comprise a major wheat-producing area, which produces 13% of the national volume. Peanuts are also an important crop. Vegetables, especially from South Carolina, are shipped to the big northern cities when the growing season in the north has ended.

The **Dairy Belt**[9] includes southern Wisconsin and most other northern states. Cattle production is widespread throughout the United States. The Great Plains between the Mississippi Valley and the Rockies is a great animal farming area. Texas leads all the other states in the production of range cattle, and Iowa and Illinois are important producers of non-range feeder cattle. Kansas is a big producer of beef.

Hog production tends to be concentrated in Iowa, Illinois, and their surrounding states. Iowa leads the United States in hog raising, accounting for about one-quarter of the national output.

Two-fifths of Iowa's annual agricultural income comes from livestock production. Chicken production is widespread, and Texas, Arkansas and Alabama are the largest producers of chicken.

By the late nineteenth century, most New England farmers were producing for urban markets, concentrating on dairy products and then on fruits, vegetables, and nuts. The middle Atlantic and "**Delmarva**[10]" states followed suit, shifting from grains and other staples toward the vegetables, fruits, dairy, and poultry that growing urban centers demanded. In the middle southern states of Kentucky, North Carolina, and Tennessee, pockets of commercial production of tobacco, cotton, and grain were surrounded by small, less productive farms. Farther south, in Florida, Georgia, Alabama, Mississippi, Arkansas, Louisiana, Texas, and South Carolina, there were also pockets of commercial production. Citrus and sugarcane in Florida, rice in Louisiana, and nuts, fruit, and corn in Georgia were especially successful in certain areas.

Of course, cotton was the primary crop in the Deep South. In 1920, 74 percent of the farmers in this area grew cotton. Certainly the soil and climate were suitable for cotton, but the persistence of cotton's dominance（优势）can't be explained by this alone. After the First World War, when agricultural promoters began to push for more industrialized farm methods, cotton growers did not mechanize or in any way industrialize the cotton fields.

Notes

1. the Appalachians 阿巴拉契亚山脉：位于美国东部，是北美洲东部的一座山系。南起美国的阿拉巴马州，北至加拿大的纽芬兰和拉布拉多省，全长约 2 600 千米。

2. The Five Great Lakes 五大湖：位于加拿大与美国交界处的 5 个大型淡水湖泊，按面积大小分别为苏必利尔湖（Lake Superior）、休伦湖（Lake Huron）、密歇根湖（Lake Michigan）、伊利湖（Lake Erie）和安大略湖（Lake Ontario）。除密歇根湖全位于美国之外，其他 4 湖都为美国和加拿大共有。

3. Big Muddy River 大泥河：位于伊利诺伊州南部，全长 156 英里（251 千米）。在墨菲伯勒以南汇入密西西比河。整个流域的大部分的河床为黄泥，故因此而得名。

4. Great Plains 大平原：北美洲中部一个广袤的平原地区，大致位于密西西比河以西、落基山脉以东、格兰德河以北。自然植被以草为主。

5. Corn Belt 玉米带：位于美国中西部的一个地区。自 18 世纪 50 年代以来，这一地区生产的主要粮食作物是玉米，因此得名。玉米带主要包括了：艾奥瓦州、伊利诺伊州、印第安纳州、俄亥俄州、密歇根州、密苏里州、明尼苏达州、威斯康星州。

6. sun belt 太阳带：指美国南部北纬 37 度以南的地区，这些地区日照时间长，大致包括了以下地区：北卡罗来纳州、南卡罗来纳州、佐治亚州、佛罗里达州、阿拉巴马州、密西西比州、路易斯安那州、得克萨斯州、新墨西哥州、田纳西州、阿肯色州、俄克拉荷马州、亚利桑那州、加利福尼亚州。

7. wheat district 小麦带：主要有两块。一块位于美国北部与加拿大交界处，是春小麦区；另一块在中部，是冬小麦区。

8. Cotton Belt 棉花带：位于美国南部，这一地区的主要经济作物是棉花，因此而得名。

美国主要的棉花产区有佐治亚州、田纳西州、阿拉巴马州、阿肯色州、密西西比州、佛罗里达州、路易斯安那州、得克萨斯州。

9. Dairy Belt 乳畜带： 分布在五大湖及东北地区。这一地区气候湿冷，土壤贫瘠，不宜耕种，适合发展畜牧业。

10. Delmarva 德玛瓦半岛： 是美国特拉华、马里兰和弗吉尼亚三州的总称。

Unit 2 The Rise of Scientific Agriculture

The Development of Agricultural Societies

When the first agricultural societies were formed in the United States, near the close of the eighteenth century, we find the beginning of recognition of the desirability of experimental inquiries for the advancement of agriculture. The society organized in South Carolina in 1785 had among its objects the establishment of an experiment farm. In 1849, the New York Agricultural Society established in Albany a chemical laboratory for the analysis of soils, manures（施肥）, etc., and an elaborate examination of maize was made there.

Two general farm organizations, **the Grange**[1] and **Farmers Alliance**[2], were pioneers in spreading cooperative principles into agricultural areas of the nation. The Granger movement started in 1867. When that driving force in cooperative development waned in the 1870s, Farmers Alliance renewed the momentum（气势）, particularly through the South in the late 1880s. One outgrowth of the Alliance was Farmers Educational and Cooperative Union of America, launched in Texas in 1902, that later became National Farmers Union.

The Granger movement was a political movement among U.S. farmers, and it was the first organized effort to address general agricultural problems. Launched in 1867 by employees of the U.S. Department of Agriculture, the Grangers focused on social activities to counter the isolation most farm families encountered. Although most of them ultimately failed, the Grangers set up their own marketing systems, stores, processing plants, factories and cooperatives. A few states passed "Granger laws" to limit railroad and warehouse fees.

The Granger laws were a series of laws passed in several Midwestern states of the United States, namely Minnesota, Iowa, Wisconsin, and Illinois, in the late 1860s and early 1870s. the Granger laws were promoted primarily by a group of farmers known as The National Grange of the Order of Patrons of Husbandry（畜牧业）. The main goal of the Grange was to regulate rising fare prices of railroad and grain elevator companies after the American Civil War.

As a non-partisan（无党派的）organization, the Grange support only policies, never political parties or candidates. Although the Grange was originally founded to serve the interests of farmers, because of the shrinking farm population the Grange has begun to broaden its range to include a wide variety of issues.

In 1823, Robert H. Gardiner founded the Gardiner Lyceum, the first American school of agriculture. In 1855, the Michigan Agricultural Society helped persuade the State Legislature to create the Michigan Agricultural College, now Michigan State University. This was the first institution of higher learning in the world to offer courses in agriculture.

Agricultural societies provided early support to teaching and research institutions. Keen interest arose within these societies about the latest techniques, fertilizers, and implements. The early societies demonstrated the usefulness of research and education in improving agriculture, while also providing political interest group support for the use of public funds for research and education in agriculture.

Land Grants

In America, starting in the 16th century, land grants were given for the purpose of establishing settlements, missions, and farms. Without supportive governmental policies, the success of American agriculture would have been impossible. These policies included generous terms for the disposal of public lands. The land grant system was organized to bring the methods of scientific research to agriculture.

The purpose of the **land-grant university**[3] was: without excluding other scientific and classical studies and including military tactic, to teach such branches of learning as are related to agriculture and the mechanic arts, in such manner as the legislature of the States may respectively prescribe, in order to promote the liberal and practical education of the industrial classes in the several pursuits and professions in life.

Departments of agricultural economics and rural sociology in many land-grant universities teach courses on marketing and agribusiness（农业综合企业）with sections on farmer cooperatives. Some have a specialized course on cooperatives. Also, these departments—often with help from supplemental Federal funds—conduct studies of cooperative activities. Several land-grant universities have special programs such as chairs or centers to emphasize cooperative activities.

The Ordinance of 1785[4] provided the first land grants for educational purposes. It stipulated that the western lands had to be ceded to the federal government and be free of Indian claims before it could be disposed. Once the land had been ceded, the territory would be divided into townships which would be subdivided into sections. The sections were to be numbered 1 to 36 with specific uses for each section, including provision for the maintenance of public common schooling. The Ordinance was designed to promote the sale and settlement of land in the West.

The Morrill Land-Grant Acts are United States statutes that allowed for the creation of land-grant colleges, including **the Morrill Act**[5] of 1862 and the Morrill Act of 1890（the Agricultural College Act of 1890）.

The Morrill Act, passed in 1862, was the vehicle to pursue educational reforms. This act provided for the establishment and support of colleges of agriculture and "mechanical arts"（engineering）in each state. The use of proportional land grants provided for perpetual funds to be established and ensured the survival of such colleges.

The original Morrill Act did not make any provision for African American farmers in the South. All the southern land-grant colleges were segregated. This concerned its sponsor, Justin Smith Morrill of Vermont, and other northern legislators（立法委员会）. Thus, in 1890 Congress amended the first Morrill Act by adding funds and requiring an end to discrimination against blacks. Within a few years, all the former slave states established separate black land-grant colleges.

The newly established land—grant colleges created a demand for research to enhance the information content of their teaching programs in agriculture and home economics. With the Morrill Act, the federal government assumed primary responsibility for agricultural research and development. The Morrill Act gave each state 30,000 acres of public land for each of its senators and representatives, with the proceeds from the sale of this land to become an endowment for an agricultural and mechanical college.

The Second Morrill Act in 1890 was also aimed at the former Confederate states. This act required each state to show that race was not an admissions criterion, or else to designate a separate land-grant institution for persons of color. Among the seventy colleges and universities which eventually evolved from the Morrill Acts are several of today's historically Black colleges and universities. Though the 1890 Act granted cash instead of land, it granted colleges under the act the same legal standing as the 1862 Act colleges.

Agricultural Experiment Stations

Soon after the first Morrill Act, several new agricultural colleges began rather extensive research and demonstration efforts in what we called experiment stations. Agricultural experiment stations first developed in Europe, especially in Germany in the mid-1800s, and served as an interesting model because they sought methods of applying laboratory science, especially chemistry, to agriculture.

Between 1875 and 1887, fourteen states established agricultural experiment stations. The Connecticut State Agricultural Experiment Station, established initially at Wesleyan University in 1875, was the first successful one.

The passage of the **Hatch Act**[6] of 1887 was the most important legislative step in institutionalizing public agricultural research in the United States. The legislation was much debated between political interest groups of the north and south and between "states rights advocates" and "federal control proponents". To gain passage of the legislation, control of state agricultural experiment stations was given to the states, leaving the USDA（美国农业部）with the relatively minor role of aiding and assisting them. Each qualified state was to receive an equal federal appropriation of $ 15,000 per year to support a station, and the stations were to be established under the direction of a state land grant college or university. The stations were mandated by the legislation to acquire and spread practical information connected to agriculture and to conduct original conduct. After passage of the Hatch Act, state agricultural experiment stations were quickly established in all states.

In the Hatch Act of 1887, Congress authorized funds to support an agricultural experiment station in each state. This act preceded the 1890 Morrill Act revisions and made no provision for black experiment stations. By subsidizing research and development in the experiment stations, Congress tried to ensure the rapid dissemination of the most advanced farming practices.

The only attempt in America to establish an agricultural experiment station through the munificence of one man deserves recognition, although it was short lived. In 1876, Mr. Lawson Valentine, a philanthropic and public-spirited native of Massachusetts, conducting a prosperous business in New York City, purchased a tract of several hundred acres in the township of Cornwall, Orange County, N. Y., to which he gave the name of Houghton Farm. Soon after, he conceived the idea of establishing at this place a series of systematic agricultural experiments. Houghton Farm was conducted for about five years. The experimental work inaugurated was grouped under four heads: (a) Agricultural physics; (b) plant growth; (c) diseases of plants; and (d) animal growth and production.

In 1899, agricultural experiment stations were in operation in all the States and Territories and in Alaska and Hawaii. In each of the States of Alabama, Connecticut, New Jersey and New York a separate station was maintained wholly or in part by State funds, and in Louisiana there were three stations receiving joint support from national and State funds. Excluding the branch stations established in several states, the total number of stations in the United States in 1899 was 56.

The stations are at present conducting a wide range of scientific research in the laboratory and plant house and an equally large amount of practical experimenting in the field, the orchard, stable and dairy. Practically, all the stations are keeping a record of meteorological data, while 10 are making special studies of problems relating to meteorological(气象学的) phenomena and climate conditions.

The agricultural experiment stations in the United States are State institutions, supported in part by funds given by the National Government to the States to be used for their maintenance. They have also received the franking privilege under federal authority. The direct management of the stations is wholly in the hands of State officers. However, the stations sustain certain definite relations to different branches of the Federal Government. The stations have much more intimate relations with the Department of Agriculture than with any other branch of the Federal Government. The Office of Experiment Stations was established as a branch of the Department to represent the Secretary of Agriculture in his relations with the experiment stations as provided by the Hatch Act.

Notes

1. the Grange 格兰其：1867 年在上密西西比河谷兴起了自称“耕作保护神”的农民组织，外界称之为“格兰其”。该组织反对垄断，反对中间商的盘剥，以保护农民利益为其宗旨。

2. Farmers Alliance 美国农场主联盟：源于1919年自发形成、并于1920年成立的一个普通的农场组织。该组织是美国农业行业内最大的农民自治组织，总部设在华盛顿。

3. land-grant universities 赠地大学：由美国国会指定，得益于《莫雷尔法案》(Morril Act)的高等教育机构。

4. The Ordinance of 1785 1785年《土地法》：美国独立后第一个公共土地出售法令，该法令确立了美国西部公共土地出售的基本制度，奠定了美国早期公共土地政策的基础，对后来的西进运动和美国经济社会的发展产生了重要影响。

5. Morrill Acts《莫雷尔法案》：美国国会于1862年颁布的(Morrill Land-Grant Act)，是美国高等教育史上最早也是最重要的法案之一，它对美国甚至世界高等教育的发展产生了深远的影响。《莫雷尔法案》有时也译作《莫里尔法案》，该法案规定，按各州在国会中参议院和众议院人数的多少分配给各州不同数量的国有土地，各州应当将这类土地的出售或投资所得收入，在5年内至少建立一所"讲授与农业和机械工业有关的知识"的学院。后来这类学院被称为"农工学院"或"赠地学院"，这些学院是《莫雷尔法案》结出的果实。当时把联邦拨地用于独立设置农工学院的就有28个州，宾夕法尼亚等州是把拨地转给原有的农业学校，有的州是在州立大学增添农工学院。农工学院的发展为美国职业技术，尤其是农工业职业技术的发展培养了不少人才。

6. Hatch Act《哈奇法》：1887年颁布的法案，旨在资助各州建立农业试验站，加强赠地学院的研究功能。

Unit 3 Agricultural Modernization in the U.S.

Agricultural Mechanization

The revolution in agriculture involved a shift from hand labor to machine farming. Between 1860 and 1890, the production of such basic commodities as wheat, corn, and cotton outstripped all previous figures in the United States. Several factors accounted for this extraordinary achievement, among which was the application of machinery to farming. The farmer of 1800, using a hand sickle (镰刀), could hope to cut 20 percent of a hectare of wheat a day. With the cradle (附在大镰刀上，使割下的谷物整齐排列的配禾架), 30 years later, he might cut 80 percent of a hectare daily. In 1840, **Cyrus McCormick**[1] performed a miracle by cutting from two to two-and-a-half hectares a day with the reaper (收割机).

Other farm machines were developed in rapid succession: the automatic wire binder, the threshing machine and the reaper-thresher or combine. Mechanical planters, cutters, manure spreaders, potato planters, hay driers, poultry incubators and a hundred other inventions. After the American Revolution, inventors perfected dozens of threshing machines. In 1844, J. I. Case marketed the first thresher that was able to winnow the grain. It became the standard model after the Civil War, and Case remained the largest producer. By 1870, a few larger steam engines, mounted on wheels, began to power threshing machines, and after 1880, they dominated threshing.

Technology played a key role in the rapid growth of farm output in the United States. Throughout the 19th century, inventions or new tools followed one another in rapid succession. The scythe and cradle replaced the sickle for harvesting grain, and then both gave way to the mechanical reaper beginning in the 1840s. The wooden plow was replaced by the cast-iron plow, and finally around 1845 by the steel plow. By the time of the Civil War, machines were utilized for haying, threshing, mowing, cultivating and planting. American agriculture saw its output increase by leaps and bounds during the second half of the 19th century.

The mechanization of farming in the early part of the 20th century was a first giant step that led to increasing intensification, concentration, and specialization of production. The industrialization of agriculture has proceeded relatively unabated from the 1920s through today, propelled by mechanization, the use of chemicals, and most recently, the introduction of advanced biotechnologies.

In the 1920s, a picking machine was developed in Texas that stripped the bolls from the plant, but unfortunately it also collected what most growers considered an unacceptable amount of dirt and trash, and it was not adopted outside of west Texas. By far, the two most important harvesting machines are the combine and the mechanical cotton picker. The combine had revolutionized wheat production in the West and on the Great Plains, when it perfectly fit the short-stem grain that was usually very dry when mature. By the Second World War, a few combines were used on the farms of the eastern United States, but they were usually smaller than their western counterparts.

Organic Agriculture

United States Department of Agriculture（USDA）is committed to helping organic agriculture grow and thrive. To help meet Secretary **Vilsack**[2]'s goal of increasing the number of certified organic operations, USDA is delivering results through its many programs which serve the growing organic sector. October 2012 marked the 10th anniversary of the USDA Organic Seal（有机食品标签）, and it has become a leading global standard.

Organic agriculture produces products using methods that preserve the environment and avoid most synthetic materials, such as pesticides and antibiotics. USDA organic standards describe how farmers grow crops and raise livestock and which materials they may use.

Organic farmers, ranchers, and food processors follow a defined set of standards to produce organic food and fiber. Congress described general organic principles in the Organic Foods Production Act, and the USDA defines specific organic standards. These standards cover the product from farm to table, including soil and water quality, pest control, livestock practices, and rules for food additives.

Organic farms and processors preserve natural resources and biodiversity（生物多样性）,

and support animal health and welfare. They also provide access to the outdoors so that animals can exercise their natural behaviors. They only use approved materials, and they don't use genetically modified ingredients. Besides, they receive annual onsite inspections and they separate organic food from non-organic food.

Over 25,000 farmers, ranchers, and other businesses get many benefits from USDA organic certification. Many receive premium prices for their products through the growing $35 billion U.S. organic retail market. Most operations that grow, handle, or process organic products and want to call their products organic must be certified. USDA has strengthened its oversight of organic products, using methods such as inspections and residue testing to ensure the integrity of organic products from farm to market.

In addition to setting the standards for U.S. organic products, USDA supports organic agriculture in all of its agencies. In May 2013, Secretary Vilsack issued new Guidance on Organic Agriculture, Marketing and Industry directing all USDA agencies to support organic agriculture and markets. USDA offers a wide variety of funding opportunities, including conservation grants, organic crop insurance, and simplified microloans.

Trade partnerships streamline organic exports and imports with other countries, increasing the market share of organic products worldwide while maintaining rigorous production standards. Additionally, foreign products certified to the USDA organic standards can access the U.S. market. USDA also provides current prices for organic apples and other market information, funds research at public and private institutions, and provides practical advice to farmers and ranchers.

Overall, USDA oversees organic farmers and businesses to make sure that organic food is produced with organic methods. Each year, organic farmers update a farm plan and complete an inspection to confirm that their practices match their records. The farmer must correct any issues to continue certification. Organic food processors meet similar requirements.

Commodity Agriculture in the U.S.

Industrialization has traditionally referred to the process whereby agricultural production has become less of subsistence activity and more of a commercial activity.

Commodity agriculture is grounded on the belief that the primary objectives of farming should be to produce as much food/fiber as possible for the least cost. It is driven by twin goals of productivity and efficiency. It produces undifferentiated products for the mass market. The current structure and landscape of commodity agriculture is the outcome of logic of production that emphasized producing standardized commodities as cheaply as possible.

Commodity agriculture is incorporated into an increasingly global and corporate-controlled food system; it is the system of production that over the past 120 years has been developed and promoted by researchers and outreach workers at agricultural colleges and universities and by government personnel affiliated with ministries and departments of agriculture, mainly in North America and Europe. It represents the accumulated knowledge and wisdom about the most widely accepted procedures and techniques for growing crops and raising livestock.

Commodity agriculture is firmly rooted and supported by the USDA, land grant universities, and large multinational agribusiness firms. Large-scale, commodity producers account for the bulk of the nation's food and fiber. However, commodity agriculture today is being propped up by tens of billions of dollars of subsidies each year. In the long run, commodity agriculture will have to accommodate the concerns raised by farmers, environmentalists, and consumers who are calling for a more socially, economically, and environmentally sustainable food and agricultural system.

Sustainable Agriculture in the U.S.

The environmental challenges facing the world are greater than any time in the nation's history. Global environmental threats such as climate change, stratospheric ozone depletion; and the loss of biological diversity, forests, and fish stocks, affect all countries regardless of their stage of development.

In June 1993, President Clinton appointed 25 leaders from business, government, environmental, civil rights and Native American organizations to the Council on Sustainable Development. Their charge was to transform the idea of sustainable development into a concrete plan of action. As a benchmark, the council adopted the definition of sustainable development proposed by the United Nations Brundtland Commission in 1987. This stated that sustainable development must "meet the needs of the present without compromising the ability of future generations to meet their own needs." The final vision statement of the council noted that: "Our vision is of a life-sustaining earth. We are committed to the achievement of the dignified, peaceful, and equitable existence. We believe a sustainable United States will have an economy that equitably provides opportunities for satisfying livelihoods and a safe, healthy, high quality of life for current and future generations. Our nation will protect its environment, its natural resource base, and the functions and viability of natural systems on which all life depends." Sustainable development theories also address the crisis of farmland mismanagement in the United States and abroad.

Farming and related activities serve as the foundation for the U.S. food and fiber industry, an industry that provides jobs for 20 percent of the workforce and contributes $820 billion to the GNP. Moreover, the nearly 1 billion acres of land in agricultural production is responsible for feeding, clothing, and housing 250 million people in the United States and millions more abroad. Yet, every minute, the United States loses three acres of productive farmland to urban sprawl—shopping malls, housing subdivisions and the like. Since the Earth Day in 1970, the United States has lost more than 40 million acres of farmland to development. In North Carolina and Florida, 283,000 acres of cropland disappear each year. In California 100,000 acres disappear. Net cropland loses in the United States between 1982 and 1992 covered an area of New Jersey. Urbanization is a leading cause of cropland loss, and cropland is also being lost because of the depletion of or diversion of irrigation water.

A sustainable agriculture must be capable of maintaining indefinitely its productivity and usefulness to society. A sustainable agriculture must possess three fundamental characteristics. It must be ecologically sound, economically viable, and socially responsible. These three dimensions of sustainability are like the three dimensions of a box. A box without height, length, or width is quite simply not a box. Any system of farming that lacks ecological, social, or economic integrity is quite simply not sustainable.

Sustainable development is seen by many as an alternative to environmental degradation. According to the social worker Richard Estes, the concept of sustainable development has succeeded in uniting differing theoretical and ideological perspectives into a single conceptual framework. In an ideological context, sustainable development promotes a process whereby natural resources are replenished and future generations continue to have adequate resources to meet their needs. While sustainable development remains an important concept, its wide use by different actors in the development process gives some pause for concern. For example, some actors use it to designate a radical restructuring a society with regard to environmental development and economic growth. Others simply use the idea of sustainable development to signal a change in attitudes and emphasis. Such different approaches are sometimes labeled **dark green strategies**[3] versus **light green strategies**[4]. Although some policy analysts claim that sustainable development is the basis for a new developmental and ecological paradigm, others caution that it is a concept not yet fully developed.

Sustainable agriculture requires that farmers find balance and harmony among the economic, social, and ecological dimensions of their farming operations—among self-interests, shared-interests, and purely altruistic interests. By pursuing their enlightened self-interest, new American farmers are not only helping to build a more sustainable agriculture but are defining the principles of a more sustainable human society.

Notes

1. Cyrus McCormick 塞勒斯·麦考密克：塞勒斯·麦考密克（1809—1884），美国企业家、发明家，收割机的发明者。1834 年他创制的一台收割机获得专利。

2. Vilsack 汤姆·维尔萨克：于 2009 年 1 月就任奥巴马内阁军团的农业部长，曾在 1998 年当选美国主要的农业州爱荷华州长，连任两届。

3. dark green strategies 深绿色理念：要求将环境与发展进行整合性思考，这是 20 世纪 90 年代以来第二次环境运动的主题。深绿色理念的本质是人与自然和谐统一的自然观。

4. light green strategies 浅绿色理念：指浅绿色的环境观念，它主要包括环境意识的觉醒以及环境保护、清洁生产等绿色行动分散展开时期。

Unit 4 U.S. Farm Bill in the 21st Century

Farm Security and Rural Investment (FSRI) Act of 2002

In May 2002 U.S. President, George Bush, signed into the law the Farm Security and Rural Investment (FSRI) Act of 2002, legislating U.S. $180 billion in government support to US farmers of major agricultural commodities, for the period 2002-2011, an increase of U.S. $54 over similar support for the previous period. The act re-introduced several measures considered to have a distorting effect on production and prices, which were discontinued under the previous Farm Bill of 1996.

The U.S. Farm Bill of 2002 covers ten titles (commodity programs, conservation, trade, nutrition programs, credit, rural development, research, forestry, energy and miscellaneous) and provides for an increase in U.S. government support to agriculture amounting to approximately U.S. $180 billion over ten years. Arguably, the Farm Security and Rural Investment Act of 2002 reverses the policy shift towards greater market liberalization which was a distinct feature of the Federal Agriculture Improvement Reform (FAIR) Act of 1996, commonly referred to as the Freedom to Farm Bill.

The Farm Bill of 2002 provides significant increases in the payments made to producers and broadens the coverage of agricultural products which could benefit from such support. The Bill provides for the payments of direct assistance to farmers who enter into production flexibility contracts for the period 2002 to 2007. It introduces a system of fixed direct payments to replace the production flexibility contract payments of the 1996 Farm Bill provided to beneficiary commodities, such as rice, corn, other grains and cotton. The commodity support program has also been extended to cover new products such as soybeans, oilseeds and peanuts. The Bill continues the marketing assistance loan program which provides **non-recourse commodity loans**[1] for selected products and loan deficiency payments, whereby a producer receives a payment equivalent to the difference between the market price of an agricultural product and an established loan rate, whenever the market price falls below that rate. The 2002 Farm Bill also includes a counter-cyclical program payment that will be triggered when market prices for selected commodities fall below an agreed threshold.

Other provisions of the 2002 Farm Bill include: Farmers who enter the production flexibility contracts would be required to continue to comply with certain conservation requirements to receive contract payments; a new conservation security program under which farmers would receive payments for adopting improved environmental practices; expansion of the Farmland Protection and Environmental Quality Incentive Programs under which farmers receive payments to keep land near urban areas in production and for manure clean-up or other improvements.

An important provision of the Farm Bill is a requirement for "country of origin" labeling

（贴标签）for meat, fruit and vegetables, fish and peanuts. The legislation requires the U.S. Secretary of Agriculture to develop mandatory labeling regulations for implementation in September 2004. In the interim, country of origin labels would be voluntary, in keeping with guidelines developed by the U.S. Secretary of Agriculture by September 2002.

Food, Conservation and Energy Act of 2008

At the time of the Farm Bill passage, the year 2008 was shaping up to be a truly exceptional one for U.S. agriculture. The 2008 Farm Bill（officially, the Food, Conservation and Energy Act of 2008）was developed in this environment of high commodity prices, but also with the inherent（内在的）uncertainties associated with price volatility（价格波动）and the expectation of continued high input costs. The legislative process was longer than it was expected, totaling 16 months. The House of Representatives and the Senate passed their versions of the farm bill on July 27, 2007, and December 14, 2007, respectively. Conference was not completed and the bill enacted until June 18, 2008.

Despite the length of time in process, the 2008 Farm Bill has many similarities with the 2002 Farm Bill regarding commodity program provisions. The 2008 Farm Bill continues counter-cyclical payments, direct payments and marketing assistance loans.

The 2008 Farm Bill contains 1,100 pages（672 pages of statutory language and 428 pages of report language）and 15 titles. As such, it is significantly larger than any prior Farm Bill passed by Congress and has, for example, 60 percent more pages in total and nearly 50 percent more provisions than that of the 2002 Farm Bill. Although some of the extra heft（内容的分量）is due to small business administration and tax provisions added by the revenue committees, there is no question that farm bills have increased in size and complexity over time.

While the provisions of the Act address a wide variety of issues, the introduction of the Average Crop Revenue Election（ACRE）program is particularly important from the risk management perspective. The **ACRE program**[2] is a revenue-based plan designed as an alternative to government support programs such as counter-cyclical payments that were introduced in the 2002 Farm Bill.

The ACRE suite（系列方案）, which was authorized for the 2009-2012 crop years, consists of: 80 percent of the traditional program's direct payments; marketing loans at 70 percent of the traditional program's loan rate; a new state revenue program. ACRE is the first revenue program authorized by a farm bill, and, unlike the fixed nominal support triggers of traditional commodity programs, has no floor on its annual revenue risk assistance levels that trigger payment eligibility.

The Agricultural Act of 2014

The Agricultural Act of 2014, also known as the 2014 U.S. Farm Bill or Farm Act, formerly the "Federal Agriculture Reform and Risk Management Act of 2013", is an act of Congress that authorizes nutrition and agricultural programs in the United States for the years of 2014-2018.

The bill authorizes $956 billion in spending over the next ten years.

The Act continues a strong overall commitment to conservation. However, unlike the previous two Farm Acts passed by Congress in 2002 and 2008, the 2014 Farm Act does not include an increase in overall funding for conservation programs, and it reduces the number of conservation programs from 23 to 13. The new Farm Act also helps maintain strong incentives for soil conservation on highly erodible land and wetland conservation by adding crop insurance premium subsides to the list of benefits that could be withheld from producers who fail to meet conservation compliance requirements. The 2014 Farm Act also creates a new "Sodsaver" provision (crop production on native sod) to help protect grasslands in the Northern Plains by sharply reducing crop insurance subsides and other limitations on crop insurance during the first 4 years of crop production. In addition, the Agricultural Act of 2014 continues the trend of assisting beginning farmers with land access by reauthorizing and increasing funding for the Conservation Reserve Program Transition Incentives Program. Beginning farmers' participation in crop insurance may increase due to new provisions that reduce their policy premiums (保险费) and administrative fees.

The Act also includes other provisions that could build and support new and growing markets. Beginning and socially disadvantaged farmers and ranchers who wish to enter value-added activities may find assistance from the Value-Added Agricultural Market Development Grants program. The Specialty Crop Block Grants is also available to help farmers become competitive producers of fruits, vegetables, tree nuts, dried fruits, horticulture and nursery crops; also, the Act includes support for organic agriculture.

The Agricultural Act of 2014 continues a strong emphasis on conservation developed during the past 30 years over the course of six major Farm Acts. While conservation funding has begun to level off after significant increases in the 2002 and 2008 Farm Acts, the new legislation continues funding for working land conservation programs. Land retirement and easement programs, however, will shrink in terms of both acreage and funding. In addition, the Act continues and expands support for beginning farmers and ranchers.

2015 Agricultural Outlook Forum—"Smart Agriculture in the 21st century"

On December 8th, 2014, the U.S. Department of Agriculture (USDA) announced speakers for the 2015 Agricultural Outlook Forum, "Smart Agriculture in the 21st Century", to be held from Feb. 19-20, 2015, at the Crystal Gateway Marriott Hotel, Arlington, Va. The forum's plenary speakers and sessions will take a global, modern look at different aspects of today's agriculture industry.

Agriculture Secretary Tom Vilsack and European Commissioner of Agriculture & Rural Development Phil Hogan are engaged in a far-ranging roundtable discussion on agriculture. Dr. Richard N. Haass, President of the Council on Foreign Relations, addressed "Food, Foreign Policy and International Order". USDA's Chief Economist Joseph Glauber delivered the 2015

Agricultural & Foreign Trade Outlooks.

The plenary panel focused on "A Discussion on Innovation, Biotechnology, and Big Data" with wide latitude for panelists to talk about the intersection of these issues. Moderated by Secretary Tom Vilsack, the panel includes: Cory J. Reed, Senior Vice President, Intelligent Solutions Group, John Deere and Company; Dr. Robert T. Fraley, Executive Vice President and Chief Technology Officer, Monsanto; Mary Kay Thatcher, Senior Director, Congressional Relations, American Farm Bureau Federation; and Dr. Robert Sutor, Vice President, Mobile, Solutions, and Mathematical Sciences, IBM Corporation.

Deputy Secretary Krysta Harden welcomed the plenary audience and moderated an afternoon session titled "Tomorrow's Opportunities", focused on the potential of agriculture as a career, and the importance of new and beginning farmers and ranchers.

The Forum's dinner speaker was Ambassador Darci Vetter, Chief Agricultural Negotiator, Officer of the United States Trade Representative.

Speaking at the 25 breakout sessions and five topical luncheons were more than 100 distinguished experts. Breakout session topics on the agenda include: Perspectives on Global and U.S. Trade; **Big Data's Impact**[3] on U.S. Agriculture; Commodity Situation and Outlooks; Food Price and Farm Income Outlooks; Moving Feed, Food and Fuel to Market; Opportunities in the Bio-Economy; Antimicrobial Resistance; and Bee/Pollinator Issues Facing Agriculture.

Additional breakout sessions cover: Conservation and Regulatory Program Updates; Water Issues and Drought, Climate Change; Nutrition Trends and New Opportunities for Producers; Regional Approaches to Rural Growth; Local Food Marketing Trends; The 100th Anniversary of USDA Market News; and Reducing Food Waste.

2016 Agricultural Outlook Forum

On Jan. 12, 2016, the U.S. Department of Agriculture announced the members of this year's Agricultural Outlook Forum Plenary Panel on "Providing Leadership for Present and Future Generations in the Transformation of Agriculture".

This year's panelists have backgrounds in academia, business, farming and media, bringing a range of expertise to this discussion on transforming the future of agriculture. The group includes Elizabeth Garrett, President of Cornell University; Ilene Gordon, CEO of Ingredion; Pamela Hess, Executive Director of the Arcadia Center for Sustainable Food and Agriculture; and Pam Johnson, an Iowa farmer and former president of National Corn Growers Association.

The Forum's plenary panelists have unique perspectives on the present and future of agriculture and rural America. Technology is the opening doors to new applications for producers and throughout the marketing chain, while demographics are changing across the country's rural landscape and farm households. These trends coupled with new markets domestically and abroad, as well as new programs under the 2014 Farm Bill, form the basis for the 92nd Agricultural Outlook Forum.

The opening plenary featured remarks from Secretary Vilsack and Deputy Secretary Krysta Harden and "The 2016 Economic Outlook for Agriculture" presented by USDA Chief Economist Robert Johansson. The Forum's keynote speaker（主旨发言人）was Howard Buffett, CEO of the Howard G. Buffett Foundation. Mitch E. Daniels, Jr., President of Purdue University and former Governor of Indiana were the dinner speaker.

Thirty concurrent track sessions supporting this theme include the Agriculture Talent Pipeline, Bioproducts, Commodities, Land & Tenure Transition, New Markets, Organics, Risk Management, Scientific Advancement, and Trade to Urban Agriculture. Deputy Secretary Harden also hosted a session on opportunities in agriculture for new and beginning farmers and hosted a Women's Agriculture Networking event.

Notes

1. non-recourse commodity loans 无追索权商品贷款：一种抵押性贷款，贷款人向主办人举办的项目提供贷款，将该项目建成投产后所产生的收益作为偿还贷款的资金来源，并以该项目的资产为贷款人设定担保。除此之外，项目主办人和其他人不向贷款人提供任何信用担保。但是，这种贷款的商业风险很大，贷款人一般都不愿接受这种方式。以农产品无追索权项目贷款为例，农场主以尚未收获的农产品作抵押，从政府的农产品信贷公司取得贷款。目标价格由生产成本和生产者利润组成。当市场价格高于目标价格时，农场主可按市场价格出售农产品，用现款还本付息。如市场价格低于目标价格，农场主可把农产品交给农产品信贷公司，政府按目标价格和市场价格之差给予差额补贴，补贴对象主要是小麦、玉米、棉花及乳制品等主要农产品。

2. ACRE program 平均作物收入选择方案：其出台的历史背景是因为美国《2002 年农业法案》中最重要和最根本的农业补贴不同程度地背离了设计初衷，没有达到预期效果，所以在美国《2008 年农业法案》中增添了该项补贴政策。

3. Big Data's Impact 大数据影响："大数据"是指信息爆炸时代产生的海量数据，能够改变组织看待和使用数据的方式，迫使公司改变商业模式。它并不是一种新技术潮流，而是在信息技术高度发展之后，人们如何开发利用数据为新的商业模式发展奠定基础的过程，是一种基于新工具的新的问题解决思路。

References

[1] CLAASSEN R. 2014 Farm act continues most previous trends in conservation [J]. Economic Research Service, 2014:1-10.

[2] CONKIN P K. A revolution down on the farm: the transformation of American agriculture since 1929[M]. Lexington: University Press of Kentucky, 2008.

[3] FITZGERALD D. Every farm a factory: the industrial ideal in American agriculture [M]. New Haven: Yale University Press, 2003.

[4] HARWOOD J. An overview of the U.S. agricultural economy and the 2008 farm bill [J]. Agricultural and Resource Economics Review, 2009, 38: 8-17.

[5] HOWARD C. An outline of American history [M]. Washington: The United States Information Agency, 1994.

[6] HUFFMAN W E. Modernizing agriculture: a continuing process[J]. Daedalus, 1998: 159-186.

[7] IKERD J E. Crisis & opportunity: sustainability in American agriculture [M]. Lincoln: University of Nebraska Press, 2008.

[8] JAMES W. Beginning farmers and ranchers and the agricultural act of 2014 [J]. Economic Research Service, 2014: 1-6.

[9] SCOTT K. Economics or education: the establishment of American land-grant universities [J]. The Journal of Higher Education, 1996, 67: 196-220.

[10] US DEPARTMENT OF AGRICULTURE. Agricultural fact book 1998[M]. United States: United States Government Printing, 1998.

[11] ATKINS V J. The US farm bill of 2002: implications for Caricom's agricultural export trade [J]. Social and Economic Studies, 2004, 53: 61-80.

[12] WANG LIREN. Agriculture and agricultural education in the U.S. [M].Changsha: Science and Technology Press, 1983.

[13] ZHU XIYAN. The United States of America—a general survey[M]. Beijing: Tourism Education Press, 1990.

[14] ZULAUF C, ORDEN D. The revenue program option in the 2008 U.S. farm bill: evaluating performance characteristics of the ACRE program [J]. Agricultural and Resource Economics Review, 2010, 39:517-533.

[15] WIKIPEDIA. National grange of the order of patrons of husbandry[EB/OL]. [2016-05-22]. https://en.wikipedia.org/wiki/National_Grange_of_the_Order_of_Patrons_of_Husbandry.

[16] WIKIPEDIA. Morrill_land-grant_acts[EB/OL]. [2016-05-22]. https://en.wikipedia.org/wiki/ Morrill_Land-Grant_Acts.

[17] USDA. Download from national agricultural library digital collections[EB/OL]. [2016-05-22]. http://naldc.nal.usda.gov/download/IND43620777/PDF.

[18] USDA. USDA announces 2015 agricultural outlook forum speakers, theme "smart agriculture in the 21st century"[EB/OL]. [2016-05-22].http://www.usda.gov/wps/portal/usda/usdahome?contentid=2014/12/0265.xml.

[19] USDA. USDA 2016 Agricultural Outlook Forum Plenary Panel Announced [EB/OL]. [2016-5-22]. http://www.usda.gov/wps/portal/usda/usdahome?contentid=2016/01/0009.xml.

Chapter Seven

American Education System

Unit 1 American Education in Colonial Era

The discovery of the new continent by Columbus in 1492 started the colonization process of the continent. Education in colonial era was the starting stage in the history of American education. Religion laid the foundations for the development of education in this period. Achieving the objectives of religion, it also emphasized the cultivation of talented people for the society.

In 1607, the first colony was established on the continent. From then on, thirteen original colonies in all were set up, which are the predecessor（前身）of the United States. During the establishment of the colonies, a great many European people immigrated, containing people from England, Scotland, Ireland, France, and Germany and so on. The immigrants mostly were the believers of **Puritanism**[1]. They endured the hardships of coming to North America from thousands of miles away and explored the continent in order to build up a society which was free and equal and could benefit descendants in all aspects of life. They put education in an important position as a way of realizing their dreams. Though different measures were taken, due to the distinct levels of economic development, the circumstances were not alike all around the colonies.

New England in the north was the district with a relatively high level of industrial and economic development, as well as education, most of whose citizens were from England. In 1635, the first Latin school was established in Boston during colonial era. Later in the year of 1642, compulsory education was mandated（命令）in Massachusetts. The towns of New England were required to establish schools where local children could be educated. In 1647, Massachusetts regulated that an elementary school should be set up in a town with 50 or more families aiming at teaching students to read and write and a Latin school should be established for the benefit of their further study in the area with at least 100 families. This was showed in **The Old Deluder Satan Law**[2].

Colonies in the middle part included New York, Pennsylvania, Delaware, and New Jersey. Because of the complexities of the immigrants in the region, languages, religion and many other aspects were diverse. In 1633, the first school was set up in New Amsterdam followed by other religious schools. In 1664, New Amsterdam was renamed as New York. Vocational education was especially valued in Pennsylvania influenced by Benjamin Franklin's thought of paying attention to practical education, which was attached great importance in the development of American education.

Southern colonies consisted of Maryland, Virginia, Georgia, North Carolina and South Carolina. With slavery existed, colonists seldom established schools for the public. In the south, education was regarded as a personal issue. Therefore, family tutors were hired to teach the children. Some of the families also sent their children to private schools and some even were sent back to England to be educated. Private schools were the main form of schooling during this period in the region.

At the beginning of the 17th century, the conflicts among the religious denominations（教派）resulted in the immigration of many Puritans. For the sake of spreading their religion and doctrines（教义）, Puritans strived to build churches and colleges. During the colonial period, the most significant step in the history of American education was the establishment of institutions of higher education. It not only cultivated a great number of people in political and economic field, but also pushed forward the economic development of colonies and the formation of the American nationality. There were nine colleges which were established during the colonial era.

The first college in the colonies was **Harvard College**[3] which was founded in 1636. The Massachusetts colonists made a decision to establish an institute like Cambridge University in U.K. with 400 pounds as funds allocated. The college was located in Cambridge. In 1638, the clergyman and one of the founders, John Harvard died away. He donated half of his savings and all the books to the college which was newly set up. Then in March 13, 1639, the college was named after the benefactor（捐赠者）to memorize him. The establishment of Harvard College was the beginning of American higher education leading the way in the field.

In 1693, the **College of William & Mary**[4] was founded in Virginia which was the first permanent colony of the British people on the continent. Thomas Jefferson, the main draftsman of ***The Declaration of Independence***[5], famous politician and the third American president, was an excellent alumnus of this college.

Yale College was founded in 1701 which later become the Yale University. In the colonies, College of New Jersey, Rhode Island College, Kings College, Academy of Philadelphia, Queens College and Dartmouth College were established one after another. These colleges are now very famous in America.

The development of education accelerated the economic improvement. The frequent communication among the 13 colonies also promoted the awareness as the American nationality which aided in the process of freeing themselves from the domination of the United Kingdom. The education of this period had great influence on the tradition of regarding education as an important part in the development of the society.

Notes

1. Puritanism 清教主义：16 世纪出现于英国，以加尔文学说为依据进行教会改革，反对国王和主教的专制，主张简化仪式，过勤俭清洁的生活。

2. The Old Deluder Satan Law 老骗子撒旦法：该法于 1647 年在马萨诸塞州颁布，要求在该法管辖的村镇内，满 50 户人家的城镇，必有一名教师来教育孩子；达到 100 户的村镇，须建立一所文法学校教育年轻人，使他们有机会进入大学学习。

3. Harvard College 哈佛学院：哈佛是美国本土历史最悠久的高等学府，诞生于 1636 年，最早由马萨诸塞州殖民地立法机关创建，初名新市民学院。为了纪念在成立初期给予学院慷慨支持的约翰·哈佛牧师，学校于 1639 年 3 月更名为哈佛学院。1780 年，哈佛学院正式改称哈佛大学。

4. College of William & Mary 威廉玛丽学院：于 1693 年由英国国王威廉三世和女王玛丽二世创立，是美国历史最悠久的大学之一，仅次于哈佛大学。1906 年该校成为公立大学，1918 年男女合校，直到 1967 年成为现代综合性大学。

5. *The Declaration of Independence*《独立宣言》：为北美洲十三个英属殖民地宣告独立的文告，由托马斯·杰斐逊起草，于 1776 年 7 月 4 日第二次大陆会议批准，这一天此后成为美国独立纪念日。

Unit 2　American Education from the Independence War to the Civil War

Both the Independence War and the Civil War had a great impact on every aspect of the United States. It was a crucial time for American education development from the Independence War to the Civil War. From the Independence War to the Civil War, American education underwent rapid development, which basically laid the foundation for modern American education. After the War of Independence, the United States became an independent country. In the colonial period, there was no doubt that education in American was influenced by Britain. At the very beginning, people in the colonial period paid attention to education. Therefore, there was a tradition that American people attached importance to education.

After the War of Independence, the United States of American won independence, politically and economically, which laid the foundation for the development of American education. As a newly independent country, the United States was ambitious in every aspect to develop and improve. After the Independence, education in the United States of America acquired great development due to the efforts both by government and people. It is obvious that in the colonial period education in the United States was mostly funded by private persons. It is evident that high-quality education in the United States deserves attention all over the world. Modern education worldwide has borrowed ideas from the United States to improve and develop their own education. The highly advanced and developed education in the United States has attracted overseas students all over the world to study. China, as a developing country, has learned advanced American teaching model and teaching methods. It is a common sense that education in terms of every aspect in the

United States developed quickly after the War of Independence and the Civil War including public education, higher education, blank education and female education and so on and so forth.

Public Education

In the colonial period, immigrants from all over Europe came to America. Until the end of 18th century, British had already established 13 colonies along the Atlantic Coast. Colonial education was influence by British teaching methods and ideas. After satisfying the basic life needs, colonial people began to pursue educational development. Education funds in the colonial period mainly came from private instead of government.

The Independence War from 1775 to 1783 was a major point in the historical development of the United States, which ended the British rule over 13 colonies. The victory of the Independence War and the establishment of the United States not only opened the way for the economic development but also provided political premise for the development of education. After the American Revolution, the colonial people gained political and economic independence, which laid the foundation for the rapid development of public education.

After the Revolution, an emphasis was put on education, especially in the North. As an independent country, America had the ability to fund and develop public education. Colonial people spared no efforts to win independence from Great Britain. After the Independence, the tradition that the United States attached great importance to education had been further carried forward, and many political leaders had advocated political development, becoming the education leaders. And the Founding Fathers spoke highly of public education. The first American President George Washington, who thought that state-owned universities were beneficial for developing the cohesive force of people and reducing the overseers studying costs, advocated the establishment of state-owned universities. Furthermore, the U.S. President John Adams said that the whole people must take upon themselves the education of the whole people and be willing to bear the expensed of it; there should not be a district of one mile square without a school in it, not founded by a charitable individual, but maintained at the public expense of the people themselves. Furthermore, after Independence, Georgia and South Carolina funded public universities. In the colonial period, educational development was mainly promoted by the private instead of the central government. The United States, as an independent country, began to develop public education including elementary education, secondary education and higher education. The education in the United States developed rapidly after the Independence despite of the failure of the initiative of funding public universities and the verdict on **Dartmouth College**[1] Lawsuit. The failure of the initiative of funding public universities restricted the role of the federal government on the higher education and the verdict on the Dartmouth College Lawsuit further restricted the rights of the states government on the private colleges.

The Civil War from 1861 to 1865 had a great impact on the historical development of the United States. The Civil War meant an end of an old time and a start of a new time. After the end of the Civil War, education in the United States had undergone a fast development including Morrill Act (Land-Grant Act) and the Second Morrill Act. Morrill Act was signed into law by President Abraham Lincoln on July 2, 1862. Under the act, each eligible state received a total of 30,000 acres of federal land to be used toward establishing and funding the educational institutions. Morrill Act promoted the establishment of land-grant universities. To some degree, it promoted educational development. In 1890, the Second Morrill Act, which stipulated that federal government allocated funds to land-grant colleges, was passed. To conclude, two Morrill Acts further promoted the development of education.

Black Education

In history, African-Americans were enslaved and deprived. At the very beginning, African-Americans were needed in the colonies because of the large scale southern plantation economy. With the end of the Civil War and the publication of **the Emancipation Proclamation**[2], African-Americans got freedom and liberation.

After the Civil War and in the time of the Reconstruction, the federal government funded public education and opened public schools for black children. Many African-American children got the opportunity to study. And the school curriculum resembled that of schools in the north. Although African-Americans got freedom after the Civil War, racial segregation was common in the South. Therefore, education in the United States was segregated and unequal.

In history, except for the efforts made by the government, African-Americans themselves made efforts to improve and develop education. **Booker T. Washington**[3], as an excellent political and educational black leader, deserved our attention. Booker T. Washington himself got good education. Through his life, he spares no efforts to promote educational development of African-Americans. He advocated Americans to fund and support black colleges and high schools all over the country.

As time went by, education in the United States developed rapidly. Until modern time, its education has become very strong.

Bilingual Education

Bilingual education in the U.S. focuses on English Language Learners (ELL).While ELL has been the dominant form to express the status of a bilingual learner, there is a new push to label the students as Emergent Bilingual. This new label will not ignore the bilingualism that these students can and must develop through schooling in the United States. The emphasis on English rejects that the student has a dominant language as part of their identity and culture that will continue to develop with time. According to the U.S. Department of Education website, a bilingual education program is "an educational program for limited English proficient students". The term "limited English proficiency" remains in use by the federal government, but has fallen out of favor elsewhere. The term "English Language Learner" is now preferred in schools and educational research to refer to a student whose first language is not English and who needs language support services in order to succeed in school.

The very first instance of bilingual education in the United States occurred with Polish immigrants in the first permanent English settlement of Virginia in what is now the United States. The Poles provided the community with manufactured pitch necessary to prevent the sinking of ships, and glass works among other industries. When **the House of Burgesses**[4] met in 1619, the rights extended only to Englishmen. The Poles, in turn, launched the first recorded strike in the New World. In dire need of their skills and industries, the Poles received the "rights of Englishmen", and established the first bilingual schools with subjects taught in English and Polish. From this first documented historic beginning, bilingual education existed in some form or another in the United States. During the 18th century, Franciscan missionaries from California to Texas used indigenous languages for translating and teaching the Catholic catechism(教义问答)to Native Americans. By the mid-19th century, private and public bilingual schools had included such native languages as Czech, Dutch, French, German, Norwegian, Spanish and Swedish. Ohio became the first state in 1839 to adopt a bilingual education law, authorizing German-English instruction at parents' request. Louisiana enacted an identical provision for French and English in 1847, and the New Mexico Territory did so for Spanish and English in 1850. By the end of the 19th century, about a dozen states had passed similar laws. Elsewhere, many localities provided bilingual instruction without state sanction, in languages as diverse as Norwegian, Italian, Polish, Czech and Cherokee. Beginning in 1959, public schools in Miami introduced bilingual programs. According to **the Bilingual Education Act**[5] of the U.S. in 1968, Congress first mandated bilingual education in order to give immigrants access to education in their "first" language.

A 1974 U.S. Supreme Court ruling, **Lau v. Nichols**[6], gave further momentum to bilingual education. Here, the Court held that San Francisco schools violated minority language students' rights when they educated students in the same classes as other students without special provisions.

Taken together, the Bilingual Education Act and the Lau v. Nichols ruling mandated that schools needed to at least provide some type of services to support English language learners, though neither specified what type of educational program needed to be provided. As such, both bilingual and English-only programs flourished after the law's passage and the court ruling.

The Bilingual Education Act was terminated in 2001 by new federal education policy, with the passage of No Child Left Behind by the U.S. Congress. This law offers no support for native language learning, but rather emphasized accountability in English only, and mandates that all students, including ELLs, are tested yearly in English.

The majority of U.S. high school students in the United States are required to take at least one to two years of a second language. The vast majority of these classes are either French or Spanish. In a large number of schools this is taught in a manner known as FLES, in which students learn about the second language in a manner similar to other subjects such as mathematics or science. Some schools use an additional method known as FLEX in which the "nature of the language and culture" are also taught.

Notes

1. Dartmouth College 达特茅斯学院：成立于1769年，是美国历史悠久的世界顶尖学府，也是闻名遐迩的私立八大常春藤联盟之一。坐落于新罕布什尔州的汉诺佛（Hanover）小镇。利扎维洛克牧师当初成立这个学校的目的，是为了培养当地印第安部落的年轻人和年轻白人。

2. *the Emancipation Proclamation*《解放黑人奴隶宣言》：是一份由美国总统亚伯拉罕·林肯公布的宣言，其主张所有美利坚联邦叛乱下的领土之黑奴应享有自由，豁免的对象包含未脱离联邦的边境州，以及联邦掌控下的诸州。

3. Booker T. Washington 布克·华盛顿：（1856年4月5日—1915年11月14日）是美国政治家、教育家和作家。他是1890年到1915年之间美国黑人历史上的重要人物之一，在政治中扮演了一个非常突出的角色。

4. the House of Burgesses 殖民地议会：独立战争之前的北美十三州都已经建立了议会制度。最早如弗吉尼亚，在1619年建立，最晚的乔治亚，也在1733年建立起来。当时，议会享有立法权，法案经由上下两院通过以后提交总督批准；议会还特别具有征税权力以及为行政费用拨款和提出有关时政法案的权力。

5. the Bilingual Education Act《双语教育法案》：1968年，美国颁布了第一部《双语教育法案》。该法案为双语教育带来了立法依据和政策支持，并正式确立了双语教育的合法地位，随后又有了1974年、1978年、1984年、1988年和1994年的五次修正案。

6. Lau v. Nichols 刘诉尼考尔斯：1974年，美国最高法院在*Lau v. Nichols*案的判决中认为，对英语学生和非英语学生提供所谓看似同等的教育，实际上并不能为他们带来平等教育的机会。判决要求采取平权步骤（affirmative steps），提供专门语言项目，使非英语的孩子享受到应得的教育。

Unit 3 American Education in Modern Period

Education of the United States is offered by federal, state and local government. Compulsory education is set up for all children in America. It can be completed in public schools, private schools which are certified by the state government or at home in an approved manner. Three levels of education in many public schools and private schools. They are elementary school, middle school or junior high school and senior high school. Children are usually divided into different grades, which is from kindergarten to the twelfth grade, namely, the final year of high school. Nevertheless, the age range may differ slightly in different states. Most children begin their education at the age of five to six years old and finish their twelfth grade in usually eighteen years old.

After the senior high schooling, students come into the stage of college education. Generally speaking, students apply to be admitted to colleges with various entrance requirements. Admissions difficulties relate to many aspects, involving standardized test scores, for instance **SAT**[1] or **ACT**[2] tests, students' **GPA**[3] in high school, ranking in their own class and the grades of the courses in high school. Most of the colleges take into consideration of other subjective factors, like the personal statement essay, or the activities in which students can show their unique characteristics or abilities.

Students study in the colleges with a field concentrated. That is to say, each student has his or her own major. Completion of the requirements of the major can lead to the award of their bachelor's degree, for instance, Bachelor of Arts or Bachelor of Science. Students of the four grades on the campus are usually called freshman, sophomore, junior student and senior student in the normal order. Some students may choose to enroll in two majors or another minor major in another field.

Community colleges[4] are the colleges which have lower standards of admissions and tuition fees. Students graduating from community colleges can be awarded the associate's degree like Associate of Science. Some of them choose to attend the community colleges for two years before further pursuing their study in another college or university to get their bachelor's degree. Many community colleges have agreements with four-year colleges or universities which provide the left years of study after students graduate from community colleges. Students may also join in the workforce as well.

The education which can lead to the award of master's degree is graduate education. The master's degree can be Master of Arts, Master of Science, and Master of Business Administration and so on. The requirements of graduate study are concerned with the academic performance as the undergraduate and the standardized test score, like Graduate Record Examination (**GRE**[5]), or Graduate Management Admission Test (**GMAT**[6]). Some graduate education can be pursued immediately students get their bachelor's degree, while in some cases, students should possess working experience of a few years before applying. After the study of master's degree, or sometimes connecting with master's degree, additional years of study can lead to students' earning doctor's degree, like Doctor of Philosophy, or Doctor of Medicine and so on.

There is no denying that the **Ivy League**[7] can not be overlooked when speaking of universities in the United States. The Ivy League commonly refers to eight institutions of higher education in Northeastern U.S. It includes Harvard University, Yale University, Princeton University, Brown University, Columbia University, Cornell University, Dartmouth College and University of Pennsylvania. Except Cornell University, the other seven universities had all been founded before the Independent War.

Harvard University is the oldest and most celebrated institution of higher education in the United States. It is a private university in Cambridge, Massachusetts. Harvard University ranks at the top of the world in university ranking in the world. Excellent graduates of this university can always be found in the elites from all walks of life. Bill Gates, the founder of Microsoft, is one of the alumni. Like Harvard University, the other universities in the Ivy League also make a great contribution in cultivating students with outstanding abilities in every aspect of the society.

Apart from the eight universities of Ivy League, there are also many other remarkable universities in the United States, such as **Stanford University**[8], **University of California-Berkeley**[9] and Massachusetts Institute of Technology（**MIT**[10]）.

Stanford University lies in state of California which is a well-known private research university, close to famous hi-tech region, the Silicon Valley. As the sixth biggest university in the United States, it provides a platform which cultivates a great number of leaders in the world, like the founder of HP, Google and eBay. University of California, Berkeley is located in San Francisco. It is a renowned public research university. Together with Stanford University, the two universities become the academic center in the western America. Massachusetts Institute of Technology, located in Cambridge, a famous private research university, should be mentioned when coming to talk about the science college in U.S. It is the leader in engineering and technological field along with the former two universities.

With the development of education in the world, American higher education is all along in the leading position. It always makes innovations in the college operation, curriculum design, and teaching modes, which can be referred to all over the world. Due to the application of multi-media and Internet technology, **MOOC**[11] is a newly used word to indicate massive open online courses. Different from traditional classroom education, this kind of new course can be completed in a more flexible environment. The place where students can get educated is not restricted. Therefore, the number of students can be extremely huge which could be unbelievable in past decades. Harvard University and Massachusetts Institute of Technology established a non-profit massive open online course platform in 2012, **edX**[12]**,** whose aim is to promote the study of students on campus, benefit more students in higher learning, and the convenience of scientific research. It attracts thousands of people to study online, some of whom can get according credits of the courses. Outstanding professors can teach anybody in any part of the world. The new model of higher learning is bringing benefit to human beings. **Coursera**[13], **Udacity**[14] and edX are the three important leading online course platforms. Coursera and Udacity were established by the professors from Stanford University. The platforms cover different subjects and fields which is a revolution in the academic world of higher education.

Notes

1. SAT 美国学术能力测验：全称“Scholastic Assessment Test”，与 ACT 都被称为“美国高考”。该考试成绩是世界各国高中生申请美国名校学习及奖学金的重要参考，成绩有效期为 2 年。

2. ACT 美国大学测验：全称“American College Test”，该考试是美国大学对申请读本科课程的学生进行的入学资格考试，是美国大学入学条件之一，也是大学发放奖学金的条件之一，既看重学生对于知识的掌握，又考虑学生的独立思考能力和判断能力。

3. GPA 平均成绩：全称“Grade Point Average”，是美国学校衡量入学申请者的参考标准之一，多数大学对此都有最低规定。

4. community college 社区学院：美国两年制短期大学，入学要求比四年制大学低，申请时间短，是美国教育体系的重要组成部分。

5. GRE 美国研究生入学考试：全称“Graduate Record Examination”，适用于法律和商业外的各专业，是大学研究生院申请时必须具备的考试成绩。

6. GMAT 研究生管理科学入学考试：全称“Graduate Management Admission Test”，美国、英国等国高校选择 GMAT 考试成绩来评估申请者是否适合商业、经济和管理研究生的学习。

7. Ivy League 常春藤盟校：由美国东北部八所名校组合而成，分别为：哈佛大学、耶鲁大学、普林斯顿大学、布朗大学、哥伦比亚大学、康奈尔大学、达特茅斯学院和宾夕法尼亚大学。除康奈尔大学，其余七所大学均是在殖民时期建立的。

8. Stanford University 斯坦福大学：一所坐落在美国加利福尼亚州斯坦福市的私立研究型大学。大学于 1891 年由时任加州参议员及州长的铁路大亨利兰・斯坦福和他的妻子简・莱思罗普・斯坦福创办。这是为了纪念他们因伤寒而于 16 岁生日前夕去世的儿子小利兰・斯坦福。学校的校园位于硅谷的西北方，邻近帕罗奥图。 校方的各个学术部门被归入七所学术学院内，而包括生物保育区及加速实验室在内的其他资产则设于主校区之外。此校同时为最富有的教育机构之一，并为第一所在一年内获得超过十亿美元捐款升幅的大学。斯坦福培养了不少著名人士，校友涵盖 30 名富豪企业家及 17 名太空员，亦为培养最多美国国会成员的院校之一。斯坦福校友创办了众多著名的公司机构，共 58 名诺贝尔奖得主现或曾于该校学习或工作。

9. University of California-Berkeley 加利福尼亚大学伯克利分校：简称“UC Berkeley”、“Berkeley” 或“加州大学伯克利分校”“伯克利加州大学”，是美国顶尖公立研究型大学，也是世界上最富盛名且最顶尖的公立大学。加州大学伯克利分校是加利福尼亚大学中最老的一所，也是美国大学协会（Association of American Universities）创始会员之一，其吉祥物蜕变自加州州旗，故其学生亦自称“小金熊”。加州大学伯克利分校与斯坦福大学、麻省理工学院一同被誉为美国工程科技界的学术领袖，常年位居上海交通大学世界大学学术排名（ARWU）前四名，泰晤士报高等教育期刊（Times Higher Education, THE）全球大学排行前十名，在美国新闻和世界报导（US News）首次发布的世界大学排名中位列全球第三名（2015 年）。该校是美国最为自由激进的两所大学之一（另一所为哥伦比亚大学）。

10. MIT 麻省理工学院：全称“Massachusetts Institute of Technology”，是美国一所综合性私立大学，创办于 1861 年，有“世界理工大学之最” 的美名，位于马萨诸塞州的剑桥市。经过近 150 多年的发展，现已有学生近万名，并且已被世界公认为与牛津大学、剑桥大学、哈佛大学等老牌大学齐名的、以理工科为主的、综合性的世界一流大学。

11. MOOC 大型开放式网络课程：全称“Massive Open Online Courses”，也称“慕课”，美国大学近几年来陆续建立的网络学习平台，在网上提供学习课程。Coursera、Udacity 和 edX 是三大课程提供商。

12. edX：是麻省理工和哈佛大学于 2012 年 4 月联手创建的大规模开放在线课堂平台。

它免费给大众提供大学教育水平的在线课堂。两所大学为这个非盈利性计划各资助三千万美元。2012 年秋天，edX 在 MITx 启动。

13. Coursera 免费大型公开在线课程项目： 由美国斯坦福大学两名计算机科学教授创办。旨在同世界顶尖大学合作，在线提供免费的网络公开课程。Coursera 的首批合作院校包括斯坦福大学、密歇根大学、普林斯顿大学、宾夕法尼亚大学等美国名校。Coursera 与另外 12 所大学达成合作协议。其课程报名学生突破了 150 万，来自全球 190 多个国家和地区，而网站注册学生为 68 万，注册课程 124 门。目前新增的大学包括了佐治亚理工学院、杜克大学、华盛顿大学、加州理工学院、莱斯大学、爱丁堡大学、多伦多大学、洛桑联邦理工学院（瑞士）、约翰・霍普金斯大学公共卫生学院、加州大学旧金山分校、伊利诺伊大学厄巴纳—香槟分校以及弗吉尼亚大学。

14. Udacity 网络公开课程： 该平台不仅有视频，还有自己的学习管理系统，内置编程接口、论坛和社交元素。

References

[1] ADAMS J. The works of John Adams, second president of the United States: with a life of the author, Notes and Illustrations[M]. Cologne: Nabu Press, 2013.

[2] ANDERSON J D. The education of blacks in the south1860–1935[M]. Chapel Hill: University of North Carolina Press, 1988.

[3] EVANS S, MCLNTYRE K. MOOCs in the humanities: can they reach underprivileged students?[J]. Convergence: The International Journal of Research into New Media Technologies, 2016, 22(3): 313-323.

[4] 徐辉，辛治祥 . 现代外国教育思潮研究 [M]. 北京：人民教育出版社，2008.

[5] 吕瑞 . 美国早期州立大学简论 (独立战争前后至 1910 年)[M]. 济南：山东师范大学出版社 , 2011.

[6] 连进军 . 从独立战争到南北战争 : 试论美国高等教育发展的一段关键历史 [J]. 煤炭高等教育 , 2004, 22(2): 47-50.

[7] 林方燕 . 浅议美国殖民地学院的教育 [J]. 科技信息，2011(12)：73-74.

[8] 水永强 . 美国普及义务教育历史研究 [D]. 兰州：西北师范大学教育科学学院，2003.

[9] 田耀 . 美国文化点滴 [M]. 天津：天津大学出版社，2009.

[10] 魏峰，王栋 . 殖民地时期的美国教育 [J]. 滨州师专学报，1995(1)：24-26.

[11] 赵文学 . 清教在美国殖民地时期教育发展中的作用 [J]. 史学集刊，2009(4)：66-78.

Chapter Eight

American Religion

In Christian world, many countries in the West have experienced declines in religious observance and increases in secularization(世俗化) in the twentieth century. This is often attributed to the influences of industrialization, **consumerism**[1], materialism, **hedonism**[2](享乐主义), mass culture, and universal education. The United States, however, seems to be an exception. Despite its materialistic image and intense worship of "mighty dollars", the U.S. still remains the most religious country in the Western countries.

Unlike other nations where religion tends to be monolithic or unitary (单一的), America is known, among other things, for its religious pluralism. There are at least three reasons for this religious diversity. For one thing, the U.S. Constitution guarantees every individual the fundamental right to practice his own religious belief. For another, the fundamental American belief in individual freedom has been at the center of American experience throughout its history. For another, as a nation of immigrants, the great diversity of ethnic backgrounds has given rise to multiplicity of religious beliefs.

The majority of Americans identify themselves as Christians, while close to a quarter claims no religious affiliation (附属). According to a 2014 study by the **Pew Research Center**[3], 70.6% of the American population identified themselves as Christians, with 46.5% professing attendance at a variety of churches that could be considered Protestant, and 20.8% professing Roman Catholic beliefs. The same study says that other religions (including Judaism, Buddhism, Islam, and Hinduism) collectively make up about 6% of the population. According to a 2012 survey by the Pew forum, 36 percent of Americans state that they attend services nearly every week or more. According to the 2013 Gallup poll, Mississippi with 61% of its population described as very religious is the most religious state in the country, while Vermont with only 22% as very religious is the least religious state.

Unit 1 Christianity

Protestantism[4]

The Protestant branch of the Christian faith broke away from the Roman Catholic Church in Europe in the sixteen century because of differences in religious beliefs and religious practices. At the time of the Protestant Reformation, the Roman Catholic Church was the center of religious life in Western European countries. The Catholic Pope and the priests played the role of parent to the people in spiritual matters. They told people what was right and wrong, and they granted them forgiveness for sins against God and the Christian faith.

The Protestants, on the other hand, insisted that every individual must stand alone before God and was solely responsible for his or her own relationship with God. If people sinned, they should seek their forgiveness directly from God rather than from a priest speaking in God's name.

After the Protestants broke away from the Catholic Church, they found that they could not agree among themselves about many things. Therefore, the Protestants began to form separate churches, called denominations（教派）. In the 1600s, the Catholic Church did not recognize the rights of such Protestant churches to exist, resulting in much bitterness among some of the religious groups. Subsequently, many Protestant denominations experienced religious persecution（迫害）, which eventually compelled many of them to leave their native countries to the New World in order to have freedom to practice their particular religious beliefs. The first of these groups was among the more radical of the English Puritans in their refusal to acknowledge the legitimacy of the Church of England itself. These "Pilgrims", or "separating Puritans", were committed to a model of church order in which each congregation（教堂会众）constituted an independent church with no need of bishops.

In the beginning, **Anglicanism**[5]（the Protestant Episcopal Church）was the established and dominant religion of the English colonies of North America, and was derived directly from the Church of England. Its adherents are often called Anglicans. Its origins can be traced to the non-rebellious element among the immigrants from England. Episcopalians（圣公会教徒）in modern America include a high proportion of people with well-paid jobs and considering themselves to be of rather high social status. This particular group is rather outside the main stream of Protestantism, though there may be a certain tendency for people who have ambitions for social status to attach them to it. But a person who wishes to be elected to political office finds membership of this group a hindrance（阻碍）rather than otherwise.

Presbyterianism[6] has had a strong presence in America since the colonial period. Reformed churches were first established in the colonies in the early 1600s and Presbyterians were instrumental in shaping the religious and political life of the fledgling nation. The only Christian minister to sign the *Declaration of Independence*, Reverend John Witherspoon, was a Presbyterian. The 18th-century "Great Awakening" was led by evangelically-minded Reformed theologians including Jonathan Edwards and George Whitefield.

The United States is in many ways founded on a Calvinist outlook: its focus was on hard work, discipline, the salvation of souls and the building of a better world. Presbyterians were instrumental in the movements for women's rights, abolition of slavery, and temperance.

During the Civil War, American Presbyterians were divided into southern and northern branches. These two churches reunited in 1983 to form the Presbyterian Church（U.S.A.）, the largest Presbyterian Reformed denomination in the United States. Other Presbyterian churches that exist today were also formed in the 20th century as some chose to move in a more liberal direction and others remained conservative.

One might have expected that the Society of Friends, or Quakers（贵格会）, would be one of the great American sects. One of the greatest states, Pennsylvania, was a Quaker foundation and for some time around 1700 the Quakers were the dominant group in New Jersey and Delaware. But the Friends do not go out to attract adherents, and, as in England, they remain a very small and select group, with little over 100,000 members. They lost political power as a group long ago, because they insisted on making a really serious attempt to follow Christian morality, but many Quakers now hold important positions outside politics, and their group is greatly respected.

Methodist churches trace their origins to John Wesley, a minister in the Church of England who sought to bring a new sense of warmth and commitment to individual's religious life. Wesley's opponents laughingly called his followers Methodists because of their discipline and seriousness. **Methodism**[7] grew with astonishing swiftness in the U.S. By 1820 it was the largest religious family in the U.S., and remained the largest one until the 1920s. Methodists hold that individual love of God and individual religious experience mean more than formal doctrine. Salvation is achieved by a life of holiness, repentance（忏悔）and faith, and is available to everyone. It has about 14 million members in the U.S.

The **Baptist**[8] family of churches is the largest Protestant family in the U.S. The Baptist Church has no recognized founder. In the U.S. the first Baptist Church was established by Roger Williams at Providence, Rhode Island, in 1639. Now the local Baptist congregations in the U.S. have great independence, determining many of their own policies. Baptists have traditionally been strong supporters of separation of church and state. The Southern Baptist Convention, a predominantly white church, is the largest Protestant denomination in the U.S. Many Baptist churches now have some 36 million members in the U.S., who mainly live in the southern and border states.

Lutherans[9] traced their churches back to the German reformer Martin Luther（1483—1546）. Luther sought to reform the doctrine and practice of the Roman Christian Church in Europe. He came to favor a marriage clergy. Lutherans regard the Bible as their sole guide; they believe that every person is a priest and can approach God directly. Immigrants from Germany and Scandinavia brought the Lutheran faith to North America, concentrating first in Pennsylvania.

Roman Catholics and the Orthodox

Roman Catholicism[10] is now the largest single Christian denomination in the United States. Many U.S. Catholics are descendents（后裔）of immigrants from Ireland, Germany, Poland, Italy and France. They are concentrated in the Northeast and Midwest and the Southwest are also predominantly Catholic. Although they are far more numerous than any single Protestant group, Catholics have always been conscious of the minority status both of their religion and of the ethnic group to which they belong. They derive vigor and cohesion from this feeling, which tends to promote intermarriage and the maintenance of their religious attachment and willingness to support their culture with money.

The problem for Catholicism is how to adapt to a religiously plural society. While Protestantism has claimed that Christ is the one true road to salvation and Judaism that it is the true way for Jews, Catholicism emphasizes another conception—the Catholic Church is the one true church, according to the traditional Catholicism, at least. The Catholic Church claims, for example, that it is the only institution with knowledge of religious and moral law. Christ is the bridge between God and man.

In the Christian religion, Orthodox Christianity, also known as **Eastern Orthodoxy**[11], began as the eastern half of Christendom, the site of the former Byzantine Empire（拜占庭帝国）. Today, the highest concentration of Orthodox Christians remains in the former Byzantine Empire（Greece, Turkey, and nearby countries）and in Russia. But Orthodoxy is found throughout the world, and approximately 225 million people are Orthodox Christians.

In 1794, a small group of missionaries landed on Kodiak Island, Alaska, bringing to the New World the Orthodox Faith of the Apostles. Over the next two hundred years, with the help of immigration from Europe and the Middle East, the Apostolic Faith spread throughout the entire North American continent.

Today, the Orthodox Church in North America, as throughout the world, is characterized by her diverse ethnic and cultural expressions of "the faith once delivered to the saints".

American Burgeoning Religions

Mormons[12] is one of the Protestant denominations that emerged between the 1820s and 1830s, also known as the Church of Jesus Christ of Latter-day Saints. Its founder, Joseph Smith, claimed that an angel led him to a buried book of revelations and to magic stone tablets to be used in translating it. He completed his translation of this *Book of Mormon* in 1827. With this new revelation, Smith quickly gathered followers, and together they moved from New York to Ohio, Missouri, Nauvoo, and finally Utah. The history of the Latter-day Saints in Utah underwent an abrupt and decisive shift in 1890, with President Wilford Woodruff's Manifesto bringing to an end the distinctive practice of polygamy（一夫多妻制）or plural marriage.

The ending of polygamy was both a symbol and a precondition of a new age in which Mormons would become much more thoroughly integrated into national life, although in a highly distinctive fashion. Mormons believe in a purposeful universe in which humans have been placed to make themselves more like God by faith and works. They hold that God was once a man, and men, too, may become gods. Missionary work is emphasized, and abstinence from coffee, tea and alcohol is considered important. Mormonism has been called the most American of religious, and has at times been treated as subversively un-American. It is clearly a community of apparent paradoxes: while its teachings strike most traditional Christians as extremely deviant（离经叛道的）, its social attitudes have brought it into increasing visibility as the American cultural and religious mood drifted rightwards in the 1970s and 1980s. Although appearing to compromise on issues such as plural marriage and, later, racial segregation, it has nevertheless continued on a conservative course that both aligns it with and estranges if from major sectors of American society. Its growing "normality" has led to higher levels of acceptability, while its aggressive evangelism and high birth rate have resulted in continuing dramatic growth. Whether its cultural "success" will lead to further erosion of its distinctiveness and the relegation of its distinctive beliefs to vestigial（残留的）symbolic status remains to be seen.

Jehovah's Witnesses[13] have been an enduring element in the American religious spectrum since their founding as the International Bible Students' Association by a Pittsburg haberdasher, Charles Taze Russell, in 1872. Russell taught that Jesus had inaugurated a "Millennial Dawn" with his return in the "upper air" in 1874, and expected the millennial consummation of the worldly order in 1914. Russell himself moved the date up four years before his own death in 1916, and his successor, Judge J.R. Rutherford, continued to adjust it as the anticipated inauguration of a new world order failed to materialize. Despite repeated "disconfirmations" the Witnesses, as they have called themselves since 1931, they have continued to flourish, in part through their aggressive door-to-door evangelism and sales of The Watchtower, and published at their Brooklyn headquarters. Their distinctive teachings, such as the restriction of full sainthood to 144,000 and their denial of a traditional interpretation of the **Trinity**[14], as well as "deviant" practices such as refusing blood transfusions, have rendered them an archetypal example of a sect in modern society. Although they have been consistently attacked by conservative Christians as a "cult", their major societal difficulties have stemmed from their alleged lack of patriotism in refusing to serve in the military and to salute the flag. These refusals result from their sense of constituting a "theocracy" in which all members are ministers and their concomitant rejection of the religious and political order of the broader when that order goes against their beliefs. The sometimes violent persecution this "deviant" behavior has incurred especially in wartime, has only strengthened their sense of rightness, and has also broadened *First Amendment* protection for such stances through the 1943 Supreme Court decision West Virginia State of Education v. Barnette. The courts have generally sustained their refusal of blood transfusions for adult believers, but not for children." By the 1980s, Jehovah's Witnesses in the United States numbered about 700,000, having benefited from the general resurgence in conservative religion of the period. They are organized into about eight thousand local congregations that meet in "Kingdom Halls", with headquarters in Brooklyn.

Notes

1. consumerism 消费主义：兴起于20世纪二三十年代的美国，五六十年代扩散到西欧、日本等地，认为社会消费力愈大对整个经济愈有利，追求消费的炫耀性、奢侈性和新奇性，并将它作为生活的目的和人生的终极价值。消费主义是资本主义从生产型社会向消费型社会转型时期和阶段所形成的一种影响深远的经济与社会文化现象。

2. hedonism 享乐主义：又叫“伊壁鸠鲁主义”（Epicureanism），19 世纪英国哲学家由他们的功利主义的伦理理论提出了享乐主义的基本原理，即所有行为皆是基于要给最多的人数获得最大的快乐，认为享乐是人类最重要的追求。

3. Pew Research Center 皮尤研究中心：美国一间独立性民调机构，总部设于华盛顿特区。该中心对那些影响美国乃至世界的问题、态度与潮流提供信息资料。

4. Protestantism 新教即基督教新教：基督教三大流派之一。该教派反对罗马教皇对各国教会的控制，宣称《圣经》为信仰的最高原则，不承认教会享有解释教义的绝对权威，强调教徒个人直接与上帝相通，不必由神父做中介。三大主流教派是指：路德宗、加尔文宗和圣公会。此外新教还有下列一些教派：福音会、清教会、卫斯理宗、卫理公会、循道公会、浸信会、公理会、福音派、布道会、宣道会、灵恩派、五旬节会、神召会、基要派、再洗礼派、门诺会、贵格会等。

5. Anglicanism 安立甘宗：常称“圣公会”，是新教主要宗派之一，与信义宗、归正宗合称新教三大流派。在英格兰为国教，称英国国教会。圣公会在宗教改革时期形成于英格兰，在英格兰称为“the Church of England”，传入美国后称为“Episcopal Church”。16 世纪早期，英王亨利八世（Henry VIII）以教皇不准他离婚为理由，实行摆脱教皇控制，夺取教会财产的改革。后又通过法案将英格兰教会立为国教，以英王为最高首领，并以坎特伯雷大主教（Archbishop of Canterbury）为名义上的领袖。圣公会只是不再服从教皇管辖，在教义和礼仪上与公教区别不大。

6. Presbyterianism 长老宗：以加尔文（Jean Calvin，1509—1564）的宗教思想为依据，亦称加尔文宗，与安立甘宗和路德宗并称新教三大主流派别。是代表大资产阶级和上层新贵族利益的政治派别，主张政教分离。

7. Methodism 循道宗：又称“卫斯理宗”，是基督教新教主要宗派之一，1783 年由英国人约翰·卫斯理（John Wesley，1703—1791）于伦敦创立。原为圣公会内的一派，后逐渐独立，主要分布于英美等国。该宗认为传统教会的活动方式已不足以应付新的社会问题，主张着重在下层群众中进行传教活动，宣称求得“内心的平安喜乐”便是幸福。

8. Baptist 浸礼宗：又称“浸信会”，是 17 世纪从英国清教徒独立派中分离出来的一个主要宗派，因其施洗方式为全身浸入水中而得名。此宗派的特点是反对婴儿受洗，坚持成年人始能接受浸礼；实行公理制教会制度，即所有信徒在教会中的地位和权利一律平等。

9. Lutherans 路德宗：经德国宗教改革家马丁·路德改革而形成的教派。16 世纪欧洲宗教改革倡导者，基督教新教路德宗创始人马丁·路德的宗教改革运动拉开了欧洲宗教改革的序幕。在信仰问题上，路德宗主张自主自治，反对教会的思想和行政控制，强调“因信称义（justification by faith）”的教义，即人在上帝面前得到救赎，不被定罪，得称为“义”，全凭内心的真正信仰，而不在于遵行教会规条，故又称“信义宗”。

10. Roman Catholicism 罗马天主教：又称“罗马公教会”，是基督宗教的三大宗派之一。该教信奉罗马天主教理论体系，包括道德、圣餐仪式以及教条。在基督宗教的所有教会之中，天主教会的人数最为庞大，全世界人数约有 11.3 亿，占世界总人口 17%，目前天主教会也是所有基督宗教的教会中最为庞大的教会。

11. Eastern Orthodoxy 东正教：是基督教三大派之一。基督教出现后不久，就逐渐分化成以希腊语地区为中心的东派教会和以拉丁语地区为中心的西派教会。1054年，东西两派正式分裂，以君士坦丁堡为中心的大部分东派教会自称"正教"，意为保有正统教义的正宗教会。因为地处东方，故又称"东正教"。

12. Mormons 耶稣基督后期圣徒教会：又称"摩门教"。摩门教是基督教在美国本土化的产物，美国第四大宗教团体，创始人为施约瑟，是目前世界上最大的新兴宗教。摩门教组织比较严谨，重视家庭。信徒接受《摩尔门经》为他们的经文，因为他们认为现在的圣经存在错误和遗漏。信徒认为自己也是信仰基督的基督信徒，但不是天主教、东正教或基督新教的基督信徒们的一部分。

13. Jehovah's Witnesses 耶和华见证人：成立于19世纪70年代，宾夕法尼亚州是它的发祥地。原来叫"守望会"，1931年改称"耶和华见证人"。其教义的最大特点是反对主流基督教的圣父、圣子和圣灵三位一体的教义。他们讨厌偶像崇拜，拒绝向上帝以外的任何偶像致敬，甚至对美国国旗也不例外，并且拒绝服兵役。

14. Trinity 三位一体：出自基督教《圣经》，基督教信仰神，是三位一体的神，透过圣经的启示，上帝包括（圣父、圣子、圣灵）三者合而为一，三个不同的位格乃是独一、真实、永恒的神。

Unit 2 Unaffiliated, Including Atheist or Agnostic

The United States federal government was the first national government to have no official state-endorsed religion. "Unaffiliated" does not necessarily mean "non-religious". Some people who are unaffiliated with any particular religion express religious beliefs and engage in religious practices. This group includes atheists, agnostics and people who describe their religion as "nothing in particular". This category included atheists, agnostics, and others with no stated religious preferences. Figures are up from 14.3 million in 1990 to 34.2 million in 2008, representing an increase from 8% of the total population in 1990 to 15% in 2008. Figures Pew study published in 2012 was described as placing the proportion at about 20% overall and roughly 33% for the 18-to-29-year-old demographic. About half of Americans say the growing number of "people who are not religious" is bad for American society. But a similar share say either that this trend is good or that it does not make much difference, according to a new survey by the Pew Research Center.

In recent years, Pew Research surveys have found evidence of a gradual decline in religious commitment in the U.S. public as a whole. For example, there has been a modest uptick over the past decade in the share of U.S. adults who say they seldom or never attend religious services. The number of Americans who do not identify with any religion also has grown in recent years; indeed, about one-fifth of the public overall—and a third of adults under age 30—are religiously unaffiliated as of 2012. Fully a third of U.S. adults say they do not consider themselves a "religious person". And two-thirds of Americans—affiliated and unaffiliated alike—say religion is losing its influence in Americans' lives.

The new, nationwide survey by the Pew Research Center's Forum on Religion & Public Life asked Americans whether having "more people who are not religious" is a good thing, a bad thing, or doesn't matter for American society. Many more say it is bad than good (48% versus 11%). But about four-in-ten (39%) say it does not make much difference. Even among adults who do not identify with any religion, only about a quarter (24%) say the trend is good, while nearly as many say it is bad (19%); a majority (55%) of the unaffiliated say it does not make much difference for society.

One important factor behind the growth of the religiously unaffiliated is generational replacement, the gradual supplanting of older generations by newer ones. But generational replacement is not the only factor at play. **Generation Xers**[1] and **Baby Boomers**[2] also have become more religiously unaffiliated in recent years. Part of the reasons that the ranks of the unaffiliated have grown in recent years is that Americans who are not particularly religious—at least by conventional measures, such as self-reported rates of attendance at religious services—increasingly describe themselves as atheist, agnostic or "nothing in particular".

The continued growth of the religiously unaffiliated is one of several indicators suggesting that the U.S. public gradually may be growing less religious. To be sure, the United States remains a highly religious country—particularly by comparison with other advanced industrial democracies—and some measures of religious commitment in America have held remarkably steady over the years. The number of Americans who currently say religion is very important in their lives (58%), for instance, is little changed since 2007 (61%) and is far higher than in Britain (17%), France (13%), Germany (21%) or Spain (22%). And over the longer term, Pew Research surveys find no change in the percentage of Americans who say that prayer is an important part of their daily life; it is 76% in 2012, the same as it was 25 years ago, in 1987. However, the same study also reported that the researchers also found acceptance or rejection of atheists is related not only to personal religiosity, but also to one's exposure to diversity, education and political orientation—with more educated, East and West Coast Americans more accepting of atheists than their Midwestern counterparts.

Notes

1. Generation Xers X一代人：指在1960—1980年间出生的人。这一代人在默默拒绝让自己的中年危机重蹈前人覆辙。

2. Baby Boomers 婴儿潮：特指美国第二次世界大战后的"4664"现象。从1946年至1964年，18年间婴儿潮使得美国人口增加7 600万人，这个人群被通称为"婴儿潮一代"。

Unit 3 Other Religions

Judaism

As we all know, the **Old Testament**[1] is the history of the Jews as a people and a large part of contemporary **Judaism**[2] celebrates this history. Many traits derived from group living have become religious customs. In this sense, Judaism is less a doctrine than a system of practices and customs, significantly different from both Protestantism and Catholicism. The basic beliefs of Judaism are a love of learning: the worships of God out of love and the performing of heartfelt good deeds without concern about rewards. Christianity broke away from Judaism, and in so doing "modernized" and "westernized" many Jewish practices. For example, certain practices such as the segregation of the sexes during worship seemed out of date when they were reintroduced into America by Judaism. Furthermore, Jews did not distinguish between the religious and secular spheres of life as Protestantism did. For instance, the traditional legal system of Judaism regulated many areas of life such as clothing and diet. Judaism, then, with its historical continuity, presented a dramatic contrast to the Christian religions. Tension was thus created, this tension between the Jews as a people with a unique cultural tradition and Judaism as a religion had to be resolved in some way on the American scene.

To know how Jews made such adjustments, it is necessary to look into their immigration experience into the United States. While Jews came to America as early as 1654, early immigration was slow, spasmodic（间歇性的）, and slight. Starting in 1836, there occurred a mass migration of German Jews to the United States, and by 1880, it was estimated that there were 250,000 Jews living in America. These Jews found it easier to divorce the idea of Jews that came later. Most of these immigrants had been minor merchants in Germany. Since they had few tie in America, many moved to the West with other pioneers, establishing small stores in the new towns they settled in. More importantly, as there were few established Jewish communities to absorb them, they saw little reason to retain their "old" way. Equally important was the fact that when these immigrants left Germany, an attack on traditional Judaism had already begun and attempts were made to adapt it to a more modern form. After arriving in the New World, these immigrants felt further encouraged to change the traditional Jewish laws and customs, thus starting what is called Reform Judaism. By dropping many traditional practices and ideas which they felt to be "un-American" in nature, Jews found themselves more acceptable in the non-Jewish world. Accordingly, Reform Judaism rejected the historic goal of the establishment of a separate Jewish nation—**Zion**[3]—where Jews could worship and live in peace. Reformed Judaism believed it had found its Zion in America, for by becoming Americanized, Jews could retain their religion and worship as they please.

Buddhism

The founder of **Buddhism**[4] was **Siddhartha Gautama**[5], who came to be known as Buddha. Buddhists share with Hinduism a belief in the cycle of **reincarnation**[6]. When a person's body dies, the soul is reborn in another person or animal. Buddha taught that a person should seek a state of detachment from worldly things and desires. Achieving this state, called **nirvana**[7], could bring contentment and would be the end of the reincarnation cycle for the soul. Buddhism entered the U.S. during the 19th century with the arrival of the first immigrations from Eastern Asia. The first Buddhist temple was established in San Francisco in 1853 by Chinese Americans. During the late 19th century Buddhist missionaries from Japan came to the U.S. Simultaneously to these processes, U.S. intellectuals started to take interest in Buddhism. The first prominent U.S. citizen to publicly convert to Buddhism was Henry Steel Olcott. An event that contributed to the strengthening of Buddhism in the U.S. was the Parliament of the World's Religions in 1893, which was attended by many Buddhist delegates sent from India, China, Japan, Vietnam, Thailand and Sri Lanka. The early 20th century was characterized by a continuation of tendencies that had their roots in the 19th century. The second half, by contrast, saw the emergence of new approaches, and the move of Buddhism into the mainstream and making itself a mass and social religious phenomenon. Estimates of the number of Buddhists in the United States vary between 0.9% and 1.2%.

Islam[8]

According to some sources, Islam is the fastest growing religion in the United States, with 20,000 converting each year, mainly among African Americans. American Islam effectively began with the arrival of African slaves. It is estimated that about 10% of African slaves transported to the United States were **Muslim**[9]. The Muslim population has increased greatly in the last one hundred years. Much of the growth has been driven by immigration, a comparatively high birth rate, and conversion. Up to one-third of American Muslim are Africans who have converted to Islam during the last seventy years, most of whom first joined the Nation of Islam, though the majority later transitioned into mainstream Sunni Islam. Research indicates that Muslims in the U.S. are generally more assimilated and prosperous than Muslims in Europe. Surveys also suggest, however, that they are less assimilated than other American subcultural and religious communities; the Islamic community has generated its own political organizations and charity organizations.

Hinduism[10]

Hinduism is a minority religion in the United States. American Hindus account for an estimated 0.4% of total U.S. population. The vast majority of American Hindus are Indian Americans, immigrants from India, Nepal, Bangladesh, Afghanistan, Caribbean and other countries, and their descendants, besides a number of converts. Currently, Hindu-Americans hold the highest education levels among all religious communities in the United States. In particular, they have the highest level of higher education. Many concepts of Hinduism such as law of karma（因果报应）, reincarnation and yoga have become prevalent among main-stream American population. For example, 24% of Americans believe in reincarnation, a core concept of Hinduism. However some scholars have criticized this concept on the basis of logic and reason. They said that there is no proof for it and it is totally an assumption.

Others

North America at the time of Columbus was a quilt of tribes with a diversity of languages and religions and ways of life. Most North American tribes hunted. Some relied upon agriculture as well; others fished; some gathered food in other ways. Through their experiences of nature, geography, and climate, as well as through their experiences within the tribe and with other tribes, and, when they came, with the Europeans, Native Americans fashioned religious worldviews. Characteristic of these worldviews is an intuition of wholeness and harmony that invests even seemingly mundane activities of life with religious meanings. But these worldviews, nevertheless, always encoded instinct meanings for the local community.

As the key unit of social organization, the tribe manifests various kinds of familial relationships. The experience of those relationships informs reflection about relationships between persons and nature, which likewise are conceived as familial bonds. The rationales for this ordering of relationships are imbedded in myths about the creation of the world, about heroes and tricksters, about monsters and ghosts, and about the end of time. Native American myths overflow with representations of kinship among nature and people; of marriages between creatures of different species; of parenting by the sun, moon and stars; and of the remembrance of ancestors by Earth itself. In Native American cultures, nature—including humanity—is conceived as an interconnected web of family relations. And it is this vision that underlies the association of each clan of a tribe with a certain animal, fish, or other living thing.

Judaeo-Christian and Islamic cosmogonies（宇宙的起源）are about the creation of the universe from nothing. Native American myths sometimes are structured in a similar way, with a cosmic creator playing the key role. Sometimes the creator is identified as female. Frequently, creation stories weave together the exploits of an extended cast of characters, each of whom has a role to play in creation. Other creation myths tell of the emergence of people and animals from places beneath the surface of the Earth. Creation stories tell more than how the world was created. They give meaning to everyday tribal life, orienting a people to the land and to spiritual values at the same time.

The religion life of Native Americans is rich with symbol, with the experience of the sacred, and with visions of kinship with people, animals, the land, and all of nature. In its ordering of the world, mythology also provides a template for morality, for guidelines about how people ought to act. Ritual transmits and confirms tribal knowledge. It expresses a religious worldview through dramatic performances, ranging from hunting rites to ritual quests for visions. Ritual is no less a language than the spoken word in terms of its effectiveness in communicating the religious meanings of events and in locating everyday life within the context of myth, the acting out of myth before an audience familiar with it. In ritual performances, persons listen to and repeat myth, shape it in new ways, adapt it, and confirm their belief in it. In ritual, a community identifies itself and rededicates itself to the tribal way of life.

Notes

1. Old Testament《旧约》: 用希伯来语写成,是基督教对《圣经》前一部分的常用称呼,后一部分称为《新约》。《圣经》旧约部分原是犹太教主要经籍《塔纳赫》,是希伯来民族文学遗产的总集。

2. Judaism 犹太教: 是世界三大神教信仰中最早而且最古老的宗教,也是犹太民族的生活方式及信仰。教义来自《托拉》,即圣经的前五卷书《摩西五经》(《创世纪》《出埃及记》《利未记》《民数记》和《申命记》)。

3. Zion 锡安山: 又称"天国",是耶路撒冷的一个迦南要塞,后泛指锡安山、耶路撒冷、以色列的土地。

4. Buddhism 佛教: 世界三大宗教之一。佛的意思是"觉者"。佛教重视人类心灵和道德的进步和觉悟。佛教信徒修习佛教的目的在于发现生命和宇宙的真相,最终超越生死轮回,断尽一切烦恼,得到解脱。

5. Siddhartha Gautama 乔达摩·悉达多:(公元前 565 年—公元前 486 年)古印度北部迦毗罗卫国(今尼泊尔境内)的王子,刹帝利种姓。佛教创始人,属于释迦族,被称为释迦牟尼佛。据佛经记载,释迦牟尼在 19 岁时,有感于人世生、老、病、死等诸多苦恼,舍弃王族生活,出家修行。35 岁时,在菩提树下大彻大悟,遂开启佛教,随即在印度北部,中部恒河流域一带传教。80 岁在拘尸那迦城示现涅磐。

6. reincarnation 轮回: 又称流转、生死轮回,意思是众生死了又生,生了又死,生死不已,像车轮一样转动不停,循环不已。轮回理论源于生命的世代轮转传承,业力是主导轮回的因,不单是现世的结果,还会生生不息地延伸至来世。佛教认为,一切有生命的东西,如不寻求"解脱",即永远在"六道(天、人、阿修罗、畜生、饿鬼、地狱)"中生死相续,无有止息地循环。

7. nirvana 涅槃: 意译为"圆寂、灭度、寂灭、无为、解脱、自在、安乐、不生不灭"等。佛教教义认为涅槃是将世间所有一切法都灭尽而仅有一本住法之圆满而寂静的状态,所以涅槃中永远没有生命中的种种烦恼、痛苦、苦行,动物、人、尸体火化后,从此不再受后有,也就是不再有下一世的六道轮回。

8. Islam 伊斯兰教: 阿拉伯语的音译,本意为"顺从",是世界性的宗教之一,与佛教、基督教并称为世界三大宗教。伊斯兰教诞生于阿拉伯半岛的社会大变动时期,以"安拉是唯一的真神"为口号,主张"施舍济贫""和平安宁"。

9. Muslim 穆斯林:"伊斯兰"一词的派生名词,意为"顺从真主者"。信奉穆罕默德是真主的使者,是传达经典《古兰经》的圣人。

10. Hinduism 印度教: 源于古印度婆罗门教,是世界主要宗教之一,诞生于公元 8 世纪。主要流行于印度,现分布在英国、巴基斯坦、孟加拉国,马来西亚、印度尼西亚、菲律宾、新加坡和美国。

Unit 4 Religion and American Society

Religion and Education

In 1925, Tennessee passed the **Butler Law**[1] outlawing the teaching of evolution—a move that set the stage for the State of *Tennessee* v. ***John Thomas Scopes***[2]. The law prohibited public school teachers from denying the Biblical account of man's origin, and also prevented the teaching of the evolution of man from what it referred to as lower orders of animals in place of the Biblical account. As **NPR**[3] notes, "the trial lasted just a week, but the questions it raised are as divisive now as they were back then." To this day, religious groups attempt to influence public education, and likewise, public schools seek to maintain a secular atmosphere that can limit religious expression. Because each state has a distinct religious makeup and laws governing the administration of public schools, some have experienced more difficulty preserving students' rights while providing a quality education.

Evolution

The theory of evolution is fundamental to biological studies, but because it conflicts with some religious views of **creationism**[4], some groups have argued against its inclusion in secular education since Darwin published *On the Origin of Species* in 1859. According to **Gallup**[5], 46% of people in the U.S. believe that God created humans independently, and only 15% believe that humans evolved with no divine intervention. Because school boards and other elected entities can change with any voting cycle, the impact these beliefs have on education can change in any given year, and they tend to vary greatly by state. In Tennessee, a bill protecting "teachers who explore the 'scientific strengths and scientific weaknesses' of evolution and climate change" passed in 2012. Kansas schools taught Intelligent Design between 2005 and 2007 but now teach mainstream science, according to the Kansas State Department of Education's website.

Sex Education

Evangelical Christian groups[6] are strong proponents for abstinence（节欲，戒酒）—only education, which encourages adolescents to abstain from sexual activity until marriage. In 2012 alone, Congress set aside $5 billion to fund abstinence-only programs, despite evidence that such programs leave young people ill equipped to protect themselves from STDs（性传播疾病）and pregnancy, according to the article, *Abstinence-Only Education Debate Resurfaces*, published on the U.S. News and World Report website. The Journal of Adolescent Health reviewed these programs and studies associated with them, finding that students who failed at abstinence were less likely to use contraception（避孕）after they did initiate sexual intercourse. This is illustrated by a University of Georgia study, detailed in the article *Abstinence-Only Education Does not Lead to*

Abstinent Behavior, UGA Researchers Find on the University of Georgia's website. The study indicates that states offering abstinence-only programs exclusively have much higher rates of teen pregnancy. Some scholars posit that this may even contribute to the high teen pregnancy rates in the U.S. compared to other industrialized countries.

Dress Codes

Some schools institute dress codes or uniforms to ensure students are dressed appropriately for a learning environment. Banning headgear（头饰）is a common dress code rule. However, some religious groups, including Muslims, Jews and some Native American tribes, consider headgear to be part of their identity. At times, this has conflicted with school dress codes; in 1997, school officials suspended a Muslim student for refusing to remove her hijab（伊斯兰头巾）. According to CNN, the school attorney at the time, D.D. Hayes, said, "As I see it right now, I don't think we can make a special accommodation for religious wear." Although other schools have taken action against students who expressed their religious identity, most schools are willing to accommodate religious garb.

Proselytizing(改变宗教)

In 1962, the Supreme Court ruled in *Engle* v. *Vitale* that prayer led by public school officials is unconstitutional. Likewise, teachers and other school employees should not promote their own religion or penalize students who do not share their religion. The law allows students to pray at school in private but does not allow them to lead mandatory prayers, pray at graduation ceremonies, actively proselytize to their fellow students or promote religious bullying. In Collier County, Florida, school officials allow groups to distribute religious literature "passively", by leaving it on tables for students to read. Despite this ruling, secular humanist groups were asked to remove their "passively" distributed secular literature from a school setting, igniting a lawsuit that cited discrimination, according to the article *Atheist Group Sues Orange Schools, Claiming Censorship* published on the Orlando Sentinel's website.

Religion and Foreign Policies

Why is U.S. foreign policy so moralistic? Why, unusually among the diplomats of the world, do American foreign policymakers appeal to ideals and values, such as the promotion of human rights and democracy, when the leaders of other nations do not? U.S. presidents have been known for their moralism for a long time—**Theodore Roosevelt**[7] was one of the first to be scolded by European leaders for it. But where does it come from?

In large part, the answer has to do with religion, particularly the pressure from below applied by ordinary religious Americans who did not wield policymaking influence or political power. The reason they were able to do so is two-fold. First, for most of its history—indeed, until the nuclear age—the United States was free from attack or invasion and thus enjoyed what national security analysts call "free security". This afforded Americans a foreign policy of almost total choice, and with it the freedom to envision the world as they wanted it to be. It also meant that foreign policymakers in Washington couldn't suppress popular causes on the grounds of national security. To be sure the advent of air power and nuclear weapons during World War II brought the age of free security to an end, but not before foreign policy habits and cultures had formed indelibly. Second, in a democracy, American officials couldn't ignore popular pressures from below, especially if they couldn't dismiss them on national security grounds. The combination of free security and republican democracy, in other words, gave religion an opening it might not otherwise have had to influence the making of U.S. foreign policy.

Conducting foreign policy is about serving the national interest, which often leads nations into morally questionable behavior. Religion, on the other hand, is about doing what's right. People of faith are inherently idealistic. Others may disagree with those ideals, but at its core religion is about believing in a set of principles that imagines the world as it should really be. When motivated by an issue they believe to be important, religious communities are indefatigable, determined, averse to compromise, highly activist, politically connected, and deeply concerned with the wider world. They relentlessly press their elected officials to protect and promote ideals that are often universal rather than national.

From antebellum evangelical and **Unitarian**[8] abolitionists who opposed territorial expansion to missionaries who dragged the U.S. government into the Chinese interior, ordinary religious Americans have advanced their own foreign policy agendas that officials in Washington have found impossible to resist. And history is littered with examples of presidents who failed to handle religious controversies adeptly, and either suffered for it at the ballot box or lost control of their foreign policy. It is, however, a relatively recent case study—the rise, fall, and reemergence of détente, from the early 1970s to the end of the Cold War in 1989—that provides perhaps the best illustration.

Notes

1. Butler Law《巴特勒法案》: 即《1944 年教育法》,英国政府于 1944 年颁布的战后教育改革法案,是英国教育制度发展史上一个极其重要的法令。它结束了战前英国教育制度发展不平衡的状况,形成了初等教育、中等教育和继续教育相互衔接的国民教育制度。此法案强调禁止在课堂上讲授人是从猴子等低等动物进化来的。

2. John Thomas Scopes 约翰·托马斯·斯科普斯: 田纳西州公立高中的老师斯科普斯违抗州法律,在课堂上教授进化论,被州政府告上了法庭,轰动美国乃至整个世界,这一历史性事件被称为"田纳西州起诉斯科普斯案",又称"猴子审判"。

3. NPR 全国公共广播电台: 全称"National Public Radio",是一家获公众赞助及部分政府资助,但独立运作的非商业性美国媒体,成立于 1970 年。节目以新闻、综述、采访为主,也有一些音乐、脱口秀等文化娱乐节目,听众数目据估计约有两千万人。

4. creationism 创造论: 也称"神创论",通常创造者被称为上帝,宇宙的创造者,与进化论相对立，被视为一种反对生物进化论的唯心学说。

5. Gallup 盖洛普民意测验：美国民意调查机构，1935 年由美国的统计学家乔治·盖洛普创办该所而得名，总部设在普林斯顿。民意测验每年举行 20 ～ 25 次，总统大选年略多。调查内容包括政治、经济、社会等。采用抽样调查方法，在全国各州按比例选择测验对象，派调查员面访，然后统计调查结果，分析并做出说明，将结果提供给用户。

6. Evangelical Christian groups 福音派宗教团体：恪守传统教义，重视《圣经》权威和学术研究。Evangelical 一词始于 16 世纪，当时的宗教改教者以此名称表明反对罗马天主教的立场，它不是一个宗派。

7. Theodore Roosevelt 西奥多·罗斯福：西奥多·罗斯福（1858—1919），人称“老罗斯福”，昵称“泰迪”（Teddy），美国军事家、政治家，第 26 任美国总统。他在总统任期内，对国建立资源保护政策，对外实行扩张政策，于 1908 年卸任。

8. Unitarian 一位论派：基督教派别之一，16 世纪产生于匈牙利和波兰。该派反对三位一体的正统基督论，只承认耶稣的人性而否认其神性，认为上帝只是一位而非三位。声称信仰的根据只能是《圣经》和理性，教会和国家无权解释教义。

References

[1] AWANA M. The influence of religion on education in public schools[EB/OL]. [2016-05-22].http://everydaylife.globalpost.com/influence-religion-education-public-schools-15541.html.

[2] Orthodoxy in American[EB/OL]. [2014-04-14]. http://orthodoxyinamerica.org/.

[3] PEW RESEARCH CENTER. Growth of the nonreligious[EB/OL]. [2013-07-02].http://www.pewforum.org/2013/07/02/growth-of-the-nonreligious-many-say-trend-is-bad-for-american-society/.

[4] PEW RESEARCH CENTER. “Nones” on the rise[EB/OL]. [2012-10-09]. http://www.pewforum.org/2012/10/09/nones-on-the-rise/.

[5] ANDREW P. Why is American foreign policy so religious? [EB/OL]. [2012-05-07]. http://religionandpolitics.org/2012/05/07/why-is-american-foreign-policy-so-religious.

[6] RELIGIONFACTS. History of Presbyterianism[EB/OL]. [2016-05-22].http://www.Religionfacts.com/christianity/denominations/presbyterian/history.htm.

[7] 刘澎 . 当代美国宗教 [M]. 北京：社会科学文献出版社 , 2001.

[8] 徐以骅 . 宗教与美国社会 [M]. 北京：时事出版社 , 2004.

[9] 徐以骅 . 宗教与美国社会 (第一辑) [M]. 北京：时事出版社 , 2004.

[10] 徐以骅 , 徐怡超 , 刘骞 . 宗教与美国社会（第七辑）[M]. 北京：时事出版社 , 2012.

[11] 约翰 · F. 威尔逊 . 当代美国的宗教 [M]. 徐以骅 , 等 , 译 . 上海：上海人民出版社 , 2013.

[12] 王恩铭 . 美国文化与社会 [M]. 上海：上海外语教育出版社 , 2009.

[13] 王晓红 . 美国社会与文化 [M]. 西安：世界图书出版西安公司 , 2010.

Chapter Nine

American Foreign Policy

Unit 1 A Brief History of American Foreign Policy

As the cultural, military and economic interdependence of the nations of the world has increased, it has become even more important for the United States to establish and carry out foreign policies to deal with external situations and to carry out its own national goals. By foreign policy, it means both the goals the government wants to achieve in the world and the techniques and strategies to achieve them. For example, if one national goal is to achieve stability in Eastern Europe and to encourage the formation of pro-American governments there, U.S. foreign policy in that area may be carried out by using various techniques, including diplomacy, economic aid, technical assistance, or military intervention. Sometimes foreign policies are restricted to statements of goals or ideas, such as helping to end world poverty, whereas at other times foreign policies are comprehensive measures to achieve particular objectives.

In the United States, the foreign policy process usually originates from the President and those agencies that provide advice on foreign policy matters. Foreign policy formulation is often affected by congressional action and national public debate.

The Formative Years

Throughout most of its history, the United States followed a foreign policy course called **Isolationism**[1]—avoiding political involvement in other nations was the best way to protect American interests. This policy, articulated by George Washington in his Farewell Address, directed the country to stay out of other nation conflicts, particularly European Wars. Of course, staying completely isolated, even in that day and age, was not an easy thing to do. In the 1820s, many European nations were expanding into Latin America. The United States saw Central and South America as its own backyard and viewed European expansion as a threat to its economic and security interests. In a historical message to Congress in 1823, President James Monroe proclaimed what has become known as the **Monroe Doctrine**[2]. In his message, President Monroe stated that the United States would not accept foreign intervention in the Western Hemisphere. He declared that the United States would look on "any attempt on the part of other nations to extend their system to any portion of this hemisphere as dangerous to our peace and security." In return, the United States would not meddle in European affairs.

Expansionism[3] and the Beginning of Interventionism[4]

While Americans were trying to avoid involvement in European affairs, they were also expanding westward across the North American continent. This expansion led the United States to the conflicts with other nations, such as Mexico, France, Spain, and Great Britain. Meanwhile, American traders were roaming the world in search of new markets, and American business were expanding across the Pacific, beginning trade with Japan, China and other Asian countries in the mid 1800s.

The first real step toward interventionism, or direct involvement in foreign affairs, came with the **American-Spanish War**[5] of 1898, when the United Nations fought to free Cuba from Spanish rule. The United States defeated Spain and gained control of several Spanish island possessions. As a result, the United States now had a colonial empire and was acknowledged as a world power.

To protect American interests in Asia, Secretary of State John Hay announced **the Open Door Policy**[6] of 1899. In the early 1900s, President Theodore Roosevelt adopted a policy that shifted the emphasis of the Monroe Doctrine. He proposed that the United States be allowed to invade Latin American countries for they believed that it was necessary to guarantee American political and economic stability. Under what came to be known as **the Roosevelt Corollary**[7] to the Monroe Doctrine, the United States began to police Latin America in the early 1900s.

Foreign Policy in World Wars and the Cold War

1.World Wars

As World War I raged in Europe in 1914, isolationism was still in a strong sentiment in the United States. For three years, the United States stayed out of the war. President Woodrow Wilson urged a policy of **neutrality**[8], or refusal to take sides in an armed conflict. When American ships in international waters were attacked without reasons by German submarines（潜艇）, however, the United States entered the war. It was the first time that the United States had taken part in a full-scale war that arose from European disputes.

World War Ⅰ ended in 1918, and during the 1920s and 1930s, most Americans did not want the United States to be involved in European affairs. The United States refused to join the League of Nations. Most Americans seemed to favor a return to a policy of isolationism.

This return to isolationism, however, was only temporary. The United States initially tried to stay out of World War Ⅱ and officially sought to remain neutral. When the Japanese attacked Pearl Harbor（珍珠港）in 1941, the United States entered the war. The United States, in alliance with Australia, Great Britain, Canada, China, France, and the Soviet Union, eventually fought Germany, Italy, and Japan. After World War Ⅱ, the United States began to play a dramatically different role in world affairs. The United States decided to participate actively in the postwar resettlement of Europe.

2.The Cold War

Although the United States and the Soviet Union were allies during World War Ⅱ , the situation deteriorated after the war. They both run after their own interests and the Cold War began.

President Harry S. Truman addressed Congress, presenting **the Truman Doctrine**[9]: "I believe that it must be the policy of the United States to support peoples who are resisting attempted subjugation by armed minorities or by outside pressures." Under the Truman Doctrine the United States began to participate actively in the postwar resettlement of Europe. The United States Secretary of State George Marshall proposed that the U.S. provided economic assistance to European countries, such as France, Germany, Great Britain and so on, which is named **the Marshall Plan**[10].

The tension created by the Cold War led the Soviet Union and the United States to try to surpass each other militarily. They began competing for more and better weapons. This phenomenon was commonly known as **Arms Race**[11].

Foreign Policy in the Post-Cold War Era

The Cold War has ended, but that does not necessarily mean that all is well and that foreign policy decision making is simpler. Indeed, some argue that foreign policy making now is more complex. During the Cold War, they knew who their "enemies" were. To a great extent, U.S. foreign policy was fashioned in response to actions taken by the Soviet Union and the Communist bloc. Today, the United States is grappling with the question of how to develop a foreign policy appropriate to the new world situation brought about by the demise of the Soviet Union. How can they best protect democracy and human rights throughout the world? Should the United States play the role of the world's "peacekeeper" ? Should economic consideration take priority over human rights issues in foreign policy making? These are just a few of the questions that foreign policymakers face today.

Notes

1. Isolationism 孤立主义：一种外交政策，通常由防务和经济两方面上的政策组成。在防务上，孤立主义采取不干涉原则，即除自卫战争外不主动卷入任何外部军事冲突；在经济文化上，通过立法最大程度限制与国外的贸易和文化交流。

2. Monroe Doctrine 门罗主义：由詹姆斯·门罗总统发表于1823年，表明美利坚合众国当时的观点，即欧洲列强不应再殖民美洲，或涉足美国与墨西哥等美洲国家之主权相关事务。而对于欧洲各国之间的争端，或各国与其美洲殖民地之间的战事，美国保持中立。相关战事若发生于美洲，美国将视为具敌意之行为。

3. Expansionism 扩张主义：一种外交政策，旨在通过单独或者兼用军事、外交及移民等手段，达到增加本国领土、殖民地或者主权，宣示霸权和扩大本国政治、经济及文化影响的效果。

4. Interventionism 干涉主义：在当前的国际环境下出现的一种以人道主义和捍卫西方

共同的价值观为借口，以武力干涉别国内政为手段，以推行霸权主义和构筑有利于西方的国际关系新秩序为目的的思潮和模式。

5. American-Spanish War 美西战争： 1898 年，美国为夺取西班牙属地古巴、波多黎各和菲律宾而发动的战争，是列强重新瓜分殖民地的第一次帝国主义战争。

6. the Open Door Policy 门户开放政策： 门户开放政策是由美国首先提出来的。它的主要内容是：在整个中国范围内，列强都有进行贸易的权利。它的主要精神是利益均沾，机会平等。

7. the Roosevelt Corollary 罗斯福推论： 是 1904 年美国总统西奥多·罗斯福对门罗主义的一个修正案，它的核心是美国可以根据自己的逻辑任意武装干涉拉丁美洲，以实现“美洲是美国人的美洲”的独霸西半球的野心。

8. neutrality 中立： 某些国家在国际关系中所持的原则和所执行的政策，即保持本国政治独立、主权完整，不参加任何军事集团，不把自己的领土作为外国的军事基地，也不对任何国家采取敌对态度。

9. the Truman Doctrine 杜鲁门主义： 第二次世界大战后，德、意、日三个法西斯国家遭到彻底失败，而英、法的力量也严重削弱，只有美国，依靠其在战争中发展起来的经济、军事实力，在资本主义世界取得了统治地位。1947 年 2 月 21 日，英国照会美国国务院，声称由于国内经济困难，3 月 31 日之后，英国无法再给希腊和土耳其以经济和军事的援助，希望美国继续给予援助。1947 年 3 月 12 日，美国总统杜鲁门在国会两院联席会议上宣读了后来被称为“杜鲁门主义”的国情咨文，发表了敌视社会主义国家的讲话。国会两院经过辩论后，分别于 4 月 22 日和 5 月 8 日通过关于援助希腊、土耳其的法案。美国国会拨款 4 亿美元援助希腊和土耳其政府，帮助它们镇压人民革命运动。“杜鲁门主义”是干涉别国内政的代名词，它的提出，标志着美苏之间的“冷战”正式开始。

10. the Marshall Plan 马歇尔计划： 官方名称为“欧洲复兴计划”（European Recovery Program），是第二次世界大战结束后美国对被战争破坏的西欧各国进行经济援助、协助重建的计划，对欧洲国家的发展和世界政治格局产生了深远的影响。该计划于 1947 年 7 月正式启动，并整整持续了四个财政年度之久。

11. Arms Race 军备竞赛： 指和平时期敌对国家或潜在敌对国家互为假想敌、在军事装备方面展开的质量和数量上的竞赛。各国之间为了应对未来可能发生的战争，竞相扩充军备，增强军事实力。是一种预防式的军事对抗。20 世纪 70 年代，美、苏核武器竞争激烈，双方拥有世界核弹头库存总数的 97%，同时双方在核武器运载工具、多弹头分导等高技术领域的研制投入大量人力和物力。冷战期间，美苏军备竞赛，两国彼此的核弹头已经太多了，美国为了从经济上拖垮苏联，就向太空发展，提出“星球大战”计划。此计划太过超前，耗资巨大，而且技术上的要求在当时的条件下很难完全达到实际运用的水平，但是也迫使苏联投入巨资向太空发展，最终将苏联从经济上拖垮了，并且导致苏联分裂解体。

Unit 2 American Foreign Policy Goals and Tools

Foreign Policy Goals

American foreign policy as a whole is guided by the overall purpose of promoting national security, or keeping the nation safe from attack or harm. Most aspects of their foreign policy are related to the need to maintain the United States as a free and independent nation, secure from unwanted external influence. The United States has worked toward his overall purpose by setting policies to achieve several goals.

Their primary foreign policy goal, like that of every other nation, is to protect their physical security. Until the era of long-range bombers and ballistic missiles(弹道导弹), achieving this goal meant preventing land invasion, and in this they have been successful.

A second goal is to help protect the physical security of their neighbors and major democratic allies. Since World War Ⅱ, they have committed themselves, through the **NATO**[1] (North Atlantic Treaty Organization), to joining the defense of Canada and Western, Southern, and now even some Eastern European nations. They also have treaty commitments to Japan, South Korea, and the nations of the South and South America.

A third goal is to protect their economic security. Although the United States is blessed with many natural resources, they must purchase such essential resources as oil, manganese, and tin elsewhere. Safe-guarding access to these resources may include stabilizing the governments of producing nations or protecting nations or protecting the sea lanes in which goods are shipped. Their economic well-being is equally dependent on selling their goods abroad, which in turn depends on how cheaply they can manufacture or grow products desired in other parts of the world and how willing the trading partners are to buy them.

A fourth overlapping goal is to extend the sphere of influence. Historically, this has meant keeping foreign powers out of the Caribbean and Latin America. Since World War Ⅱ, their sphere of interest has extended around the world. They have sought to influence security arrangements on all continents. Even after the post-Cold War base closures, they still have more military bases and more troops outside their borders than any other country. They also try to spread their influence by promoting democracy, capitalism, and Western cultural values.

Their specific foreign policy objectives, such as protecting access to oil in the Middle East, drying up funding sources for terrorist operations, removing trade barriers and increasing U.S. exports, are almost always related to achieving one or more of these four general goals.

Foreign Policy Tools

The major goal of American Foreign Policy is to protect national security. The United States uses several tools to achieve this and other foreign policy goals. These tools include diplomacy, foreign aid, alliances and pacts, trade agreements, and military force.

1.Diplomacy

Diplomacy is the total process of conducting political relations with other countries, including settling differences and conflicts through peaceful means. It is the most important tool of American foreign policy. Many other foreign policy tools, such as alliances and trade agreements, result from diplomatic negotiations with other countries. True diplomacy involves working with people through various forms of compromise and negotiation. When disagreements between nations arise, each nation usually sends representatives, known as diplomats, to speak with diplomats from other nations about the issues.

2.Foreign Aid

Economic aid to other countries has been an American foreign policy tool for over fifty years. It began with **the Lend-Lease Program**[2] for the early 1940s, in which the United States gave nearly 50 billion dollars in food, munitions, and other supplies to their allies in World War Ⅰ, World War Ⅱ. After World War Ⅱ, the Marshall Plan promoted economic recovery in Europe. Under the Marshall Plan, the United States gave billions of dollars to sixteen Western European nations between 1948 and 1952. This aid helped with Western Europe's postwar economic recovery and increased its ability to trade with the United States.

American foreign aid goes primarily to nations that support U.S. foreign goals. Aid has been given to prevent the establishment of governments with political ideals contrary to their own and to help countries fight against aggression. The United States also gives economic aid to establish friendly relations with nations.

3.Alliances and Pacts

American foreign policy also seeks security through alliances and pacts. A mutual defense alliance is a military alliance formed among countries to protect against a common threat to their security. Under such an alliance, nations become allies and pledge to support each other in case of an attack by enemy forces. The United States has signed mutual defense treaties with at least forty-two nations in various regions. These treaties are multilateral treaties in that they are signed by a group of several nations.

After World War Ⅱ, the United States and leaders of Western European nations gathered in Washington to create the NATO. The chief objective of NATO was the collective defense of Western Europe, particularly against Soviet aggression. In 1948, the nations that have signed the Rio Pact established the **OAS**[3] (The Organization of American States). The goal of the OAS is to promote economic development and strengthen peace and security in the Western Hemisphere, to prevent conflicts to settle them peacefully through negotiation, and to seek isolation for political, judicial and economic problems.

4.Trade Measures

Another foreign policy tool involves the terms under which the United States trades with other countries. Two aims of American trade policies are to increase sales of American goods to other countries, which promote economic prosperity, and to persuade trading partners to support its other foreign policy goals. Trade terms include how much of tariffs, or taxes, will be levied on the products.

Not surprisingly, the United States has been at the forefront in pushing for freer world trade. The United States was a leading member of the General Agreement on Tariffs and Trade (**GATT**[4]), which formed the World Trade Organization (**WTO**[5]). Sometimes, the United States punishes other nations by withdrawing trade benefits. For example, in 1986, Congress initiated and passed a bill instituting economic sanctions against South Africa to pressure that nation into ending apartheid(种族隔离政策). In 1990, President Bush imposed severe economic sanctions against Iraq in an effort to force Iraq's leader, Saddam Hussein, to withdraw his force from Kuwait.

5.Military Force

On a number of occasions, the United States has used military force to achieve foreign policy goals. On five of these occasions, the United States has declared war. American troops have been used abroad without declaration of war many times.

Notes

1. NATO 北大西洋公约组织：英文全称"North Atlantic Treaty Organization"，中文简称"北约组织"或"北约"，是美国与西欧、北美主要发达国家为实现防卫协作而建立的一个国际军事集团组织，是资本主义阵营在军事上实现战略同盟的标志，是马歇尔计划的发展，是美国得以控制英国和法国为首的欧盟的防务体系，是美国世界超级大国领导地位的标志。

2. the Lend-Lease Program 租借法案：美国国会在第二次世界大战初期通过的一项法案，目的是在美国不卷入战争的同时，为盟国提供战争物资。

3. OAS 美洲国家组织：英文全称"The Organization of American States"，由美国和拉丁美洲的国家组成的区域性国际组织，其前身是美洲共和国国际联盟。成立于 1890 年 4 月 14 日，1948 年在波哥大举行的第 9 次泛美大会上改称现名。

4. GATT 关税与贸易总协定：英文全称"General Agreement on Tariffs and Trade"，是一个政府间缔结的有关关税和贸易规则的多边国际协定，简称"关贸总协定"。它的宗旨是通过削减关税和其它贸易壁垒，削除国际贸易中的差别待遇，促进国际贸易自由化，以充分利用世界资源，扩大商品的生产与流通。

5. WTO 世界贸易组织：英文全称"World Trade Organization"， 1994 年 4 月 15 日成立，取代成立于 1947 年的关贸总协定。是当代最重要的国际经济组织之一，目前拥有 159 个成员国，成员国贸易总额达到全球的 97%，有"经济联合国"之称。

Unit 3 Makers and Shapers of American Foreign Policy

As in domestic policy, foreign policy making is a highly pluralistic arena. First there are the official players who comprise the "foreign policy establishment"; these players and the agencies they lead can be called "makers" of foreign policy.

Who Makes Foreign Policy?

1.President

Although many foreign policy decisions can be made without so much as the President's fingerprint on them, these decisions must be made and implemented in the name of the president. In **Iran-Contra Affair**[1], much of the action took place far from the White House and was hidden from the president. But those decisions and actions were taken of further a goal that the president wanted. That all foreign policies come from the President is a necessity in making any foreign policy. All heads of state must have some confidence that each head of state has enough power and stability to negotiate, to make agreements, and to keep those agreements.

2.Congress

In foreign policy making, Congress has to be subdivided into three parts. The first part is the Senate. For most of American history, the Senate was the only important congressional foreign policy player because of its constitutional role in reviewing and approving treaties. Since World War II and the continual involvement of the United States in international security and foreign aid, Congress as a whole has become a major foreign policy maker because most modern foreign policies require financing , which requires both the House of Representatives and the Senate. Congress has also become increasingly involved in foreign policy making because of the increasing use by the president of executive agreements to conduct foreign policy. The third congressional player is the foreign policy and military policy committees: in the Senate there are **the Foreign Relations Committee**[2] and **the Armed Services Committee**[3]; in the House, there are the International Relations Committee and the Armed Services Committee.

3.The Bureaucracy

The major foreign policy players in the bureaucracy are the secretaries of the departments of State, Defense, and the Treasury; the Joint Chiefs of Staff(**JCOS**[4]), especially the chair of the JCOS; and the director of the Central Intelligence Agency(**CIA**[5]). A separate unit in the bureaucracy comprised of these people and a few others is the National Security Council (**NSC**[6]), whose main purpose is to iron out the differences among the key players and to integrate their positions in order to confirm or reinforce a decision the president wants to make in foreign policy.

In addition to these top cabinet-level officials, key low-level staff members have policy-making influence as strong as that of the cabinet secretaries; some may occasionally exceed cabinet influence. These includes the two or three specialized national security advisers in the White House, the staff of NSC, and a few other career bureaucrats in the Department of State and Defense whose influence varies according to their specialty and to the foreign policy issue at hand.

Who Shapes Foreign Policy?

The shapers of foreign policy are the nonofficial, informal players, but they are typically people of groups that have great influence in the making of foreign policy. Of course, the influence of any given group varies according to the party and the ideology that is dominant at a given moment.

1.Interest Group

Far and away the most important category of nonofficial player is the interest group—that is, the interest groups to whom one or more foreign policy issues are of long-standing and vital relevance. The type of interest group with the reputation for the most influence is the economic interest group. Yet the myths about their influence far outnumber and outweigh the realities. The actual influence of organized economic interest groups in foreign policy varies enormously from issue to issue and year to year. Most of these groups are "single-issue" groups and are therefore most active when their particular issue is on the agenda.

Another type of interest group with a well-founded reputation for influence in foreign policy is made up of people with strong attachments and identification to their country of national origin. A third type of interests group, one with a reputation that has been growing in the past two decades, is human rights interest group. Such groups are made up of people who, instead of having self-serving economic or ethnic interests in foreign policy, are genuinely concerned for welfare and treatment of people through the world—particularly those who suffer under harsh political regimes. The related type of group with a fast-growing influence is the ecological or environmental group, sometimes called the "Greens". Groups of this nature often depend more on demonstrations than on the usual forms and strategies of influence in Washington—lobbying and using electoral politics.

2.The Media

Here again, myth may outweigh truth about media influence in foreign policy. The most important element of the policy influence of the media is the speed and scale with which the media can spread political communications. In that factor alone, the media's influence is growing—more news reaches more people fast, and people's reaction times are therefore shorter. When we combine this ability to communicate faster with the "feedback" medium of public opinion polling, it becomes clear how the media have become so influential—they enable the American people to reach the president and the other official makers of foreign policy.

There is one other aspect of media influence to consider. Many unhappy politicians complain bitterly of "media bias". The complaint most often heard is the journalists have a liberal bias. Although this general complaint has never been adequately documented, one aspect of media bias has been shown. One proper influence of the media on foreign as well as domestic policy has been to make the American people far more cynical and skeptical than they would otherwise have been. Of any medium of communication or any one influential journalist or news program varies from case to case.

3.The Public Opinion and Action

Public opinion also influences U.S. foreign policy. Some scholars argue that public opinion on issues of foreign policy has two dimensions, militarism and non-militarism, isolationism and internationalism, creating four opinion groups. Others say that a third dimension, unilateralism and multilateralism, is also important. The public is not equally divided among these opinion groups, but foreign policy usually has to appeal across these dimensions to two or more groups to achieve widespread popular support.

As a rule, the American public is more interested in domestic affairs than foreign policy. Nevertheless, public opinion is often on the president's mind when creating or implementing foreign policy. Public opinion rarely determines what an administration does, but it often influences the emphasis that an administration places on a foreign initiative.

Public action sometimes shapes foreign policy, as in the widespread resistance to the draft during the Vietnam War. Growing public opposition to the war over time made it difficult to draft soldiers and reach the personnel levels that military desired.

Notes

1. Iran-Contra Affair 伊朗门事件: 美国向伊朗秘密出售武器一事被揭露，从而造成里根政府严重政治危机的事件，因人们把它与尼克松水门事件相比，故名“伊朗门事件”。它给人们留下了许多难以解开的谜团，也留下了许多值得思考的问题。

2. the Foreign Relations Committee 美国参议院外交委员会: 美国参议院外交关系委员会是美国参议院的一个常务委员会。它负责领导外交政策立法和在参议院辩论。外交关系委员会负责的是监督而不是管理工作，还负责对外援助以及武器销售的筹资。

3. the Armed Services Committee 美国军事委员会 : 通常称为众议院或参议院军事委员会，是美国常务委员会之一。它负责对国防部、美国武装力量、能源部大部分机构提供资金以及实施监督。

4. JCOS 参谋长联席会议: 全称“Joint Chiefs of Staff”，是分布在美国各军事力量主要兵种的首长小组。其机构与英联邦国家的参谋长委员会相类似，主要职能是兵种的协调和进行合作参谋。

5. CIA 中央情报局: 英文全称“Central Intelligence Agency”，通常是指美国政府的情报、间谍和反间谍机构，前身为战略情报局。主要职责是收集和分析全球政治、经济、文化、军事、科技等方面的情报，协调美国国内情报机构的活动，并把情报上报美国政府各部门。中情局的根本目的是透过情报工作维护美国的国家利益和国家安全。

6. NSC 国家安全委员会: 英文全称“The National Security Council”，1947 年 7 月成立，主要职责是统一有关美国国家内政、军事和外交政策，向总统提出建议，但不是决策机构，不能制定政策，只是总统有关安全政策的统筹、协调、参谋机构。

Unit 4 Instruments, Institutions and Values of American Foreign Policy

Instruments and Institutions of American Foreign Policy

1.The United Nations

The utility of the United Nations (**U.N.**[1]) to the United States as an instrument of foreign policy can too easily be underestimated. During the first decade or more after its founding in 1945, the United Nations was a direct servant of American interests. The most spectacular example of the use of the United Nations as an instrument of American foreign policy was the official U.N. Authorization and sponsorship of intervention in Korea with an international "peacekeeping force" in 1950.

The United States provided 40 percent of the U.N. Budget in 1946 and 26 percent of the $1.2 billion U.N. budget in 1997-1998. Many Americans feel that the United Nations does not give good value for the investment. But any evaluation of the United Nations must take into account the purpose for which the United States sought to create it—to achieve power without diplomacy. After World War Ⅱ, when the United States could no longer remain aloof from foreign policy, the nation's leaders sought to use their power to create an international structure that could be run with a minimum of diplomatic involvement—so that Americans could return to their normal domestic pursuits. As one constitutional scholar characterized the founding of the American republic in 1787, so can we say of the effort to found the United Nations—the U.S. sought to create "a machine that could go of itself".

2.The International Monetary Structure

Fear of a repeat of economic devastation that followed World War Ⅰ brought the United States together with its allies (except the **U.S.S.R.**[2]) to Brenton Woods, New Hampshire, in 1944 to create a new international economic structure for the postwar world. The result was two institutions: the International Bank for Reconstruction and Development (commonly called **the World Bank**[3]) and the International Monetary Fund.

The World Bank was set up to finance long-term capital. Leading nations took on the obligation of contributing funds to enable the World Bank to make loans to capital-hungry countries.

The International Monetary Fund (**IMF**[4]) was set up to prove means by aide for the short-term flow of money. After the war, the dollar, instead of gold, was the chief by which currencies of one country would be "changed into" currencies of another country for purpose of making international transactions. To permit debtor countries with no international balances to make purchases and investments, the IMF was set up to lend dollars to other appropriate currencies to needy member countries to help them to overcome temporary trade deficits. For many years after World War Ⅱ, the IMF, along with U.S. Foreign aid, in effect constituted the only international medium of exchange.

3.Economic Aid

Commitment to rebuilding war-torn countries came as early as commitment to the basic postwar international monetary structure. This is the way President Franklin Roosevelt put the case in a press conference in November 1942, less than one year after the United States entered World War II .

The particular form and timing for enacting American foreign aid was heavily influenced by Great Britain's sudden decision in 1947 that it would no longer be able to maintain its commitments to Greece and Turkey. Within three weeks of that announcement, President Truman recommended a $400 million direct aid program for Greece and Turkey, and by Mid-May of 1947, Congress approved it. Since President Truman had placed the Greek-Turkish action within the larger context of a commitment to help rebuild defend all countries the world over, wherever the leadership wished to develop democratic systems or to ward off communism, the **Greek-Turkish aid**[5] was followed quickly by the historically unprecedented program that came to be known as the Marshall Plan, named in honor of Secretary of State George C. Marshall.

The Marshall Plan—officially known as the European Recovery Program (ERP)—was essential for the rebuilding of war-torn Europe. By 1952, the United States had spent over $34 billion for the relief, reconstruction, and economic recovery of Western Europe. The emphasis was shifted in 1951, with passage of the Mutual Security Act, to building up European military capacity. Of the $48 billion appropriated between 1952 and 1961, over half went for military assistance, the rest for continuing economic aid. Over those years, the geographic emphasis of U.S. aid also shifted, toward South Korea, the Philippines, Vietnam, Iran, Greece, and Turkey for its political and economic purpoes. Many critics have argued that foreign aid is really aid for political and economic elites, not for the people. Although this is to a large extent true, it needs to be understood in a broader context.

The Values in American Foreign Policy

1.Legacies of the Traditional System

Two identifiable legacies flowed from the long tradition based on anti-statism(反国家主义), federalism and client status. One is the intermingling of domestic and foreign policy institution. The second is unilateralism—America's willingness to go to it alone. Each of these reveals a great deal about the values behind today's conduct of foreign policy.

2.Intermingling of Domestic and Foreign Policy

Because the major European powers once policed the world, American political leaders could treat foreign policy as a mere extension of domestic policy. The tariff is the best example. A tax on one category of imported goods as a favor to interests in one section of the country would directly cause friction elsewhere in the country. But the demands of those adversely affected could be met without directly other goods that would placate those who were complaining about the original tariff. In this manner, Congress was continually adding and adjusting tariffs on more and more classes of commodities.

An important aspect of the treatment of foreign affairs as an extension of domestic policy was amateurism. Unlike many other countries, America refused to develop a tradition of a separate foreign service composed of professional people who spent much of their adult lives in foreign countries, learning foreign languages, absorbing foreign cultures, and developing a sympathy for foreign points of view. Instead, Americans have tended to be highly suspicious of any American diplomat or entrepreneur who spoke sympathetically of any foreign viewpoint. No systematic progress was made to create a professional diplomatic corps until after the passage of the Foreign Service Act of 1946.

3.Unilateralism[6]

Unilateralism, not isolationism, was the American posture toward the world until the middle of the twentieth century. Isolationism means trying to cut off contacts with the outside, to be a self-sufficient fortress. America was never isolationist; it preferred unilateralism, or "going it alone". Americans have always been more likely to rally around the President in support of direct action rather than for a sustained, diplomatic involvement.

4.The Great Leap to World Power

The traditional era of U.S. Foreign policy came to an end with World War Ⅰ for several important reasons. First, the "balance of power" system that had kept the major European powers from world war for a hundred years had collapsed. Second, the United States was no longer a client state but in fact one of the great powers. Third, the United States was quick to shed its traditional system of American foreign policy. Yet there were no discernible changes in America's approach to foreign policy in the period between World War Ⅰ and World War Ⅱ. After World War Ⅰ, as one foreign policy analyst put it "the United States withdraws once more into its insularity".

The Great Leap in foreign policy was finally made thirty years after conditions demanded it and only then after another world war. Following World War Ⅱ, pressure for a new tradition came into direct conflict with the old. The new tradition required foreign entanglements; the old tradition feared them deeply. The new tradition required diplomacy; the old distrusted it. The new tradition required acceptance of antagonistic political systems; the embraced democracy was aloof from all else.

The values of the new tradition were all apparent during the Cold War. Instead of unilateralism, the United States pursued **multilateralism**[7], entering into treaties with other nations to achieve its foreign policy goal. What's more, furthering capitalism has long been one of the values guiding American foreign policy and this might be true at the end of twentieth century than at any time before.

Notes

1. **U.N. 联合国：**英文全称“United Nations”，是1945年第二次世界大战后成立的国际组织，是一个由主权国家组成的国际组织。1945年10月24日，在美国旧金山签订生效的《联合国宪章》标志着联合国正式成立。联合国致力于促进各国在国际法、国际安全、经济发展、社会进步、人权及实现世界和平方面的合作。

2. **U.S.S.R. 苏联：**全称“苏维埃社会主义共和国联盟”（Union of Soviet Socialist Republics）。1922年12月30日由俄罗斯苏维埃联邦社会主义共和国、白俄罗斯苏维埃社会主义共和国、乌克兰苏维埃社会主义共和国、外高加索苏维埃社会主义联邦共和国合并而成的社会主义联邦制国家，于1991年12月25日解体。

3. **the World Bank 世界银行：**成立于1945年12月27日，是一个国际组织。其一开始的使命是帮助在第二次世界大战中被破坏的国家的重建。今天它的任务是资助国家克服穷困，它的各机构在减轻贫困和提高生活水平的使命中发挥着独特的作用。

4. **IMF 国际货币基金组织：**英文全称“International Monetary Fund”，根据1944年7月在布雷顿森林会议签订的《国际货币基金协定》，于1945年12月27日在华盛顿成立。与世界银行同时成立，并列为世界两大金融机构之一，其职责是监察货币汇率和各国贸易情况，提供技术和资金协助，确保全球金融制度运作正常。

5. **Greek-Turkish aid 希腊和土耳其援助：**二战后整个东欧基本都属于苏联的势力范围，而西欧独立自主的国家基本也只有法国、德国西部、丹麦、瑞典和波兰。希腊和土耳其境内共产党势力十分强大，有着推翻资本主义政权，建立共和主义政权的可能，所以以美国为首的资本主义大国援助希腊和土耳其，实际是要抢在苏联之前在这片东欧地中海沿岸的国家建立立足点。

6. **unilateralism 单边主义：**指举足轻重的特定大国，不考虑大多数国家和民众的愿望，单独或带头退出或挑战已制订或商议好了的维护国际性、地区性、集体性和平、发展、进步的规则和制度，并对全局或局部的和平、发展、进步有破坏性的影响和后果的行为与倾向。

7. **multilateralism 多边主义：**原指不完全依赖俄罗斯或者独联体内部来解决问题，而是谋求多边发展，利用外部世界一切可能利用的因素和机会，既为自己吸收更多的发展动力，又可避免单方面依赖而受制于俄罗斯。

References

[1] BARDES B A, SCHMIDT S W, et al. American government and politics today: the essentials [M]. Connecticut: Thomson Wadsworth, 2002.

[2] HOLMES J, ENGELHARDT M J, ELDER R E. American government: essentials & perspectives[M]. New York: McGraw-Hill, Inc.,1994.

[3] JAMES M. The Obamians：the struggle inside the White House to redefine American power[M]. New York: Viking Adult, 2012.

[4] JENTLESON B W. American foreign policy: the dynamics of choice in the 21th century[M]. New York: London,2000.

[5] KEGLEY W C J. American foreign policy[M]. New York: St. Martin's Press,1996.
[6] LASSER W. Perspectives on American government[M]. Massachusetts: D.C.Heath and Company,1996.
[7] GINSBURG L. American government [M]. New York : London, 2000.
[8] LOWI T J, GINSBURG B, SHEPSLE K A. American government: power and purpose [M] New York: London, 2004.
[9] MILLER R L. American government[M]. Texas: National Textbook Company, 2002.
[10] PATERSON T G, CLIFFORD J G, MADDOCK S J, et al. American foreign relations: a history to 1920（Volume 1）[M]. Boston: Houghton Mifflin Company, 2000.
[11] SCHMIDT S, BARDES B A. American government and politics today[M]. Texas: Thomson Wadsworth ,2008.
[12] WELCH S, GRUHL J. Understanding American government[M]. Connecticut: Thomson Wadsworth, 2008.
[13] WILSON J Q, DILULIO J J. American government[M]. Boston: Houghton Mifflin,1998.
[14] WOOLLEY P J, PAPA A R. American politics: core argument & current controversy[M]. New Jersey: Prentice Hall,1998.
[15] 拉塞尔・邓肯，约瑟夫・戈达德 . 当代美国 [M]. 北京：中国人民大学出版社，2009.
[16] 亨利・基辛格 . 美国的全球战略 [M]. 胡利平，凌建平，等，译 . 海口：海南出版社，2012.
[17] 江宁康 . 美国概况——美国历史、社会与文化 [M]. 南京：东南大学出版社，2013.
[18] 王俊生，刘沛富 . 最新英美概况 [M]. 北京：外语教学与研究出版社，2012.
[19] 王玮，戴超武 . 美国外交思想史 [M]. 北京：人民出版社，2007.
[20] 吴心伯 . 21 世纪的美国与中美关系 [M]. 北京：时事出版社，2013.
[21] 周琪 . 意识形态与美国外交 [M]. 上海 : 上海人民出版社，2006.
[22] 熊志勇 . 美国政治与外交决策 [M]. 北京：北京大学出版社，2011.
[23] 周柏林 . 美国新霸权主义 [M]. 天津：天津人民出版社，2002.
[24] 赵学功 . 当代美国外交 [M]. 北京：社会科学文献出版社，2012.

Chapter Ten

Major Diplomatic Events

Unit 1 American-Spanish War

Spanish-American War happened in 1898. The United States launched the war to capture the Spanish territory of **Cuba[1], Puerto Rico[2]** and the **Philippines[3]**. It is the first imperialist war launched by the powers to carve up the world. There are three main reasons for this war: firstly, at the end of 19th century, the United States entered a period of imperialism. American monopoly capital consortium urgently needed to open up new markets, outlets of investment and sources of raw materials. Secondly, people's struggle in Spain created a favorable environment for the United States. Thirdly, Spanish army's brutal repression of the Cuban insurgents irritated the American people, and endangered the economic interests of American capitalists. So the United States sent **USS Maine[4]** to protect the interests of American businessmen. However, on February 15th, 1898, USS Maine in Cuba exploded and sank in Havana harbor. The Explosion of USS Maine aroused strong repercussions of American press and great domestic anger.

On March 27th, 1898, the United States required Spain through the Spanish minister of a cease-fire and abolishment of the concentration camp law in Cuba. In order to avoid combat with America, on April 9th Spain announced a truce. But the U.S. Congress announced the resolution which recognized Cuban independence, demanded the Spanish withdrawal（撤离）from Cuba, granted the President the right to use force, and at the same time declared that the U.S. had no intention to annex Cuba. On April 22th, the **U.S. Navy[5]** blocked Cuban ports and captured Spanish merchant ships. On April 24th, Spain declared the war on the United States, and the next day the United States declared the war as well.

America had been ready for war. The United States had established a strong fleet known as the world's third and they were deployed on different strategic points in the world. Among which the one in Hong Kong had been ready for a war for a very long time. Congress had conscripted 200,000 soldiers and had rapid-fire artilleries（大炮）, telegraph, telephone and other advanced equipment. Conversely, Spain was totally unprepared. Only 12,000 of 200,000 soldiers in Cuba could fight, and the rest were old and sick. They owned only a few old-fashioned wood warships. In the Philippines, there were only 42,000 troops, and Spain was in anarchy. Military profession generally believed that Spain had no chance of winning in the war with the United States. Wars took place in the Philippines, Cuba and Puerto Rico simultaneously.

1. The Philippines

On August 13th, 1898, under the joint Strike of the United States Army and Navy, the Spanish army in Manila only took symbolic resistance before the ceasefire announced. Later, the U.S. Army took three years to suppress the Philippines' resistance. What the Philippines wanted was independence, not imperialist masters. Then, after about 50 years, the United States recognized that the Philippines had the ability of self-government. However, according to the provisions related to the Philippines in the "peace treaty", the United States wanted to intervene in affairs of the Far East for a long time.

2. Cuba

Cuba is the main battlefield of the Spanish-American War. The United States set up Expeditionary Forces consisting of 2.5 million people, and trained them intensely in Tampa, Florida and subsequently dispatched them to Cuba. The U.S. Army wanted to attack Havana, but the Navy was requested to attack Santiago, and they reached an agreement to attack Santiago together. At this time, the Cuban army had liberated almost all of the land, and surrounded Santiago. After the negotiation with each other, the American troops and Cuban insurrectionary（暴动的）army began to combat together. On July 16th, the Spanish troops exhausted their supplies and ammunition and 24,000 troops laid down their arms and surrendered. The United States did the same thing to Cuba just as what they had done to the Philippines. The United States left aside the Cuban insurrectionary army and negotiated with Spain alone, and they prohibited the Cuban insurrectionary army from going into the city. Again, America pocketed the fruit of victory without sharing with anyone else.

3. Puerto Rico

On July 25th, 1898, 3,000 American soldiers under the command of Nelson Myers landed in Puerto Rico and established a military base. In early August, the United States dispatched another 10,000 troops there. All the troops together besieged the capital of Puerto Rico, San Juan from four different directions. After several skirmishes, the United States captured the island of Puerto Rico at the price of 50 casualties.

On December 10th, the two sides signed the *Peace Treaty* in Paris. The provisions were: Spain recognized Cuban independence and transferred the possession of Puerto Rico, Guam and the Philippines to the USA. America paid 20 million to Spain as compensation of owning the Philippines.

The Spanish-American War marked that the world had entered the age of imperialism. Both sides taking part in this war were imperialist countries, so it was regarded as the first imperialist war in which the powers wanted to re-divide the world. It marked American rising as a major military power. This Maritime conflict made the U.S. caught in the complex problems of the Far East, and warned the European powers who dared to contend against the U.S. Military. For Americans, it marked that America would be more involved in world affairs and began to set foot on the road of external expansion.

Notes

1. Cuba 古巴： 即古巴共和国，意为“肥沃之地”“好地方”。是北美洲加勒比海北部的群岛国家，哈瓦那是古巴的经济、政治中心和首都。古巴是现存的世界上为数不多的社会主义国家之一，而且是美洲唯一的社会主义国家。在历史上以20世纪60年代的猪湾事件和古巴导弹危机闻名。

2. Puerto Rico 波多黎各： 位于加勒比海大安的列斯群岛东部。包括波多黎各岛及别克斯、库莱夫拉等小岛。北临大西洋，南濒加勒比海，东与美属、英属维尔京群岛隔水相望，西隔莫纳海峡，同多米尼加共和国为邻，首府为圣胡安。

3. the Philippines 菲律宾： 位于西太平洋，是东南亚的一个群岛国家，也是一个多民族国家。菲律宾人的祖先是亚洲大陆的移民。在14世纪前后，建立了海上强国苏禄王国。1565年，西班牙侵占菲律宾，统治300多年。1898年美国占领菲律宾。1942年，日本占领菲律宾。二战后，菲律京重新沦为美国殖民地。1946年，菲律宾独立。

4. USS Maine 缅因号： 1898年，美军战舰缅因号在古巴哈瓦那离奇沉没（现时相信是船内锅炉爆炸），它的爆炸成为美国发动战争的借口之一。

5. U.S. Navy 美国海军： 美国武装力量的一个重要军种，负责管理所有与海上军事行动有关的事务。其职责是配备、训练和武装一支有能力赢得战争、阻止入侵和保证海域自由的海军战斗部队。美国海军下设七个舰队，约500,000现役和预备役军人、279艘现役军舰和4,000架飞机，是目前世界上规模最庞大、吨位最高、装备最先进、总体实力远超于其他国家的世界上最强的海军。

Unit 2 World War Ⅰ and World War Ⅱ

1. World War Ⅰ

When the First World War broke out in Europe in 1914, the United States at first remained neutral. It was a European War, according to most Americans, and no U.S. interests were involved. In addition, the United States was largely a nation of European immigrants, and Americans were deeply divided about whom to support. It thus makes sense for both foreign policy and domestic political reasons to stay out of the war. Indeed, when Present Woodrow Wilson ran for a second term in 1916, he used the slogan "he kept us out of the war" to win reelection.

Nevertheless, several events, especially Germany's policy of unrestricted submarine warfare, under which German subs sank U.S. ships carrying cargo to Great Britain and France, caused immense problems in U.S.-German relations. Finally, declaring that the United States was fighting "a war to end all wars", Wilson in 1917 led the nation into the conflict. American troops and supplies began to arrive just when the human and material resources of the United States' main allies, Great Britain and France were nearly exhausted. Even though the United States entered the war late, its armed forces and economic assistance swung the tide of victory to the Allies' side.

After World War Ⅰ, Wilson put great faith in **Collective Security**[1] to maintain the peace. To Wilson, collective security was based on the premise that if one country attacked another, the other countries in the international community should all unite against the attacking country. Countries would thus ensure their security collaboratively.

At the Paris Peace Conference following the war, Wilson was instrumental in creating a new international organization, **the League of Nations**[2], to implement collective security. However, he failed to build support for the League in the United States. A Democratic President with a Senate controlled by Republicans, Wilson failed to include GOP senators among the U.S. delegates to the peace to conference. Besides, partisan reasons, many senators believed that U.S. membership in the League of Nations would fly in the face of traditional U.S. isolationism and unilateralism. The Senate thus refused to give the necessary two-thirds vote to ratify the Treaty of Versailles, which formalized the terms of the end of the war, and the United States never joined the League.

2. The Inter-War Years

Following rejection of the *Treaty of Versailles*, most Americans thought that U.S. interests were best served by isolationism and unilateralism. Nonetheless, new U.S. industries sought more raw materials from foreign countries and American businesses sought new markets overseas. During the 1920s, the United States became the world's leading source of credit and goods as the American economy prospered.

As Europeans rebuilt their economics, they presented a challenge to U.S. industry. Consequently, the Republican-controlled Congress during the 1920s raised tariffs to protect U.S. industry from foreign competition. In 1930, Congress passed the extremely high **Smoot-Hawley Tariff**[3]**,** and other countries responded by raising their tariffs. The impact that higher tariffs had on world trade, in conjunction with **the Great Depression**[4], was dramatic. By 1932, trade dropped to about one-third of its former level.

As the Great Depression of the 1930s worsened, some Americans concluded that isolationism and unilateralism were wrong. They argued that the Depression was worse than it may have been because of the decline in trade brought about by high tariffs. Some also attributed the rise of Germany's Adolf Hitler（希特勒）and Japanese and Italian leaders bent on world domination to the economic turmoil of the times. In addition, they argued that without the United States, the League of Nations had proven incapable of preserving peace.

The United States and the rest of the world did little to oppose German, Japanese, and Italian aggression in the 1930s, and the world slid toward war. Congress was particularly isolationism, passing *Neutrality Acts* to keep the United States from becoming involved in foreign conflicts. President Franklin D. Roosevelt occasionally warned against this mentality, but he also knew that the American people and Congress were unwilling to get pulled into another world war without a more direct threat to America itself.

3. World War Ⅱ

The World War Ⅱ began on September 1st, 1939, when Nazi Germany invaded Poland.

Great Britain and France immediately declared war on Germany. In the United States, strong isolationism sentiment persisted. The country remained formally neutral even though it tilted more and more toward Great Britain. Despite the tilt, the United States stayed out of the war for over two years after it had begun in Europe. This changed on December 7th, 1941, when Japan bombed Pearl Harbor. The next day, the United States declared war on Japan. A few days later, Germany and Italy declared war on the United States, and the United States responded. The United States was fully engaged in a global war, participating in the Grand Alliance of the United States, Great Britain, the Soviet Union, and several other allied nations against **the Axis**[5] powers of Japan, Germany and Italy.

This global conflict transformed the United States' role in the world. Before World War Ⅱ, the United States was an essentially isolationist country. By the end of the war, the United States was the leader of the most powerful military coalition that the world had ever seen. What's more, the United States had the only major economy in the world that had not been decimated by war. These realities forced the United States to reassess the principles that had guided its foreign policy for the previous century and a half.

After the United States entered the World War Ⅱ, its phenomenal industrial and military mobilization secured victory. The war also transformed American society. The war ended in Europe on May 8th, 1945, with the Allies bruised and victorious. The war against Japan ended after the United States dropped two atomic bombs on Japan, one on Hiroshima（广岛）on August 6th, 1945, and the other on Nagasaki（长崎）three days later. On August 15th, Japan surrendered. The birth of nuclear age made it more important that, in building the postwar world, the victorious powers somehow found a way to keep the peace.

One way to do this, many believed, was to create an improved version of the League of Nations, this time with the participation of all of the world's great powers, including the United States. Thus, even before the war ended, the United States and fifty-one of its allies met in San Francisco to create the United Nations（UN）, an international governmental organization, whose purpose was to guarantee social well-being around the world. Believing that the collapse of international trade in the 1930s created conditions that led to the rise of dictators and the beginning of the World War Ⅱ, the victorious powers also created new international economic organizations to encourage trade, which mainly included the International Monetary Fund（IMF）, the World Bank, and the General Agreement on Tariffs and Trade（GATT）. The IMF was created to stabilize exchange rates among major currencies and set their value in terms of the dollar and gold, and the World Bank tasked to help the world recover economically from the destruction of World War Ⅱ. The GATT led to negotiations that substantially reduced tariffs. GATT remained in place until the World Trade Organization（WTO）was created in 1995. The IMF and World Bank continue to operate today.

The U.S. intention to participate in these institutions indicated a shift in U.S. attitudes regarding isolationism and unilateralism. To participate in these institutions, the United States had to be less isolationist and less unilateralist than before the war. Gradually, then, the country moved toward internationalism and multilateralism—a belief that foreign and military policy actions should be taken cooperation with other states.

Notes

1. Collective Security 集体安全政策：又称"集体安全保障"。众多国家对国家安全和国际和平的集体相互保障。在集体安全保障下，侵略者进攻集体安全体系中任何一个国家即被视为侵犯所有国家。

2. the League of Nations 国际联盟：简称"国联"，是《凡尔赛条约》签订后组成的国际组织，1934 年 9 月 28 日至 1935 年 2 月 23 日的最高峰时期，国联曾拥有 58 个会员国。宗旨是减少武器数量、平息国际纠纷及维持民众的生活水平。美国没有加入国际联盟。二战结束以后，国际联盟的角色被联合国取代。

3. Smoot-Hawley Tariff 斯姆特—霍利关税法：于 1930 年 6 月 17 日经签署成为法律，该法案将 2 000 多种进口商品关税提升到历史最高水平。一些经济学家认为，斯姆特—霍利法案是导致美欧之间贸易规模从 1929 年的历史高位急遽衰退到 1932 年历史低位的催化剂，这次衰退伴随着的是大萧条的开始。

4. the Great Depression 大萧条：指 1929 年至 1933 年之间发源于美国的经济危机。

5. the Axis 轴心国：指在第二次世界大战中结成的法西斯国家联盟，领导者是纳粹德国、意大利和日本及与他们合作的一些国家和占领国。名称源于 1936 年 11 月 1 日意大利法西斯独裁者墨索里尼在与纳粹德国达成协调外交政策的同盟条约后不久对此评价的一次演说："柏林和罗马的垂直线不是壁垒，而是轴心"，因柏林和罗马在同一经度线上，因此，后人就把法西斯同盟称为"轴心"，参加国称为"轴心国"。

Unit 3 The Cold War and Containment, Cuba, and Vietnam

1. The Cold War and Containment: 1947—1960

As mentioned at the first unit of this chapter, the relationship between the United States and the Soviet Union deteriorated（恶化）after the World War Ⅱ. The Cold War began.

The Truman Doctrine and the Marshall Plan were the linchpins of the strategy of containment. As postulated by diplomat George Kennan（乔治凯南）, who liked many Americans believed that the Soviet Union wanted to dominate the world. The United States would apply "counterforce" wherever the Soviet Union applied pressure. Containment had other key elements. In 1949, the United States and eleven other countries signed **the North Atlantic Treaty**[1], which stated that all signatories considered an attack against one an attack against all. This was the first occasion when the United States joined a political and military alliance during peacetime. The following year, treaty members created the North Atlantic Treaty Organization（NATO）, a defense alliance to implement the treaty.

When the Koren War broke out in 1950, the United States sent troops under UN auspices to defend South Korea. When U.S. Forces arrived, they pushed back the North Korea forces, but the United States then changed its war aims from defending South Korea to unifying Korea. When U.S. forces drove north and approached Korea's border with China, however, China entered the war and pushed the Americans back. Finally, the warring parties reached a truce in 1953, dividing Korea almost exactly where it had been divided. It remains divided today, with U.S. Troops deployed along the border to protect South Korea.

Starting in the 1950 s, much of the U.S. military strategy was based on nuclear weapons and deterrence. Deterrence was the theory that a potential enemy wanted to attack but knew that it would in turn be attacked, it would not attack. During the 1950s and 1960s, as the United States and the Soviet Union developed large nuclear arsenals, a new version of deterrence developed called **Mutual Assured Destruction (MAD[2])**. Under MAD, both the United States and the Soviet Union were deterred from launching a nuclear attack because each knew that if they attacked first, the other would still have enough nuclear weapons remaining to destroy the attacker as a functioning society.

Throughout the 1950 s and into the 1960 s, the world seemed divided into two camps, one led by the United States and the other by the Soviet Union. Containment was the core U.S. foreign policy. With some modifications, it remained so until the Cold War ended. Meanwhile, moralism（道德主义）and pragmatism（实用主义）remained key principles of U.S. foreign policy. Isolationism and unilateralism had been discarded as principles of foreign policy.

2. Containment, Cuba, and Vietnam: 1961—1969

Containing the Soviet Union and at the same time establishing cordial relations with it to lesson the peril of nuclear war was a top issue on President Kennedy's foreign policy agenda in the period of 1960s. Thus, in 1961, leaders from the United States and the Soviet Union had a meeting in Vienna, Austria. The meeting did not go well. Both leaders returned to their respective countries and increased military spending. In 1962, the Soviet Union began to deploy intermediate-range ballistic missiles in Cuba, only ninety miles from Florida, leading to **the Cuba Missile Crisis[3]**. The United States reacted strongly, placing a naval blockade around quences. After several days during which the world was closer to nuclear war than it had ever been, the Soviet Union backed down and withdraw the missiles. The world breathed a sigh of relief.

The Cuba Missiles Crisis led a period of improved U.S.-Soviet relations. During the crisis, the United States and the Soviet Union had marched to the edge of nuclear war. Thus, in 1963, the two nations concluded a partial nuclear test ban treaty and installed a "hot line" between Washington and Moscow to allow the leaders of the two countries to talk directly during crisis.

The Cuba Crisis confirmed the majority of American belief that the Soviet Union was an expansionist power. Despite its danger, most Americans believed that containment was the correct strategy, and that the United States remained the moral defender of liberty and justice, acting pragmatically but always with restrains to prevent communist expansion.

The Vietnam War started in the 1950 s, but it was in the mid-1960 s that U.S. bombing and ground operations began, and they escalated quickly. While many in South Vietnam were grateful for U.S. assistance, The United States became embroiled in a civil war in which it was difficult to determine friend from foe. Eventually, the U.S. presence in Vietnam grew to more than 500,000 troops, 58,000 of whom were killed. As deaths mounted and costs grew, many Americans asked questions they had rarely asked before. Was the United States on the side of justice in Vietnam, or had it only replaced France there as a colonial power? How much killing and how great a cost would be to the United States? Increasingly, U.S. citizens became less persuaded that their mission in Vietnam was moral. By the end of 1960s, Americans were not as sure of their moral superiority as they had been, nor were they sure that containment was the proper strategy on which to base their foreign policy.

Notes

1. the North Atlantic Treaty 北大西洋公约：是北约组织签订的条约。北约组织是一个为实现防卫协作而建立的国际组织。1949 年 3 月 18 日美国和西欧国家公开组建北大西洋公约组织，于 1949 年 4 月 4 日在美国华盛顿签署《北大西洋公约》后正式成立。为与以前苏联为首的东欧集团国成员相抗衡，使成员国一旦受到攻击时，其他成员国可以作出即时反应。但这一条款在 9•11 事件之前，一直都未动用过。

2. MAD 核威慑：英文全称"Mutual Assured Destruction"，即指核国家基于核武器的威力为国家利益和政治目的的行为。核威慑是指美国和苏联在冷战时期所使用的一种战略，即把拥有核武器作为威慑对方的一种重要手段，往往需要相当数量的核弹。

3. the Cuba Missile Crisis 古巴导弹危机：1962 年，加勒比海地区发生了一场震惊世界的古巴导弹危机。它由苏联在古巴部署导弹、美国则坚持要求撤除导弹而引发。这是冷战期间美苏两大国之间最激烈的一次对抗。

Unite 4 Détente and Containment Revisited and Renewed

1. Détente[1] and Human Rights: 1969—1981

When Richard M. Nixon was inaugurated as President in 1969, he declared it was time to move from "an area of conformation" to "an area of negotiation" in relations with the Soviet Union. And he undertook policies that began this transformation. The improvement in U.S.-Soviet relations were called Détente（缓和）. As Nixon calculated how to achieve these objectives, some criticized his approach as cynical. Emphasizing pragmatism to the virtual exclusion of moralism, Nixon's approach remained many of old-style European its earliest days. Critics pointed to **the Nixon Doctrine**[2]—that the United States would provide military aid to countries but not do the fighting for them—as evidence of this cynicism.

The changed nature of U.S.-Soviet relations brought about by Détente was best illustrated by the frequency of summit meetings. From 1972 to 1979, American and Soviet leaders met six times, but Détente was more than summitry. It also included increased trade, arms control agreements. Détente improved East-West relations in Europe as well.

When Jimmy Carter became President in 1977, he too intended to pursue détente. However, he rejected Nixon's foreign policy cynicism. Carter instead emphasized **human rights**[3], that is, the protection of people's basic freedoms and needs. This found a sympathetic ear among many Americans. Once again, they believed, the United States would emphasize morality in foreign policy.

Détente finally died in 1979 when the Soviet Union invaded Afghanistan. Described by Carter in his 1980 States of the Union Address as "the most serious threat to peace since the Second World War", the Soviet invasion led to an immediate increase in U.S. defense spending. Carter also adopted a more hard-line approach to foreign policy, announcing the **Carter Doctrine**[4] under which the United States would fight to prevent any further Soviet expansion toward the Persian Gulf.

2. Containment Revisited and Renewed: 1981—1989

The tense U.S.-Soviet relations during Jimmy Carter's last year as President became confrontational during President Ronald Reagan's first term in office. Reagan accelerated the U.S. arms buildup and initiated an activist foreign policy in response to Soviet influence in developing countries. In addition, Reagan emphasized morality in American foreign policy and pushed to create an open international economic system.

By 1984, however, relations between the United States and the Soviet Union were beginning to improve. The two countries upgraded their hot-lines and agreed to expand arms-control talks. Most importantly, the rhetoric from both capitals deescalated. What happened? First, the 1984 U.S. presidential election constrained U.S. rhetoric. Second, U.S. foreign policy initiatives had an impact on Moscow as, in addition to its arm buildup, the United States implemented **the Reagan Doctrine**[5], under which the United States provided arms to anti-Soviet movements fighting pro-Soviet governments in Afghanistan, Angola（安哥拉）, Mozambique（莫桑比克）, and Nicaragua（尼加拉瓜）. These programs increased the cost of Soviet involvements there and led Soviet leaders to rethink their foreign policy. Finally, the Soviet Union had serious internal problems. Its economy was performing poorly and it had a leadership crisis. These problems had to be addressed. To do this, the Soviet Union needed a less confrontational relationship with the United States.

Recognizing this, Soviet President **Mikhail Gorbachev**[6] worked with Reagan to improve relations after Gorbachev became the Soviet leader in 1985. Gorbachev introduced "perestroika"—reforms in domestic, foreign and military policies that transformed the Soviet Union and U.S.-Soviet relations. Although the reforms were intended to address the serious problems that the Soviet Union faced, they eventually led to the end of the Cold War and the demise of the Soviet Union.

Notes

1. Détente 美苏关系的缓和：这一时期的美国，由于受经济危机的冲击，经济增长趋于缓慢，侵越战争受到严重挫折，军事力量被苏联赶上，美国在美苏争霸中从战略进攻转为战略防御。

2. the Nixon Doctrine 尼克松主义：美国第37届总统理查德·尼克松执政时期所提出的调整美国对外战略的指导原则，收缩美国全球义务、调整国际关系的外交新方针。尼克松主义的实质是美国霸权地位衰落的产物和表现。

3. human rights 人权：人权（基本人权或自然权利）是指"人，因其为人而应享有的权利"。它主要的含义是：每个人都应该受到合乎人权的对待。人权的这种普适性和道义性，是它的两种基本特征。在当今的国际社会，维护和保障人权是一项基本道义原则。是否合乎保障人权的要求已成为评判一个集体（无论是政治上的还是经济上的）优劣的重要标准。但是，在具体实践的层面上，对于人权的具体定义以及保障人权的具体方式都存在着相当大的争议，甚至引发了很严重的冲突。

4. Carter Doctrine 卡特主义：美国总统卡特1980年1月在国情咨文中提出的一项对海湾地区的政策声明。鉴于苏联军队于1979年12月侵入阿富汗，卡特在这份咨文中警告苏联不要利用伊朗和阿富汗的动乱作为借口，谋求实现苏联长期以来企图获得一个温水港的目标。

5. the Reagan Doctrine 里根主义：主要内容是与苏联争夺第三世界。认为苏联在20世纪70年代势力伸展过长，内外交困，难以巩固已经取得的进展；美国应准备以"低烈度战争"阻止和反击苏联在第三世界对美国利益的威胁，遏制它的扩张主义，把它取得的政治和军事进展推回去；鼓励第三世界亲美右翼政府的活动，加强对其他第三世界国家和抗苏武装的经济、军事援助，稳定局势。

6. Mikhail Gorbachev 米哈伊尔·谢尔盖耶维奇·戈尔巴乔夫：1931年3月2日生于苏联南部斯塔夫罗波尔边疆区普利里沃利诺耶村，苏联最后一任总书记、总统。

Unit 5 Searching for a New International Order: 1989—2001

George Bush, vice president during President Reagan's two terms, assumed that the presidency in 1989 pledged to continue Reagan's foreign policy directions. However, the pace and scope of change in Eastern Europe and the Soviet Union raised questions about the entire direction of U.S. foreign policy. The first question came from Eastern Europe. In 1989, the people of many Eastern European states revolted against their governments. During previous rebellions, Soviet troops stationed in Eastern Europe subdued rebellions. This time, Gorbachev ordered Soviet troops to remain in their barracks. The rebellions continued, and the government of several countries in Eastern Europe fell.

The United States was not quite sure how to respond. At first, Bush proceeded cautiously. As it became clear that the revolutions were irreversible, the United States and other western states helped these Eastern European states try to establish the so-called "democratic political and free market economic systems". Remarkably, in matter of months, the so-called "**Iron Curtain**[1]" in Europe had collapsed, with almost no serious bloodshed.

The 1990 Iraqi invasion of **Kuwait**[2] produced a new challenge. The Bush Administration believed that the invasion threatened vital U.S. interests, and the United Nations passed a resolution authorizing the use of force to expel Iraq from Kuwait. Shortly after Congress voted to support the use of military force against Iraq, the **Persian Gulf War**[3] began in January 1991. U.S. and allied force defeated Iraq in a matter of weeks. The objective—expelling Iraq from Kuwait—had been achieved with few U.S. casualties.

Meanwhile, starling events were unfolding in the Soviet Union. Under Gorbachev, the Soviet Union posed less and less of a threat as the United States and Soviet Union forged an increasingly close relationship. Weakened by a failed coup at tempt against Gorbachev in the summer of 1991, its economy was in shambles, and was torn by internal dissent and the desires for nationalities for independence, the Soviet Union collapsed. The Cold War was over, as was the need for containment. Once again, Americans asked questions: What would U.S. strategy be? With the Cold War over, should the United States cut defense spending, and if so, how much? How much aid should the United States send to its former enemy to help it survive its collapse? What criteria would guide decisions about where and when to employ U.S. forces abroad in a world with only one remaining superpower?

These were the complex questions Bill Clinton faced when he assumed the presidency in 1993. Defining the American role in this world presented a challenge. Clinton's agenda centered on implementing **Engagement and Enlargement**[4], shaping new international economic relationships, deciding when U.S. armed forces should be used overseas, and puzzling over what role the United States should play in the post-Cold War world. Engagement meant that the United States would not retreat into isolationism as it did after World War I and for a short time after World War Ⅱ. Engagement implied that the United States relied on negotiations and cooperation rather than confrontation and conflict, although it would use force, when necessary. Enlargement meant that the United States would promote democracy, open markets, and other Western political, economic, and social values. In practice, Engagement and Enlargement led to the implementation of the Partnership for Peace program with countries in Eastern Europe and the former Soviet Union and the expansion of NATO.

International economic issues were another focus of Clinton's activities. With help from members of his own Democratic Party as well as congressional Republicans, he guided **the North American Free Trade Agreement** (**NAFTA**[5]) into law, establishing the free flow of goods among Canada, Mexico, and the United States. The United States under Clinton also played a major role in initiating two other major free trade areas: the Free Trade Area of the Americans and the Asia-Pacific Economic Cooperation agreements, as well as creating the World Trade Organization (WTO), charged with overseeing world trade, judging trade disputes, and lowering tariffs.

Notes

1. Iron Curtain 铁幕: 原意为封锁某国家或某集团，后转为某国家或某集团对自己实行铁桶似的禁锢。该词出现于第二次世界大战后。当时法国总理克列孟梭在众议院宣称:"要在布尔什维克主义周围装上铁幕。"1946 年 3 月 5 日,英国前首相邱吉尔在美国富尔顿城威斯敏斯特学院的演说中,变"铁幕" 一词之意而首先公开使用,攻击苏联和东欧社会主义国家"用铁幕笼罩起来"。此后,西方国家用"铁幕国家"来蔑称社会主义国家。

2. Kuwait 科威特: 位于阿拉伯半岛东北部、波斯湾西北部的君主专制国家。在南部与沙特阿拉伯、北部与伊拉克分别接壤。该国首都科威特城与该国名称同名。科威特的石油和天然气资源丰富。科威特的已探明石油储量 940 亿桶,约为世界总储量的 10% 。石油、天然气工业为国民经济的支柱,其产值占国内生产总值的 45%。

3. Persian Gulf War 海湾战争: 指以美国为首的多国部队于 1991 年 1 月 17 日—2 月 28 日在联合国安理会授权下,为恢复科威特领土完整而对伊拉克进行的局部战争,同时也是人类战争史上现代化程度最高、使用新式武器最多、投入军费最多的一场战争。主要战斗包括历时 42 天的空袭和历时 100 小时的陆战。海湾战争是美军自越南战争后主导参加的第一场大规模局部战争。在战争中,美军首次将大量高科技武器投入实战,展示了压倒性的制空、制电磁优势。通过海湾战争,美国进一步加强了与波斯湾地区国家的军事、政治合作,强化了美军在该地区的军事存在。海湾战争对冷战后国际新秩序的建立产生了深刻影响,同时,它所展示的现代高科技条件下作战的新情况和新特点,对军事战略、战役战术和军队建设等问题带来了众多启示。

4. Engagement and Enlargement 参与与扩展战略: 利用冷战后对美国总体有利的国际形势,加强介入和参与国际和地区事务的力度,扩展自由世界的疆界,实现美国的世界领导地位。

5. NAFTA 北美自由贸易协定: 英文全称" North American Free Trade Agreement",由美、加、墨三国组成,经过几年协商,在 1994 年 1 月 1 日正式生效。

Unit 6 The War on Terrorism and Wars in Iraq and Afghanistan

1. The War on Terrorism: 2001 to the Present

During his first months as President, George W. Bush conducted an active foreign policy. By September 2001, the Bush administration had full foreign agenda. Relations with Latin America, Europe, Russia and China all loomed large, as did security, international economics, immigration, drugs and the environment. However, the new administration had not sorted through this considerable agenda to determine which items it considered most important. Suddenly and unexpectedly, on the morning of September 11st, the Bush administration's foreign priorities became clear.

On September 11st, 2001, members of **al-Qaeda**[1], a terrorist network founded and funded by Muslim fundamentalist **Osama bin Laden**[2], hijacked four jetliners, flying two into the twin towers of New York's Trade Center. The impact destroyed the towers and killed almost 3,000 people.

Another hijacked plane slammed into the Pentagon, killing 189 individuals. The fourth plane headed toward Washington, D.C., but crashed into a field in Pennsylvania after passengers charged the hijackers and forced them to lose control of the plane.

After **the 9/11 attacks**[3], President Bush, declaring a war on terrorism, organized a coalition of nations to combat the threat posed by terrorist groups such as al-Qaeda. He dememded that Afghanistan's **Taliban**[4] government, which had provided safe haven for bin Laden and al-Qaeda's terrorist training camps, turned bin Laden over to the United States. When Taliban refused, the Bush administration launched Operation Enduring Freedom against al-Qaeda and the Taliban regime in October 2001. The military operation included air strikes against Taliban and al-Qaeda targets and support for Northern Alliance, an Afghan opposition force battling Taliban control. By the end of 2001, the Taliban were overthrown and the United States was committed to peace enforcement in Afghanistan and assistance with the transition to a democratic government.

The terrorist attacks of September 11st, 2001, had a profound impact on U.S. foreign policy. Despite its superpower status and nuclear superiority, the United States appeared vulnerable in a way it had not previously. President Bush responded by inaugurating a global campaign against terrorists and supporters. Comparing with other presidents before him, George W. Bush was putting his distinctive stamp on how the country should address threats to national security. The Bush administration advocated a proactive doctrine of preemptive（先发制人的）military action. This bold but controversial strategy was commonly referred to as **Bush Doctrine**[5].

The 9/11 terrorist attacks gave the United States two overarching foreign policy priorities: defense of the homeland and pursuing the global war on terrorism. Few Americans disagree with these priorities. But, disagreements and controversies continue regarding the means to these ends and the effectiveness of government policies. Moreover, other foreign policy issues, such as the threat of nuclear-armed Iran, hostilities between Israel and Lebanon, and the humanitarian crisis in Sudan, have also captured the public's attention.

2. Wars in the Persian Gulf

On August 2nd, 1990, the Persian Gulf became the seeing for a major challenge to the international system set up after World War Ⅱ. President Saddam Hussein of Iraq sent troops into the neighboring oil sheikdom of Kuwait, occupying the country. This was the most clear-cut case of aggression against an independent nation in half a century.

（1）The Persian Gulf—the First Gulf War

At the formal request of the king of Saudi Arabia, American troops were dispatched to set up a defensive line at the Kuwaiti border. After the UN approved a resolution authorizing the use of force if Saddam Hussein did not respond to sanctions, the U.S. Congress reluctantly also approved such an authorization. On January 17th, 1991, two days after a deadline for Hussein to withdraw, U.S.-led coalition forces launched a massive air attack on Iraq. After several weeks, the ground offensive began. Iraqi troops retreated from Kuwait a few days later, and the First Gulf War ended, although many Americans criticized President George H. W. Bush for not sending troops to Baghdad(巴格达)to depose Saddam Hussein.

As part of the cease-fire that ended the Gulf War, Iraq agreed to abide by all UN resolutions and allowed UN weapons inspectors to search for and oversee the destruction of its medium-range missiles and all weapons of mass destruction, including any chemical and nuclear weapons, and related research facilities. Economic sanctions were to be imposed on Iraq until the weapons inspectors finished their work. In 1999, however, Iraq placed so many obstacles in the path of the UN inspectors that they withdrew from the country.

(2)The Persian Gulf—the Second Gulf War

After the terrorist attacks on the United States on September 11st, 2001, President George W. Bush called Iraq and the Saddam Hussein part of an "axis of evil" that threatened world peace. In 2002 and early 2003, Bush called for "regime change" in Iraq and began assembling an international coalition that might support further military action in Iraq.

Having tried and failed to convince the UN Security Council that the UN should take action to enforce its resolution. Bush decided to take unilateral action against Iraq. In March 2003, supported by a coalition of thirty-five other nations, including Britain, the United States invaded Iraq. Within three weeks, the coalition forces had toppled Hussein's decades-old dictatorship and were in control of Baghdad and most of the other major Iraqi cities.

The process of establishing order and creating a new government in Iraq turned out to be extraordinarily difficult, however. In the course of the fighting, the Iraqi army, rather than surrendering, disbanded itself. Soldiers simply took off their uniforms and made their way home. As a result, the task of maintaining law and order fell on the shoulders of a remarkably small coalition expeditionary force. Coalition troops were unable to put an immediate halt to the wave of looting and disorder that spread across Iraq in the wake of invasion. Although Hussein himself was found and arrested in December 2003, his capture did nothing to end the insurgent resistance movement that had begun against the coalition forces.

That the United States launched its war against Saddam Hussein's regime signaled the implementation of the Bush Doctrine. The U.S.-led invasion of Iraq was part of a new strategy that sought to promote American security through preemptive military strike against potentially dangerous nations. Believing that the Hussein regime was developing weapons of mass destruction (**WMDA**[6])—nuclear, chemical, or biological weapons—and that Iraq was a safe harbor and potential breeding ground for terrorists, the U.S. government chose to act even though the UN Security Council refused to endorse the recourse to war, and even without the support of key allies such as France and Germany. The failure of the United States to win approval from the Security Council for the 2003 invasion of Iraq led to vigorous debate at home and abroad, and the United States actions created hard feelings among many of America's traditional allies.

Over time, coalition forces failed to find evidence of an active nuclear weapons program in Iraq—the original justification provided by Bush administration for a preemptive military strike—but it is clear that Hussein possessed chemical weapons, engaged in genocide, and brutally oppressed the Shiite majority in Iraq. As evidence of WMDs failed to materialize, the Bush administration changed its justification for war, arguing that Saddam Hussein posed a severe danger to the world because of his long history of brutality, and emphasizing the goal of promoting democracy in the Middle East through his removal from power.

In the month after President Bush declared an end to major combats, soldiers from the United States and its allies found themselves under attack from mortar fire, roadside bombings, and suicide missions by various insurgents. As the American military presence in Iraq continued, war death and injuries mounted. By the end of 2006, more than 2,900 U.S. service men and women had lost their lives in Iraq and more than 22,000 had been injured.

A positive development, however, was the January 2005 election in which the Iraqi people chose representatives for a 275-member National Assembly. The election marked an important step in the process of turning over control of the country from the U.S.-led coalition to Iraqis themselves. But the hope for an end to the growing civil unrest and a withdrawal of U.S. troops declined.

On August 31st, 2010, President delivered a speech from the Oval Office, announcing that the American combat mission in Iraq had ended, that operation Iraqi freedom was over.

3. Wars in Afghanistan

On September 11st, 2001, four U.S. commercial airliners were hijacked. They were used as human-guided missiles: Two were flown into twin towers of the World Trade Center in New York City and one was crashed into the Pentagon in Arlington, Virginia. The fourth aircraft, which was apparently targeting the U.S. capital for the White House, crashed in rural Pennsylvania when passengers attempted to wrest control from the hijackers. Approximately 2,893 people were killed in the World Trade Center attack. An additional 189 people were killed in the attack on the Pentagon, and 44 passengers and crew members died in the Pennsylvania crash. The hijackers were quickly identified as members al-Qaida (Arabic for "the Base"), which was described as a terrorist organization by the U.S. Government. At the time of the attacks, al-Qaida was led by Osama bin Laden, a multimillionaire Muslim extremist.

On September 12nd, 2001, President George W. Bush remarked, "We have just seen the first war of the twenty-first century," and on September 20th, he made a televised Address to a Joint Session of Congress to announce the nation's new war footing and to pledge that the battle would be taken to Taliban and al-Qaida. In the days following September 11th, U.S. military forces were deployed to strategic positions from which they could attack Afghanistan. The Bush administration made a successful diplomatic effort to secure the support of many nations in prosecuting a "war against terror". On October 7th, the United States attacked Taliban targets in Afghanistan. U.S. and British aircraft targeted military objective, including al-Qaida camps and Taliban installations. During November, U.S. and Northern Alliance attacks against Taliban positions made significant headway. On November 13th, the Afghan capital city of Kabul was occupied. But Osama bin Laden and many other al-Qaida leaders remained at large.

After the Taliban regime was removed, a pro-Western interim government was installed in Afghanistan, which was ratified in 2005 by the first free elections held in Afghanistan in thirty-three years. Despite this achievement, in 2006 Afghanistan remained a dangerous and unstable place, in which elements of the Taliban remained active.

The war in Afghanistan was the offensive phase of the war on terror. Defensive measures included a $40 billion emergency spending bill passed by Congress on September 14th, 2001, that made "emergency supplemental appropriations for fiscal year 2001 for additional disaster assistance, for anti-terrorism initiatives, and for assistance in the recovery from the tragedy that occurred". Several laws were quickly passed to expand the investigative powers of U.S. law enforcement agency, such as the *USA Patriot Act* and *Homeland Security Act*.

Notes

1. Al-Qaeda "基地" 组织：成立于1988年，由本·拉登创建，在阿拉伯有10多处训练基地，对从各国来到阿富汗的成员进行恐怖活动训练。拉登成立该组织的最初目的是以此组织为基地，来训练和指挥与入侵阿富汗的苏联军队战斗的阿富汗义勇军。苏军撤退后，目标转为美国和伊斯兰世界的"腐败政权"。

2. Osama bin Laden 奥萨马·本·拉登：沙特阿拉伯王国利雅得行省人，是基地组织的首领，该组织被认为是全球恐怖组织。

3. the 9/11 Attacks 9·11 事件：指美国东部时间2001年9月11日上午（北京时间9月11日晚上）恐怖分子劫持的4架民航客机撞击美国纽约世界贸易中心（双子塔）和华盛顿五角大楼的历史事件。

4. Taliban 塔利班：发源于阿富汗的坎大哈地区的伊斯兰原教旨主义运动组织。 塔利班，在波斯语中是"学生"的意思，它的大部分成员是阿富汗难民营伊斯兰学校的学生，故又称"伊斯兰学生军"。美国等西方国家认定其为恐怖组织。

5. Bush Doctrine 布什主义：指布什政府从美国共和党保守主义和现实主义思想出发，奉行"共和党色彩的国际主义"路线，在国家安全政策和对外交往中遵循"美国利益至上"和"以实力求和平"两大原则，在对待恐怖主义和谋求核武器、大规模杀伤性武器的不友好国家采取先发制人的打击政策，在全球地缘战略格局上以更具进攻性的军事部署为基础，采用强硬和保守的态度追求美国的国家利益。

6. WMDA 大规模杀伤性武器：指用来大规模屠杀的武器，一般针对的是平民，但是也可以针对军事人员。它包括三类武器：核武器（包括放射性武器）、化学武器、生物武器。美国入侵伊拉克是以萨达姆拥有大规模杀伤性武器为借口的，后经证实此消息并不准确，2016年英国前首相为此而道歉。

Unit 7 Sino-American Relations

1. First Contact in 1784 to Anti-Communism Policy in 1940s

As early as 1784, the U.S. merchant boat **"Empress of China[1]"** visited Guangzhou. It brought American ginseng to China and took Chinese silk, tea and porcelain back. This was the first contact between the two countries. China-U.S. ties had been basically friendly and equal until 1844 when the U.S. taking advantage of China's defeat in the **First Opium War**[2], forced the Qing government into the unequal treaty of Wangxia and later the Treaty of Tianjin in 1858.

Back in the U.S. in 1870s and 1880s, Chinese were made scapegoat for economic crisis because of their diligence and low demands on payment and working conditions. Disregarding the great contribution of Chinese workers to its development, the U.S. Congress passed a law in 1882 to stop Chinese immigrants.

By the end of the 19th century, China was almost divided by major Western powers and Japan as spheres of influence, leaving none to the U.S.. To help American business expansion and to protect its existing interests in China, the U.S. put forward the privileges Western powers and Japan had already had. The U.S. also joined seven other powers (**the Eight-Nation Alliance**[3]) in invading China in 1900 to suppress the Boxer Uprising and forced China into conceding more privileges and huge reparations.

In WW Ⅰ and at the beginning of WW Ⅱ, the U.S. appeased Japan's expansionism. It simply made protests without real action when its interests were not seriously damaged. It was not until Japan's attack at Pearl Harbor that the U.S. allied with China for the fist time. President Roosevelt once commented on China's role in WW Ⅱ to the effect that the U.S. could have suffered much more if China had not contained millions of Japanese soldiers on the Chinese soil.

During the Second World War China received about $1.6 billion worth of war materials from the United States under the *Lend-Lease Act*, which greatly helped China's War of Resistance against Japan. The American Volunteer Group, a voluntary air force financed by the U.S. government, well known to China as the Flying Tigers, helped China train pilots, protected China's airspace, and engaged in air battles with Japanese planes. Toward the end of WW Ⅱ, the U.S. wanted to develop China as its major ally in Asia to contain possible future threats from Japan. That explained why, at the founding of the UN, president Roosevelt insisted that China become one permanent member of the Security Council, so China would be grateful and follow it in the UN.

In December 1945, President Harry Truman sent his Secretary of State, George C. Marshall, to China to broker a coalition government between the KMT (Nationalist Party) government and the CCP (Chinese Communist Party). Chiang Kai-shek had no real intention to make peace and refused to abide by the peace agreement with the CCP. Another Chinese Civil War broke out. The U.S. decided to support the KMT regime in China Civil War from 1946 to 1949. Despite advanced American weapons and other direct and indirect American aid, the KMT regime was defeated and fled to Taiwan, quite to American disappointment.

2. 1949 to the End of 20th Century: from Confrontation to Containment & Engagement

The CCP soon liberated China and established People's Republic of China. Amid U.S. enmity and isolation by most capitalist countries, the new China chose to ally itself with the Soviet

Union, America's archenemy（主要敌人）. The Truman administration decided not to recognize the New China and remained hostile to it while supporting the exiled KMT government in Taiwan.

During the Korean War, the U.S.-led UN forces, ignoring China's repeated warnings of entering the war if UN forces crossed the 38° Parallel, spread the flames of war to Yalu River. Feeling greatly threatened, the New China, though poor and weak, sent its Chinese People's Volunteer Army to fight alongside the Korea People's Army against the UN forces and forced them back to the 33° Parallel and to the negotiation table. A truce was signed in 1953.

After China's entry in the Korean War, Washington decided to strengthen its support to Chiang Kai-Shek's regime in Taiwan so it could better intervene in China's internal affairs. The U.S. sent its Seventh Fleet to Taiwan Straits to prevent liberation of Taiwan by the People's Liberation Army. In 1954, the United States signed a mutual defense treaty with Taiwan so it could "defend" Taiwan. During the "First Taiwan Straits crisis" (also called the "1954—1955 Taiwan Straits Crisis"), the U.S. even threatened a possible nuclear strike at the mainland of China. During the "Second Taiwan Straits Crisis" in 1958, the U.S. sent its navy vessels to protect the KMT troops. The U.S. and the New China remained enemies until 1970 s.

At the height of the Cold War, the U.S. was deeply mired in the Vietnam War while the Soviet Union was aggressively expanding. The U.S. was forced to make strategic retreats. It also began contact with China to balance the Soviet influence. Under such circumstances, President Nixon paid a historic visit to China in February 1972, breaking the ice of over two decades of hostility and mutual hatred. The two sides signed **the Shanghai Joint Communique**[4] in which the U.S. agreed to recognize the One-China Policy and that Taiwan is a part of China.

In 1978, the Carter administration, after years of tough negotiation, finally decided to cut relations with Taiwan, withdrew its soldiers from Taiwan, and established diplomatic relations with Beijing. In the Joint Communique on the Establishment of Diplomatic Relations between the USA and the China as the sole legal representative of China and that Taiwan is a part of China. About the same time, China started its opening up and reform process with a shift of focus toward economic development.

Regarding China as the key to its successful containment of the Soviet Union, the Reagan administration attached great importance to the China-U.S. ties and even lifted bans of arms sales and transfer of high-technology to China. It also agreed to reduce arms sales to Taiwan. On August 17th, 1982, the Reagan administration signed a Joint Communique with China. The U.S. promised to gradually "reduce the arms sales to Taiwan, leading, over a period of time, to a final resolution". China-U.S. relations entered a honeymoon period.

Since the establishment of diplomatic relations between China and the U.S., two-way trade has grown rapidly. Personal and cultural exchanges as well as interchange in many other filed further enhanced the mutual understanding and friendship between the two countries.

China-U.S. relations, however, has never been entirely smooth. Just about three months after the establishment of China-U.S. Diplomatic relations, the U.S. Congress passed the so-called Taiwan Relations Act. This was seen by Chinese officials as an excuse to intervene in China's domestic affairs. The Reagan administration and succeeding administration continued sales of high-tech weapons to Taiwan under the so-called Taiwan Relations Act and in violation of its solemn promise in the U.S.-China Joint Communique of August 17th, 1982. The American government often blamed China for human rights abuses, trade imbalances, ect. In April, 2001, a U.S. espionage plane spying over China's South-Sea waters hit a Chinese fighter watching over it. A Chinese pilot died. Sino-U.S. ties fell to a low point.

With China's overall national strength increased, American Presidents realized China's growing importance after assuming presidency and began to improve its relations with China. President Bush and President Clinton granted unconditional Most-Favored Nation (MFN) treatment to China and advocated full "engagement" with China amid great domestic pressure. The U.S. set up the Constructive Strategic Partnership with China in November 1996. After the bombing of the Chinese embassy in Belgrade on May 8th, 1999, President Clinton made repeated apologies to China and compensations were made to the victims and the Chinese government.

3. The Sino-U.S. Relations in 21st Century to Present

When running for his second term, President George W. Bush changed his China Policy in his platform to "we welcome the emergence of a strong, peaceful, and prosperous China". Staring from 2005 to the end of the Bush administration, the two countries conducted high-level strategic dialogues six times and Strategic Economic Dialogue five times. The two dialogues were combined into one, *China-U.S. Strategic and Economic Dialogue* when President Obama took office. From November 15th-18th, 2009, President Obama paid a state visit to China, within a year after assuming presidency, which demonstrated the importance the U.S. attached to the relations with China and to China's growing influence. In the *China-U.S. Joint Statement* concluding his state visit, the two sides agreed that respecting each other's core interests is extremely important to ensure steady progress in China-U.S. Relations. Sino-U.S. relations reached a new height.

Despite the relatively smooth China-U.S. relations in 2009 and the successful state visit to China by President Obama, structural problems in the bilateral relations remain and stand out with China's rapid rise and the relative decline of the U.S.. The beginning of 2010 saw numerous conflicts between the two countries which could be mainly summarized as three "T"s, namely, Taiwan, trade and Tibet. Owing to the needs of domestic politics, the Obama administration launched anti-dumping investigations on many Chinese products and led the West in pressing China to appreciate its currency to solve world trade imbalances; the U.S. sold advanced weapons worth $6.4 billion to Taiwan in January, 2010, and what was more, the U.S. government sold $5.85 billion worth of advanced arms to Taiwan in September, 2011 just a month after its vice-president Joe Biden visited China in August, 2011. On January 18th, 2010, President Obama met with the Dalai Lama at the White House despite China's strong opposition, which reoccurred on July 16th, 2011. More problems between the U.S. and China expected to emerge.

Complex and difficult as it has been, Sino-U.S. relationship is too important to get out of control. As permanent members of the UN Security Council and influential nuclear powers, China, the largest developing country, and the US, the largest developed country, have to cooperate in a wide range of issues to ensure the well-being of the people of both countries and the people of rest of the world. These issues include denuclearization of Korea peninsula, nuclear non-proliferation, war on terrorism, Darfur peace process, and environment protection, to name a few. Not only the people in both countries but also people elsewhere look forward to closer cooperation between the two countries.

Under the context and at the invitation of U.S. President Barack Obama, President Hu Jintao paid a state visit to the U.S. from January 19th to 22nd, 2011. The two countries signed a joint statement, in which the U.S. reiterates its policy of welcoming "a strong, prosperous and successful China that plays a greater role in world affairs". The two sides also pledge to forge a China-U.S. cooperative partnership based on mutual respect and mutual benefit for the interests of the two countries and the rest of the world. President Hu's visit came at a time of rapid rise of China's strength and influence versus an America standard in record high fiscal deficit and international trade deficit, near double-digit unemployment rate, and the largest public debt in the history of the world, which increased to about $15.7 trillion by June, 2012, and increased by $4 billion every passing day. Obama visited China in 2014, and Xi Jinping visited America in 2016. Both countries are learning to adjust to the new situation and make sure cooperation instead of confrontation will be the key tone for China-U.S. relations in the coming decade. Only in this way can people expect the fundamental interests of the two sides, of the entire Asia-Pacific region and the world to be guaranteed.

Notes

1. Empress of China 中国皇后号：中美两国的首次通商是从 1784 年开始的。那时，美国刚刚获得独立。在这百废待兴的日子里，美国的一些人士便急于要同远在万里以外的中国通商。担负这次具有历史意义通商的是一艘原在海军服役的帆船，改装后被命名为"中国皇后"号，含有对中国皇室尊重之意。

2. First Opium War 第一次鸦片战争：第一次鸦片战争（1840 年 6 月—1842 年 8 日），英国经常称第一次中英战争（First Anglo-Chinese War）或"通商战争"，是中国近代史的开端。"闭关锁国"后的清朝逐步落后于世界大潮，但是在外贸中，一直处于贸易顺差地位。为了扭转对华贸易逆差，英国开始向中国走私毒品鸦片，获取暴利。1840 年 6 月，英军舰船 47 艘、陆军 4 000 人在海军少将懿律（Anthony Blaxland Stransham）、驻华商务监督义律（Charles Elliott）率领下，陆续抵达广东珠江口外，封锁海口，鸦片战争开始。虽然这场战争只是鸦片战争的一部分，但有时也经常把它称作鸦片战争。这场战争一直断断续续进行，其间的一系列战斗和军事行动相互之间并无关联。

3. the Eight-Nation Alliance 八国联军：指 1900 年（光绪二十六年）以军事行动侵入大清国的大英帝国、法兰西第三共和国、德意志帝国、俄罗斯帝国、美利坚合众国、日本帝国、意大利王国、奥匈帝国的八国联合军队。

4. the Shanghai Joint Communique 中美上海联合公报：1972 年 2 月，美国总统尼克松应周恩来总理的邀请访华，中美交往的大门重新打开。尼克松访华期间，中美双方于 1972 年 2 月 28 日在上海发表了《中美联合公报》(《上海公报》)，美国承认台湾是中国的领土，承诺从台湾撤军。标志着中美关系开始走向正常化。

Unit 8 American New Foreign Policy in Twenty-first Century

1. Twenty-first Century Challenges

As President, George W. Bush has grappled with many of the same issues as his two predecessors. When should the United States intervene military overseas? When should the United States act unilaterally and when should it act multilaterally? What can the United States do to promote peace between Israelis and Palestinians? What is the best way to prevent nuclear proliferation and the attempts of rogue states like Iran to develop nuclear capabilities? As the international community has grown more interconnected over time, forging U.S. foreign policies that both protect American interests and benefit those outside their borders have become more consequential and increasingly challenging.

2. Identifying Policies to Pursue in the National Interest

Throughout the post-World War Ⅱ era, most Americans agreed that it was the United States's national interests to attain economic prosperity, defend the homeland, and protect American values. Further, with occasional exceptions, such as the Vietnam War, they generally agreed with the policies put into place to attain these goals. In the post-Cold Ware era, prosperity, homeland defense, and protecting national interests remain key elements of U.S. foreign policy.

Before the 9/11 terrorist attacks, there was disagreement about what policies should be adopted in pursuit of these interests. Post-9/11 consensus regarding the need for strong homeland defense and for effective prosecution of the war on terrorism has largely eclipsed earlier debates about which foreign policy should prioritize. Nevertheless, the Bush administration's support of preemptive military actions has generated debate about how to address emerging threats that include saber-rattling from North Korea, Iran's quest for enriched uranium(铀), humanitarian crises such as the genocide(种族灭绝) in Darfur region of Sudan, and the reemergence of the Taliban and its regime of violent intimidation in rural regions of Afghanistan. These are a few of questions that policy makers ponder as they debate which policies should be implemented in the national interest.

3. Deciding When to Intervene Overseas

Between the end of World war Ⅱ and the demise of the Soviet Union, U.S. military intervention overseas usually was tied to the containment of eastern European countries. But, the demise of the Soviet Union eliminated this easy benchmark for deciding when to intervene. Following the Cold War, President George Bush, Bill Clinton, and George W. Bush all faced the problem of when to use the U.S. military overseas and none of these presidents hesitated to commit U.S. forces to overseas action.

In 2001, the decision to intervene was relatively easy in the case of Afghanistan, whose Taliban government supported and sheltered Osama bin Laden and al-Qaeda terrorist training camps. The Bush administration's preemptive defense strategy aroused more debate when the United States and several partner countries invaded Iraq in 2003. This intervention was controversial with many U.S. allies and fueled criticism in the United States. Supporters of the U.S. Action in Iraq argued that the display of American resolve would be an object lesson for other countries that were not behaving as the United States wanted. According to Richard Perle, a senior adviser to the Bush administration, "It's always been at the heart of the Bush Doctrine that a more robust policy would permit use to elicit greater cooperation from adversaries." When Libyan leader **Muammar Qaddafi**[1] indicated his willingness to abandon the development of weapons of mass destruction in late 2003, some viewed this as proof that Bush Doctrine worked.

Critics, however, believed the Bush Doctrine is misguided for several reasons. First, they pointed to the frightening precedent of launching preemptive wars, and the dangerous lesson that might teach other countries who fear and hate their adversaries. Second, they question the morality of invading another country based solely on what it might do. Third, they question whether such an aggressive strategy might create lasting problems with allies, and deepening hatred of the United States by adversaries.

Beyond the war on terrorism, the same quandaries confront U.S. policy makers after 9/11 attacks that they struggle with before. Should the United States intervene overseas to stop human rights violations? Should the United States intervene overseas to overthrow dictatorial government or support democratic governments? Except for the Bush administration's strategic doctrine of preemptive defense, there are no easy guidelines, and decisions will undoubtedly be made on a case by case basis.

4. Promoting Democracy in the Middle East

Promoting democracy in the Middle Est is a difficult task that can have unexpected consequence. In a surprising outcome, the Islamic resistance movement **Hamas**[2] won a decisive victory in Palestinian elections in early 2006. Long identifies as a terrorist organization by the United States and the European Unions because of its commitment to the destruction of Israel, Hamas gained control of the majority of seats in a Hamas-controlled government unless it renounces violence and agrees to recognize Israel as a legitimate nation.

Though the Hussein government in Iraq was easily toppled in 2003, the situation there is far less secure than initially predicted by the Bush administration. Many Iraqis, even those who are glad to be free of Hussein's tyrannical rule, are troubled by the lawlessness unleashed by **Hussein**[3]'s overthrow. Many resent the U.S. occupation and remain skeptical of the democratically elected government's ability to manage the growing violence. Some attacks appear to be the work of individuals who entered Iraq specially to fight U.S. Forces, but increasingly the violence has been characterized by sectarian warfare and the marks of civil war. While some parts of Iraq are successfully rebuilding and remain relatively calm thanks to help from the U.S.-led coalition, the overall situation remains enormously volatile. Oil pipelines are routinely sabotaged, Iraqi police forces often come under attack, and Iraqis face great uncertainty about the future.

The elections of representatives to the National Assembly in 2005 gave some life to the democratic process despite the fact that the election was boycotted by most Sunni Iraqis. After the swearing in of the al-Maliki national government in May 2006, the United States began serious talks with Iraq officials about increasingly turning over control of security to Iraqi forces to decrease violence by insurgents opposed to the presence of U.S. and other coalition forces. Whether the new Iraqi government has the capacity and the legitimacy to reverse the country's slide toward civil war is an open question.

Iraq remains an unfinished piece of business, as does Afghanistan. As Iraq struggles with continued insurgent and sectarian violence, Afghanistan is under assault from recognized Taliban militias. It is unclear how long the United States will need to station troops or how many more Americans will die in the struggle to make Iraq and Afghanistan democratic havens in the Arab world.

5. Transnational Threats to Peace

Terrorist organizations represent an ever evolving threat that is not easily contained or defeated with traditional military activities. Operating as non-state actors, terrorists "blur the line between civilians and the military" and "confound war plans and diplomatic practices based upon enemies with fixed territory and political sovereignty". And military resources are relatively seeking to obtain weapons of mass destruction—nuclear, chemical, or biological weapons. Meeting these threats is a key element of the war on terrorism, which will be both long and costly.

Because of its reliance on computers, the United States is in vulnerable to information warfare: attacks on information systems. These threats have led officials to warm about the danger of an "**Electronic Pearl Harbor**[4]" in which information warfare could bring some sectors of the United States to a halt. Indeed, computers and web sites used by the U.S. Government as well as business such as **CNN**[5], **Home Depot**[6], and **Amazon.com**[7] often have come under attack from individual hackers.

How serious is the threat of information warfare? Government studies have highlighted the vulnerabilities of U.S. infrastructures, including communications and telephones, baking, power grids, water system, fuel supply networks, and other systems that rely on computers.

6. Drug and Environmental Problems

During the late 20th century, international efforts to address the illegal drug trade and the quality of the world's environment emerged as issues that challenged U.S. policy makers. The United States has a mixed record on both.

American policy makers use three tactics against illegal drugs. The first concentrates on reducing demand in the United States and rarely is involved with foreign affairs. The second one emphasizes stopping the flow of drugs into the United States. A third tactics is helping countries stop drug production within their borders. The United States provided economic and military help.

Since the U.S. overthrow of the Taliban regime in Afghanistan in 2001, opium production has surged. The U.S. government officials have identified the resurgence in opium productions and trafficking as one of the greatest challenges currently Afghanistan is facing. Today, Afghanistan is the world's largest producer of opium. According to the IMF, drug revenue accounts roughly 60 percent of the country's economy and opium trafficking has contributed to government to corruption at all levels. The United States has committed millions to counter-narcotics programs in Afghanistan and continued to work with the Afghan government to eradicate opium production.

Environment issues such as global warming, ocean pollution, deforestation, desertification, and the loss of biodiversity moved onto foreign policy agenda in the late 20th century. At times, the United States has been a leader in international efforts to address environment issues. Since the United States is responsible for approximately one-third of the pollutants that are thought to contribute to global warming, it is an especially important player in any international efforts to improve climate conditions.

George W. Bush opposes the Kyoto Agreement and withdrew U.S. support when he became President. As the European community has moved forward with the implementation of the **Kyoto Protocol**[7], the United States has continued to distance itself from international efforts to limit greenhouse gas emission. In 2002, the European Union, Canada and Japan ratified the Kyoto Protocol, but for its provisions to become internationally binding, participation by the United States or Russia was necessary. In 2004, Russia formally ratified the treaty. Because the United States is not a signatory to the treaty, the United States is not bound by its provisions. However, support among the American public and at the state level—including Bush's home state of Texas—for limiting carbon dioxide emissions and for renewable energy programs means that global climate issues are bound to remain a part of the political agenda for the foreseeable future.

7. Obama's Foreign Policy

In evaluating Obama and his foreign policy, the questions of change have several different dimensions. How much did the Obama administration really change from the George W. Bush administration? How much did the Obama administration as a whole change during its time in office? And how much did the president change his own ideas and strategy?

Many people now respond to the first question by claiming Obama is not much different from Bush. That answer comes from both political directions: Liberals mourn the fact that there has not been more change; Republicans such as Dick Cheney gloat about how little of the Bush legacy has been undone. Yet this perception of continuity is too simplistic: Clearly, Obama has not been the same as Bush. Indeed, in a few instances Obama has been more hawkish. He vastly expended both the use of drone for targeted killings and the areas where these drone killings are carried out. Moreover, he was less collaborative and more unilateral than Bush in dealing with

Pakistan: Bush's approach was to inform and work with Pakistani leaders; it was Obama who achieved the success of the Bin Laden raid.

More generally, however, the Obama administration relied on multilateralism in its foreign policy where the Bush administration did not, at least during Bush's tumultuous first term. It is hard to image George W. Bush intervening in Libya in the fashion that Obama did. Under Bush, the United States either would have spurned the British and French appeals to act against Gaddafi or, if he decided to join them, would have dominated the military operation and thus paid most of the costs for it. That was how America has always done since World War II.

Still, on quite a few issues, the continuities from Bush to Obama were striking. Certainly, in the field of counter-terrorism, Obama changed American policies far less than it had been expected when he took office. Few could have predicted, for example, that the prison at Guantanamo would remain open three years into Obama's presidency, or that he would continue so many of Bush's other policies, including targeted killings, rendition and warrantless surveillance.

Why is it that Democratic presidential candidates hold out the prospect of a new American foreign policy, and yet often wind up with ones that are not fundamentally different from the Republicans'? It is worth keeping in mind that during presidential campaigns, both Democrats and Republicans always have an interest in emphasizing the differences between the two parties. Both parties seek to frame foreign policy issues in simplistic ways that will arouse their own supporters. The candidates tend to talk less about the policies of their opponents that they will continue. Moreover, people tend to remember the parts of a candidate's message they like and ignore the parts they don't.

Americans tend to assume that a change in administration represents a wholesale change in personnel and viewpoints. But that is not always true, and especially not in the case of Obama administration. Even when the personnel do change with a new administration it does not automatically produce a change in outlook or assumptions about the world. In short, the people Obama appointed and the assumptions they carried with them into office were far less conducive to far-reaching change than the rhetoric of the Obama presidential campaign had led people to anticipate.

During the course of his first three years in the White House, Obama altered some of his own ideas and strategies. His calm demeanor obscured this reality. In 2009, Obama was determined to avoid sounding like George W. Bush. As one part of that effort, he clearly de-emphasized the importance of promoting democracy overseas, both in his speeches and in dealing with countries like Iran. His acknowledged model in foreign policy was the realist approach pursued under President George H. W. Bush and Brent Scowcroft.

The President also changed his military strategy in a fundamental way, so that the Obama of 2011 was not the same as the Obama of 2009. At the start of his administration, Obama bought heavily into the strategy of counterinsurgency that had seemed to work for Petraeus in Iraq. He ordered troops to Afghanistan in early 2009 and then more at the end of the year, hoping to win support of the Afghan people in a way that would turn the war. At that time, Obama rejected the arguments of some officials to rely on more heavily on a counter-terrorism strategy-using fewer ground troops and relying more heavily on special operations forces, drones and missiles to attack al-Qaeda.

In mid-2011, however, Obama shifted in Afghanistan toward counter-terrorism, the approach that succeeded in killing Osama bin Laden in Pakistan and, five months later, Anwar al-Awlaki in Yemen, the Obama team minimized the significance of this change in military strategy, probably because calling attention to it would have raised questions about whether he should have sent so many more American troops to Afghanistan in the first place.

The senior positions in the Obama administration changed hands too. The personnel moves were so gradual that few people bothered to put them all together, but the result was that by the end of Obama's third year in office, only one of the top eight officials in the government's foreign policy apparatus was in the same job as at the start of the administration. By contrast, there was considerably more continuity in Obama's inner circle.

If a single word captured the view of overall strategy of Obama's administration in dealing with the world, from the very start of the administration, it was the concept of "re-balancing". They used "re-balancing" in a variety of contexts. In general, they said, America should re-balance its priorities toward a greater emphasis on domestic concern. In foreign policy, America needed to re-balance from an over-reliance on the military toward diplomacy and other means of statecraft. The United States also needed to re-balance away from a preoccupation with the Middle East and toward the prosperous region of East Asia. In economics, Obama and his aids spoke of the need to re-balance the international economy, the global markets, the distribution of imports and exports, the values of various countries' currencies.

After several years in office, the Obama administration could point to several successes in its foreign policy. The principal one is in counter-terrorism, where Obama's overall strategy and the specific choices he made have clearly weakened al-Qaeda's leadership and capacities. He'd managed to smooth over the animosities with Europe that had been aroused by the Iraq War. By the end of 2011, he had withdrawn American troops from Iraq.

On other goals, he achieved only middling success. He wanted to reorient American policy toward Asia, yet the continuing needs of the war in Afghanistan, which he chose to expand, made it considerably more difficult to achieve his goal. He sought to restore America's standing in the Middle East, but the results were limited; critics remained cynical about American motives, because of continuing U.S. links to undemocratic regimes in places like Saudi Arabia and Bahrain. The Obama administration had hoped that a conciliatory approach to China would produce a better working relationship, but had to make adjustments after finding that China was emboldened by America's eagerness to avoid conflict. Obama worked hard to forge a relationship with Russian president Dmitry Medvedev, hoping that he could emerge as a leader in his own right with a degree of independence from Prime Minister Vladimir Putin-only to discover in the fall of 2011 that Putin re-installed himself as president and Russia's unchallenged leader for another twelve years.

During his presidential campaign in 2008, Obama promised that as President of the United States, he would push the Cuban government to embrace democratic reforms and free political prisoners. After his election, former Cuban President Fidel Castro said he was "open" to the idea of meeting with the president-election. However most of his policies towards Cuba before 2014 were changed little from the Bush policies. Obama visited Havana, Cuba for two days in March 2016, becoming the first sitting U.S. President to arrive since Calvin Coolidge in 1928.

There were notable failures, too, in what had been some of Obama's highest priorities at the time he took office. He wanted to bring about significant movement toward a Middle East peace settlement. Yet after three years, his efforts had not yet achieved any substantial change. So, too, Obama wanted to induce Iran to stop its nuclear weapons it had already had. Through the end of 2011, he had succeeded in obtaining tighter economic sanctions, but had made little if any headway toward the ultimate goal of persuading the leaders of Iran and North Korea to change course.

Notes

1. Muammar Qaddafi 奥马尔·穆阿迈尔·卡扎菲: 奥马尔·穆阿迈尔·卡扎菲(1942年6月7日—2011年10月20日),利比亚政治家、军事家、政治理论家。逊尼派穆斯林,利比亚革命警卫队上校,利比亚九月革命的精神领袖,前任利比亚最高领导人。

2. Hamas 哈马斯: 伊斯兰抵抗运动,它的目的是要创造有利于解放巴勒斯坦人民的内外部环境,收复被以色列占领的所有领土。"哈马斯"就其广义来说,是一个圣战组织,是伊斯兰教复兴运动的一部分,如果说得更准确,它实际是伊斯兰世界穆斯林兄弟会运动的延伸,因此,它的基础可追溯到20世纪40年代。该组织坚信,伊斯兰教复兴是解放巴勒斯坦的基础。

3. Hussein's 萨达姆·侯赛因: 伊拉克第五任总统,革命指挥委员会主席,伊拉克武装部队总司令,阿拉伯复兴社会党伊拉克地区领导机构总书记。萨达姆·侯赛因1937年4月28日出生于萨拉丁省提克里特县一个农民家庭,是前总统贝克尔的外甥。自幼丧父,由叔父抚养成人。

4. Electronic Pearl Harbor 电子珍珠港: 对联系一国的计算机基础设施进行的闪电式袭击。多年以来,美国非常重视它。

5. CNN 美国有线电视新闻网: 英文全称"Cable News Network",由特纳广播公司(TBS)特德·特纳于1980年6月创办,通过卫星向有线电视网和卫星电视用户提供全天候的新闻节目,总部设在美国佐治亚州的亚特兰大。

6. Home Depot 家得宝: 即美国家得宝公司,为全球领先的家居建材用品零售商,美国第二大零售商,家得宝遍布美国、加拿大、墨西哥和中国等地区,连锁商店数量达2 234家。家得宝连续9年被美国《财富》杂志评为"最受欢迎的专业零售商"。

7. Amazon.com 亚马逊公司: 一家财富500强公司,总部位于美国华盛顿州的西雅图。

它创立于 1995 年，目前已成为全球商品品种最多的网上零售商和全球第三大互联网公司，亚马逊及其他销售商为客户提供数百万种独特的全新、翻新及二手商品，如图书、影视、音乐和游戏、数码下载、电子和电脑、家居园艺用品、玩具、婴幼儿用品、食品、服饰、鞋类和珠宝、健康和个人护理用品、体育及户外用品、玩具、汽车及工业产品等。

8. Kyoto Protocol 京都议定书：又译《京都协议书》《京都条约》，全称《联合国气候变化框架公约的京都议定书》)，是《联合国气候变化框架公约》的补充条款。是 1997 年 12 月在日本京都由联合国气候变化框架公约参加国三次会议制定的。其目标是"将大气中的温室气体含量稳定在一个适当的水平，进而防止剧烈的气候改变对人类造成伤害"。2011 年 12 月，加拿大宣布退出《京都议定书》，成为继美国之后第二个签署但后又退出的国家。

References

[1] BRESLER F, KARLESKY S J, TUNER L. Understanding American government[M]. New York: Horizon Textbook Publishing, 2007.

[2] EDWARDS G, WATTENBURG M P, LINEBERRY R L. Government in America[M]. New York: Addison Wesley Longman,1999.

[3] JENTLESON W B. American foreign policy: the dynamics of choice in the 21th century[M]. New York: London, 2000.

[4] KEGLEY W C J, WITTKOPE E R. American foreign policy[M]. New York: St. Martin' s Press,1996.

[5] GINSBURG L. American government [M]. New York : London, 2000.

[6] THEODORE L J, GINSBURG B, SHEPSLE K A. American government: power and purpose [M] New York: London, 2004.

[7] O' CONNOR K, SABATO L J, HAAG S D. American government: continuity and change[M]. Texas: Pearson Longman, 2004.

[8] O' CONNOR K, SABATO L J, HAAG S D. American government: continuity and change[M]. Texas: Pearson Longman, 2006.

[9] O' CONNOR K, SABATO L J, HAAG S D. American government: continuity and change[M]. Texas: Pearson Longman, 2008.

[10] SCHMIDT S, BARDES M. American government and politics today[M]. Texas: Thomson Wadsworth, 2008.

[11] WELCH S, GRUHL J. Understanding American government[M]. Connecticut: Thomson Wadsworth, 2008.

[12] WILSON Q J, DILULIO J J. American government[M]. Boston: Houghton Mifflin,1998.

[13] WOOLLEY J P, PAPA A R. American politics: core argument & current controversy[M]. New Jersey: Prentice Hall,1998.

[14] 乔治 • F. 凯南 , 约翰 • J. 米尔斯海默 . 美国大外交 [M]. 雷建锋 , 译 . 北京：社会科学文献出版社，2013.

[15] 亨利 • 基辛格 . 美国的全球战略 [M]. 胡利平 , 凌建平 , 等 , 译 . 海口：海南出版社，2012.

[16] 江宁康 . 美国概况——美国历史、社会与文化 [M]. 南京：东南大学出版社，2013.
[17] 玛雅 . 美国的逻辑：意识形态与内政外交 [M]. 北京：中国经济出版社，2011.
[18] 汤闯新 . 美国新全球战略 [M]. 北京：三联书店，2012.
[19] 陶文钊 . 冷战后的美国对华政策 [M]. 重庆：重庆出版社，2006.
[20] 王晓德 . 美国文化与外交 [M]. 天津：天津教育出版社，2008.
[21] 王知津 . 世界通览 [M]. 哈尔滨：哈尔滨工程大学出版社 ,2004.
[22] 熊志勇 . 美国政治与外交决策 [M]. 北京：北京大学出版社，2011.
[23] 周柏林 . 美国新霸权主义 [M]. 天津：天津人民出版社，2002.
[24] 赵学功 . 当代美国外交 [M]. 北京：社会科学文献出版社，2012.
[25] 张小明 . 美国与东亚关系导论 [M]. 北京：北京大学出版社，2011.
[26] 张哲 . 美国国会与台湾问题 [M]. 上海：复旦大学出版社，2005.

Chapter Eleven

American Literature

Unit 1 Colonial Period to 1815

In 1620, a group of Puritans from European countries came to America by "Mayflower" to escape religious persecution. The **Puritanism**[1] they believed in greatly influenced American literature. Most of the colonial literature was in the form of narratives or journals at that time. It recorded the life experiences of the early settlers, for example, History of Plymouth wrote by **William Bradford**[2] (1590—1526) showed Puritans' bravery and persistence during the process of establishing the settlements.

In the 18th century, America went through two big events, one was the Independent War and the other was **the Enlightenment movement**[3] which was originated from the Europe. It was an age of reason. People paid more attention to the human reason, scientific methods and discoveries rather than the Omnipresence of God. The Enlightenment freed the Americans from the Puritanism and pushed the development of American literature. Some literary figures who were also the political leaders stepped on the social stage.

Essay

Born in a poor family, Benjamin Franklin(本杰明·富兰克林)(1760—1790) was a jack-of-all-trade(多面手). As a scientist, he invented the Franklin stove, bifocal glasses, a miniature printing press and many other things. What's more, he founded the first circulating library(巡回图书馆) and a club for discussion of scientific, economic and political ideas. In politics, he participated in the draft of The Declaration of Independence with others. As a writer, he published an annual collection of proverbs which was called **Poor Richard's Almanac**[4] (《穷理查年鉴》). His *Autobiography* wrote how a poor man rose to wealth and fame. The words of Benjamin Franklin were simple but honest, smooth and humorous.

Thomas Paine(托马斯·潘恩)(1737—1806) was the most influential writer and thinker during American revolutionary period. His political pamphlets **Common Sense**[5] and *American Crisis* encouraged lots of soldiers to fight for the freedom of the United States.

Thomas Jefferson (托马斯·杰斐逊)(1743—1826), the third president of America, was the main drafter(起草者) of *The Declaration of Independence*(《独立宣言》). There was no doubt that *The Declaration of Independence* was an excellent political essay. Apart from his political ideas, the writing style of his was elegant and concise（简洁的）.

Poetry

As a poet and political journalist in the period of revolution, Philip Freneau（菲利普・弗瑞诺）（1752—1832）wrote many patriotic poems. He was considered to be "the poet of revolution". His most famous poems *The Wild Honey Suckle*（《野忍冬花》）presented his natural and simple writing skills.

Notes

1. Puritanism 清教主义：起源于英国，在北美殖民地得以实践与发展。美国清教主义从一开始就是一种精神运动，它不仅仅是一种宗教信仰，且还是一种极端民主与共和的理论。清教徒在自己的祖国遭受迫害，对英国严酷的社会现实不满而移民到美国。他们希冀按自己的意欲信仰上帝。于是，他们致力于建立一个乌托邦式的重视伦理和精神生活的社会模式。他们崇尚真正的自由——这种真正的自由涵盖了广泛的道德的含义。他们把一切破坏和蔑视这种自由信念的行为一概斥责为对权威的亵渎。他们奠定了今日美国主流文化价值观念的基础，铸就了美国民族特性。

2. William Bradford 威廉・布拉德福德：威廉・布拉德福德（1590—1657），五月花号公约签署人之一，于1620年参与创立了普利茅斯殖民地，并在长达30余年的时间里担任普利茅斯总督。他所撰写的"普利茅斯垦殖记"是关于欧洲新世界殖民史的早期著作之一。这是新英格兰殖民活动的早期最重要的编年史之一。这部史书以其倾向于将宗教事务与世俗关怀分开编写而著称。与保守的马萨诸塞海湾殖民地所编写的类似文章不同，布拉德福德并没有凡事皆以上帝的眷顾加以解释。褪去说教的企图和清教徒大迁徙的宗教激情，布拉德福德领导普利茅斯殖民地走上了一条界乎于马萨诸塞神圣共和国以及罗德岛的宽容的世俗生活之间的中间道路。

3. the Enlightenment movement 启蒙运动：通常是指在17世纪至18世纪法国大革命之前的一个新思维不断涌现的时代，与理性主义等一起构成一个较长的文化运动时期。这个时期的启蒙运动，覆盖了各个知识领域，如自然科学、哲学、伦理学、政治学、经济学、历史学、文学、教育学等等。启蒙运动同时为美国独立战争与法国大革命提供了框架，并且导致了资本主义和社会主义的兴起，与音乐史上的巴洛克时期以及艺术史上的新古典主义时期是同一时期。

4. Poor Richard's Almanac《穷理查年鉴》：由美国资本主义精神最完美的代表——本杰明・富兰克林所写，他作的年鉴是作为一个虚构的理查德・桑德斯（因此叫"穷理查德"）的著作从1733—1758年在费城年年发表。这些年鉴在殖民地居民中极受欢迎。典型的年鉴包含有日历、天气预测，忠告、食谱以及其他许多有用的知识。穷理查德的谚语、格言和箴言有的是他自己创作的，有的不是。它们使富兰克林实用、宽容和令人快活的妙语和哲学得到传播普及。

5. Common Sense《常识》：美国独立战争期间，托马斯・潘恩撰写了铿锵有力并广为流传的小册子《常识》，极大地鼓舞了北美民众的独立情绪，也被广泛视为美国开国元勋之一。

后来受到法国大革命影响，潘恩撰写了《人的权利》，成为启蒙运动的指导作品之一。今日之美国是自由民主的代名词，而最早提出“自由民主论”的，便是这位“美国体制之父”，他将半生心血，都倾注在《常识》这本不到50页的政论小册子里。

Unit 2 Romanticism (1815—1865)

The first thriving phenomenon of American literature appeared during the 19th century due to the impact of romanticism. The literary forms were colorful and the themes were various. Romanticism laid emphasis on freedom, individuals and imagination. It advocated that the natural world was the source of beauty. Accompanied by the development of romanticism, transcendentalism was born on American soil. It exalted feeling over reason, individual expression over the restrains of law and custom and praised the divinity of nature.

Novel

Washington Irving（华盛顿·欧文）（1783—1859）was the first American writer to earn the international reputation during the early romantic period. His *The Sketch Book*（《见闻札记》）brought him great success. Two short stories in it, *Rip Van Winkle*（《瑞普·凡·温克尔》）and *Legend of Sleepy Hollow*（《睡谷的传说》）were most significant. Irving was a highly skillful writer. His stories were usually set in a Gothic and supernatural atmosphere and his characters were vivid. In addition, the use of the humor in his works entertained readers a lot.

James Fennimore Cooper（詹姆斯·费尼莫尔·库柏）（1789—1851）was regarded as the first important American novelist. *The Leathestocking Tales*（《皮袜子故事集》）which was a collection of five novels made him popular. It was made up of The Pioneer, *The Last of Mohicans, The Prairie, The Pathfinder and The Deerslayer*. Natty Bumppo who was the central role of the five novels symbolized American hope for the pursuit of ideal society.

Nathaniel Hawthorne（纳撒尼尔·霍桑）（1804—1864）was the first writer to stress on the moral tradition in his works during the romantic period. Sin was his major theme of his novels. In his opinion, evil or sin was at the core of human life. Whenever there was sin, there was punishment. His masterpiece, **The Scarlet Letter**[1] told a story that a woman was expelled from the community as a result of adultery. Furthermore, it displayed a psychological insight into moral isolation and human emotions. Hawthorne liked to tell stories in a multiple point of view and symbolism was his main writing feature. He was good at using metaphors and similes in his novels to reveal the characters' psychology.

Herman Melville（赫尔曼·梅尔维尔）（1819—1891）was born in New York. As a sailor, his personal experiences brought him abundant material for his writings. His representative work **Moby Dick**[2] is a novel of symbolism. It reflected the process of the author's understanding about himself, society and human beings. The story was tragic but inspiring, and was regarded as one of the classics of American literature.

As one of the famous short story writers, O. Henry（欧·亨利）（1862—1910）was hailed as the father of American modern short novels. Like Mark Twain, he has another name William Sydney Porter which was his real name. More than 300 of his works were collected in Cabbages and Kings, The Voice of the City and other volumes. The stories that people liked most were *The Gift of the Magi*, *The Last Leaf* as well as *The Cop and the Anthem*. O. Henry was good at telling stories in a romantic way and many of his stories were involved with the life of ordinary people in New York City. His works were known for their wit, wordplay and the clever use of twist endings. Because the ending of his story was so surprising that it was called **"O. Henry ending"**[3].

Poetry

As one of the most controversial and influential American writers, **Edgar Allen Poe**[4]（1809—1849）lived a short and unhappy life. He was not only a great writer of fiction but also a poet. Besides, he was the first important critic in American literature. Poe wrote several books of poetry. The most famous ones were *The Raven*（《黑鸦疑云》）, *To Helen* and *Annabel Lee*. He was well known for his horror stories, for example, *The Fall of the House of Usher* and *The Black Cat*. He was also "the father of detective fiction", because he was so interested in deduction and induction. *The Murders in the Rue Morgue* was one of the best of this kind. As a critic, Poe put forward his principles for poetry and short story writing. In accordance with his principles, poems should be short, concise and readable at one sitting. The goal of poem writing was to create beauty and the most beautiful thing was the death of a beautiful woman. He stressed the rhythm of the poem. In terms of short story, he argued that short story should give the readers the totality of impression. What's more, the first sentence should bring out the "single effect" and the last sentence should leave a sense of finality with the readers.

Walt Whitman（沃尔特·惠特曼）（1819—1892）was a great experimentalist of poetry of his age. *Leaves of Grass* was his most popular work. Whitman was a reformer in American poetry history. He was the first one to employ free verse（自由体）in his poetry. In his works, he extolled equality, democracy, dignity, self-reliant spirit and so on. As far as the language concerned, it was always direct, plain and even vulgar（老百姓的）. The influences Whitman exerted on the readers and future writers were immeasurable.

Emily Dickenson[5]（艾米莉·狄金森）（1830—1886）who had a reclusive（隐遁的）personality received little attention when she was alive. She wrote 1775 poems but only 7 were published. However, she was considered to be one of the greatest poets in 19th century of America. Many of her poems were related to the nature, immortality, love, etc. She was especially obsessed with the theme of death which accounted for about two-thirds of her writings, such as:

I Had a Fly Buzz When I Died and Because I Could Not Stop for Death...

Emily's poems were quite distinguished from other poets'. Her poems had no titles, thus were always quoted by their first line. And there were abundant uses of dashes, irregular punctuations and capitalization in her writings.

Essay

Ralph Waldo Emerson(拉尔夫·沃尔多·爱默生)(1803-1882) and Henry David Thoreau(亨利·戴维·梭罗)(1817-1862) were the most outstanding advocates of **American Transcendentalism**[6]. As the spokesman of this movement, Ralph Waldo Emerson's first book *Nature* has been called "the manifesto of American transcendentalism". His essay *The American Scholar* has been regarded by Oliver Wendell Holmes as "America's declaration of intellectual independence". Emerson's thoughts have inspired many Americans. The other talented essayist of transcendentalism was Henry David Thoreau. He was a man who put his beliefs into the practice. His most marvelous writing **The Walden**[7] was based on his two years' residence at Walden Pond. In this collection of essays, he explained that independence and self-reliance of people's minds were the most critical factors to find out one's own way of living.

Notes

1. The Scarlet Letter《红字》: 19 世纪美国浪漫主义作家霍桑的长篇小说。发表于1850年。《红字》讲述了发生在北美殖民时期的恋爱悲剧。女主人公海丝特·白兰嫁给了医生奇灵渥斯,他们之间却没有爱情。在孤独中白兰与牧师丁梅斯代尔相恋并生下女儿珠儿。白兰被当众惩罚,戴上标志"通奸"的红色A字示众。然而白兰坚贞不屈,拒不说出孩子的父亲。《红字》的开篇一章的一句话:"新殖民地的开拓者们,不管他们的头脑中起初有什么关于人类品德和幸福的美妙理解,总要在各种实际需要的草创之中,忘不了划出一片未开垦的处女地充当墓地,再划出另一片土地来修建监狱。"表明了霍桑的基本态度:人人皆有罪,罪恶与人类如影相随。小说惯用象征手法,人物、情节和语言都颇具主观想象色彩,在描写中又常把人的心理活动和直觉放在首位。因此,它不仅是美国浪漫主义小说的代表作,同时也被称作是美国心理分析小说的开创篇。

2. Moby Dick《白鲸》:19 世纪美国最重要的小说家之一——赫尔曼·梅尔维尔于1851年发表的一篇海洋题材的小说,小说描写了亚哈船长为了追逐并杀死白鲸(实为白色抹香鲸)莫比·迪克,最终与白鲸同归于尽的故事。故事营造了一种让人置身海上航行、随时遭遇各种危险甚至是死亡的氛围,是作者的代表作。1956年06月27日发行的电影《白鲸记》,就是改编自这篇小说。《白鲸》中的哥特式自然书写表现了梅尔维尔对美国19世纪中期自然生态恶化的忧虑意识。

3. O. Henry ending 欧·亨利式结尾: 欧·亨利(1862年9月11日—1910年6月5日),有时又译奥亨利,原名威廉·西德尼·波特(William Sydney Porter), 19世纪末20世纪初美国著名短篇小说家,美国现代短篇小说创始人。与法国的莫泊桑、俄国的契诃夫并称为世界三大短篇小说巨匠。"含泪的微笑"是欧亨利小说的创作风格,是作品喜剧形式和悲剧内涵的有机结合"微笑"是其喜剧形式。 他少年时曾一心想当画家,婚后在妻子的鼓励下开始写作。后因在银行供职时的账目问题而入狱,服刑期间认真写作,并以"欧·亨利"为笔名发表了大量的短篇小说,引起读者广泛关注。他是一位高产的作家,一生中留下了一部长篇小说和近三百篇的短篇小说。他的短篇小说构思精巧,风格独特,以表现美国中下层人民的生活、语言幽默、结局出人意料，即“欧·亨利式结尾”而闻名于世。

4. **Edgar Allen Poe 埃德加·爱伦·坡**：（1809—1849），19世纪美国诗人、小说家和文学评论家，美国浪漫主义思潮时期的重要成员。在世时长期担任报刊编辑工作。其作品形式精致、语言优美、内容多样，在任何时代都是“独一无二”的风格。坡以神秘故事和恐怖小说闻名于世，他是美国短篇故事的最早先驱者之一，又被尊为推理小说的开山鼻祖，进而也被誉为后世科幻小说的始祖。象征主义所谓“纯诗”的主张，最早是由爱伦·坡提出来的。爱伦·坡认为：“天下没有、也不可能有比这样的一首诗——这一首诗本身——更加是彻底尊贵的、极端高尚的作品——这一首诗就是一首诗，此外再没有什么别的了——这一首诗完全是为诗而写的。”爱伦·坡关于诗歌音乐性的主张及实践，对法国象征主义影响深远，以至于音乐性成为象征主义一个非常重要的共同艺术特征。

5. **Emily Dickenson 艾米莉·狄金森**：又称“狄更生”（1830—1886），美国传奇诗人。出生于律师家庭。青少年时代生活单调而平静，受正规宗教教育。从25岁开始拒绝社交，闭门不出，在孤独中埋头写诗30年，留下诗稿1 700余首；生前只是发表过7首，其余的都是她死后才出版，并被世人所知，名气极大。狄金森的诗主要写生活情趣，自然、生命、信仰、友谊、爱情。诗风凝练婉约、意向清新，描绘真切、精微，思想深沉、凝聚力强，极富独创性。她被视为20世纪现代主义诗歌的先驱之一。美国诗人最著名的佼佼者是美国文学之父欧文，以及惠特曼和狄金森。她深锁在盒子里的大量创作诗篇是她留给世人的最大礼物。在她有生之年，她的作品未能获得青睐，然而周遭众人对她的不解与误会，却丝毫无法低损她丰富的创作天分。根据统计，艾米莉惊人的创作力为世人留下1 800多首诗，包括了定本的1 775首与新近发现的25首。

6. **American Transcendentalism 美国超验主义**：也称“新英格兰超验主义”或者“美国文艺复兴”，是美国的一种文学和哲学运动。与拉尔夫·沃尔多·爱默生和玛格丽特·富勒有关，它宣称存在一种理想的精神实体，超越于经验和科学之处，通过直觉得以把握。领导人是美国思想家、诗人拉尔夫·沃尔多·爱默生。美国超验主义是美国的一个重要思潮，它兴起于19世纪30年代的新英格兰地区，但波及其他地方，成为美国思想史上一次重要的思想解放运动。它是与拉尔夫·沃尔多·爱默生以及梭罗相关的一种文学和哲学运动，宣称存在一种理想的精神实体，超越于经验和科学之处，通过直觉得以把握。

7. **The Walden《瓦尔登湖》**：19世纪美国作家梭罗的一部文学名作。作为他的主要著作之一，《瓦尔登湖》是梭罗在瓦登湖林中两年零两个月又两天的生活和思想纪录。这是一本清新、健康、引人向上的书，它向世人揭示了作者在回归自然的生活实验中所发现的人生真谛——如果一个人能满足于基本的生活所需，其实便可以更从容、更充实地享受人生。梭罗的文章是关于自然的艺术创作。他把关于自然的观察与体验详细地记录下来，并赋予通俗的哲学意义，这是梭罗的书真实可爱之处。梭罗积极倡导一种生活观念，一种与现代物质生活日益丰富对立的简朴的生活方式，他堪称超验主义的实践家。《瓦尔登湖》是一门独特的艺术，它是美国现代文学中散文作品最早的典范之一。与其同时代的伟大作家们相比，此书的风格独特甚至比霍桑、梅尔维尔和爱默生这些天才作家们更富于20世纪散文的气息。

Unit 3 Realism (1865-1914)

The American Civil War brought an end to the romantic period and raised the curtain of realistic period in American literature. After the war, the industrialized North had conflicts with the agrarian South. The capitalism developed in an amazing speed. A large number of people flooded into the cities in search of the jobs. More and more people realized that beneath the glittering surface of prosperity, sufferings could be seen everywhere. Thus "**the gilded age**[1]"(镀金时代) was another name of this period. For writers, they attempted to expose the society as it really was. William Dean Howells, Henry James and Mark Twain created a new century of American literary realism together. At the same time, as an important part of American realism, localism appeared. It reached its high point after the Civil War. Local color writers were inclined to present the local characters of a certain region. In addition to this, people had new understanding in respect to the society. Furthermore, under the influence of **Darwinism**[2], some people began to find out that human's life was out of control owing to the heredity and environment. They were helpless and hopeless in the vast universe. The ugly side of life was exposed to the readers. As a result, when realism went to extreme, **naturalism**[3] surfaced. Stephen Crane, Jack London and Theodore Dreiser were well-known writers of American naturalism.

Novel

William Dean Howells(威廉·迪恩·豪威尔斯)(1871-1881) was the pioneer who advocated the realist literature in America. He had great influence on many writers, including Mark Twain and Henry James. Howells was a writer, an editor as well as a critic. His masterpiece *The Rise of Silas Lapham* (《塞拉斯·拉帕姆的发迹》)was considered to be full of "keen observation" and "well-intentioned criticism". In a word, Howells earned his prestigious position in the late 19th century through successfully influencing the American literary public taste.

Mark Twain (马克·吐温)(1835-1910) was definitely one of the giants in American literary history. He was honored as the greatest novel writer of American realism. In fact, Mark Twain was the pen name of Samuel Langhorne Clemens. Being the sailor along the Mississippi river once before, he successfully put his personal experiences into his works. **The Adventures of Tom Sawyer**[4] and its sequel(续篇) *The Adventures of Huckleberry Finn* were welcomed warmly by different readers. Ernest Hemingway once spoke highly of *The Adventures of Huckleberry Finn*. He said this novel was "all modern American literature comes". Mark Twain was known as a local color writer for he used colloquial(口语的)language and lots of dialects in his works. His words were simple, brief or even ungrammatical. In face of social injustice, Mark Twain was good at criticizing it in a humorous manner.

Henry James (亨利·詹姆斯)(1843-1916) was born and raised in a wealthy and well-educated family thus provided him ample(足够的) opportunities to travel widely in England, France and Italy. Therefore, his novels were involved with the international theme which was about the confrontation of American and European culture. Although he published a large number of books, the most remarkable ones were The American, Daisy Miller and The Portrait of a Lady. In his view, writers should be familiar with life so as to create vivid characters. He also attached great importance to the individual psychology. His language was always highly refined and well-polished. The writing style of his was often intricate(错综复杂的).

Harriet Beecher Stowe(哈丽叶特·比切·斯托)(1811-1896) who was living in the critical period of American civil war wrote the novel **The Uncle Tom's Cabin**[5]. This book exposed the cruelty of slavery in southern plantation and the misery of the slaves and showed Stowe's strong sympathy for the encounter of theirs. The importance of this novel in American history was remarkable. It pushed American anti-slavery struggle but meanwhile the slander from the slavery owners was also hash. To some extent, public sentiment about the Civil War was aroused. Therefore, President Lincoln said in 1862 to Stowe, "So you're the little lady who wrote the book that started this Great War!"

Stephen Crane(斯蒂芬·克莱恩)(1871-1900) was a pioneer of American naturalism. He witnessed the people's miserable life in slums of New York, hence, provided him rich writing material. In his *Maggie: A Girl of the Street*(《街头女郎梅季》), he conveyed the idea that human beings were so insignificant that they couldn't battle against the environment. The *Red Badge of Courage*(《红色英勇勋章》,又译《红色的英勇标志》) was one of his greatest novels. In this book, it described how an ordinary soldier became mature spiritually little by little in the war. The story revealed that the war was blind and brutal; the battlefield was like a slaughterhouse that it made people lose their humanity.

Jack London(杰克·伦敦)(1876-1916) was a prolific American novelist and short story writer. He got little education when he was young but he was quite fond of reading. When he was 19 years old, he began to study by himself. His life was full of hardships but his strong-will and hard work made him successful eventually. Jack London's works dealt with the overwhelming power of nature and struggle for survival. **The Call of the Wild**[6] told a story that a giant pet dog Buck found his survival instincts. His masterwork Martin Eden(《马丁·伊登》) was somewhat autobiographical. It brought the pretense and decay of capitalist society to light. Based on Jack London's experiences and his own insights into life, his novels were exciting, well-detailed and vividly told.

Theodore Dreiser(西奥多·德莱塞)(1871-1945) was born in a poor family whose parents were German immigrants. Being a journalist broadened his version and made him realize the wide gap between the poor and the rich. Therefore, he showed his sympathy for the poor and the helpless from time to time in his writings. For Dreiser, man was a "victim of forces over which he has no control". His works were true to the social conditions of his age. **Sister Carrier**[7] which was his first novel presented the modern life of the United States at the end of the 19th century. In "*The Trilogy of Desire*"(《欲望三部曲》) which includes *The Financier*, *The Titan* and *The Stoic*,

Dreiser continued to criticize the society. Among all of his books, The American Tragedy won the best appraisement. The intriguing plot was one of the reasons contributed to the success of its popularity. This book tried to tell people that American tragedy was the result of American society itself rather than somebody's. And the American dream was a big setup that it hurt the innocent people. Although Dreiser's writing style has been controversial since the beginning and his language at times was awkward, he still remains to be one of the most important writers in American literature.

Notes

1. the gilded age 镀金时代：《镀金时代》是马克·吐温发表于1873年的的一部长篇小说，通过对一位企业家兼政客的描写，揭露了西部投机家、东部企业家和政府官吏三位一体掠夺国家和人民财富的黑幕。后来人们用这个词来形容从南北战争结束到20世纪初的那一段美国历史。南北战争为美国资本主义发展扫清了道路，加上不断涌入的移民和西部新发现的矿藏，这一切使得美国的工业化极速发展，国家财富迅速增长。到20世纪初，美国已经是世界上最强的工业国了。历史学家认为，在这一历史时期，商业上的投机风气猖獗，政治上腐败严重，不少人以不正当手段发财致富，并以炫耀财富为荣，有些人口中的这个“黄金时代”不过是“镀金时代”罢了。

2. Darwinism 达尔文主义：英国生物学家C.R. 达尔文创立的以自然选择为中心的生物进化理论，即通常所指的“进化论”。达尔文主义第一次把生物学放在完全科学的基础上，它的产生不仅是生物学的伟大革命，也是人类思想史上的伟大革命，具有巨大的哲学意义。它用自然选择的进化学说合理地说明生物的多样性和适应性，从而有力地打击了唯心主义的特创论和目的论利用生物的多样性和适应性长期宣扬的上帝有目的地创造生物的观点，这是唯物主义世界观的伟大胜利。

3. naturalism 自然主义：产生于19世纪，它排斥浪漫主义的想象、夸张等主观因素，自认为比现实主义更真实地描写客观生活。实际上是以实证主义哲学和生物进化论来分析人，把人视为动物，认为人的品性与命运只由两种自然力量即遗传和环境决定。

4. The Adventures of Tom Sawyer《汤姆·索亚历险记》：美国小说家马克·吐温1876年发表的代表作品，小说的故事发生在19世纪美国密西西比河畔的一个普通小镇上。主人公汤姆·索亚天真活泼、敢于探险、追求自由，不堪忍受束缚个性、枯燥乏味的生活，幻想干一番英雄事业。小说的时代在南北战争前，写的虽是圣彼得堡小镇，但该镇某种程度上可以说是当时美国社会的缩影。小说通过主人公的冒险经历，对美国虚伪庸俗的社会习俗、伪善的宗教仪式和刻板陈腐的学校教育进行了讽刺和批判，以欢快的笔调描写了少年儿童自由活泼的心灵。《汤姆·索亚历险记》以其浓厚的深具地方特色的幽默和对人物敏锐观察，一跃成为最伟大的儿童文学作品，也是一首美国“黄金时代”的田园牧歌。《汤姆·索亚历险记》自出版以来，就广受追捧，是史上最经典的历险记之一。该书大获成功之后，马克·吐温又创作了《密西西比河上的生活》（1883年）和《哈克贝利·费恩历险记》（1884年），被后人推崇为“密西西比河三部曲”，还原了19世纪中后期最真实的美国社会。而《哈克贝利·费恩历险记》中的主人公正是《汤姆·索亚历险记》中的哈克贝利·费恩，因此也被认为是《汤姆·索亚历险记》的续篇。

5. The Uncle Tom's Cabin《汤姆叔叔的小屋》：又译作《黑奴吁天录》和《汤姆大伯的小屋》，此书于 1852 年首次在《民族时代》刊物上连载，赢得了成千上万的热情的读者。当时几乎每个识字的美国人都争先恐后地阅读这部"扣人心弦"的小说。《汤姆叔叔的小屋》既描写了不同表现和性格的黑奴，也描写了不同类型的奴隶主嘴脸。它着力刻画了接受奴隶主灌输的基督教精神、逆来顺受型的黑奴汤姆；也塑造了不甘心让奴隶主决定自己生死的具有反抗精神的黑奴；同时，也揭示了各种类型的奴隶主的内心世界和奴隶主不完全相同的表现。《汤姆叔叔的小屋》的流传使斯托夫人成了一位世界注目的人物。当然，在对《汤姆叔叔的小屋》的一版赞美声中也夹杂着阵阵责骂的喊叫，代表南方奴隶主利益的宣传喉舌《南方文学通讯》等，指责斯托夫人"歪曲事实"，小说是"幻觉的反映"。林肯总统后来接见斯托夫人时戏谑地称她是"写了一本书，酿成了一场大战的小妇人"，这一句玩笑话充分反映了《汤姆叔叔的小屋》这部长篇小说的巨大影响。

6.Thc Call of the Wild《野性的呼唤》：又名《荒野的呼唤》，美国著名作家杰克·伦敦所著。作品以一只狗的经历表现文明世界的狗在主人的逼迫下回到野蛮，写的是狗，也反映人的世界。热望本已在，蓬勃脱尘埃；沉沉长眠后，野性重归来。巴克原是米勒法官家的一只爱犬，经过了文明的教化，一直生活在美国南部加州一个温暖的山谷里。后被卖到美国北部寒冷偏远、盛产黄金的阿拉斯加，成了一只拉雪橇的狗。小说中的狗是有着生命自主赏识的。狗，不再是传统意义上简单的工具和附庸，而是具有自身价值和意义的生命强者。

7. Sister Carrier《嘉莉妹妹》：美国现实主义作家西奥多·德莱塞的重要作品之一，描写了农村姑娘嘉莉来到大城市芝加哥寻找幸福，为摆脱贫困，出卖自己的贞操，先后与推销员和酒店经理同居，后又凭美貌与歌喉成为演员的故事。作家以嘉莉为代表深刻揭露了美国资本主义制度对贫苦人民压榨的残酷性和资产阶级生活方式对小资产阶级分子的腐蚀性。小说中不乏现实主义的描写。它以新兴的工商业城市芝加哥为背景，展现了在工业扩张和自由经济的黄金时代里，百万富翁第一次被人们当成崇拜的偶像，吸引着四面八方的人。农民纷纷涌入城市，成为了资本家廉价的劳动力。结果芝加哥商业区失业者到处流浪，向行人行乞，这一切仿佛是一幅生动的城市风景画，小说通过嘉莉妹妹、杜洛埃和赫斯特伍德三人的关系深刻的揭示了这一主题。

Unit 4 American Modernism (1914-1945)

In 1914, Van Wyck Brooks（范·威克·布鲁克斯）visited London and there he wrote in London, America's Coming of Age, was published the following year（1915）. The book was considered the new "American Scholar"（after Emerson's essay with the same title）for that generation. He attacked the Genteel（文雅的）tradition and rooted it, right or wrong, in Puritanism. He was also militantly（激进地）resistant to the classicism of Irving Babbitt and Paul Elmer More who had deeply shaped the thinking of **T. S. Eliot**[1]. Then, world war came（America did not get involved in it until 1917）. The war, with its horror of mechanical warfare and mass slaughter, negatively impacted the aesthetic sensibility, especially among American writers or would-be writers who served in the Europe theatre. After the war, much of the new modern writing would be primarily a reaction to that dirty war. From the 1920s till the end of World War II American modern fiction reached a level of accomplishments as illustrious as that in American modern poetry. While the basic impulse of literary modernism emerged in 19th century Europe, notably in such authors as Baudelaire, Flaubert, Dostoevsky, Nietzsche, Proust and others. This impulse became the roots of **American modernism**[2]. From 1914 (the beginning of World War I) till 1945 (the end of World War II), American literature began to merge into the mainstream of Western modern culture. Compared with realists, literary modernists have a more complex view of reality. They believe that reality is experienced from different perspectives and at different levels. They are willing to include multiple perspectives, to keep the structure of their stories open-ended and to experiment with other narratives options to avoid a totalization of reality. Understanding American modernist style (forms) is extremely important for a proper understanding of modern literature. It is impossible to list all stylistic features here, but several features are highly discussed, for example, the first person point of view, the inclusion of perspectives, literary exploration of the psychological depths, open-endedness and using irony and so on. If American Romanticism was the first flowering of American literature, American modernism was the second flowering. It began with the rebellion of naturalist before 1917, thrived along with the rise of **the Lost Generation**[3] in the 1920s, attained the zenith of prosperity on the 1930s, and ended with the Second World War.

Realistic Fiction

After the Civil War, American authors and scholars turned against the irrationality and vanity of contemporary literature. They blamed the convention of romanticism for fostering a national vision which inevitably led to war, causing Americans to fight when they might have negotiated, to seek empty glory though it cost them their lives. Realism offered detailed verisimilitude, close social notation, analysis of motives, and unhappy endings.

Sherwood Anderson(舍伍德·安德森) who began to explain characters from psychology aspect is famous for his work of *Winesburg Ohio*(1919). He portrayed the small-town Middle Westerners' unfulfilled and twisted lives. Twistedness and sweetness constitutes Anderson's central concept of the "grotesque", which was absorbed by Faulkner, Flannery O'Connor, Carson McCullers and others in their creation of character types. The first American author to win the Nobel Prize for Literature, Sinclair Lewis was a sociological writer. His novels form a segment of American social history. Lewis never wrote before he acquainted himself thoroughly with his material. For several decades Lewis nibbled like a silkworm at the mulberry(桑树) leaf of American middle-class life so that he got to know it inside out. Main Street(1920) deals with parochial small-town life; Babbitt(1922) paints a truthful picture of the middle-class business world of post-war America.

In a sense the thirties can be called the decade of John Dos Passos(约翰·多斯·帕索斯). He was the leading naturalist of the Depression. While he, to some extent, is a political writer. His writings were communist-oriented for a long period. In *Three Soldiers*(1921), he sought experimental forms to break out of the perspective of his own social class. And the source of inspiration for his formal experimentation was political radicalism. *Manhattan Transfer*(1925) was his significant attempt to broaden his social perspective. The novel's protagonist is not an individual but Manhattan itself, dazzling and alienating. The best-known work by Dos Passos is a trilogy consisting of *The Forty-Second Parallel*(1930), 1919(1932), and *The Big Money*(1936). The three books attempted to introduce into fiction the sweep of scenes and the quick shifts of focus that one often finds in movies.

During the depression of the 1930s, fiction that dealt with social and economic themes came to the fore. The outstanding author in this field is John Steinbeck(约翰·斯坦贝克). He placed faith in the oppressed to be able to use political democracy for the improvement of their condition. His novel is the novel of protest, also the document of social condition and development. The *Grapes of Wrath*(1939) is the story of those migrant farm workers who were driven from the dust bowl of Oklahoma to California. The trip to California was filled with hardships, however their courage endures. The novel is full of bitterness and pain but not exactly despair. Another two famous novels are *In Dubious Battle*(1936) and *Of Mice and Men*(1937). In 1962, he won the Nobel Prize.

Lost Generation

During the 1920s, a group of literary notables known as "Lost Generation" gained popularity. The Lost Generation was born with its specific social and historical background. Two important factors made it distinctive: World War I and the sense of life being dislocated(混乱) and fragmented.

Gertrude Stein(格特鲁德·斯泰因) settled down in Paris in 1903. She met many more talented young American writers who lived in Paris and came to her with letters of introduction. She called them "the lost generation"—young people lost and embittered in a world that had been shaken to its foundations by World War I. Her term "lost generation" applied to a group of great writers, such as F. Scott Fitzgerald, and Ernest Hemingway and so on. *Three Lives*(1909) is one of her best, most readable works.

F. Scott Fitzgerald[4](弗朗西斯·斯科特·菲茨杰拉德) is the novelist who best captured the fashion, the wealth, the changing sexual habits, the charm, the deceit, and confusion in the social life of the 1920s. In addition, he revealed the deeply invested dreams, the illusions, romantic vulgarities and spiritual restlessness of his generation. This *Side of Paradise*(1920), his first novel expressed perfectly the feverish , excitement-craving lives of the youth of the **"Jazz Age[5]"**. His most important work is *The Great Gatsby*(1925). The main character, Jay Gatsby is striving to recapture a beautiful dream he once believed in. He wanted to capture the past exactly as it was. Fitzgerald's novel shows the nature of American dream, a deeply paradoxical thing.

Ernest Hemingway(欧内斯特·海明威) is the recipient of the Nobel Prize for Literature in

1954 for his writing of *The Old Man and Sea*(1952). Hemingway's style is not just a style of writing but also a style of living, which is spare, understate, and direct. Though simple on the surface, he effectively conveys some intense and complex emotions. Two of his novels are about bullfighting: The *Sun Also Rises*(1926) and *Death in the Afternoon*(1932). The former one was his first novel, which tells of the sadness and isolation of young Americans living in Paris after World War I. For *Whom the Bell Tolls*(1940) is an important novel about Spanish Civil War, while *A Farewell to Arms*(1929) recalls the suffering and destruction of World War I. In his writing, Hemingway created a **Code Hero**[6], who would adhere to a set of rules of conduct. The character must act in a way that is acceptable when he is faced with the fact of death, which means the hero is a man's man. Through his novel, he also tried to show **the tip of iceberg**[7]. In an interview, Hemingway said: " I always try to write on the principle of the iceberg. There is seven-eighths of it under water for every part that shows."

Southern Literature

Southern literature is defined as American literature about the Southern United States or by writers from this region. They displayed the conservative romanticist spirit, reflected simultaneously the universal truth of humanity, and constructed the myth of keeping the land pure from industrial corruption. Since the beginning of the 20th century, there have emerged a few generations of southern writers who have all tried to root their works in the south with a view to achieving universal applicability.

Ellen Glasgow(艾伦·格拉斯哥), with her series of novels set in Virginia, focused more on the future rather than keeping casting a backward glance. This is what her novels such as *Virginia*(1913) and *Barren Ground*(1925) try to represent. Glasgow also made her unique contribution to the emergence of William Faulkner.

William Faulkner(威廉·福克纳), as a novelist, has achieved the status of a literary giant. He wrote about a mythical Mississippi town called Jefferson, in a mythical county called **Yoknapatawpha**[8]. He secretly presents his real hero: the spirit of tragedy in such novels as The *Sound and the Fury*(1929), *Light in August*(1932), *Absalom, Absalom!*(1936), *The Hamlet*(1940), and *A Fable*(1954). Through these novels, he showed the true life about the South. In 1949 he was awarded the Nobel Prize for Literature.

Flannery O'Connor(弗兰纳里·欧康纳) was also a Southern writer, but she did not explicitly resort to the Southern dialect. Rather, she conveyed the sound of Southern speech by choosing the words and word order the characters would use. *Good Country People* proves a patterned theme in O'Connor: redemption can be achieved through catastrophe or sanctity through great sinfulness. *A Good Man Is Hard to Find* is another example. It is a story about a family of six which, on its way to Florida, gets wiped out by an escaped convict named the Misfit.

Eudora Welty(尤多拉·威尔蒂) was born in Jackson, Mississippi, in the Deep South which historically placed its women in a sheltered environment. She managed to stand outside all politics and causes throughout her life. Although she was virtually the next-door neighbor of William Faulkner, she did not have too strong a sense of Southern ancestry as Faulkner did. *Delta Wedding* (1946) offers a whimsical (异想天开的) portrait of a family, the Fairchilds, who live in Fairchild (fictional town), Mississippi, near Delta City.

African American Literature

Economic hard times in the 1930s and the 1940s gave rise to more active social movements, further boosting **Harlem Renaissance**[9]. Harlem is an African American community in New York. Harlem Renaissance blossomed between the wars in several cities, not just in Harlem. The movement showed a pride in African heritage and in African American culture. *Jean Toomer's Cane* (1923) signaled the beginning of black writing known as the Harlem Renaissance. Richard Wright is a pioneer in African literature. Struggling against the deprived upbringing with talent, courage and character, Wright became increasingly aware of the conditions under which African Americans were oppressed. This literary pursuit let to the success of his first novel *Native Son* (1940), a novel that explores the complex social and psychological factors involved in a black boy's horrendous crimes.

Modern Poetry

Although at the very beginning of the 20th century, American poetry was overshadowed by novel for a while, the second decade of the century, however, began to witness a poetry renaissance. American Poets of the 20th century who had always felt a compulsion "to justify his existence as poet" began to come to terms with the significant social, economic and political changes of the modern era.

Traditional Poets

Edwin Arlington Robinson (埃德温·阿林顿·罗宾逊), had nothing but scorn for the tradition of "pretty" poems. The words and rhythms of his poems matched the New England speech of the day. His *The Man Against the Sky* (1916) let him receive adequate recognition of his genius. However, he struggled for 25 years before he gained wide recognition in 1922 when he won the first of his three Pulitzer Prizes. He is best known for his poems about a fictional New England "Tilbury Town" and its inhabitants.

Robert Frost[10] (罗伯特·弗罗斯特) is the most popular modern poet in America. His first collection of poetry was *A Boy's Will*, published in 1913. With the help of Ezra Pound, he published his second volume *North of Boston* (1914). His *The Road Not Taken* is also very famous. Frost's poetry addresses familiar subjects, makes use of an accessible language, and shows, on the surface, a simple thought process, but beneath the surface simplicity is the complexity of life. To him, a poem was an expression that "begins in delight and ends in wisdom." He became the nation's unofficial **Poet Laureate**[11] when he was invited to read his poem at President Kennedy's inauguration in 1961.

Imagist

Ezra Pound（埃兹拉·庞德）exerted tremendous influence on modernism, particularly on modern verse. He developed the term Imagism and headed a group of poetic experimentalists, who called themselves **imagists**[12], for they expressed themselves through a series of clear, exact images, or likenesses. Pound's In a Station of the Metro has been regarded as a classic specimen of imagist poetry. He has great influences on Rober Frost and T. S. Eliot.

Early in his poetic career, William Carlos Williams（威廉·卡洛斯·威廉姆斯）imitated Pound, gradually he developed his own effective style of free verse. Beginning in 1951 when Book Four of his epic, Paterson-the longest poem, appeared, he was perceived to be a major poet. His shortest serious poem, The *Red Wheelbarrow*（1923）highlighted images or things, avoided the direct presentation of ideas and described a picture with a plain factual statement.

Symbolist

Wallace Stevens[13] was a symbolist（象征主义）, which means that words in his poems frequently carry special meanings. He wrote a series of poems predicated on the theme that reality is an integration of imagination and the external world, such as Anecdote of the Jar.

The Fugitive Group

From the end of World War I till the end of World War II, T. S. Eliot was regarded as the iconic figure in poetry, for his portrayal of the post-war era as a despiritualized desert in his long poem. The *Waste Land*（1922）echoed a sense of loss and despair that many felt in that time period. In his poem, there are two more noteworthy stylistic features. One is Eliot's ability to fuse the past into the present. The other is his use of mythology as a way to give poem structure and unity. Eliot influenced a whole generation of younger American writers, including Ernest Hemingway, F. Scott Fitzgerald, and William Faulkner. His work *Four Quartets*（1943）won him the Nobel Prize.

Adopting much of Eliot's approach, a group of young south Agrarians（平均地权论者）, teachers and students at Vanderbilt University in Tennessee made it popular in most American universities and elite intellectual circles in about forty years. This was the Fugitive Group（逃逸派）. The central figure of this group is **John Crowe Ransom**[14]. He began writing poetry in about 1916, and in the early 1920s, he discovered his own poetic voice, publishing two important books of poetry: *Chills and Fever*（1924）and *Two Gentlemen in Bonds*（1927）. The Fugitives concerned with producing and publishing poems, but the focus of the group gradually shifted from the study of poetry to literary criticism and initiated the movement of New Criticism.

Prairie Poets(草原诗人)

Carl Sandburg[15] was one of the Mid-West prairie poets that became known in the Chicago

Renaissance. He did not become known as a poet until his first volume, Chicago Poems, was put out by a nationally known publisher in 1916. He was also associated with the imagists and wrote well-known Imagist poems such as Fog, Lost, and The Harbor.

African Poets

Langston Hughes[16] is widely acclaimed as a great African American writer in the 20th century with a national and international fame. He was often referred to as "Poet Laureate of the Negro Race". The 1921 publication of his *The Negro Speaks of Rivers* marks the beginning of the first phase of Hughes' literary career, the Harlem Renaissance Period, throughout the whole 1920s.

Drama

American drama has often been regarded as the poor stepchild in the family of American literature. In 1915, American drama found its artistic feeling with the founding of three new theatrical groups. It was not until 1920（the year of Eugene O'Neill's *Beyond the Horizon*）that American produced a playwright.

Eugene O'Neil[17] was America's first dramatist of world renown. In 1936, he won the Nobel Prize. His dramas are poetic and romantic. *Long Day's Journey into Night*（1956）is one of O'Neil's longest and most serious plays. It is basically the story of a young writer's attempt to understand and eventually escape from his nightmarish home. In part, it is also the story of a period in O'Neil's own life.

Notes

1. T. S. Eliot 托马斯·斯特尔那斯·艾略特：诗人、剧作家和文学批评家，诗歌现代派运动领袖。出生于美国密苏里州的圣路易斯。艾略特自称在宗教上是英国天主教徒，政治上是保皇派，文学上是古典主义者。他的诗受法国象征派诗歌、文艺复兴后期英国剧作家和玄学派诗歌的影响，形象具体准确，思想和感情融合，用联想和暗示为联系，反映了 20 世纪 20 年代资本主义社会中存在的怀疑和幻灭的情绪，到了三四十年代又有向宗教中求解脱的情绪。《荒原》（1922）是 20 世纪西方文学里一部划时代的作品，是现代派诗歌的里程碑，也是艾略特的成名作。艾略特的剧作多采用诗体，最著名的诗剧是《大教堂凶杀案》（1935），为坎特伯雷大教堂节日活动而作。艾略特还提出两个重要的诗歌批评概念："感受的分化"和"客观对应物"。艾略特的创作和评论对英美 20 世纪现代派文学和新批评派评论起了开拓作用，对整个西方文坛的影响，很少有人能和他相比。

2. American modernism 美国现代主义：美国现代主义时期以第一次世界大战为起点，经历了大萧条一直延续到第二次世界大战。这一时期最引人注目的文学运动就是作家的自我流放，也称"第二次美国文艺复兴"。格特鲁德·斯坦因所称"迷惘的一代"中最著名的代表人物有诗人埃兹拉·庞德、依·依·肯明斯，小说家海明威、威廉·福克纳。美国现代主义作家通过形式、技巧和风格的大胆实验，与习俗和传统决裂。弗洛伊德的心理分析，威廉·詹姆斯的意识流学说以及荣格的原型象征理论对美国现代主义作家的文学创作产生了巨大影响。他们特别注重对人们的内心世界的挖掘。

3. the Lost Generation 迷惘的一代：又称“迷失的一代”“失落的一代”，是美国文学评论家格特鲁德·斯坦因提出的，指第一次世界大战到第二次世界大战期间出现的美国一类作家的总称。他们共同表现出的是对美国社会发展的一种失望和不满。他们之所以迷惘，是因为这一代人的传统价值观念完全不再适合战后的世界，可是他们又找不到新的生活准则。他们认为，只有现实才是真理，可现实是残酷的。于是他们只能按照自己的本能和感官行事，竭力反叛以前的理想和价值观，用叛逆思想和行为来表达他们对现实的不满。海明威在其创作的小说《太阳照常升起》中使用了“迷惘的一代”作为题词，从而使这一名称广为人知。其代表人物例如弗朗西斯·斯科特·菲茨杰拉德、T. S. 艾略特、约翰·多斯·帕索斯、沃尔多·皮尔斯、艾莎道拉·邓肯、亚伯拉罕·伍克威兹、阿兰·西格和埃里希·玛利亚·雷马克等。

4. F. Scott Fitzgerald 弗朗西斯·斯科特·菲茨杰拉德：（1896 年 9 月 24 日—1940 年 12 月 21 日），20 世纪美国最杰出作家之一。他年轻时试写过剧本。读完高中后考入普林斯顿大学。在校时曾自组剧团，并为校内文学刊物写稿。后因身体欠佳，中途辍学。1917 年入伍，终日忙于军训，未曾出国打仗。退伍后坚持业余写作。1920 年出版了长篇小说《人间天堂》，从此出了名，小说出版后他与吉姗尔达结婚。婚后携妻寄居巴黎，结识了安德逊、海明威等多位美国作家。1925 年《了不起的盖茨比》问世，奠定了他在现代美国文学史上的地位，成了 20 世纪 20 年代“爵士时代” 的发言人和“迷惘的一代” 的代表作家之一。菲兹杰拉德成名后继续勤奋笔耕。他不仅写长篇小说，短篇小说也频有特色。除上述两部作品外，主要作品还有《夜色温柔》（1934）和《末代大亨的情缘》（1941）。他的小说生动地反映了 20 世纪 20 年代“美国梦” 的破灭，展示了大萧条时期美国上层社会“荒原时代” 的精神面貌。

5. Jazz Age 爵士时代： 般指 战以后，经济大萧条以前的约 10 年的时间。第一次世界大战结束了（1918），经济大萧条（1929）还没有到来，传统的清教徒道德已经土崩瓦解，当时爵士乐与舞蹈逐渐受到欢迎，享乐主义开始大行其道。用菲茨杰拉德自己的话来说：“这是一个奇迹的时代，一个艺术的时代，一个挥金如土的时代，也是一个充满嘲讽的时代。”菲茨杰拉德称这个时代为“爵士乐时代”，他自己也因此被称为爵士乐时代的“编年史家” 和“桂冠诗人”。

6. Code Hero 硬汉形象：指海明威作品中出现的一系列人物形象。这些人物有拳击师、斗牛士、猎人、渔人等，他们都具有一种百折不挠、坚强不屈的性格，面对暴力和死亡，面对不可改变的命运，都表现出一种从容、镇定的意志力，保持了人的尊严和勇气。《老人与海》中的主人公老汉桑提亚哥更是集中体现了海明威心中的硬汉形象，从而成为海明威作品中众多硬汉形象最突出而独特的代表。桑提亚哥的名言“人可以被毁灭，但不能被打败”，即是这种“硬汉”形象的精神境界。

7. the tip of iceberg 冰山原则：1932 年，海明威在他的纪实性作品《午后之死》中，提出著名的“冰山原则”。他以“冰山” 为喻，认为作者只应描写“冰山” 露出水面的部分，水下的部分应该通过文本的提示让读者去想像补充。他说：“冰山运动之雄伟壮观，是因为他只有八分之一在水面上。”文学作品中，文字和形象是所谓的“八分之一”，而情感和思想是所谓的“八分之七”。前两者是具体可见的，后两者是寓于前两者之中的。

8. Yoknapatawpha 约克纳帕塔法：是美国小说家威廉·福克纳笔下虚构的一个县，名字借自约克纳帕塔法河，这条河流过密西西比州拉斐特县南部。Yoknapatawpha 来自乔克托语或奇克索语，按照一般当代语言学家的解释，Yokna 意为“土地”，“patawpha”意为“犁开”。不少拉斐特县人认为它的名字意思是“分裂的土地”，但没人知道准确的意思。福克纳对它的解释是“河水缓缓流过平原”。

9. Harlem Renaissance 哈莱姆文艺复兴：又称“黑人文艺复兴”，20 世纪 20 年代到经济危机爆发这 10 年间美国纽约黑人聚居区哈莱姆的黑人作家所发动的一种文学运动。它的内容主要可以概括为两点：一是在黑人的觉悟和民族自尊心大为提高的情况下，一些黑人青年知识分子开始重新评价自己的艺术创造才能，并要求在文学艺术中塑造“新黑人”的形象——一个不同于逆来顺受的汤姆叔叔型的、有独立人格和叛逆精神的新形象；二是在报刊上广泛开展了“是艺术还是宣传”的讨论，大多数作家都认为必须加强黑人文艺作品的艺术表现能力。

10. Robert Frost 罗伯特·弗罗斯特：罗伯特·弗罗斯特（1874 年 3 月 26 日—1963 年 1 月 29 日）是 20 世纪最受欢迎的美国诗人之一。他曾当过新英格兰的鞋匠、教师和农场主。他的诗歌从农村生活中汲取题材，与 19 世纪的诗人有很多共同之处，相比之下，却较少具有现代派气息。他曾赢得 4 次普利策奖和许多其他的奖励及荣誉，被称之为“美国文学中的桂冠诗人”。只是在他的下半生才赢得大众对其诗歌作品的承认。在此后的年代中，他树立起了一位伟大的文学家的形象。代表作品：《诗歌选集》《一棵作证的树》《山间》《新罕布什尔》《西去的溪流》《又一片牧场》《林间空地》和诗剧《理智的假面具》《慈悲的假面具》《诗歌全集》《未选择的路》。

11. Poet Laureate 桂冠诗人：经由政府官方任命的诗人及其称号。自欧洲中古世纪，在皇帝的侍从队伍内也有诗人，他们的工作就是写下纪念某事或某节日的诗歌，这种诗人在英国就称之为“桂冠诗人”，其职位由国王任命。现在把优秀诗人和桂冠诗人挂上等号，则是源自更早的习俗——在古希腊和古罗马，把桂叶编成花环，挂于优胜者或优秀艺术家的头上——此种意义上的桂冠诗人重现于 1670 年，首位得到这种称号的是英国诗人、评论家、剧作家约翰·德莱顿。

12. imagists 意象派：1909—1917 年间的一个文学流派。意象主义运动是一些英美诗人发起并付诸实践的文学运动，它是当时盛行于西方世界的象征主义文学运动的一个分支。其宗旨是要求诗人以鲜明、准确、含蓄和高度凝炼的意象生动及形象地展现事物，并将诗人瞬息间的思想感情溶化在诗行中。它反对发表议论及感叹。意象派的产生最初是对当时诗坛文风的一种反拨，代表人物是埃兹拉·庞德。在 19 世纪后期英国文坛，象征主义、唯美主义与浪漫主义结成一体，形成新浪漫主义。意象派是在其基础上演变而成的。

13. Wallace Stevens 华莱士·史蒂文斯：美国著名现代诗人，1879 年 10 月 2 日出生于美国宾夕法尼亚州的雷丁市。大学时就读于哈佛，后在纽约法学院获法律学位。1904 年取得律师资格后，在康涅狄格州就业于哈特福德意外事故保险公司，1934 年就任副总裁。在 1955 年，他获得了普利策诗歌奖。代表作有《冰激凌皇帝》等。他的第一本诗集《风琴》，在

1923 年出版，流露出英国浪漫主义和法国符号学派对他的影响，显示了他对审美哲学的倾向，还有一种完全原始的风格和感觉：异乎寻常、想入非非，浸透着印象主义绘画的色彩光亮。与其他现代诗人相比，史蒂文斯更为关注想像的转换能力。

14. John Crowe Ransom 约翰·克罗·兰赛姆：约翰·克罗·兰赛姆（1888—1974），20 世纪著名文艺批评家、诗人、文学理论“新批评”派领军人物，生前曾长期担任美国梵德比尔大学文学教授。兰赛姆认为，诗的本质、精华，及其表现世界的本质存在的能力，都在于肌质，而不在构架。在兰赛姆看来，构架与肌质无关，也就意味着内容和形式无关，内容比起形式来，其重要性极低。所以批评家要忘掉那些道德、哲学、伦理、功利等，集中精力去看到诗的肌质、诗的形式，从而也就看到了诗的本体性存在。

15. Carl Sandburg 卡尔·桑德堡：美国诗人、传记作者和新闻记者。被誉为“人民的诗人”的卡尔·桑德堡对表达中西部的乐观和民主精神尤为感兴趣。他运用通俗语言和平常讲话时的节奏描绘了先驱开拓的日子里的赤裸而又强有力的现实主义以及美国工业化扩张。1940 年，卡尔·桑德堡因作品《亚伯拉罕：战争的年代》（四卷，1939 年）获得普利策历史著作奖。1951 年他再次因《诗歌全集》（1950 年）而获得普利策诗歌创作奖。

16. Langston Hughes 兰斯顿·休斯：兰斯顿·休斯（1902 年 2 月 1 日—1967 年 5 月 22 日）在美国文坛，尤其是黑人文学方面，是一个举足轻重的人物。他写过小说、戏剧、散文、历史、传记等各种文体的作品，还把西班牙文和法文的诗歌翻译成英文，甚至编辑过其他黑人作家的文选，但他主要以诗歌著称，被誉为“黑人民族的桂冠诗人”。休斯的诗歌从黑人的音乐和民歌中汲取营养，把爵士乐的节奏融入于自由诗中，因而他的诗开阔，舒展，节奏热情得像爵士乐那样强烈。他的诗格调清新，意境深远，具有震撼人心的感人力量，对美国现代黑人文学与非洲黑人诗歌的发展都产生了重大影响。

17. Eugene O’ Neil 尤金·奥尼尔：尤金·奥尼尔（1888—1953），美国著名剧作家，表现主义文学的代表作家。主要作品有《琼斯皇》《毛猿》《天边外》《悲悼》等。尤金·奥尼尔是美国民族戏剧的奠基人。评论界曾指出：“在奥尼尔之前，美国只有剧场；在奥尼尔之后，美国才有戏剧。”一生共 4 次获普利策奖（1920，1922，1928，1957），并于 1936 年获诺贝尔文学奖。奥尼尔是美国史上的一座丰碑。他卓有成就的戏剧创作，标志着美国民族戏剧的成熟，并使之赶上世界水平。奥尼尔的戏剧师承斯特林堡和易卜生的艺术风格，把传统的现实主义手法和现代的表现主义技巧结合起来，开掘人类心灵的底层。

Unit 5 1945 to the New Millennium

For the development of American literature from the end of World War II till today, a period of more than half a century, it is difficult to find a single phrase to describe the general literary trends. To understand the conditions, this period can be divided into two parts: the first is the 1950s and 1960s; the second is the several decades beginning in the late 1960s.

In the first half of the period, the United States assumed leadership of the Western capitalist world and invested much of its energy engaging in wars, such as the Cold war, the Korean War and the Vietnam War. The psychological fear was real, tense and omnipresent. Anxiety was variously manifested. Furthermore, some social activities, such as Civil Rights Movement, produced new energies, new ideas and new conditions. And a wider variety of intellectual and stylistic forms emerged. However, since the late 1960s and early 1970s, the world has undergone some dramatic changes. Colonialism in the old forms has come to an end, and Cold War has ended, too. Yet, the Cold War mentality continues and legacies of colonialism persist. Then postcolonial literature has come into being and has become a main feature of cultural production in the last 30 years. Consequently, the event of 9/11 in 2001 has pushed the United States and the rest of the world into a war against terrorism（恐怖主义）. These new changes made large numbers of immigrants from different parts of the world arrive in the United Sates, which increased the political weight of minority groups. With African American literature being the precursor and leader, ethnic literature—including Native American literature, Asian American literature, and others—became an important part of the American culture.

Drama

Tragedy is the major theme in several modern American dramatists' work. **Tennessee Williams**[1]（田纳西・威廉斯）was the most important dramatist that emerged after World War II. Postwar American drama has been said to begin with the staging of *The Glass Menagerie*（玻璃动物园）(1945), which is a "memory play" using the technique of broken chronology. The narrator recollects and comments on incidents taken from his earlier life. This play was based on Tennessee Williams' family circumstances in 1935-1936. It is his attempt to transform life into art. Another of his famous drama is *A Streetcar Named Desire*（1947）, which illustrates many of the thematic and stylistic characteristic of Williams. A drama which Chinese people are very familiar to is *Death of a Salesman*（1949）written by Arthur Miller, who with Tennessee Williams led the post new drama. Its protagonist, Willy Loman was drove to death by a sense of failure. It is a sad version of the American Dream.

The two preeminent（卓越的）playwrights that have impacted contemporary American theater are Sam Shepard（山姆・夏普德）and David Manet. Sam Shepard tends to explore the world of the subconscious and the repressed. Over the years, Shepard has written a good number of plays like *Buried Child*, *Fool for Love* and *A Lie for the Mind* and so on. David Mamet is the most important playwright to emerge in the 1970s. Mamet's major concern relates to his pessimistic view of the dilemma with which contemporary America is faced in the areas of social, economic, and human relationships. He has written many plays such as *House of Games*, *Sexual Perversity in Chicago*, and *American Buffalo*, and so on.

Frank Chin（赵健秀）has played an important role in the development of Asian American literature. In his plays and other works, Chin has attempted to overthrow the stereotypes imposed on Chinese American by the white society. In *The Chickencoop Chinaman* and *The Year of the Dragon*, he presents characters who struggled with the history of Asians in the United States, and who strove to get an essentially American identity that recognized their cultural roots.

War Novels

War novels explore the theme of war. Writers have all experienced the war in person, therefore their description of the scenes of battlefield and the psychological characteristics are vivid and real.

War novels become an important genre after World War II, represented by **Norman Mailer**[2], who has, by virtue of his enormous imagination and immense literary output, become part of the American consciousness. *The Naked and the Dead* became a spectacular success in 1948. It tells the story of a fourteen-man platoon that land on the barren beach of Anopopei, a small Japanese-held island in the South Pacific for a reconnaissance mission behind the Toyaku Line.

Black Humor Literature

In the United States, **black humor**[3] as a literary genre came to prominence in the 1950s and 1960s. Black humor regards the world as absurd and unreasonable and gives a smile after feeling extremely and thoroughly pessimistic.

Joseph Heller[4], author of *Catch-22*, was born in New York's Coney Island. Heller enlisted in the United States Air Force in 1942 at the age of 19. His experience as a B-25 wing bombardier during World War II provided the inspiration for *Catch-22*. *Catch-22* is an anti-war novel which is built on alternating play of black humor and horror of hopelessness.

Thomas Pynchon[5]（托马斯·品钦）is one of the contemporary writers whose life is little known. He has published five novels so far: *V*（1963）, *The Crying of Lot 49*（1966）, *Gravity's Rainbow*（1973）, *Vineland*（1990）, and *Mason & Dixon*（1997）. Some of his short stories were collected in *Slow Learner: Early Stories*（1984）. The publication of the *Gravity's Rainbow*, which won the National Book Award and has since received a good deal of critical attention, ensured Pynchon's prominence in American postmodern fiction.

Metafiction

Metafiction[6] namely is a piece of fiction that is concerned with revealing the devices and conventions of making fiction and the process of making fiction. Put it simply, metafiction is fiction about fiction.

John Barth[7] is a postmodern writer, who uses more metafiction. **The Literature of Exhaustion**（《枯竭的文学》）, which Barth wrote in 1967, signaled the beginning of postmodern and metafictional fiction in the US and declared the death of traditional realism. *Lost in the Funhouse*（1968）, which the narrator Ambrose Mensch created from memory and imagination a funhouse with "real" characters, echoed the author's ideas expressed in The Literature of Exhaustion.

Postmodern Realism

Postmodern Realism（后现代现实主义）or Magical Realism is a technique popular among

Latin American writers in which supernatural elements are treated as mundane.

Joyce Carol Oates[8] has obtained the reputation as an author known for her literary use of violence in depicting American life. Her first novel, *With Shuddering Fall*(1964), depicts an intense and violent love affair between a 17-year-old girl and a 30-year-old car racer, exposing emotional derangements(紊乱), compulsive behaviors, and tragic love.

Raymond Carver[9] is perhaps the most accomplished fiction writer since the 1960s. In 1967 his story *Will You Please Be Quiet, Please?* was included in the Best American Short Stories. His style is minimalist, like Hemingway's, in which the sentences are short, direct, without too many adjectives, and the dialogues are terse but suggestive.

Realistic Fiction

Mention should be made to two realists in contemporary U.S. Literary circle: J. D. Salinger and John Updike. They followed the tradition of the realism before the 20th century to depict the characters, to reflect the reality and to reveal certain motif(主题).

J. D. Salinger[10](杰罗姆·大卫·塞林格)wrote *The Catcher in the Rye*(《麦田里的守望者》)(1951), which critical acclaim and attracted almost a cult(受特定群体欢迎的) following. It relates the painful story of a high-school boy growing up in the world of decadent New York. Through the novel, he expresses a complexity: growing out of childhood innocence is not a pathway to experience but to corruption. While this matches to the mood of trouble realism, which suits a time of a continuing nuclear threat and spiritual vulgarity(庸俗).

John Updike[11] is best known for his Rabbit books: *Rabbit, Run*(1960); *Rabbit Redux*(1971); *Rabbit Is Rich*(1981); *Rabbit at Rest*(1990). Updike's fiction depicts the American Protestant(美国新教教徒) small-town middle class holding on to their style of while trying to adjust to new ideas and new social realities. He is considered a "neo-realist"(新现实主义), for his prose is distinguished by precision, clarity of expression and satire.

Beat Generation[12]

Among those breaking news about the new age of postmodernism were two "Beat" writers who, with their sheer rebellious energy, chose the road not taken and broke new ground. These two were William Burroughs and Jack Kerouac.

William Burroughs(威廉·巴勒斯) was the oldest of the Beat writers. His works reveal a mind thinking and communicating differently from accepted standards. He enjoyed shocking his readers out of their normal grooves of perception and took immense delight in distracting them from their cozy complacency. Burroughs' most well-known novel is *The Naked Lunch*. It is a book of a peculiar kind in novel writing, which best illustrates Burroughs' thematic and formal features.

Jack Kerouac(杰克·凯鲁亚克), Burroughs' friend, was born and raised in Massachusetts in a French Canadian family. He wrote many genres of works, such as fiction, poetry and novel and so on. He was strictly autobiographical: he converted his own experience with life and people into fictions. Jack Kerouac has been noted and will continue to be for his book, *On the Road* (1957). The book is a prose narrative with not much of a dramatic interest, not much of a plot line, but there are unsettled tension, unnerving conflicts and unconventional subject matter that keep a palpable hold on the imagination of the readers. It is a story of freedom from the pressure of life. Dean and Sal are never able to hold their job positions long because they find it difficult to keep to schedules and deadlines. Dean believes that life should be lived in the present or in the moment. They set out in search of truth, but always come back to square one, disillusioned and desperate.

Other notable writers at the turn of the century include Michael Chabon, whose Pulitzer Prize-winning *The Amazing Adventures of Kavalier & Clay*(2000) tells the story of two friends, Joe Kavalier and Sam Clay, as they rise through the ranks of the comics industry in its heyday; Denis Johnson, whose 2007 novel *Tree of Smoke* about falsified intelligence during Vietnam both won the National Book Award and was a finalist for the Pulitzer Prize for Fiction and was called by critic Michiko Kakutani "one of the classic works of literature produced by [the Vietnam War]"; and Louise Erdrich, whose 2008 novel *The Plague of Doves*, a distinctly Faulknerian, polyphonic examination of the tribal experience set against the backdrop of murder in the fictional town of Pluto, North Dakota, was nominated for the Pulitzer Prize, and her 2012 novel *The Round House*, which builds on the same themes, was awarded the 2012 National Book Award.

Postmodern Poetry

When Elizabeth Bishop(伊丽莎白·毕肖普) started publishing her poetry in 1946, the era of high modernism was almost over. Yet, the convincing dispassion in her poetry is evidence that she is still linked with the modernist sensibility. Her poetry is in large measure a response to her personal. "The Fish" is Bishop's best known poem.

In the 1950s and 1960s, poets who adapted certain techniques of the novel for their poems were called **Confessional Poets**[12]. Confessional Poets closed the gap between the poet and the speaker, which makes them to be able to explore more intensely their dark selves. Robert Lowell (罗伯特·洛威尔) is foremost among these poets. When *Life Studies*(1959) appeared, he had switch form the new critical style to open form, and had inadvertently(漫不经心地) initiated a new school of verse, the confessional poetry. A series of studies on life and survival, Lowell's Life Studies, a masterpiece of Confession poetry, becomes eventually a scrutiny of American life in general.

Adrienne Rich candidly explores her emotional lifer in her poems. From the mid-1970s, she turned her attention towards the liberation of women and wrote to alert readers to feminist issues. Today she is foremost among feminist poets in the United States. "Aunt Jennifer's Tigers", published in 1951, is a good example of Rich's feminist concerns and of her modernist learning.

Allen Ginsberg (艾伦·金斯堡) was a rebel, a trailblazer and an explorer of the unknown.

He is one of the poets that belong to the "Beat" counterculture. The term "Beat Generation" refers to a group of American poets and artist in the 1950s and 1960s who waged a rebellion, in a romantic fashion, against American middle-class values and their tastes in poetry. His best and most influential poem is *Howl*(《嚎叫》). With engaged hyperbole, the poem denounces the life-denying effects of American culture on the minds of the young. The genesis (起源) of Howl is archetypal of Ginsberg's life as a whole.

The so-called New York School (纽约派诗人) became well known with the publication of Donald Allen's (唐纳德・艾伦) 1960 anthology (诗集). The poetry of the New York School reveals something in common. First, they were all vehemently (激烈地) up against the dominant New Critical values such as the impersonal presentation of images; second, they introduced the popular and the low features of life into their writings like popular songs; third, they exhibited a huge sense of humor, offering room as their poems did for elements like the vulgar and the sentimental; fourth, they experimented with surrealism, for a while. The central figure of this school was **Frank O'Hara**[13] who was born in Maryland and grew up in Massachusetts. He made less effort to get his works published, and his uncollected poems were found either from scraps of paper in boxes and trunks or retrieved from letters. These were put together and became the five-hundred-page Collected Poems.

One group of poets active on the contemporary were either associated with Black Mountain College, or with Black Mountain Review (edited by Robert Creeley), they have become known as the "**Black Mountain Poets**[14]". The leading figure of this school of poetry was Charles Olson (查尔斯・奥尔森), who joined the college in 1951 and was its rector (院长) until 1956 (year of its closure). He wrote the well-known essay *Projective Verse* (1950), one of the most significant statements in postwar American poetry, and fought for the birth of a new poetry almost single-handedly against the New Critical hegemony of the publishing world then. His *The Maximus Poems* (1953-1968) is a collection of lyrical, sociological, and experimental poems which has, together with the works of *Ezra Pound* and *William Carols Williams*, made up the basic poetics of a good deal of contemporary American poetry.

Regarding poetry, the most prolific (多产的) Asian-American poet today is probably Garrett Hongo, a Japanese American. As a poet, he is motivated by his search for ethnic and familial roots and cultural identity and poetic inspiration. He feels the need for a life of the mind. His poetry reveals his deep attachment to the places and people he calls his own. His works include *The Buddha Bandits Down Highway 99* (1978, in collaboration with Lawson Inada and Alan Lau), *Yellow Light* (1982), and *The River of Heaven* (1988).

Another interesting component of multiethnic American literature is Spanish-American or **Chicano literature**[15]. One prominent Chicano poet is Luis Omar Salinas (路易斯・奥玛尔・萨利纳斯), whose involvement in the Chicano movement began with his book of verse, *Crazy Gipsy*(《疯狂的吉普赛》) (1970), which contains his two best poems, "*Aztec Angel*" and "*Quixotic Expectations*".

Notes

1. Tennessee Williams 田纳西·威廉斯：美国剧作家托马斯·拉尼尔·威廉斯三世的笔名。田纳西·威廉斯是美国20世纪最伟大的三大戏剧家之一（另外两位是尤金·奥尼尔和阿瑟·米勒），同时也是全世界范围内最重要的剧作家之一。威廉斯的大部分作品都以20世纪上半期的美国南方为背景，描写南方的没落，充满了怀旧情绪。剧作家眷恋着南方美好的过去，对它的败落感到惋惜和痛心。密西西比三角洲的景色和气息融入了威廉斯的生命之中。威廉斯的戏剧作品无不流露出对伴随现代物质文明而来的"文明病"——人际情感冷漠的感慨，这种悲哀和凄凉的心痛隐现在每一部剧中。作家孜孜不倦地在自己的作品中探寻，提供如何面对生活的答案，将之作为永不衰竭的主题，也昭显了自己的价值观。田纳西·威廉斯一生的剧作在前期是接近现实主义的。反对单纯因袭现实主义的传统，力求广泛采用象征主义、表现主义、浪漫主义，兼及现实主义的各种艺术手法。

2. Norman Mailer 诺曼·梅勒：美国著名作家，国际笔会美国分会主席，美国"全国文学艺术院"院士，"美国文学艺术研究院"院士。1923年1月31日生于新泽西州朗布兰奇，童年在纽约犹太人居住区度过。他毕生将写作视为一项英雄般的事业，不仅苛求自己与同时代的同行竞争，也把自己视为托尔斯泰和陀思妥耶夫斯基式的人物。他的作品之多，创作期之长，让其他作家惊叹，1948年即以《裸者与死者》出名。1968年和1979年凭借《夜幕下的大军》和《刽子手之歌》两度获得普利策奖。作为记者，梅勒还成功地将小说的写作技巧融入到纪实作品中，如今这样一种写作手法被许多记者所模仿。他被誉为20世纪最伟大的美国作家之一的同时，也被称为20世纪伟大的记者。

3. black humor 黑色幽默：产生于20世纪60年代，繁荣于70年代，有其特定的时代背景。当时美国在朝鲜战争结束后，一方面社会矛盾、劳资矛盾频繁；另一方面麦卡锡主义使整个社会形成了压抑窒息的氛围。20世纪60年代初期，美国卷入越南战争，战事的失利和美军惨痛的伤亡，更使全国反战情绪高涨，局势比较动荡，社会状况比较混乱。在无所适从的社会背景下，产生了对现实采取嘲笑抨击、揭露和讽刺、幻想和否定结合在一起的"黑色"的"幽默"。

4. Joseph Heller 约瑟夫·海勒：美国当代最著名的小说家之一，1923年5月1日出生于纽约布鲁克林的科尼岛区，父母是俄国犹太移民。1961年发表长篇小说《第二十二条军规》令他一举成名，这部小说被视为黑色幽默的经典名著，对20世纪世界文坛有着巨大的影响。"第二十二条军规"一词现在已经是英语语言中的一个常用词，按《美国新世界辞典》的解释，该词的意思是"法律、规则或实践上的一个悖论，不管你做什么，你都会成为其条款的牺牲品"。这一定义具有深远的生存内涵，意指人类困境是模糊的、迂回的、不可名状的。

5. Thomas Pynchon 托马斯·品钦：美国后现代主义文学代表作家，以其晦涩复杂的后现代小说著称。1937年出生于美国长岛，曾于美国海军服役两年。1960年起开始着手创作第一部长篇小说《V.》（1963）。作品《万有引力之虹》（1973）荣获1974年度美国全国图书奖，但拒绝领奖，最后由人代领。1975年，获美国艺术文学院的豪威尔斯奖，亦拒绝领奖。品钦对自己的个人生活讳莫如深，成名后深居简出。其作品往往以神秘的荒诞文学与当代科学的交叉结合为特色，包含着丰富的意旨、风格和主题，涉及到历史、哲学、自然科学、数学等不同领域。代表作《万有引力之虹》为后现代主义文学中的经典之作，西方评论界称其为20世纪最伟大的文学作品。主要作品还有《拍卖第四十九批》(1966)、《梅森和迪克逊》(1997)、《抵抗白昼》(2006)等。

6. Metafiction 超小说：又称“元叙述”或“元小说”(又译“超小说”、自反小说)，“元小说”是有关小说的小说，是关注小说的虚构身份及其创作过程的小说。传统小说往往关心的是人物、事件，是作品所叙述的内容；而元小说则更关心作者本人是怎样写这部小说的，小说中往往喜欢声明作者是在虚构作品，喜欢告诉读者作者是在用什么手法虚构作品，更喜欢交代作者创作小说的一切相关过程。小说的叙述往往在谈论正在进行的叙述本身，并使这种对叙述的叙述成为小说整体的一部分。当一部小说中充斥着大量这样的关于小说本身的叙述的时候，这种叙述就是“元叙述”，而具有元叙述因素的小说则被称为元小说。

7. John Barth 约翰·巴思：美国小说家。一般认为他是美国后现代主义小说家，是反讽、戏拟、元小说作家。他的创作反映了二战以来不同历史时期的时代特征。巴思虽然一度由于作品的实验性而成为读者关注的对象，他的作品也往往被界定为“滑稽讽刺”“黑色幽默”甚或者“荒诞”。不过，无法否认的是，巴思的创作的确颠覆了小说创作的传统范式，然而严格地讲来，巴思的作品在美国并没有得到畅销，某些评论家甚至认为，他的作品偏离了传统小说的创作轨道，一味追求形式上的标新立异而忽略了内容上的深刻性。

8. Joyce Carol Oates 乔伊斯·卡罗尔·欧茨：出生于1938年，美国当代著名小说家，被誉为“女福克纳”。欧茨是一位多产作家，自1963年出版首部短篇小说集《北门边》以来，一直活跃于美国文坛，她勤于笔耕，不断有作品问世，迄今为止已发表长篇小说四十余部。代表作品：《表姐妹》《他们》《人间乐园》《漆黑的水》《大瀑布》等。曾多次获提名诺贝尔文学奖。她素以揭露美国社会的暴力行径和罪恶现象而闻名，敢于探索创新，涉及不同文体，采用不同的写作技巧。从表现形式上看，美国文化传统对欧茨的影响显而易见，在继承马克·吐温、德莱塞、斯坦贝克等作家的批判现实主义传统的同时，她还深受福克纳的意识流和哥特式风格的影响，作品大量运用心理分析、内心独白等意识流手法，尤其擅长营造神秘恐怖气氛，使用心理现实主义手法，注重用多样化的艺术形式刻画人物内心世界。

9. Raymond Carver 雷蒙德·卡佛：雷蒙德·卡佛(1938—1988)，“美国20世纪下半叶最重要的小说家”和小说界“简约主义”的大师，是“继海明威之后美国最具影响力的短篇小说作家”。《伦敦时报》在他去世后称他为“美国的契诃夫”。 美国文坛上罕见的“艰难时世”的观察者和表达者，并被誉为“新小说”创始者。《大教堂》是他最著名的短篇之一。卡佛看到了平民日常生活的乏味、琐碎、无聊，背后的愚昧、平庸、悲哀、无奈；他认认真真地记流水账，仿佛没有情绪，内心压抑的郁闷不时通过主人公及其难听的话或歹毒之至的小动作表现出来。“极简主义”是评论家给他的定义。

10. J. D. Salinger 杰罗姆·大卫·塞林格：杰罗姆·大卫·塞林格(1919—2010)，美国作家，其著名小说《麦田里的守望者》被认为是二十世纪美国文学的经典作品之一。小说主人公霍尔顿是当代美国文学中最早出现的反英雄形象，这一形象尤其得到青少年的普遍认同。

11. John Updike：约翰·厄普代克1932年3月18日—2009年1月27日)，美国长篇小说、短篇小说作家、诗人。一生发表了大量体裁多样的作品，包括系列小说《兔子四部曲》《贝克三部曲》以及一些短篇小说集、诗集和评论集等。其中，《兔子富了》和《兔子歇了》使他分别于1982年和1991年两度获得普利策小说奖。厄普代克被公认为美国最优秀的小说家之一，他的文风对许多作家产生了巨大影响。

12. Beat Generation 垮掉的一代：第二次世界大战后风行于美国的文学流派。这一名称最早是由作家杰克·克鲁亚克于1948年前后提出的。该流派的作家都是性格粗犷豪放、落拓不羁的男女青年，他们生活简单、不修边幅，喜穿奇装异服，厌弃工作和学业，拒绝承担任何社会义务，以浪迹天涯为乐，蔑视社会的法纪秩序，反对一切世俗陈规和垄断资本统治，抵制对外侵略和种族隔离，讨厌机器文明，他们永远寻求新的刺激，寻求绝对自由，纵欲、吸毒、沉沦，以此向体面的传统价值标准进行挑战，因此被称作垮掉的一代。代表作家有金斯堡及其作品《嚎叫》。

12. Confessional Poets 自白诗：美国20世纪五六十年代流行的一种诗歌，内容为自传体，题材包括精神疾病、性和自杀。1958年，美国诗人罗伯特·洛威尔的诗文集《生活研究》出版，在诗坛掀起一股"自白热"，成为"自白派"的创始人。另一位诗人约翰·贝里曼1953年发表的诗歌中已有自白诗的倾向，此后花用十几年工夫创作的《梦歌》，成为自白诗的名篇。西尔维娅·普拉斯、安·塞克斯顿更是任人皆知的自白派诗人。

13. Frank O'Hara 弗兰克·奥哈拉：弗兰克·奥哈拉（1926—1966），美国最著名的纽约派诗人，曾在哈佛大学和密执安大学攻读英文，1951年定居纽约，其诗采用口语及开放的结构，即兴、反理性，在幽默机智中又有荒诞感、梦幻感，突出地表现了诗人的个性，开创了反文雅反高贵的诗风，影响很大。国内翻译了弗兰克·奥哈拉的诗作包括：《死亡》《脾脏》《喜欢》《我的心》《文学自传等》《拥有一个可乐和你》等。

14. Black Mountain Poets 黑山派诗人：美国当代诗坛三大主流派别之一。黑山派崛起于20世纪50年代初，是当代最有影响的诗歌流派之一。20世纪50年代后期，他们与"垮掉派"诗人合流，引起较大的影响。该派代表诗人有查尔斯·奥尔森、罗·邓肯、罗伯特·克里利等。1950年，查尔斯·奥尔森发表了《投射诗》一文，这篇文章被看作是黑山派的成立宣言。黑山派诗人在破旧立新上比垮掉派诗人更激进，也更有建树，他们强调自我和非个性的自然融合。黑山派诗学理论的提出可以说是一场名副其实的诗歌革命，对英美当代诗歌产生了深远的影响。

15. Chicano literature 奇卡诺文学："奇卡诺"（Chicano）一词是20世纪中期以后墨西哥裔美国人的代名词。特殊的时代连同墨西哥裔美国人所具有的特殊的历史和血统，造就了"奇卡诺"奇特的文化现象。作为一种称谓，"奇卡诺"开始被使用是在20世纪40年代，当时许多生活在美国具有美国国籍的墨西哥后裔喜欢用这个词表明自己的种族身份。60年代，美国墨西哥族裔兴起一场旨在争取平等权利的社会运动，"奇卡诺"迅速成为运动的文化标志，更加广泛地出现在政府文件、主流文化媒体及社会的各个方面，以至代替了传统的"墨西哥裔美国人"的称谓，成了具有特定时代与文化内涵的专用名词。

Unit 6 Literature of Ethnic Groups

Jewish American Literature

Saul Bellow[1]（索尔・贝洛）was a leading novelist in post-World War II America. Growing up in Montreal and Chicago, Bellow received a trilingual heritage of Yiddish, English and French. In his writings, they involve the use of Jewish fables and romance with the Europe intellectual fictional tradition. Culturally, he was a Jewish writer. His *Mr. Sammler's Planet*（1970）was believed to be his best novel. It brings readers to the inner process of a Holocaust survivor who wonders about the Earth's future. To Bellow, freedom and love are his larger concerns. By the 1960s, his novels became a very important gauge（标准）of the energy and quality of American fiction. In 1976, he won the Nobel Prize in Literature.

Bernard Malamud[2] is another major American Jewish writer. Like Bellow, Malamud creates the American Jew as a symbol of the modern man's struggle. The theme that he more inclined to express is the hope of redemption（救赎）. The *Assistant*（1957）tells a story of conversion, and redemption. Frank Alpine, who was brought up in a Catholic orphanage on the West coast, comes to New York where, initially, he commits a crime but gradually struggles out of evil into good and becomes a Jew.

Isaac Bashevis Singer[3] wrote almost exclusively in Yiddish, trying to revitalize a 1,000-year-old language and the cultural heritage related to it. In 1978, he won the Noble Prize. He was the first Yiddish writer. His famous writings involve *Forward*（1945-1948）, *The Slave*（1962）, *The Manor*（1967）, *The Estate*（1970）etc.

African American Literature

Ralph Ellison[4] gained reputation as a fiction writer due to his work of *Invisible Man*（1952）. It describes an American black from a southern background involved in the horror of a race riot in New York's Harlem. It is a widely established perception that this novel deeply embedded in African American culture and experience, is not just representative of the African America, and not even just representative of America, white and black, but it is also a highly pertinent commentary on the human condition in the 20th century.

Harlem is also the setting（背景）of *Go Tell It on the Mountain*（1953）, whose author is **James Baldwin**[5]. This is his first writings, whose main plotline follows the religious conversion of John Grimes. *The Fire Next Time*（1963）, a part of *Go Tell It on the Mountain*, had positive influences on the civil rights legislations.

Toni Morrison[6] is the winner of the 1993 Nobel Prize in Literature as an African American novelist. The most important contribution Morrison makes to American and word literature is that she has fictionalized a territory in which African Americans are not marginal anomalies but a genuine human society. *Beloved*(1987) is her best novel. With the community's help, Sethe escapes the violence and the ghost disappears. The novel is an allegory(寓言) of how African Americans struggle with the nightmare legacies of slavery.

Alice Walker[7] is a feminist African American writer. The black woman struggling towards self-realization in a hostile environment is a recurrent theme in her novels. She is best known as the author of *The Color Purple*(1982), in which the heroine, Celie, suffers not only from poverty and racism but also from the sexual abuse and ignorance of her sharecropper family. Yet, she endures it all and rises to a serene accommodation in the end.

Native American Literature

The man who initially helped set the stage for the Native American Renaissance of the 1960s was D'Arcy McNickle, the writer who devoted his life to improving the lot of his fellow American Indians. He wrote a number of nonfiction works, the most important of which is *Native American Tribalism: Indian Survivals and Renewals*(1973). But he is best known as the author of the novel, *The Surrounded*(1936), a milestone in the history of Native American literature.

Natachee Scott Momady is a Native American writer of poetry and fiction. Most of his stories focus on the power of myth and language in shaping reality. His major fictional works include: *House Made of Dawn*(1968), The *Way to Rainy Mountain*(1969), and *The Ancient Child*(1989).

Leslie Marmon Silko is a native writer of the Laguna Pueblo tribe. She is interested in preserving the rituals and ceremonies of the Laguna Pueblo natives. In her novels, the protagonist's return to the oral and mythical traditions of the past is meant to rediscover the basis of his cultural heritage and to heal. Her important novels include: *Ceremony*(1977), *Storyteller*(1981) and *Almanac of the Dead*(1991). Another Native American writer is Lousie Erdrich. She wrote: *Love Medicine*(1984), *The Beet Queen*(1986) and *Antelope Woman*(1998).

Asian American Literature

Maxine Hong Kingston (汤亭亭) is a Chinese American writer. Her publication of ***The Women Warrior***[8] in 1976 signaled the Asian American writers had finally broken into the mainstream. This book is a fictionalized autobiography, freely mixing memories, stories and dreams to outline a young Chinese American girl growing up with the ambition to become a woman warrior like Hua Mulan.

Amy Tan (谭恩美) is a daughter of Chinese immigrant parents. Tan's stories often depict the relationship between a Chinese American daughter and her Chinese mother, such as ***The Joy Luck Club***[9] (1989), *The Kitchen God's Wife*(1991) and *The Bonesetter's Daughter*(2001).

Mu Xin[10] (木心), residing in the suburbs of New York since 1982, writes essays, fiction and poetry in Chinese. This style brings out a kind of internalization, invention and unconventionality reminiscent of the best in modern Western literature. His famous works include *SanweYiji* (Collected Sanwen: Volume I, 1983), *Balong*(Parron, 1998), and *MalageJihua*(The Malaga

Project, 1999) and so on.

Chang-Rae Lee[11], a Korean American fiction writer, now enjoys a great deal of favorable attention from both the general readership and from the academic establishment. Lee poignantly portrays his Asian American characters in their feelings as "foreigners". In *Native Speaker* (1995), Park's alienation from the Korean culture and history that is a component of him is the biggest trouble. The theme of "foreignness" helps the reader explore what is alienation in the context of an American society.

Multiethnic American Literature

Richard Rodriguez(理查德·罗德里格斯) is a Mexican American writer. His ***Hunger of Memory***: The *Education of Richard Rodriguez*(1982) tells his education experience. Much of Vladimir Nabokov's life is described in his autobiography *Speak, Memory*(1952). While his most sensational and influential work is his *Lolita*(1955).

Jhumpa Lahiri[12]'s first novel, *Namesake* was published in 2003 and made into a movie in 2007. The storyline revolves around two generations of the Gangulis, and shifts between the United States and India.

Czeslaw Milosz[13] is widely considered the greatest Polish poet in the 20th century. Before 1955, he published two novels, *The Seizure of Power*(1952) and *The Issa Valley*(1955). While in his autobiography *Native Realm*(1958), Milosz makes it evident that his method of depicting reality, in poetry as in prose, is to go beyond the limits of the "I" and to study himself as a sociological object in the context of collective history. In 1980, he won the Nobel Prize.

Notes

1. Saul Bellow 索尔·贝洛：或称"索尔·贝娄"(1915—2005)，美国作家，被称为美国当代文学发言人。贝娄父母是来自俄国圣彼得堡的犹太移民。1952 年，获美国国家文学艺术院奖。1954 年，贝娄以《奥吉·马奇历险记》小说获得美国国家图书奖。1971 年，长篇小说《赛姆勒先生的行星》获美国国家图书奖。1976 年，贝娄获"普利策小说奖"，同年获得诺贝尔文学奖，颁奖词指出：索尔·贝娄"把丰富多彩的流浪汉小说与对当代文化的精妙分析结合在一起"。1977 年，贝娄获美国文学艺术院金质奖章。贝娄的文学世界与贝娄自身的犹太身份相关，即他所塑造的世界是一个洋溢着浓郁的人文精神和犹太民族特色的世界。在美国文学史上，贝娄作品的意义主要体现在他所构建出来的崭新的文学世界和所塑造出来的迥然不同的人物形象。

2. Bernard Malamud 伯纳德·马拉默德：伯纳德·马拉默德(1914—1986)，美国小说家，其作品有长篇也有短篇。他的大部分作品用怜悯而扭曲的幽默描绘美国犹太人及他们对美好生活的追求。《店员》(*The Assistant*，1957 年)描写一个纽约的犹太店主和他的意大利裔美国店员的故事。《房客》(*TheTenants*，1971 年)讲述了住在纽约一个废弃的公寓里，一个犹太作家和一个黑人作家的故事。1959 年马拉默德因其短篇小说集《魔桶》而获得国家图书奖，1967 年又因其长篇小说《修配工》(*Fixer*)再次获得该奖项。《修配工》还获得了

1967 年的普利策奖。

3. Isaac Bashevis Singer 艾萨克·巴什维斯·辛格：艾萨克·巴什维斯·辛格(1904—1991)，美国犹太作家，被称为 20 世纪"短篇小说大师"。于 1978 年获得诺贝尔文学奖。代表作品有《傻瓜吉姆佩尔》《莫斯卡特一家》《庄园》《撒旦在戈雷》等。辛格是一位具有强烈民族使命感的作家。身为一名犹太人，辛格对于自己民族的命运和前途感到深深的忧虑，他的小说创作也处处体现了这一点。

4. Ralph Ellison 拉尔夫·埃里森：拉尔夫·埃里森(1914—1994) 是美国 20 世纪 50 年代以来最重要的黑人文学作家，同时是一个卓有成效的美国文学评论家，还是 20 世纪美国文化研究的重要开拓者之一。他对美国黑人文学和美国文学做出了里程碑式的贡献，在整个美国非裔文学创作及文学理论的发展演变过程中起到了承前启后的作用；其作品《无形人》的问世标志着黑人文学脱离现实主义和自然主义文风，迈入了现代文学的殿堂。

5. James Baldwin 詹姆斯·鲍德温：美国黑人作家、散文家、戏剧家和社会评论家。1924 出生在纽约市黑人聚居区，一生著述颇为丰厚，共写有六部长篇小说、四部剧本和十几部散文集，其作品涉及的范围非常广泛。他的小说《向苍天呼吁》与赖特的《土生子》和埃里森的《无形人》被并列为 20 世纪四五十年代美国黑人文学的典范。在二战后的美国黑人文学发展进程中，鲍德温起着承上启下的作用，是一个"真正的必不可少"的作家。

6. Toni Morrison 托妮·莫里森：美国黑人女小说家。生于俄亥俄州洛雷恩。霍华德大学毕业。20 世纪 60 年代末登上文坛，其作品情感炽热，简短而富有诗意，并以对美国黑人生活的敏锐观察闻名。主要作品有《最蓝的眼睛》(1970)、《苏拉》(1974)、《所罗门之歌》(1977) 和《柏油孩子》(1981) 等。她所主编的《黑人之书》(The Black Book)，记叙了美国黑人 300 年历史，被称为"美国黑人史的百科全书"。1993 年获诺贝尔文学奖。

7. Alice Walker 艾丽斯·沃克：普利策奖得主、小说家、诗人和社会运动人士，她在作品中反映黑人妇女为自身权利而奋斗，获得广大的回响，著有《紫色》(*The Color Purple*)。小说改编成剧本《紫色》是美国电影史上第一部黑人题材的电影，主要演员几乎全部为黑人之外，参与影片摄制的工作人员也大半为有色人种。

8. *The Women Warrior*《女勇士或译女斗士》：作者汤亭亭 1940 年出生于美国加利福尼亚州蒙士得顿市。汤教授从青少年时代，从母亲所讲的故事中所听到许多有关中国的种种神话和传说、戏剧内容情节、中国风俗习惯及有关她的祖先们飘洋过海、希望在国外发财致富的传奇式的经历，她将这些内容和材料配合起来而创作了三部传记性的长篇小说，因而蜚声美国和欧洲文坛。她的三部作品被评为美国最佳非小说作品。她的第一部作品是回忆录式的小说 *The Woman Warrior*(《女勇士或译女斗士》)。此书于 1976 年出版后，获当年美国及全国书评界的一项最佳奖和安士菲尔德—任尔夫种族关系奖和女教师杂志奖。小说故事情节是表现华裔母女两代人由于生活道路和文化教养的歧异而产生的矛盾冲突。1980 年第二部作品 *China Men*(《金山华人》，或译《中国佬》，又译《金山勇士》)。获 1981 年美国书籍奖。作者用生动、细致、引人入胜的笔调，描写先辈与同辈在美国的传奇性苦难经历，为修筑美国四通八达的铁路网立下不可磨灭的功劳。1989 年她的第三部 *Tripmaster Monkey*

(《孙行者》,或译《西游记》)出版,获美国西部国际笔会奖。此书描述美国华裔青年惠特曼·阿新的生活奇遇。

9. *The Joy Luck Club*《喜福会》: 著名美籍华裔女作家谭恩美的作品。作者1952年出生于美国加州奥克兰。1987年,她根据外婆和母亲的经历,写成了小说《喜福会》(*The Joy Luck Club*),并于1989年出版该书。

10. Mu Xin 木心: 1927年生于浙江桐乡。本名孙璞,字仰中,号牧心,笔名木心。毕业于上海美术专科学校,陈丹青的导师。1982年定居纽约,在中国台湾和美国纽约华人圈中被视为深解中国传统文化的精英和传奇人物。曾出版多部著作。中国当代文学大师之一。2014年2月14日,广西师范大学出版社推出了《温故》第二辑。本辑纪念专号首次发表了木心的《海伯伯》(未完成)、《如是我灯(序)》

11. Chang-Rae Lee 李昌来: 1965年出生于韩国,3岁时随家人移民美国。他就读于耶鲁大学和俄勒冈大学,获得艺术硕士学位。目前,他在普林斯顿大学路易斯艺术中心教授创作。他凭借第一部小说《说母语的人》获得1996年美国笔会海明威最佳新人小说作品奖和美国图书奖。他的第四部小说《幸存者》获得2011年普利策奖最终提名。1999年,他的第二部小说《手势生活》出版以后,他被《纽约人》杂志评选为"20位40岁以下美国著名作家"之一。他凭借《手势生活》和《漂浮》(2004年出版)获得了2005—2006年度亚太美国文学奖。

12. Jhumpa Lahiri 拉赫瑞: 印度裔美国作家,生于1967年7月11日。拉赫瑞的处女作短篇小说集《疾病解说者》(1999)获得2000年普利策小说奖;她的第一部小说《同名同姓》(2003),被改编成当红的同名电影。她由奥巴马总统任命为总统艺术和人文委员会的成员。她于2013出版的小说《低地》,被提名布克奖和美国国家图书奖。

13. Czeslaw Milosz 切斯瓦夫·米沃什: 切斯瓦夫·米沃什(1911—2004),美籍波兰诗人、散文家、文学史家。1911年6月30日,切斯瓦夫·米沃什生于立陶宛维尔诺。曾参加左派抵抗组织,从事反法西斯活动。后任波兰驻美国、法国外交官。1951年向法国申请政治避难,1970年加入美国国籍。1980年获诺贝尔文学奖,主要作品有《被禁锢的头脑》《伊斯河谷》《个人的义务》《务尔罗的土地》等。

Unit 7 Some of the Contemporary Authors

Mike Grinti is a Russian immigrant. His first novel, *Claws*, was published in 2012. The twelve-year-old Vietnamese American Emma wonders what happened to her sister, Helena, after the older girl goes missing one day. She learns how to use her powers as she hunts down her sister's whereabouts. In 2014 he published *Jala's Mask*. Political upheavals wracks the archipelagic nation after Azi, the kayet King of the wealthy five-and One Islands, marries Jula of Bardo tribe against the wishes of their families. The chaos comes to an end, however, when invading sorcerous ships arrive loaded with corpses.

Andrew Dice Clay (born as Andrew Silverstein) is known for his controversial, raunchy, and to many, offensive stand-up comedy routines. In 2014 Clay published his self-proclaimed unapologetic and uncensored autobiography, the *Filthy Truth*, with David Ritz. With no-holds-barred humor and honesty, the memoir chronicles his youth in Brooklyn, rise to fame, fall, and eventual comeback. His big break came with an appearance on the Rodney Dangerfield HBO special Nothing Goes Right. From there Clay rose to become king of comedy.

In 2015, Allegra Jordan published *The End of Innocence: A Novel, Sourcebooks Landmark*, which combines a love story with a commentary about war. It is commented as "… a thought-provoking and emotional memorial to the Great War that affected so many lives…" and "… a beautiful writing, almost poetic" by the critics.

S.M. Hulse's *Black River: a Novel* was published in 2015. It is her first extended work of fiction described as a contemporary western by reviewers. Critics have also called the novelist's debut a sign of the emergence of a major new talent in the field of western literature. Critics celebrated Hulse's accomplishment in her debut novel.

Michael Bazzett is an American educator and poet and the author of the 2014 poetry collection *You Must Remember This: Poems*. This collection earned Bazzett the 2014 Lindquist & Vennum Prize for Poetry, awarded annually by the Minneapolis-based publisher Milkweed Editions.

Katie Coyle's debut novel, *Vivian Apple at the End of the World*, established the author as a rising star in the world of young adult fiction. The novel is the story of a sixteen-year-old girl whose parents and their fellow Believers have disappeared overnight. The story is set in a dystopian version of the contemporary United States. Natural disasters, warfare, and other kinds of violence are rampant, as is economic hardship.

Rebecca Scherm is a novelist whose first book, *Unbecoming*(2015), tells the story of Grace, who is living in Paris as the novel begins. In her previous life, Grace planned a heist of rare antiques. Thc only problcm is that hcr husband, Rilcy, and his friend, Alls, were caught and went to jail in Tennessee. Grace, however, got away and is working in Paris restoring antiques and calling herself Julie, claiming she is from California. Eventually, Grace learns that Riley and Alls have been released from prison. She is certain that they blame her for them getting caught and will come after her, especially since she has a valuable painting, the only item not recovered from the heist. Further complicating matters is the fact that Grace is in love with Alls.

References

[1] TONG M. A history of American literature[M]. Beijing: Foreign Language Teaching and Research Press, 2008.

[2] 常耀信 . 美国文学简史 [M]. 3 版 . 天津：南开大学出版社 , 2008.

[3] 王卓 , 李权文 . 美国文学史 [M]. 武汉：华中师范大学出版社 , 2010.

[4] 朱永涛 . 英美文化基础教程 [M]. 北京：外语教学与研究出版社 , 1991.

[5] 王蕾 , 刘著研 . 美国文学选读 [M]. 天津：天津大学出版社 , 2007.

Chapter Twelve

Historical Events

Unit 1 The American Revolution

English Settlements

The first English permanent colony was planted in Virginia, named after Elizabeth Ⅰ, the "Virgin Queen" On May 6th, 1607, three ships loaded with about 100 men reached Chesapeake Bay after four months' voyage across the Atlantic Ocean. They landed by the James River and began to build the Jamestown which they named both after their King James Ⅰ who chartered the London Company which financed this settlement. The London Company expected a return from gold and other wealth in the new colony. However, the colonists found no gold but 73 deaths of hunger and disease within seven months of their first arrival. But the colony limped along and gradually discovered a way to make a profit by growing tobacco, which they began shipping to England in 1614.

Meanwhile, far to the north of the Chesapeake, quite different colonies were taking shape in New England. The Pilgrims who established Plymouth Colony were determined not to find gold or make a fortune but to build an ideal Christian community—**"a city upon a hill"** [1]. They belonged to the most uncompromising sect of Puritans, the Separatists, who severed all ties with the Church of England. The Pilgrims sailed to the new world in the ship Mayflower and settled at Plymouth, Massachusetts in 1620. A much larger Puritan colony was established in the Boston area in 1630. The ethics of Puritans were working hard, spending little, and living a moral life, therefore they strictly punished drunks, adulterers, and heretics. The Puritans believed that governments should enforce God's morality.

Roger Williams, one of the Puritans who protested that the state should not interfere with religion, was forced to leave Massachusetts in 1635. He set up the neighboring Rhode Island colony where religious freedom and the separation of church and state were guaranteed. Lord Baltimore founded the colony of Maryland in 1634 as a refuge for Roman Catholics. And the colony of Pennsylvania was founded for Quakers by William Penn who advocated religious toleration. This toleration attracted many non-British settlers to North America. German farmers settled in Pennsylvania, Swedes founded the colony of Delaware, and African slaves arrived in Virginia in 1619. In 1626 Dutch settlers purchased Manhattan Island from local Indian chiefs to build the town of New Amsterdam which was to be captured by the English and renamed New York in 1664.

The American War of Independence

By the early 1760 s, English settlers had occupied 13 colonies along the Atlantic coast, from New Hampshire in the north to Georgia in the south while the French controlled Canada and Louisiana. The Seven Years' War between Britain and France from 1756 to 1763, known in America as the French and Indian War, ended with the Peace of Paris which confirmed Britain the possession of Canada and all of North America east of the Mississippi River. The American colonists shared in the euphoria of victory, but the moment of celebration served to mask festering resentments and conflicts. Underneath the pride in the glowing British Empire a sense of American nationalism was maturing. For over a generation, the colonists had essentially governed themselves through an elected assembly in cooperation with governors appointed by the English King.

The British government argued that Britain invested soldiers and money to defend the American colonies in the French and Indian War, therefore the colonists should pay a part of those expenses. This led to a series of Acts. New taxes were charged on sugar, tea, textiles and other imported goods. *The Stamp Act*（印花税法）attached special tax stamps to all newspapers, pamphlets, legal documents and licenses. *The Quartering Act* forced the colonists to house and feed British soldiers. These new Acts aroused colonists' suspicion that new taxes would make trade difficult, and that British troops stationed in the colonies might crush the civil liberties. Colonists insisted that they could be taxed only by their own assemblies, which was "**no taxation without representation**[2]."

In early winter of 1773, a group of colonial patriots protested the tea taxes by commencing the Boston Tea Party. They disguised themselves as Indians, boarded three British vessels, and threw 342 chests of tea into Boston Harbor. To reassert its authority, Parliament passed the *Coercive Acts*（强制法案）, dubbed in the colonies the *Intolerable Acts*（不可容忍法案）which handed over the Massachusetts colonial government to royal officials, closed Boston Harbor to all oceangoing traffic, and allowed the housing of British troops in private homes in all the colonies. To fight against what the colonists perceived as British oppression, in September 1774, 55 delegates to the First Continental Congress gathered in Philadelphia. These delegates urged colonists to disobey the *Intolerable Acts* and to boycott British trade. Colonists began to organize militias and collect and store weapons and ammunition.

On April 19th, 1775, the first shot was fired at the village of Lexington when 700 British soldiers marched from Boston to capture a colonial arms depot in Concord. Thus the American War of Independence began. On May 10th, 1775, the Second Continental Congress met in Philadelphia and began to assume the role of a national government. It founded a Continental Army and Navy under the command of **George Washington**[3], a Virginia planter and veteran of the Seven Years' War. On July 2nd, 1776, the Congress resolved that "these United Colonies are, and of right ought to be free and independent states". **Thomas Jefferson**[4], along with **John Adams**[5] and **Benjamin Franklin**[6], drafted *Declaration of Independence*, which was adopted by Congress on July 4th, 1776.

The Declaration[7] officially proclaimed the independence of the 13 North American colonies and served as the defense of the American Revolution. It included detailed grievances against the British King, George III. Most significantly, it explained the philosophy behind the revolution—that men have a natural right to "life, liberty and the pursuit of happiness"; that governments can rule only with "the consent of the governed"; that any government may be dissolved when it becomes destructive to people's right. This guiding principle and political theory came from John Locke, an English political philosopher in the 17th century.

Britain's old rival, France had been secretly supplying the Continental Army with guns and ammunition since the spring of 1776. The news of Britain's surrendering an entire army at Saratoga, New York, finally convinced France that the Americans might well reap the fruits of victory. In February 1778, France signed a treaty of commerce and friendship and a treaty of alliance, which Congress approved in May.

On October 19th, 1781, 8,000 British troops under General George Cornwallis were defeated at Yorktown, Virginia, by a French fleet and a combined French-American army under George Washington's command. Soon afterward the British government pursued peace negotiations in Paris in early 1782. On April 15th, 1783, Congress approved the final treaty, and Britain and its former colonies signed it on September 3rd. Known as the *Treaty of Paris*, the peace settlement acknowledged the independence, freedom and sovereignty of the 13 former colonies, now states, to which Britain granted all the territory north of Florida, south of Canada and east of the Mississippi River.

A New Nation

After the War of Independence, the United States was not yet a united nation. George Washington wrote of the period between the *Treaty of Paris* and the writing of Constitution that the states were united only by a "rope of sand". This "rope of sand" was the *Articles of Confederation* which set up a very weak central government—Congress, which couldn't make laws or raise taxes. The individual states were almost independent.

To revise the *Articles of Confederation*, 55 delegates from the 12 states (Rhode Island refused) gathered in Philadelphia in May 1787, thus the Constitutional Convention began. But the delegates, among whom were George Washington, **James Madison**[8] and Benjamin Franklin, simply threw the Articles aside and devised a wholly new Constitution. It set up a stronger federal government empowered to collect taxes, regulate foreign trade and commerce among the states, and conduct diplomacy. Most importantly, it established the principle of "balance of power" to be maintained among the three branches of government—the legislative, the executive, and the judicial.

After bitter debate, the Constitution was ratified in 1788. Many Americans feared that the powerful central government would trample on the liberties of the people, and in 1791 ten amendments to the Constitution—the *Bill of Rights*—were adopted. This document guaranteed Americans freedom of religion, of speech and of the press, the right to assemble, to own weapons, to a fair trial by jury, and to protection against illegal house searches.

During the Napoleonic Wars, British and French warships harassed American merchant ships. President Jefferson embargoed all trade with the warring nations. After the Jefferson Embargo Act was repealed in 1809, President James Madison went to war with Britain over this issue in 1812. The war achieved little militarily, and Britain and the United States agreed on a compromise peace in December 1814. **The War of 1812**[9] was, in a sense, a second war of independence. Britain's recognition of American sovereignty after 1815 ended the threat of foreign interference in America's internal affairs, and brought America independence from British control that had commenced with the Revolution.

After the War of 1812, America enjoyed a new surge of economic prosperity. A national transportation network was linking various regions of the nation: canals, roads, steamboats and eventually railroads. The first steam railroad opened in Baltimore, Maryland, in 1830. The Industrial Revolution began reshaping the American economy. From 1790 to 1860 the United States Patent Office granted more patents than England and France combined. Factories were producing rubber goods, sewing machines, shoes, clothing, farm implements, guns and clocks.

Notes

1. a city upon a hill 山巅之城: 清教徒先驱希望把他们的殖民地建成一个理想的社会。这种传统对美国有很大影响。至今,一些美国人仍把自己的政治制度,价值观念看作是最好的。

2. no taxation without representation 没有代表权就不交税: 英国政府要求北美殖民地人民纳税,但同时剥夺其选派代表进入英国议会的权利。

3. George Washington 乔治·华盛顿: 弗吉尼亚人,独立战争时期的大陆军总司令,美国制宪会议的主席,美利坚合众国的第一位总统(1789—1797)。

4. Thomas Jefferson 托马斯·杰斐逊: 弗吉尼亚人,《独立宣言》的主要作者,美国第三任总统(1801—1809)。他被认为是美国民主的先驱,在起草《独立宣言》时曾把反对奴隶制写进宣言里,终因南方奴隶主的反对未能实现。

5. John Admas 约翰·亚当斯: 约翰·亚当斯(1735 年 10 月 30 日—1826 年 7 月 4 日)是美国第一任副总统(1789—1797),其后接替乔治·华盛顿成为美国第二任总统(1797—1801)。同时,亚当斯也是第一位由总检察长带领宣誓的美国总统。他是由托马斯·杰斐逊组成的《独立宣言》起草委员会的成员。被誉为"美国独立的巨人"。由于他任职期间在内政、外交方面均无明显成就, 1800 年竞选总统时被托马斯·杰斐逊击败。亚当斯于 1826 年 7 月 4 日去世。约翰·亚当斯是《独立宣言》签署者之一,被美国人视为最重要的开国元勋之一,同华盛顿、杰斐逊和富兰克林齐名。他的长子约翰·昆西·亚当斯后当选为美国第六任总统。

6. Benjamin Franklin 本杰明·富兰克林：美国开国元勋之一，参与起草《独立宣言》，是制宪会议的重要成员。他出身贫寒，后在印刷业中获得成功，在政治、科学及哲学等领域也卓有建树。

7. The Declaration《独立宣言》：分为四个部分：第一部分是前言，说明北美殖民地人民必须独立的基本原因；第二部分阐释独立的哲学原则和政府原则；第三部分列出二十七条英王乔治三世侵犯北美殖民地人民权利的罪状；最后一部分宣布和英国处于战争状态。

8. James Madison 詹姆斯·麦迪逊：詹姆斯·麦迪逊（1751—1836），美国第四任总统。他担任总统期间曾领导进行第二次美英战争，保卫了美国的共和制度，为美国赢得彻底独立建立了功绩。他在1776年参加弗吉尼亚宪法的制定，在大陆的国会提供，并且是弗吉尼亚会议的一位领导人。他还是出席大陆会议的代表，是制宪会议的主要人物、北部联邦党人文件的起草人之一、众议院议员、民主共和党的组织者。

9. The War of 1812 1812年战争：又称“第二次独立战争”，是美国与英国之间发生于1812至1815年的战争。是美国独立后第一次对外战争。美国正式向英国宣战，但是英国军队的50%兵员是加拿大的民兵。同时，美洲印地安部落由于种种原因也卷入了战争。1812年6月18日，美国向英国宣战。1812至1813年，美国攻击英国北美殖民地加拿大各省。1813年10月至1814年3月，英国在欧洲击败拿破仑，将更多的兵力增援北美战场。英国占领美国的缅因州，并且一度攻占美国首都华盛顿。但是英国陆军在美国南部的路易斯安那州战场、尚普兰湖战役、巴尔地摩战役、新奥尔良战役中多次遭到挫败，并且海军也遭受败局。1815年双方停战，边界恢复原状。

Unit 2 The Civil War

The Rise of the Slavery Issue

After the War of 1812, Americans began to transform their young republic into a sprawling nation. By 1850 the national territory stretched over forest, plain and mountain. Within these far-flung limits dwelt 23 million people in a union comprising 31 states. In the North, industry boomed. In the South, agriculture flourished. One issue, however, exacerbated the regional and economic differences between North and South: slavery. The Northern states gradually abolished slavery, but the Southern plantation economy relied on slaves to grow cotton, rice, tobacco and sugar.

As far back as 1820, Southern and Northern politicians disputed the question of whether slavery would be legal in the western territories. Congress finally reached the *Missouri Compromise*: Slavery was permitted in the new state of Missouri and the Arkansas territory, while it was forbidden everywhere west and north of Missouri. However，slavery was inherently a system of brutality and coercion in which beatings and the breakup of families through the sale of individuals were commonplace. While Northern humanitarians organized themselves into abolitionist societies, Southern whites defended their way of life which was well over 200 years old.

The victory of **the Mexican War**[1]（1846—1848）gained America a vast new territory of 1.36 million square kilometers encompassing the present-day states of Arizona, Nevada, California, Utah and parts of New Mexico, Colorado and Wyoming. But it was also a poisoned acquisition because it revived the most explosive question in America of the time: would the new territories be slave or free? This dispute was settled down by the Compromise of 1850: California entered the Union as a free state; the remainder of the new annexation was divided into two territories of New Mexico and Utah whose inhabitants would decide the issue themselves. The Compromise also included the *Fugitive Slave Act*, which established more effective machinery to catch runaway slaves and to return them to their masters.

This Compromise, however, was not a final settlement to which North and South were reconciled permanently. The *Fugitive Act* deeply offended many Northerners, who refused to have any part in catching slaves. Some Northern states didn't enforce the Act, and abolitionists continued to help fugitives escape through the Underground Railroad. This Act had the tremendous effect of widening and deepening the antislavery impulse in the North.

Antislavery forces found their most persuasive appeal not in opposition to the *Fugitive Act* but in the novel of *Harriet Beecher Stowe's Uncle Tom's Cabin*（1852）. Although sentimental and full of stereotypes, Uncle Tom's Cabin portrayed with undeniable force the cruelty of slavery and the fundamental conflict between free and slave societies. It inspired widespread enthusiasm for the antislavery cause, appealing as it did to basic human emotions—indignation at injustice and pity for the helpless individuals exposed to ruthless exploitation. The issue of slavery became, in American social, economic and political life, the central point of contention, which would culminate in a crisis of the Union.

The Civil War

The crisis between the two sections steadily worsened before the 1860 presidential election. In 1857 the Supreme Court delivered its **Dred Scott decision**[2]. Scott was a Missouri slave who had been taken by his master to live in the free Illinois and the Wisconsin territory. Returning to Missouri and becoming discontented with his life there, Scott sued for liberation on the ground of his residence on free soil. The Supreme Court decided that the laws of a free state had no effect on his status because he was the resident of a slave state; and that slaveholders had the right to take their "property" anywhere in the federal territories. This denial of the citizenship of slaves was a great victory for the Southern Democrats but it stirred fierce resentment throughout the North. On October 16th, 1859, John Brown, an abolitionist fanatic（狂热信徒）led a band of followers in an attack on the federal arsenal in West Virginia. Brown's goal was to use the weapons seized to lead a slave uprising. After two days' fighting, Brown and his surviving men were taken prisoner. Brown was quickly tried for treason, convicted, and sentenced to be hanged, whereupon some Northerners hailed him as a martyr. Tensions between North and South were growing.

Amid emotional hysteria, the nation approached a presidential election destined to be the most fateful in its history. In 1860 Abraham Lincoln won a four-way race and became the first Republican to be elected President. Following Lincoln's triumph, South Carolina seceded. It was soon joined by Mississippi, Florida, Alabama, Georgia, Louisiana, Texas, Virginia, Arkansas, Tennessee, and North Carolina. These 11 states proclaimed themselves as the Confederate States of America. When Lincoln was sworn in as president of the United States of America on March 4th, 1861, he refused to recognize the secession, considering it legally void. His inaugural speech closed with a plea for restoration of the bonds of union. But the South turned deaf ears. On April 12th, guns opened fire on the federal troops stationed at Fort Summer, South Carolina. The Civil War began.

Lincoln's first priority was to defend and maintain the supremacy of the Constitution and to preserve the Union—"my paramount object in this struggle is to save the Union, and is not either to save or to destroy slavery." But as the war ground on, Lincoln eventually decided that complete emancipation was required to win the Union support at home and abroad. On January 1st, 1863, Lincoln issued the Emancipation Proclamation, which freed all slaves in areas still controlled by the Confederacy and authorized the recruitment of blacks into the Union army.

On April 2nd, 1865, General **Robert E. Lee**[3] was forced to abandon Richmond, the Confederate capital. On April 9th, surrounded by huge Union armies, Lee surrendered to General **Ulysses S. Grant**[4] at Appomattox Courthouse. Although scattered fighting continued elsewhere for several months, the Civil War was over. On April 14th, Lincoln was assassinated by John Wilkes Booth, a Virginia actor embittered by the South's defeat.

The assassination capped four years of bloody war, which remains the costliest war in the experience of the American people. The Civil War was the first total war in history, whose outcome depended not just on armies but on the mobilization of each society's human, economic, and intellectual resources. One out of every twelve American males served in the war, and few families were unaffected by the event. Over 630,000 men on both sides lost their lives, almost as many as in all the other wars the nation has fought from the Revolution through Vietnam combined. Southern wealth declined 43 percent, transformed what had been the richest section in the nation to the poorest, which was now subjected to military occupation.

The war firmly resolved two fundamental questions: the right to own slaves and the right of a state to secede. It ended slavery, which was completely abolished by the *13th Amendment to the Constitution* in 1865. It also proclaimed, once and for all, that America was not a voluntary confederacy of sovereign states, but a single indivisible nation.

Reconstruction

Although the Civil War settled two important questions-secession and slavery, it raised a great many new ones. What was to happen to the South? How were freed blacks to be treated? And who would decide, the President or Congress?

In his *Proclamation of Amnesty and Reconstruction*, issued in December 1863, Lincoln sought to quickly restore the broken union by offering a full pardon to rebels willing to renounce secession and to accept the abolition of slavery. Lincoln's assassination elevated Andrew Johnson to the presidency who believed in white supremacy and followed policies designed to restore the old planter class to power. According to Johnson's reconstruction plan, in the summer of 1865, state governments across the South drew up a series of laws known as "black codes" which kept the freed slaves from participating in economic and political life.

When Congress assembled in December 1865, it repudiated Johnson's state governments and eventually enacted its own program of Reconstruction, which included the principle of black suffrage. *The 14th Amendment to Constitution*, which passed Congress in 1866, nullified the Dred Scott decision of 1857 by making blacks national citizens, thus protecting blacks against their own state governments. But this congressional reconstruction was bitterly resented by most Southern whites, who united into organizations such as the Ku Klux Klan to protect white interests. They intimidated blacks, prevented them from exercising their rights and making social advances.

Despite constitutional guarantees of their rights, the failure of land reform left blacks a propertyless laboring class. Without economic resources of their own, many Southern blacks were forced to become sharecroppers on land owned by their former masters. And sharecropping became the primary means of organizing black labor in the South.

The 1890s and early 1900s saw a profusion of *Jim Crow Laws* in Southern states that segregated public schools forbade or limited black access to many public facilities, such as parks, restaurants and hotels, and denied most blacks the right to vote by imposing poll taxes and arbitrary literacy tests. In ***Plessy V. Ferguson***[5] (1896), the Supreme Court decided that blacks' equal rights under the Fourteenth Amendment were not violated if the separate facilities on railroads (and, by implication, in schools and other public places) were equal. In *Cumming v. County Board of Education*(1899), the Supreme Court formally extended the philosophy of "separate but equal" to schools.

By 1870, practical and business-minded Republicans were replacing the band of reformers prominent in 1860s. While Northern commitment to defend black freedom eroded, Southern commitment to white supremacy intensified. The election of 1876 both confirmed and completed the collapse of Reconstruction.

The Civil War remained only a half accomplished revolution. With the failure of Reconstruction, the nation did not fulfill the promise of emancipating blacks. The struggle of African Americans for equality and freedom was deferred until the 20th century, when it would become a national, and not a Southern issue.

Notes

1. the Mexican War 墨西哥战争： 美墨战争是美国与墨西哥之间于 1846—1848 年爆发

的一场战争。美国通过这场规模不算很大的战争夺取了 230 万平方千米的土地。

2. Dred Scott decision 斯科特判决案：斯科特判决案是美国联邦最高法院于 1857 年对“D. 斯科特控告 J. 桑福德案”的判决。这一判决实际上宣布《密苏里妥协案》违宪，引起北部各州人民的抗议，加剧了南部和北部围绕奴隶制度的斗争。

3. Robert E. Lee 罗伯特·爱德华·李：罗伯特·爱德华·李（1807 年 1 月 19 日—1870 年 10 月 12 日），美国军事家，出生于弗吉尼亚。他在美墨战争中表现卓越，并在 1859 年镇压了约翰·布朗的武装起义。在美国南北战争中，他是美国南方联盟的总司令。内战中，他在公牛溪战役、腓特烈斯堡战役及钱瑟勒斯维尔战役中大获全胜。1865 年，他在联盟军弹尽粮绝的情况下向尤里西斯·辛普森·格兰特将军投降，从而结束了内战。战后，他积极从事教育事业，任华盛顿大学（现名华盛顿与李大学）的校长。1870 年病逝，葬在弗吉尼亚列克敦。

4. Ulysses S. Grant 尤里西斯·辛普森·格兰特：尤里西斯·辛普森·格兰特（1822 年 4 月 27 日—1885 年 7 月 23 日），美国军事家、陆军上将、第 18 任美国总统，他是美国历史上第一位从西点军校毕业的总统。在美国南北战争后期任联邦军总司令，屡建奇功。但能征惯战并不等于善于理政，格兰特的平平政绩与他的赫赫战功成为明显对照。特别是在第二次总统任期内，他对南方奴隶主妥协让步以及对贪污腐化的属员采取姑息纵容态度，引起了选民的普遍不满。格兰特卸职后曾周游世界，并想在政治上东山再起，但未能如愿。晚年经商失败，抑郁病逝。

5. Plessy V. Ferguson 普莱西诉弗格森案：简称“普莱西案”，是美国历史上一个标志性案件，对此案的裁决标志着“隔离但平等”原则的确立。1892 年 6 月 7 日，具有八分之一黑人血统的荷马·普莱西故意登上东路易斯安那铁路的一辆专为白人服务的列车，根据路易斯安那州 1890 年通过的相关法律，白人和有色种族必须乘坐平等但隔离的车厢。根据该条法律，普莱西被认定为“有色种族”，遭到逮捕和关押。于是他将路易斯安那州政府告上法庭，指责其侵犯了自己根据美国宪法第十三、十四条修正案而享有的权利。但是法官约翰·霍华德·弗格森裁决州政府有权在州境内执行该法，普莱西最终败诉，以违反隔离法为名被判处罚金 300 美元。普莱西接着向路易斯安那州最高法院控告弗格森法官的裁决，但该法院维持了弗格森的原判。1896 年，普莱西上诉至美国最高法院。5 月 18 日，最高法院以 7：1 的多数裁决：路易斯安那州的法律并不违反宪法第十三、十四条修正案，因为“隔离但平等”并不意味着对黑人的歧视，而只是确认白人和黑人之间由于肤色不同而形成差别。该案的裁决事实上确认了种族隔离政策的合法性，直到 1954 年布朗诉托皮卡教育委员会案后，这一政策方才失去其合法地位。

Unit 3 The Great Depression and the New Deal

Affluence and Anxiety

Between two great wars—the Civil War and World War Ⅰ—the United States of America came of age. It transformed from a rural republic to an urban state. The frontier vanished. Great factories and steel mills, transcontinental railroad lines, flourishing cities and vast agricultural holdings marked the land. The decade after World War Ⅰ was a time of prosperity. Changes in industrial economy—**Henry Ford**[1]'s automobile revolution, advertising, mass production-propelled fundamental change throughout society. Living standards rose-Americans enjoyed pleasures from latest household goods and fashions, attending baseball and football games and boxing matches, gathering around the radio, and going to the movies. But Americans were growing increasingly suspicious of and hostile towards Bolsheviks, immigrants and others who may destroy the American way of life. Some of the anxiety grew out of wartime patriotism, and some reflected the postwar economic and political turmoil.

The "Red Scare[2]" was one manifestation of a general fear of internal subversion that swept the nation in 1919, when the Bolsheviks advocated worldwide revolution, and many Americans feared that the Communists planned to take over the United States. In January 1920, Attorney General A. Mitchell Palmer ordered a series of raids that netted 6,000 alleged subversives who were foreign-born political radicals, anarchists, socialists and communists. Though most of them were innocent of any conspiracy, Palmer nevertheless ordered 500 noncitizen suspects deported. Although Palmer's warnings continued to fuel the "Red Scare", the threats never materialized; and by the summer of 1920, it collapsed in its excesses.

Between 1900 and 1915, more than 13 million people immigrated to the United States, with the preponderance from Southern and Eastern Europe. Many of these people were Jewish or Catholic, which alarmed many older Anglo-Saxon, Protestant Americans. Some resented these newcomers because they competed for low-wage jobs, others because the new immigrants often lived in urban ethnic enclaves, and seemed to resist assimilation into the larger American culture. As a result of this immigration surge, a reorganized Ku Klux Klan emerged, which restricted its membership to native-born white Protestants, and campaigned against Catholics, Jews, blacks and immigrants. Anti-immigration sentiment culminated in the *Immigration Quota Law* of 1924 and a 1929 act. These laws limited the annual number of immigrants to 150,000 and favored immigrants from Britain, Ireland, Scandinavia and Germany. Small quotas were reserved for eastern and southern Europeans; none at all for Asians.

The 1920s was a contradictory decade, when hedonism coexisted with a puritanical conservatism. It was the age of Prohibition. The Eighteenth Amendment banned the manufacture and sale of alcohol in January 1920. But drinkers evaded the law in thousands of speakeasies, and gangsters made fortunes supplying illegal liquor. It was a time when intellectuals felt disillusioned with America, yet it was one of the most creative periods for American literature. F. Scott Fitzgerald captured the energy, turmoil and disillusion of the Jazz Age in *The Great Gatsby*. He was one of the "Lost Generation"—writers and intellectuals who were shocked by the carnage of World War Ⅰ and dissatisfied with what they perceived to be materialism and spiritual emptiness of life in America. Many of them—such as their most celebrated member, Ernest Hemingway—travelled to Europe and lived as émigrés in Paris. At the same time, an African American literary and artistic movement, termed the "Harlem Renaissance" emerged. Like the "Lost Generation," these writers rejected middle-class values and conventional literary forms.

The Great Depression

Just as the dazzle of the Roaring Twenties hid divisions in society, extravagant prosperity masked structural flaws in the economy. Farm receipts had already bottomed out, and farmers throughout the 1920s had to deal with large surpluses, declining prices, and higher expenses. For many years chronic unemployment had characterized certain industries, in particular textiles and coal mining.

In the 1920s, the uneven distribution of income suggested an economic disaster. The slowly rising real wages of industrial workers were outdistanced by the salaries, savings, and profits of those higher on the economic ladder. In 1929, the 24,000 richest families had an aggregate income more than three times as large as that of the nearly 6 million poorest families. The purchasing power of Americans did not keep up with the production potential of the industrial plant and the flood of commercial advertising. Those who were getting rich, meanwhile, found their savings piled up out of proportion to need. Looking for opportunities for sound investment, they turned to speculation in real estate and securities, both blown up into a bubble sure to burst.

The federal government failed to deal with these matters. Tax policies favored the rich, making even more unequal the distribution of income. Labor policies were anti-union. The economic situation abroad only aggravated the domestic crisis. European nations needed goods and credit from America to restore their economies and stabilize their currencies. But American tariffs such as **the Hawley-Smoot Tariff**[3] of 1930 passed during the Hoover administration, presented obstacles to European exports and limited Europe's buying power. American manufacturers found it even more difficult to sell abroad. The American and European economies were so closely linked that the crisis soon became worldwide.

On October 24th, 1929— "Black Thursday"—a wave of panic selling of stocks swept the New York Stock Exchange. President Hoover tried to assure the public that there was no reason to panic. He struggled tirelessly, but the Great Depression deepened. Confidence evaporated and many lost their life savings. Business houses closed their doors, factories shut down and banks failed. Farm income fell some 50 percent. By 1932 approximately one out of every four Americans was unemployed. By 1932 the Depression had nearly brought the nation to its knees. This worst crisis since the Civil War, in turn, led to the most profound revolution in American social thought and economic policy.

The New Deal

The presidential campaign of 1932 was chiefly a debate over the causes and possible remedies of the Great Depression. Hoover depended largely on natural processes of recovery. But his Democratic opponent, Franklin D. Roosevelt, already popular as the governor of New York during the developing crisis, was prepared to use the federal government's authority for bold experimental remedies. The election resulted in a smashing victory for Roosevelt, who won 22,800,000 votes to Hoover's 15,700,000.

In 1933 the new President Franklin Roosevelt, who is charming, self-assured, energetic, and fearless, brought an air of confidence and optimism that quickly rallied people to the New Deal. Within the first three months of Roosevelt's administration, termed "the Hundred Days", a bewildering number of bills were rushed through Congress to aid the recovery of the economy.

To deal with the banking and finance crisis, New Dealers drafted the *Emergency Banking Act*, which empowered the secretary of the treasury to decide which banks could be safely reopened and to release funds from the Reconstruction Finance Corporation (RFC). To secure the confidence of depositors, Congress passed the *Glass-Steagall Banking Act*, setting up the Federal Deposit Insurance Corporation (FDIC), which guaranteed bank customers that federal government would reimburse them for deposits if their banks failed. The National Recovery Administration (NRA) regulated fair competition among businesses and ensured bargaining and minimum wages for workers.

The relief measures included the Federal Emergency Relief Administration (FERA), which Congress authorized with an appropriation of $500 million in direct grants to cities and states. The Public Works Administration (PWA) was more a pump-priming than a relief agency, whose duties include planning bridges, hospitals, dams, and other public projects and contracting private companies to construct them. The Civilian Conservation Corps (CCC) was the most popular work relief program established in 1936, which offered unemployed young men a chance to earn wages while working to conserve natural resources. The Tennessee Valley Authority (TVA) built dams along the Tennessee River to control floods and to generate electricity.

In areas of agriculture, the Agriculture Adjustment Administration (AAA) paid farmers to cut back production to the level of domestic needs, thus raising crop prices. The *New Deal* was also characterized by the reform of Social Security, which provided a modest income to relieve the poverty of the elderly people. The *Social Security Act* required that pensions for the elderly be funded not by direct government subsidies but instead by tax contributions from workers and their employers. Social Security also created unemployment insurance, paid for by employers' contributions, to provided modest benefits for workers who lost their jobs.

The *New Deal* had three interrelated objectives: to provide relief to the destitute; to foster the economic recovery of farms and businesses, thereby creating jobs and reducing the need for relief; and to reform the government and economy in ways that would reduce the risk of devastating consequences in future economic slumps. But the *New Deal* never fully achieved these goals of relief, recovery, and reform. Full recovery was finally brought by the defense buildup prior to America's entering the Second World War.

The most durable achievements of the New Deal were reforms that stabilized agriculture, encouraged the organizations of labor unions, and created the safety net of Social Security. In its efforts to bring the nation out of Depression, the *New Deal* vastly expanded the size and influence of federal government, especially the executive branch. But the most impressive achievement of the *New Deal* was what did not happen. Authoritarian governments and anticapitalist policies were common during the 1930s outside America, but they were shunned by the *New Deal*. The greatest economic crisis the nation had ever faced did not cause Americans to abandon democracy, as happened in Germany, where **Adolf Hitler**[4] seized dictatorial power. Nor did the nation turn to radical alternatives such as socialism or communism.

Notes

1. **Henry Ford 亨利·福特**：福特汽车公司的建立者。他是世界上第一位使用流水线大批量生产汽车的人，这种生产方式使汽车成为一种大众产品，它不但革命了工业生产方式，而且对现代社会和文化产生了深远影响。

2. **The Red Scare 红色恐慌**：又名"红色恐怖"，是指于美国兴起的反共产主义风潮，分为两个阶段。第一个阶段自1917年俄国十月革命爆发后延续至1920年，恐慌受到欧洲的影响，美国工人以及社会主义者可能爆发政治激进主义或革命运动。第二个阶段是指开始于1947年，并几乎贯穿全部1950年代的麦卡锡主义后遗症。恐慌来自于美国国内外共产主义者对美国社会的影响以及对联邦政府的间谍行为。

3. **the Hawley-Smoot Tariff 斯姆特—霍利关税法**：该法案将2 000多种进口商品的关税提升到历史最高水平，在该法案通过之后，许多国家对美国采取了报复性关税措施。

4. **Adolf Hitler 阿道夫·希特勒**：纳粹党首，1934—1945年间任德国元首，二战时兼任德国武装力量最高统帅。

Unit 4 Social Movements in the Mid-Twentieth Century

The Civil Rights Movement

African Americans' quest for equality influenced the postwar struggle for civil rights by all other groups in America. Stemming from an effort dating back to the Civil War and Reconstruction, the black movement gained momentum in the postwar years. During the war they had challenged discrimination in the military services and in the work force, and they had made limited gains. Millions of blacks had left southern farms for northern cities, where they hoped to find better jobs. They found instead crowded conditions in urban slums. Now, black servicemen returned home, intent on rejecting second-class citizenship, as other blacks began to argue that the time was ripe for racial equality.

The legal strategy of the major civil rights organization, the National Association for **the Advancement of Colored People (NAACP)**[1], reached its crowning achievement with the Supreme Court decision in **Brown v. Board of Education**[2] in 1954. The Court unanimously declared that "separate facilities are inherently unequal" and declared that the "separate but equal" doctrine could no longer be used in public schools. A year later, the Supreme Court demanded that local school boards move "with all deliberate speed" to implement the decision.

Another milestone in the Civil Rights Movement occurred in 1955 in Montgomery, Alabama. Rosa Parks, a 42-year-old black seamstress, who was also secretary of the state chapter of the NAACP, sat down in the front of a bus in a section reserved by law and custom for whites. Ordered to move to the back, she refused. Police came and arrested her for violating the segregation statues. Black leaders organized a boycott of the bus system which cut gross bus revenue by 65 percent. About a year later, the Supreme Court ruled that bus segregation, like school segregation, was unconstitutional.

The struggle of black Americans for equality reached its peak in the mid-1960s. After progressive victories in the 1950s, blacks became even more committed to nonviolent direct action. Groups like the Southern Christian Leadership Conference (SCLC), made up of black clergy, and the Student Nonviolent Coordinating Committee (SNCC), composed of younger activists, sought reform through peaceful confrontation.

On February 1st, 1960, black college students sat down at a segregated Woolworth lunch counter in North Carolina and refused to leave. Their sit-in mushroomed into hundreds of similar demonstrations, all designed to desegregate public facilities and transportation. In 1961, civil rights workers organized "freedom rides", in which blacks and whites boarded buses heading South towards segregated terminals, where confrontations might capture media attention and lead to change.

They also organized rallies, the largest of which was the "March on Washington" in 1963. More than 200,000 people gathered in the nation's capital to demonstrate their commitment to equality for all. The high point of a day of songs and speeches came with the address of **Martin Luther King Jr.**[3], who had emerged as the preeminent spokesman for civil rights. "I have a dream that one day on the red hills of Georgia, sons of former slaves and the sons of former slave owners will be able to sit down together at the table of brotherhood," King proclaimed. Each time he used the refrain "I have a dream," the crowd roared.

The Civil Rights Movement achieved tremendous legislative success in the 1960s. The sweeping *Civil Rights Act* of 1964 guaranteed access for all Americans to public accommodations, public education, employment, and voting, which sounded the death knell for the South's system of segregation and discrimination. The *Voting Rights Act* of 1965 authorized the U.S. attorney general to appoint federal examiners to register voters where local officials were obstructing the registration of blacks. The year after passage, 400,000 blacks registered to vote in the Deep South; by 1968 the number reached a million.

The New Wave of Feminism

After ratification of the Nineteenth Amendment in 1920 which guaranteed women's right to vote, feminism receded from national attention, but small groups of women continued to work for women's rights and opportunities in such areas as employment, jury service, and electoral politics.

Beginning in the 1940s, large demographic changes laid the preconditions for a resurgence of feminism. Women did not abandon the workplace after World War II , as more and more women, especially wives and mothers, took jobs. Moreover, the democratization of higher education brought more women to college campuses, where their aspirations expanded beyond the confines of domesticity and of routine, subordinate work. In the 1960s and 1970s, a new wave of feminism re-emerged. One of the major inspirations for this reemergence was the Civil Rights Movement, which had focused the nation's attention on issues of injustice, inequality, and second-class citizenship.

The publication in 1963 of Betty Friedan's The Feminine Mystique sounded the clarion call of the modern women's movement. Utilizing a variety of case studies, Friedan articulated the frustrations and disaffection, the boredom and anguish of American women. Friedan encouraged readers to seek new roles and responsibilities, to seek their own personal and professional identities rather than have them defined by the outside, male-dominated society.

In 1966, 28 professional women, including Betty Friedan, established the National Organization for Women (NOW) to "take action to bring American women into full participation in the mainstream of American society now". By the next year, 1,000 women had joined; four years later membership reached 15,000. NOW and other similar organizations helped make women increasingly aware of their limited opportunities and strengthened their resolve to increase them.

This new wave of feminism, or organized activity on behalf of women's rights, reached high tide in the early 1970s. A flurry of publications spread the principles of the women's movement. In 1972, journalist Gloria Steinem and several other women founded a new magazine, Ms., which had already 200,000 subscribers by 1973. Our bodies, ourselves, a handbook published by a women's health collective, encouraged women to understand and control their bodies; it sold 850,000 copies between 1971 and 1976.

The women's movement also won support from the legislative and judicial branches of government. In 1972, Congress passed Equal Rights Amendment (ERA) to the Constitution which declared, "Equality of rights under the law shall not be denied or abridged by the United States or by any State on account of Sex". In 1973 the Supreme Court in **Roe v. Wade**[4] sanctioned women's right to abortion during the early months of pregnancy—a significant victory for the women's movement.

The Latino Movement and the Native American Movement

The Civil Rights Movement's undeniable moral claims helped to make protest respectable, while its impact on public opinion and government policy encouraged other groups with grievances such as Latinos and Native Americans.

The fastest-growing minority group in the 1960s was Latinos, or Hispanic Americans, a varied population encompassing people of Mexican, Puerto Rican, Caribbean, and other Latin American origins. They were often unskilled, Spanish-speaking groups. Some worked as farm laborers and were cruelly exploited; other gravitated to cities, only to encounter serious difficulties in their quest for a better life.

Chicano, or Mexican-American, protest drew national attention to California, where Cesar Chavez founded the United Farm Workers（UFW）in 1962 to improve the wretched conditions of migrant agricultural workers. UFW struck for better pay and working conditions, and union recognition. Chavez skillfully appealed to middle-class consumers nationwide to boycott grapes, which won the workers a wage increase in 1970. Similar boycotts of lettuce and other products harvested by exploited labor were also successful. In 1975, the long struggle on behalf of farm workers culminated with the enactment in California of a measure requiring growers to bargain collectively with the elected representatives of the workers.

Protest was not new to the group of Americans with the oldest grievances, but Native American activism took on fresh militancy and goals in the 1960s. Contrary to the intention of Indian policy established in the 1940s and 1950s to assimilate Native Americans, the termination policy stirred Indian resistance, and the relocation programs stimulated a sense of Indian identity across tribal lines and a desire to preserve traditional culture among those who moved to cities.

In 1961, a new, more militant generation of Native Americans expressed growing discontent with the government and with the older Indian leadership by forming the National Indian Youth Council（NIYC）. The cry "**red power**"[5] reflected the influence of black radicalism on Native Americans who rejected the goal of assimilation and sought the freedom to control their own circumstances.

In 1968, the American Indian Movement（AIM）was founded to attack problems in cities, where about 300,000 Indians lived. AIM sought to protect Indians from police harassment, secure antipoverty funds, and establish "survival schools" to teach Indian history and values. The new movement's appeal quickly spread beyond urban areas and seized many Indians, especially young people with a sense of purpose.

The wave of Indian protest produced the end of relocation and termination policies; greater tribal sovereignty and control over community services; enhanced health, education, and other services; and protection of Indian religious practices. A number of laws and court decisions restored rights to ancestral lands or compensated Indian tribes for land seized in violation of treaties. The right of the first Americans to remain Indians while exercising their rights as Americans gained nationwide recognition.

Notes

1. the National Association for the Advancement of Colored People（NAACP）全国有色人种协进会：一个由美国白人和黑人组成的旨在促进黑人民权的全国性组织，总部设在纽约。

2. Brown v. Board of Education 布朗诉托皮卡教育局案：堪萨斯州一位名叫布朗的女孩因是黑人而被当地小学拒之门外。由此引起的布朗与教育局的官司一直打到最高法院。该案于 1954 年 5 月 17 日由美国最高法院做出决定，原告与被告双方所争执的"黑人与白人学童不得进入同一所学校就读"的种族隔离法律违反宪法。因此，由普莱西诉弗格森案所建立的“隔离但平等”的先例被推翻。

3. Martin Luther King Jr. 小马丁 • 路德 • 金：民权运动是美国 20 世纪 60 年代最为重要的运动之一，最早由罗莎 • 帕克斯女士引起，后由青年学生将其推向全国。该运动主张种族平等，社会公正，在小马丁 • 路德 • 金的领导下，以非暴力为主要手段，金因此于 1964 年获得诺贝尔和平奖，1968 年遭到暗杀。

4. Roe v. Wade 罗诉韦德案：美国联邦最高法院于 1973 年对于妇女堕胎权以及隐私权的重要案例，对于妇女堕胎的问题，美国联邦最高法院承认妇女堕胎权，受到宪法隐私权的保护。

5. “red power” “红人权力”：即印第安人权力，20 世纪 60 年代，印第安人在民权运动的影响下，成立了各种争取印第安人应有权利的组织，他们仿效”黑人权力”的口号，提出了“红人权力”的口号以鼓舞他们的同胞。

Unit 5 September 11th and the war on terrorism

9•11

Before September 11th few Americans had paid much attention to terrorism or terrorist movements—that is, movements that used violent attacks against civilian populations to bring about changes in the political and social order. Indeed few American radicals had resorted to terrorist tactics. During the Red Scare following WW Ⅰ anarchists exploded bombs, including one detonated on Wall Street in New York City. Thirty people died, but no other major incidents had followed. Most twentieth-century terrorist attacks had taken place abroad such as in Palestine, Northern Ireland and Lebanon. However, in the Middle East terrorist movements increased during the 1980s and 1990s. The spread of Western goods, culture, and values into the Muslim world, along with the 1991 **Gulf War**[1] against Iraq and the stationing of American troops in Saudi Arabia, bin Laden's homeland, enraged Islamic extremists. Acting on a distorted interpretation of one of the world's great religions, bin Laden sought to rid the Middle East of Western influence and install puritanical Muslim control. High levels of poverty ignored by undemocratic and corrupt governments provided bin Laden a pool of disaffected young Muslims who saw the United States as the evil source of their misery and the supporter of Israel's oppression of Palestinian Muslims. The technological advances accompanying globalization and people's increased mobility facilitated bin Laden's worldwide coordination of his Al Qaeda（a radical Islamic organization）network and eased the hijackers' entrance into and activities in America, who were responsible for the September 11 attack in 2001.

On that sunny Tuesday morning, nineteen hijackers seized control of four commercial jets that had taken off from East Coast airports. At 8:46 a.m. one plane crashed into the 110-story North Tower of the World Trade Center in New York City, causing a huge explosion and fire. At 9:03 a.m., a second plane flew into the South Tower. In less than two hours, both buildings collapsed, killing thousands of office workers, firefighters, and police officers. At 9:43, the third plane crashed into the Pentagon, leaving a huge hole in its west side. The fourth plane was also headed toward Washington, but several passengers—learning of the World Trade Center attacks through cell-phone conversations—stormed the cockpit; in the scuffle that followed, the plane crashed in Somerset County, Pennsylvania, killing all aboard. More than three thousand people died, making this the deadliest act of terrorism in history. Not since the Japanese assault on Pearl Harbor in 1941 had the United States experienced such a shocking and devastating attack on its soil.

The tragedy of September 11 changed America profoundly. Before the attack the booming economy of the 1990s had already shown serious signs of strain especially the telecommunications companies. The disruptions of the attack and its aftermath only worsened the situation. Even before September 11, George W. Bush pursued a unilateral approach to foreign policy. In addition to withdrawing from the Kyoto Protocol on global warming in 1997, it scrapped the 1972 Antiballistic Missile Treaty in order to develop the space-based missile-defense system—SDI—first proposed by **Ronald Reagan**[2]. After the attack, counter-terrorism features prominently in American policy, which has made the U.S. stuck in the war on terror from the Afghanistan War, the Iraq War, the Libya War, to the ongoing Syria War.

The Afghanistan War and the Iraq War

The attack on the World Trade Center and the Pentagon reoriented American priorities, causing the Bush administration to wage a war on terror both at home and abroad.

On September 11th, President Bush declared that, "the United States will hunt down and punish those responsible for these cowardly acts." Bush demanded that Afghanistan, ruled by **Taliban**[3] since 1996, hand over bin Laden and his key associates. After the Taliban leadership refused, the U.S. and allied forces initiated aerial bombing of suspected al Qaeda targets on October 7th. They also joined anti-Taliban groups within Afghanistan to overthrow the regime militarily. Using sophisticated new technology, they discovered a network of hidden caves and destroyed underground bunkers. Under this deadly assault the Taliban government quickly collapsed. America established a coalition government in **Kabul**[4] to help in the slow and expensive process of rebuilding Afghanistan.

With Afghanistan conquered, Bush's focus shifted from bin Laden to Iraq's brutal dictator, Saddam Hussein, who had violated UN resolutions from the 1991 Gulf War requiring Iraq to destroy and stop further development of nuclear, chemical, and biological weapons. Because these weapons enabled "even weak states and small groups to attain a catastrophic power to strike great nations", it was necessary for the United States to "be ready for preemptive action".

In November 2002, the United States got the UN Security Council to pass a resolution requiring Iraq to disarm or face "serious consequences". When Iraq failed to comply fully with new UN inspections, the administration decided on war. Claiming that Hussein had links to Al Qaeda and harbored terrorists and that Iraq possessed weapons of mass destruction, Bush insisted that the threat was immediate and great enough to justify **preemptive action**[5]. Without the UN sanction, America and Britain invaded Iraq on March 19th, 2003. Although Saddam Hussein remained at large until December 2003, the coalition forces won an easy and decisive victory, and Bush declared the end of the war on May 1st. However, the U.S. didn't formally withdraw all combat troops from Iraq until December 2011. The failure to find any weapons of mass destruction and the continuing chaos in Iraq led critics to question the validity of the war. Hillary Clinton, the 2016 Democratic presidential candidate, describes her voting as then Senator to give the then President George W. Bush authority in Iraq as her greatest regret as well as a mistake in an interview in Good Morning America of the ABC News on April 21st, 2016.

The War on Terrorism at Home

While waging the war on terrorism abroad, the Bush administration also declared it at home. Domestically the war faced a daunting task. In an open society, where citizens travelled freely and valued their privacy, Americans debated how aggressively the government should act to prevent further terrorist incidents. For its part, Congress gave strong approval to broader governmental powers to wage the war on terrorism by passing the USA Patriot Act（美利坚合众国爱国者法案）in October 2001. The Act broadly expanded government powers to monitor electronic communications, such as tapping telephones and tracking e-mails; to investigate bank transactions; to monitor suspected terrorists and their associates through prying personal information from libraries, universities, businesses, and the like; and to allow more exchange of information between criminal investigators and those investigating foreign threats. This law weakened civil liberties, however, in late 2001, security appeared more crucial than civil rights to most members of Congress as they sought ways to combat any domestic terrorist threat.

The government also focused on the problem of securing the United States from any further terrorist attacks by a major reorganization of the executive branch, the biggest since 1948. In November 2002, Congress authorized a new Department of Homeland Security combining 170,000 federal employees from 22 agencies through which responsibilities for different aspects of domestic security had been dispersed. Chief among the duties of the new department were intelligence analysis; overseeing immigration and border security; chemical, biological, and nuclear countermeasures; and emergency preparedness and response.

The War in Syria

Before the Afghanistan War and the Iraq War were officially ended respectively in 2014 and in 2011, conflicts broke out in Syria. Pro-democracy protests erupted in March 2011 in the southern city of **Deraa**[6] after the arrest and torture of some teenagers who painted revolutionary slogans on a school wall. Soon the unrest triggered nationwide protests demanding President **Assad**[7]'s resignation. The government's use of force to crush the dissent merely led opposition supporters to take up arms first to defend themselves and later to expel security forces from their local areas. Later violence escalated and the country descended into civil war as rebel brigades were formed to battle government forces for control of cities, towns and the countryside.

The civil war in Syria is more than a battle between those for or against Mr. Assad. It has acquired sectarian overtones, pitching the country's **Sunni**[8] majority against the president's Shia **Alawite**[9] sect, and drawn in regional and world powers. For example, Iran and Russia have propped up the Alawite-led government of President Assad and gradually increased their support. The Sunni-dominated opposition has, meanwhile, attracted varying degrees of support from its international backers-Turkey, Saudi Arabia, Qatar and Jordan, along with the US, UK and France.

The rise of the jihadist group Islamic State（IS）has added a further dimension, since IS has been accused by the UN of waging a campaign of terror. It has inflicted severe punishments on those who transgress or refuse to accept its rules. Its fighters have also carried out mass killings of rival armed groups, members of the security forces, religious minorities, and beheaded hostages, including several Westerners.

In September 2014, a US-led coalition launched air strikes inside Syria in an effort to degrade and ultimately destroy IS. But the coalition avoided attacks that might benefit Mr. Assad's forces. Russia began an air campaign targeting terrorists in Syria a year later, but opposition activists said its strikes mostly killed Western-backed rebels and civilians.

To fight the IS terrorism, the US and Russia searched for a political solution in Syria. The US and Russia led efforts to get representatives of the government and the opposition to attend proximity talks in Geneva in January 2016 to discuss a Security Council-endorsed road map for peace, including a ceasefire and a transitional period ending with elections.

Notes

1. Gulf War 海湾战争：以美国为首的多国部队于 1991 年 1 月 17 日—2 月 28 日在联合国安理会授权下，为恢复科威特领土完整而对伊拉克进行的局部战争。

2. Ronald Reagan 罗纳德·威尔逊·里根：1911 年 2 月 6 日生于美国伊利诺伊州坦皮科城。美国杰出的右翼政治家，曾担任第 33 任加利福尼亚州州长，第 40 任（第 49—50 届）美国总统（1981—1989）。他也是一名伟大的演讲家。在踏入政坛前，里根也担任过运动广播员、救生员、报社专栏作家、电影演员、电视节目演员、励志讲师，并且是美国影视演员协会的领导人。他的演说风格高明而极具说服力，被媒体誉为“伟大的沟通者”。历任总统之中，他就职年龄最大。他是历任总统中唯一一位演员出身的总统。

3. Taliban 塔利班：发源于阿富汗的坎大哈地区的伊斯兰原教旨主义运动组织，自 1996 年至 2001 年，塔利班在阿富汗建立全国性政权，正式名称为“阿富汗伊斯兰酋长国”。

4. Kabul 喀布尔：阿富汗首都，喀布尔省省会和阿富汗的最大城市。它是一座有 3 000 多年历史的名城，1773 年以后成为阿富汗首都。“喀布尔”在新德语中是“贸易中枢”的意思。 根据 2012 年的统计，喀布尔城市总人口达到 320 多万人。喀布尔在世界城市规模中排名第 64 位，也是世界上第五大发展最快的城市。

5. preemptive action 先发制人的行动：指当美国认定某个对美国敌对的国家已经掌握了或生产了大规模杀伤武器，或者具备拥有这样武器的潜力时，美国应该使用武力排除这种对美国的威胁。美国不应该等待这些危险逼近，或者等待美国遭受了攻击，才采取行动。

6. Deraa 德拉：叙利亚西南边境城市，德拉省省会，是一个重要交通枢纽、商业中心与边防重镇。经由铁路或公路，向北可到大马士革，向南可达约旦首都安曼及耶路撒冷，向西可达地中海沿岸的海法港。德拉地处内陆高山，受副热带高气压带和信风带的影响，形成炎热干燥的热带沙漠气候，气温年较差较大。

7. Assad 巴沙尔·阿萨德：阿拉伯复兴社会党总书记、叙利亚总统、叙利亚武装部队总司令，元帅军衔，是哈菲兹·阿萨德的次子。2000 年 7 月，巴沙尔以 97% 的得票率当选叙利亚总统，并于 2007 年获得连任。巴沙尔就任叙利亚总统后，开始改革。曾一度被誉为“大马士革之春”。2011 年 1 月，叙利亚爆发了反政府示威。巴沙尔·阿萨德表示，叙利亚政府在努力推动叙全国政治对话的同时，将继续打击叙境内旨在破坏国家安全稳定的恐怖主义。叙利亚当地时间 2014 年 7 月 16 日下午，巴沙尔·阿萨德宣誓就任叙利亚总统，开启第三个 7 年总统任期。

8. Sunni（伊斯兰）逊尼派教徒：伊斯兰教主要教派之一，全称“逊奈与大众派”。人数约占全世界穆斯林的 85% 以上。与什叶派并称为不同的两大政治、宗教派别。“逊尼”系阿拉伯语的音译，原意为“遵守逊奈者”，亦即“遵循传统者”。穆斯林大多属逊尼派。该派有四大教法学派：哈乃斐教法学派、马立克、沙斐仪、罕百里学派。

9. Alawite 阿拉维派教徒：伊斯兰教什叶派的一个分支派系。

References

［1］ ALEXANDER J. The United States its history and constitution [M]. Charleston: BiblioLife, 2009.

［2］ BETH M. A people and a nation: a history of the United States [M]. New York: Cengage learning, 2009.

［3］ DAVIDSON J, CHRISTINE H. Nation of nations: a narrative history of the America republic [M]. New York: Mcgraw-Hill College, 1997.

［4］ DAVIDSON J, CHRISTINE H. Nation of nations: a narrative history of the America republic [M]. New York: Mcgraw-Hill College, 2004.

［5］ DIVINE R. America, past and present[M]. Boston: Addison-Wesley, 2005.

［6］ NASH G, JEFFREY J. The American people: creating a nation and a society[M]. New York: Pearson, 2003.

［7］ ROARK J, JOHNSON M. The American promise: a history of the United States [M]. Boston: Bedford/St Martins, 2005.

［8］ TINDALL G, SHI D. America：a narrative history [M]. New York: W. W. Norton & Company, 2000.

Chapter Thirteen

American Social Welfare

Unit 1 What Is American Social Welfare?

Poverty has always been one of the most serious social problems in the United States. It is a state of privation, or a lack of the usual or socially acceptable amount of money or material possessions. The most common measure of poverty in the U.S. is the "**poverty threshold**[1]" set by the U.S. government. This measure recognizes poverty as a lack of those goods and services commonly taken for granted by members of mainstream society. According to **Reuters**[2] report, the U.S. poverty rate rose to 14.3% (43.6 million) in 2009 from 13.2% (39.8 million) in 2008. In November 2012, the U.S. **Census Bureau**[3] said more than 16% of the population lived in poverty, including almost 20% of American children. An alarming concern is that there has been an increase in the proportion of the population that is poor.

Certain population categories correlate(与相关联) with high poverty rate in the United States, including one-parent families, children, the elderly, large families, and people of color. Besides, educational level, unemployment, and place of residence are also related to poverty. Poverty interacts with almost all other social problems-emotional problems, alcoholism, unemployment, racial and sex discrimination, medical problems, crime, and so on. As indicated that being poor intensifies the effects of those social problems, the U.S. government has the resources to eliminate poverty. To some extent, almost every existing social service works to combat poverty.

Social welfare can be viewed as an institution or an academic discipline. The **National Association of Social Workers**[4] gives the following definition of social welfare as an institution: a nation's system of programs, benefits, and services that helps people meet those social, economic, educational, and health needs that are fundamental to the maintenance of society. In the academic discipline context, social welfare is "the study of agencies programs, personnel, and policies which focus on the delivery of social services to individuals, groups, and communities". All in all, the goal of social welfare is to fulfill the social, financial, health, and recreational requirements of all individuals in a society.

The American government establishes social welfare policy, a government funded project, to assist the less fortunate citizens in various ways without the stigma (烙印) of charity. This welfare can include healthcare, special payments for young mothers and pregnant women, and food stamps, etc. The beneficiaries of all the welfare programs should apply and meet certain requirements.

Notes

1. poverty threshold 贫困线:美国的贫困线与家庭人口和家庭收入为基本要素，2011 年美国贫困人口标准是四口之家税前年现金收入低于 22 314 美元或两口之家低于 14 218 美元。

2. Reuters 路透社: 是世界前三大的多媒体新闻通讯社，提供各类新闻和金融数据，在 128 个国家运行。路透提供新闻报导给报刊、电视台等各式媒体，向来以迅速、准确享誉国际。

3. U.S. Census Bureau 美国人口普查局: 美国商务部下属的一个机关。它的任务是每十年进行一次人口普查，相应的美国众议院的成员数由这个调查结果决定。除此之外它还提供美国国家、人民和经济的统计数据。

4. National Association of Social Workers 美国社会工作者协会: 首要使命是增强人的福祉并帮助满足所有人的基本需求，尤其是关注那些脆弱的、受压迫的和生活贫困的人的需要。1996 年 8 月由美国社会工作者协会会员大会通过伦理守则。

Unit 2 Development of Social Welfare

Early History—Pre- and Industrial Revolution

Humanitarianism is an important value throughout history, which has considerable relevancy for social welfare-ascribing a high value to human life and benevolently helping those in need. Before the Industrial Revolution, the responsibility of helping those who are unable to be self-sufficient was met largely by the family, by church and by neighbors.

From the first English colony Virginia established in 1607 to Georgia colony established in 1732, 13 colonies along the eastern Atlantic coast constituted the original Union. The settlers in the New World hoped to found an ideal community unlike the Old World. From the beginning of the colonial period, everyone including priests, traders, millers and anyone others could gain their own land. Even the indenture（契约）servants could change into an independent land owner after they worked for 4-7 years in return for their passage to America. The community also can be granted land to be able to hold some social welfare services like schools, churches.

Despite the fertile soil and the unique natural resources, the new settlers were poorly trained and equipped to cope with life in the wilderness. They suffered tremendously from poor food, hard work, infectious diseases, and bitterly cold weather. At the beginning, most European immigrants sustained their life by various social communities, relatives and neighbors. As the population increased and colonial life became complicated, the former approaches were unsuccessful at meeting the needs of many who were unable to be self-sufficient. Several Motherland's

Poor Laws were begun to be imitated, adopted and practiced. The fundamental provisions of **Elizabethan Poor Law**[1] of 1601, the most significant law enacted (颁布) during the reign of Queen Elizabethan I, were incorporated into the social welfare policies of the American colonies. Towns were assigned to be responsible for the needy, almshouse were built, orphaned children were apprenticed out, and a system of legal residency was established to make it clear that towns had no responsibility for destitute strangers. The *Elizabethan Poor Law* has had a significant influence on American current approaches to public assistance and other social legislation.

In the 17th century, the Industrial Revolution flourished in America. Except for the technological advances, two themes—the protestant ethic and the laissez-faire (无干涉主义) economic view also had important effects on the Industrial Revolution, as well as on social welfare. The former one emphasized individualism that one is master of one's own fate. The social welfare implication of it reached their most inhumane level in a theory that Herbert Spenser extended Charles Darwin's theory of evolution. The theory stated that the strong (the wealthy) survived because they were superior, whereas the weak (the needy) deserved to perish. Although leaving the weak to perish was never advocated on a wild scale, the theory did have a substantial influence in curbing the development of innovative and more humane social welfare programs. The laissez-faire economic theory asserted that private businesses and industries were permitted to develop as they desired and any government regulation of business practices was discouraged. Because of the lack of development of public social welfare, private social welfare services began to spring up in the 1800s, primarily at the initiation of the clergy and religious groups, and provided most of the funds and services to the needy until the 1930s.

The Great Depression and the Social Security Act

At the turn of the 20th century, some theorists objected to social Darwinism and laissez-faire economics, such as Lester Ward who drew a sharp distinction between purposeless animal evolution and human evolution. Ward declared that humans, unlike animals, could and should provide social welfare programs to help the needy. The federal government was also called on to take on new functions to regulate business practices and to provide social welfare programs. Although the federal government began to place some limited funds into such programs as health, housing and slum clearance, the social services were provided primarily by churches and voluntary organizations before 1930.

After the New York Stock Exchange (纽约证券交易所) crashed on October 24th, 1921, the American economy was heading for a severe depression. By 1932, unemployment had reached 23.6% and it peaked in early 1933 at 25%, drought persisted in the agricultural heartland, businesses and families defaulted on record numbers of loans, thousands of banks failed, and many farmers and business owners went bankrupt. Then some measures had to be taken to deal with the economic collapse.

The Republican President, Herbert Hoover resisted proposals for federally funded relief and work projects（救济项目）, while he believed that only private charity should meet the needs of the unemployed. However, because of so many unemployed people and the inadequate protection from local and state funds, private charity also had trouble raising necessary funds to help the jobless. Millions of unemployed people fell into hunger, cold, and despair, even many middle-class people became penniless.

In 1933, after Democratic President Franklin D. Roosevelt took office, 40% of the population in some states was receiving local and state public relief money. Within three months—the historic "Hundred Days"（百日新政）—Roosevelt had rushed through Congress a great number of laws to aid the recovery of the economy. The Great Depression brought about profound changes in social welfare. Although the view of individualism was still widely held, after the depression, people realized that the federal government must play a role in providing financial assistance and social welfare. As a result, the *Social Security Act*（社会保障法案）was passed in 1935, which established contributory old-age and survivor's pensions, as well as a joint federal-state program of unemployment insurance. The Act forms the basis of most of American current public social welfare programs, and federal legislation for the programs like social insurance, public assistance, and public health and welfare services was enacted.

War on Poverty

Before the mid-1960s, Americans were characterized by optimism that the United States was the best of all possible places; that Americans had never fought an unjust war; that Americans were always on the side of right and ruled by noble motives. However, the late 1960s was a shock: Martin Luther King, Jr., and Robert Kennedy were assassinated; there were race riots in many cities and student riots on many campuses; public protests occurred as various groups (women, blacks, Indians, etc.) pointed out that they had always been discriminated; other social ills such as drug problem and environment pollution also emerged.

In the social welfare field, a major push for expansion of social welfare programs came in the 1960s, when President Lyndon Johnson announced the War on Poverty—a major, wide-ranging campaign that made the elimination of poverty one of the highest priorities of the nation and generated such programs as **VISTA**[2] (Volunteers in Service to America), **Neighborhood Youth Corps**[3], **Job Cops**[4], and **the Community Action Program**[5]. The social welfare system was renewed to change the environment to better meet the needs of clients rather than enable clients to better adapt and adjust to their life situation.

Conservatism in the 1970s and 1980s

After the end of the Vietnam War and the turmoil of the late 1960s, the hope that government programs could cure all the social ills was destroyed and citizens began to doubt the capacity of the government. Hence, the liberalism of the 1960s, when new social welfare programs were expanded and developed, was replaced by a more conservative administration in 1970s, 1980s, or even in the early 1990s, when no new, large-scale social welfare programs were initiated.

Johnson's successor, President Nixon's proposal **Family Assistance Plan**[6] (FAP), which would guarantee a minimum income to all American, was opposed by different interest groups and was defeated in a Senate subcommittee in 1970. By 1978 President Carter's plan, which called for a classification of welfare recipients into those who are able to work and those who are not and also included provision for a guaranteed minimum income, was again encountered strong resistance from several quarters and Congress shelved the issue. During President Jimmy Carter's administration, there was increased recognition that the federal government simply did not have the power to cure all the country's social ills.

The Reagan and the George Bush administrations adopted same social welfare policies that the federal government is not a solution to social problems but in fact is part of the problem. They believed that federally funded social welfare programs led recipients to become dependent on the government rather than industrious and productive. They held an economic program that cut taxes and provided incentive to the private sector for expansion and greater employment, which aimed to create a period of prosperity that would benefit the lowest stratum. The result, however, was that the gap between the rich and the poor widened, because the latter failed to benefit from the prosperous rich. Both the current and the former recipients were hurt by cutbacks in federally financial social welfare programs.

The Devolution Revolution in the 1990s

In 1992, President Bill Clinton resolved social problems with a moderate liberal orientation. He proposed a universal health insurance program for all Americans, which was eventually defeated by a Republican-controlled Congress. President Clinton also claimed "**Devolution Revolution**[7]", which shifted the provision of key social welfare programs from the federal to the state government.

From 1935 to 1996, the federal government required all states to provide the **AFDC**[8] (Aid to Families with Dependent Children), a federal assistance program created by the 1935 *Social Security Act* and provided financial assistance to children whose families had low or no income. In 1996, President Clinton negotiated with the Republican-controlled Congress to pass the *Personal Responsibility and Work Opportunity Act* which drastically restructured the program: each state sets its own parameters and amounts for financial assistance; while federal government provides block grants to states to assist in financing the programs. In 1996 federal legislation dismantled the AFDC and replaced it by more restrictive program Temporary Assistance for Needy Families (**TANF**[9]), which asserted that single mothers (and fathers) have an obligation to work for a living rather than stay at home to raise their children. The reform granted states wide discretion of how to distribute TANF entitlement and authority to eliminate payments to recipients, who are required to find a job within 24 months of receiving aid.

Notes

1. Elizabethan Poor Law《伊丽莎白济贫法》：于 1601 年英国颁布的第一个有关济贫的法律，不仅是这一法律制度的发端，也为这一法律制度的发展确定了基本原则，因此也被称为世界上最早的社会保障法，并在早期美国殖民地时期得以效仿。

2. VISTA：于 1964 年由美国政府成立的一个项目机构，为美国贫困地区的穷人提供扶贫服务志愿人员，被称为美国国内的"和平队"。

3. Neighborhood Youth Corps 邻里青年队：负责提高年青人的文化水平，为他们提供各种咨询。

4. Job Corps 工作队：是培训青年人，为他们提供一定工作技能的培训中心，后被尼克松总统废除。

5. the Community Action Program 社区行动计划：为穷人提供各种活动或工作，旨在使他们摆脱贫困状态。

6. Family Assistance Plan 家庭援助计划：在尼克松政府上台后，为克服美国家庭福利制度的弊端而提出的改革方案。该计划以负所得税理论为依据，以现金支付为手段，以接受工作培训为条件，对福利制度进行革命性的改革。由于威胁到南部和东部权势集团和一些社会利益集团的利益，最终在参议院阶段遭到否决。

7. Devolution Revolution 放权革命：克林顿总统上台后，提出了"放权革命"的口号，决心调整政府系统的权利关系，一方面集成了"新联邦主义"的权利下放目标，同时又对"新联邦主义"作出了调整。

8. AFDC 抚养未成年儿童家庭援助：1935 年到 1996 年美国的一项联邦补助项目，由美国卫生及公共服务部所管理。该项目对于贫穷家庭的子女进行经济上的援助。1997 年被贫困家庭临时援助（TANF）所替代。

9. TANF 贫困家庭临时援助：一个以现金方式救助项目，受益家庭多为单亲或父母中有一人无劳动能力或长期失业，这类家庭的户主多为女性。另外，该项目还对受益者采取了严格的受助时间和工作小时等限制，并将重点放在督促和帮助失业者再就业方面，旨在通过提高受助人的工作愿望和增加他们的个人责任来减低他们对福利救助的依赖，使他们树立"以工作求自立"的理念。

Unit 3 Social Welfare Today

Although the United States spends more on social welfare than any other countries in the world, it ranks very low in the percentage of gross national product spent on social welfare programs among industrial nations, such as Sweden, which proportionately spends over twice as much as the United States.

In 2011, federal spending on means-tested（资产调查）welfare, plus state contributions to federal programs, reached $927 billion per year. Roughly half of this welfare assistance, or $462 billion went to families with children, most of which are headed by single parents. While the

American welfare state effectively reduces poverty, the ranks of America's poor are greater than previously known, reaching a new level of 49.1 million—or 16 percent—due to rising medical costs and other expenses. During 2012, total benefits of $786 billion were paid out versus income (taxes and interest) of $840 billion, a $54 billion annual surplus. Excluding interest of $109 billion, the program had a cash deficit of $55 billion. Thus the U.S. has the weakest social safety net of all developed nations.

Social Welfare Programs

Because poverty relates to almost every other social problem, there have been many government and nongovernment efforts to reduce poverty and its effects in the United States. Those existing social welfare programs working to combat poverty are too numerous to describe fully. Reform proposals continue to circulate with some urgency, due to a long-term funding challenge faced by the program. Starting in 2011 and continuing thereafter, program expenses were expected to exceed cash revenues, due to the aging of the baby-boom generation (resulting in a lower ratio of paying workers to retirees). This section will introduce some main social insurance programs and public assistance programs.

Social Insurance Programs

Social insurance programs are financed by taxes on employers, on employees, or on both. Social insurance is a system whereby people are compelled to insure themselves against the possibility of their own indigence(贫穷), including 4 key social insurance programs: Social Security, Medicare, Unemployment Insurance, and Workers Compensation.

Social Security is also referred to **OASDI**[1] (Old-Age, Survivors, and Disability Insurance), created by the *1935 Social Security Act*. With few exceptions, all legal residents working in the United States now have an individual Social Security number. Income derived from Social Security is currently estimated to keep roughly 20% of all Americans, age 65 or older, above the federally defined poverty level. Based on previous earnings, payments are provided to fully insured workers at age 65 or older, dependent husbands or wives over age 62 and dependent children under age 18.

Social Security is funded through the *Federal Insurance Contributions Act* tax (**FICA**[2]), a payroll tax. Employers and employees are responsible for making equal FICA contributions. During 2012, Social Security taxes were levied on the first $110,100 of income for employment; amounts earned above that are not taxed. Covered workers are eligible for retirement and disability benefits. If a covered worker dies, his or her spouse and children may receive survivors' benefits. Social Security accounts are not the property of their beneficiary and are used solely to determine benefit levels. Social Security funds are not invested on behalf of beneficiaries. Instead, current receipts are used to pay current benefits (the system known as "pay-as-you-go"), as is typical of some insurance and defined-benefit plans

In 1965 Congress enacted *Medicare to the Social Security Act*. Medicare is the U.S. government's health insurance program for people age 65 or older. Some people under age 65 can qualify for Medicare, too. They include those with disabilities, permanent kidney failure, or amyotrophic lateral sclerosis. Medicare helps with the cost of health care. It does not cover all medical expenses or the cost of most long-term care. The program has four parts: Part A is hospital insurance; Part B helps pay for medical services that Part A doesn't cover; Part C is called Medicare Advantage. If you have Parts A and B, you can choose this option to receive all of your health care through a provider organization, like an HMO (Health Maintenance Organization); Part D is prescription drug coverage, which helps pay for some medicines.

Unemployment Insurance was also created by the *1935 Social Security Act* in response to the Great Depression, when millions of people lost jobs and couldn't buy goods and services. In addition to helping workers and their families, this program plays a key role in helping business, communities, and the nation's economy. Now, as then, the program helps cushion the impact of economic downturns and brings economic stability to communities, states, and the nation by providing temporary income support for laid off workers. The eligible unemployed should: (a) have worked a certain number of weeks in covered employment; (b) be ready, willing and able to work; (c) file a claim for benefits and be registered in a public employment office; (d) demonstrate that unemployment is due to a lack of work for which he or she is qualified. Financed by a tax on employers, the amount and duration of weekly benefits vary from states to states. In many states, the unemployed are eligible for benefits for about one year.

The first Workers' Compensation Insurance was the *Federal Employees Compensation Act* of 1908, but it was not until 1948 that all states had such laws. This program provides both income and assistance in meeting medical expenses for injuries sustained on a job. Financed by a tax on employers, cash benefits are paid for total or temporary disability or death. As key stakeholders in the worker's compensation program, insurance carriers(保险公司) and self-insured (自行承保) employers have the primary responsibility for the administration of workers' compensation claims for injured workers. The responsibilities include: making payments that are due to workers promptly and accurately; interfacing with the Worker's Compensation Division by sending required reports and by replying promptly to all correspondence.

Public Assistance Programs

Public Assistance Program benefits are paid from general government revenues. The applicants must have a "means test", an examination of their income and assets, to determine whether their financial needs meet the eligibility requirements. Except for federal, state, and local guidelines on eligibility, the staffs who administer public assistance also have substantial discretion in deciding whether a client will receive special allowances in addition to basic benefits, as well as in deciding which social services and other resources might be mobilized on behalf of the client. Unlike social insurance, to which recipients are viewed as legally entitled, public assistance are perceived as charity, because in U.S., the poor are not considered to be protected by government to have right to a minimum income. The main public assistance programs include **SSI**[3] (Supplemental Security Income), **GA**[4] (General Assistance), Medicaid, Food Stamps, Housing Assistance, and **TANF**[5] (Temporary Assistance for Needy Families, created by the *Personal Responsibility and Work Opportunity Reconciliation Act* to replace Aid to Families with Dependent Children).

SSI officially began operation as the first federally administered assistance program in January 1974, and replaced such programs created by the *1935 Security Act* as Old-Age Assistance, Aid to the Blind, and Aid to the Permanently and Totally Disabled. In order to be eligible to receive SSI benefits, the applicants must: (a) be over 65 years of age, or blind, or disabled; (b) legally reside in one of the 50 states, the District of Columbia, Northern Mariana Islands, or are the child of military parent(s) assigned to permanent duty outside of the US, or are a student (certain restrictions apply) temporarily abroad; (c) have income and resources within certain limits.

GA, also known as General Relief, is the only public assistance program that receives no federal funds, but is funded by property taxes. It is used to benefit adults without dependents (single persons, or less commonly, childless married couples) as opposed to families with children, who receive assistance from the federal program AFDC or its successor TANF. This program is supposed to serve those needing temporary, rather than long-term, financial support. In any event, the person(s) seeking General Assistance must first apply for any other programs — state or federal — for which alternate eligibility may or may not exist; only if all such applications are denied is the applicant then permitted to receive General Assistance benefits, which usually include food stamps (食品救济券), and often, assistance in paying for rental housing. In some states, General Assistance programs are not universal, and the policies of different counties or cities therein may differ widely. For example, California provides such program, while San Francisco, a state once paid the most generous benefits, drastically reduced the benefits in 2003.

Medicaid is a social health care program, providing hospital and medical care to families and individuals with low income and resources. As the largest source of funding for medical and health-related services for poverty-stricken people, it is a means-test program that is jointly funded by the state and federal government and administered by the states. A low income is not the only requirement to enroll in the program. The enrollees include low-income children below a certain age, pregnant women, parents of Medicaid-eligible children, the disabled, the blind, and the aged. Although all states must follow the same basic frame, the eligibility rules differ significantly from state to state. Unlike Medicare, a social insurance program funded at federal level, Medicaid is a program that is not solely funded by federal government, but by states, which provide up to half of the funding for the Medicaid program. During the 2008—2009 recession, loss of income and medical insurance coverage resulted in a substantial increase in Medicaid enrollment in 2009. Nine U.S. states showed an increase in enrollment of 15% or more, resulting in heavy pressure on state budgets.

Food Stamp is a federal aid program, providing food-purchasing assistance for low- and no-income people living in the U.S. There are income (130% or less of the federal poverty level) and resource requirements for the program, as well as specific requirements for immigrants, elderly persons and persons with disabilities. As an entitlement program, it benefits cost $76.4 billion in fiscal year 2013 and supplied roughly 47.6 million Americans with an average of $133.08 per month in food assistance.

Housing Assistance is an "in-kind" program rather than a cash program to help low-income households that are forced to spend too much of their budget on rent. The federal government offers housing assistance through **HUD**[6] (the Department of Housing and Urban Development). HUD also contracts with state and local agencies to make sure everyone has access to safe and affordable housing. HUD places families into one of three categories, based on a metropolitan area or county's median income. If a family earns an annual wage that is at or below 80% of its area's median income, HUD labels the family "low-income"; Yearly earnings at or below 50% of its area's median, "very low-income" category; while income at or below 30% of the median, "extremely low-income". For public housing, HUD takes applications from all three groups.

TANF is one of the United States of America's federal assistance programs. It began on July 1st, 1997, and succeeded AFDC (the Aid to Families with Dependent Children) program, providing cash assistance to indigent American families with dependent children through the United States Department of Health and Human Services. This cash benefit is often referred to simply as "welfare". TANF was created by the *Personal Responsibility and Work Opportunity Act* instituted under President Bill Clinton in 1996. The Act provides temporary financial assistance while aiming to get people off of that assistance, primarily through employment. There is a maximum of 60 months of benefits within one's lifetime, but some states have instituted shorter periods. The reform granted states wide discretion of how to distribute TANF entitlements. States also have the authority to eliminate payments to recipients. Under the new act, TANF recipients are required to find a job within 24 months of receiving aid. In enforcing the 60-month time limit, some states place limits on the adult portion of the assistance only, while still aiding the otherwise eligible children in the household.

Notes

1. OASDI 联邦社保基金：全名“联邦老年、遗属和伤残人保险信托投资基金”，产生于20世纪30年代”经济大萧条”时期，目前主要通过强制征收工薪税形成。

2. FICA 联邦保修捐助条例：属于收入税的一种，是美国政府强制征收的税种。为退休、残疾、死亡工人的子女支付的联邦基金，用于维持社会保险和医疗。

3. SSI 补充社会保障收入：美国非缴费型福利制度中最大的现金福利，在全国范围内向最需要帮助的老人、盲人和残疾人提供最低收入保障，被誉为“社会安全网”。

4. GA 一般性援助：也称“通用救援”，美国没有家属的成年人（单身或没有子女的已婚夫妇）受益的福利项目，自1996年以来，正式称为贫困家庭临时救助。

5. TANF 贫困家庭临时援助：一个现金救助项目，受益家庭多为单亲或父母中有一人无劳动能力或长期失业，这类家庭的户主多为女性。另外，该项目还对受益者采取了严格的受助时间和工作小时等限制，并将重点放在督促和帮助失业者再就业方面，旨在通过提高受助者的工作愿望和增加他们的个人责任来减低他们对福利救助的依赖，使他们树立"以工作求自立"的理念。

6. HUD 美国住房与城市发展部：英文全称"The Department of Housing and Urban Development"，于 1965 年通过合并政府原有机构而成立，是美国内阁的一个部，办公地点位于华盛顿。其职责主要是为美国国民建立一个合理的住房体系和合适的居住环境，通过其抵押贷款担保方案为中低收入家庭拥有住房提供担保，在支持居民获得房屋所有权方面起到了重要作用。

References

[1] EDWIN S D, ELIZABETH N F. American government and politics today [M]. Stamford: Thomson Wadsworth, 2008.

[2] WELCH S, GRUHL J. Understanding American government [M]. Stamford: Thomson Wadsworth, 2008.

[3] GOLDIN F, SMITH D, SMITH M S. Imagine: living in a socialist USA. New York: Harper Perennial, 2014.

[4] 王恩铭 . 美国文化与社会 [M]. 上海：上海外语教育出版社 , 2007.

[5] 王恩铭 . 美国社会文化 [M]. 北京：北京大学出版社 , 2010.

[6] 江康宁 . 美国概况：美国社会、历史与文化 [M]. 南京：东南大学出版社 , 2013.

[7] 田耀 . 美国文化点滴 [M]. 天津：天津大学出版社 , 2009.

[8] 吴斐 . 美国社会与文化 [M]. 武汉：武汉大学出版社 , 2003.

[9] 江涛 . Listen to speeches in Massachusetts Institute of Technology [M]. 北京：石油工业出版社 , 2013.

Chapter Fourteen

American Mass Media

Unit 1 Newspapers and Magazines

Mass media is a term used to denote a section of the media specifically envisioned and designed to reach a very large audience such as the population of a nation state. It was coined in the 1920s with the advent of nationwide radio networks, mass-circulation newspapers and magazines, although mass media, like books and manuscripts, were present centuries before the term became common. The term public media has a similar meaning: it is the sum of the public mass distributors of news and entertainment across media such as newspapers, television, radio, broadcasting, which may require union membership in some large markets such as Newspaper Guild（同业公会）, a labor union founded by newspaper journalists in 1933 aimed to improve wages and working conditions, its constitution says its purpose is to fight for honesty in journalism and the news industry's business practices. While some internet media nowadays may include: television, personal webpages, message boards, podcasts, blogs and video hosting services.

The U.S media today is frequently known as the **"Fourth Estate"** [1], suggesting that the press shares equal status with the other branches of government created by the constitution. The press, or "Fourth Estate" plays a vital role as a guardian（监护人）of U.S democracy. The powerful influence of mass media comes, in a sense, as a result of the Constitution that ensures the Americans of the public's right to know what has happened or is taking place in the United States. The *Bill of Rights*, or the first 10 Amendments to the Constitution of the United States, guarantees a healthy and uninhabited flow of information as James Madison states that people should be their own governors and "must arm themselves with the power knowledge gives". The first Amendment provides an American citizen with the law to protect him from any kinds of information control, regardless of his political stance, religious belief, or economic status. The government and the media often engage in confrontations when reporters disclose classified information or pursue investigative reporting to uncover injustices and corruption within American institutions. The Washington Post's role in uncovering the Watergate scandal illustrates the media's involvement in national events.

In history, America's earliest media audiences were the colonies' upper class and community leaders, who are capable of reading and purchasing printed stuff. The first regular newspaper was the Boston News-Letter, a weekly started in 1704 by the city's postmaster, John Campbell. This weekly published shipping information and news from England but most Americans rarely saw a newspaper and had to depend on travelers or passing townsmen for their news. In 1734, publisher of New York Weekly Journal, **John Peter Zenger**[2], faced a trial for his openly criticizing and attacking the colony's governor Sir William Cosby, a trial that many historians regard as the birth of America's free-press tradition.

In the late 19th century, popular culture appeared with the publication of a penny paper New York Sun in 1833, which paid special attention to the low level of society. After that, the press switched soon from a small upper class readership to mass readership and the majority of the Americans, including workers and immigrants, had rights and opportunities to learn the world and the way of American life.

Today, there are approximately 9,800 newspapers operating in the United States. Of these about 17% are dailies, 77% weeklies, and 6% semiweekly. There are three national daily papers that enjoy large circulations（发行量）and significant social and political impact. The oldest and most respected is the Wall Street Journal, whose focus is on the world of business, though the definition of business is broad. Following that is the **Christian Science Monitor**[3]（基督教科学箴言报）, which continues to holds its founding principle as a paper of serious journalism. Equally influential are large metropolitan dailies, such as the New York Times, the Chicago Daily News, the Washington Post, and the Philadelphia Bulletin. These dailies not only sell newspapers in the metropolitan areas, but also publish zone edition—suburban versions of the paper to attract readers and to combat competition for advertising dollars from the suburban papers.

Also, the newspaper was the first mass medium to rely on advertising for financial support, changing the relationship between audience and media from then on. The reason why Americans have such a great number and variety in newspaper is that readers value them. When newspapers prosper financially, it is because advertisers recognize their worth as an ad medium. Newspapers account for more than 50% of all advertising spending in the United States. That is more than 50 billion a year, more than all other media combined. The biggest newspapers advertisers are retail stores and telecommunications, auto, computer and entertainment brands.

Popular American Newspapers

The U.S. has never had a national newspaper with a mass national circulation like The Time and The Daily Telegraph in Britain or the leading papers in other countries, most notably The New York Times, The Washington Post, and Wall Street Journal has increased so that these papers come close to constituting a national press. These **papers syndicate**[4] their staff-written stories to regional newspapers all over the country. Most newspapers rely heavily on two major new services, the Associated Press（AP）, and the United Press International（UPI）, which gather national and international news stories and sell them to subscribing newspapers. Some of the largest newspapers are at the same time news-gathering businesses. They not only print newspapers, but also collect and sell news, news features, and photographs to hundreds of other newspapers in the

United States and even abroad. The better-known of these are The New York Times', The Washington Post's, and the Los Angeles Times' news services. In one famous example, an expose of the CIA (Central Intelligence Agency) published in The New York Times' also appeared in 400 other American papers and was picked up or used in some way by hundreds more overseas. In this way, the major American newspapers are enabled to have their influence spread out nationwide, or even worldwide, thereby (借此) establishing themselves as "national presses".

During recent years, however, newspapers have encountered many problems, such as loss of competition and hyper-commercialization. In 1923, 502 American cities have two or more competing dailies. Today, only 20 have separate competing papers. Currently, the nation's 126 newspaper chains control 82% of daily newspaper circulation, own the biggest circulations papers in the country, and own 1,200 of the nation's 1,600 dailies. Another serious problem with newspapers concerns hyper-commercialization. Many papers, such as USA Today, the Orange Country Register, and the Oakland Press, have begun selling their space on the front page, once the exclusive province of the news. Some papers now even permit and charge for the placement of pet obituaries (讣告) alongside those of deceased humans. But the greatest fear expressed by critics of concentration and hyper-commercialization is the eroding (侵蚀) of the firewall between newspapers' editorial and advertising mission. Probably due to competition from other media, the number of daily newspapers in the U.S. has declined over the past half-century, according to Editor & Publisher, the trade journal of American newspapers.

In the mid-1700s, magazines were a favorite medium of the British elite, and two prominent printers hoped to duplicate (复制) that success in the New World. In 1741 in Philadelphia, Andrew Bradford published American Magazine, followed by Benjamin Franklin's General Magazine. Composed largely of reprinted British material, these publications were expensive and aimed at the small number of literate colonists. Lacking an organized postal system, distribution was difficult, and either magazine was successful. American Magazine produced 3 issues, General Magazine. Yet, between 1741 and 1794, 45 new magazines appeared, although no more than 3 were published in the same period. Entrepreneurial printers hoped to attract educated, cultured, moneyed gentlemen by copying the successful London magazines. Even after the Revolutionary War, U.S. magazines remained clones of the British forerunners.

In 1821, the Saturday Evening Post appeared. Among other successful early magazines were Harper's (1850) and Atlantic monthly (1857). In 1825, there were 100 magazines; by 1885, the number rose to 3300. Mass circulation popular magazines began to prosper in the post-Civil War years. The reasons for their phenomenal (惊人的，非凡的) growth were manifold (多方面的). As with books, widespread literacy was one reason. The *Postal Act of 1879*, which permitted mailing magazines at cheap second-class postage rates from 35 cents apiece to 10 to 15 cents, and the spread of the railroad, which carried people and publications westward from the East Coast, were two others. Finally, urbanization and industrialization provide people with more leisure time and higher personal income, facilitating the process of mass circulation. An additional factor in the success of the early magazines was the spread of social movements such as abolitionism and labor reform. These issues provided compelling content, and a boom in magazine publishing began.

Magazine industry research indicates that among people with at least some college education, 94% read at least one magazine and average more than 11 different issues a month. Nearly the same figures apply for households with annual incomes of over $40,000 and for people in professional and managerial careers, regardless of educational attainment.

Until recently the U.S has had three leading weekly newsmagazines: TIME, Newsweek and U.S News & World Report. Time is well-known for naming a "person of the year" each year, while U.S News & World Report publishes annual ratings of American colleges and universities. Other popular magazines include: Readers Digest, National Geographic Magazine, Modern Maturity, People Magazine, etc.

One of the most influential magazines to appear during the early years of magazine history was National Geographic, in 1899. Largely through the high-quality photo essays it pioneered, this publication opened up new vistas of cultural awareness and understanding. The National Geographic Society uses proceeds from the magazine to pursue cultural and wildlife research, and to produce their famous documentary films. During the 1980s and 1990s, more and more media operations have come under the hands of just a few media conglomerates(企业集团). The declining value of the dollar, the lack of rules concerning foreign ownership of America publishing firms, and the general financial attractiveness of the print media lured foreign investors as never before. The News Corporation of Australia, headed by Rupert Murdoch, led the way when it acquired papers in Chicago and New York, a book publishing company, and a large number of magazines, including TV guide. Hachette, a French company, bought most of the magazines that were formerly owned by CBS. Reed International of Great Britain also acquired several consumer and about fifty trade magazines. Magazines, though less concentrated than newspapers, are also moving toward centralization.

The biggest news of the mid-1990s concerned the move of newspapers and magazines on the information superhighway. Many newspapers and magazines like Time and Mother Jones started to offer online services, offering special interactive features not available to their hard copy readers. Research revealed that about 8,000 people a day were browsing the electronic racks during its first week online. Exclusive online magazines have yet to produce a profit, and many industry analysts think it will be a long time before they do.

Notes

1. "Fourth Estate" 第四权: 第四权所指的即是媒体、公众视听。源于西方"国民等级"(estates of the realm)的概念。传统三个等级分别是神职人员(上议院中的神职人员)、世俗议员(上议院中的其他人员)和下议院议员。目前一般认知是指在行政权、立法权、司法权之外的第四种政治权力。

2. John Peter Zenger 皮特曾格案： 皮特曾格案件是北美殖民地时期有关法律和出版自由的著名案例，对此后西方（尤其是美国）影响深远。北美本土派势力（商人和地主）兴起后，要求对殖民地事务享有更大的控制权，但由于本地仅有的一份报纸是布雷德福所有的《纽约公报》，而且是由殖民当局所控制。于是 1733 年秋，商界在和曾格磋商后，1733 年 11 月 5 日，曾格的《纽约新闻周报》出版。风格犀利的《新闻周报》使得当局越发不满，总督威廉科·斯比爵士指控曾格"对政府进行无耻中伤和恶毒谩骂，试图煽动反政府情绪"，曾格以"煽动闹事" 罪名被捕。最后，费城律师主动要求做曾格的辩护律师，在他精彩的辩护下，陪审团做出无罪裁决，曾格获得自由。

3. The Christian Science Monito《基督教科学箴言报》： 美国面向全国的颇有影响的四开日报。1908 年 11 月由科学基督教创始人玛丽·贝克·埃迪夫人在美国的马萨诸塞州的波士顿创刊，由基督教科学出版社出版，报名便由此而来。它虽与宗教团体有关，而且报名上有"基督教"字样，但并不是纯宗教性的报纸，而是一份面向"世俗"的一般性报纸，自称是"国际性的报纸"。

4. paper syndicate 报业辛迪加： 报业辛迪加就是不同的报纸杂志，有偿共享新闻报道、新闻图片和专栏文章，从而打破各家媒体细分市场的格局，并形成规模，催生出优秀的新闻作品。

Unite 2 Radio

Audio broadcasting began experimentally in the first decade of the 20th century. By the early 1920s radio broadcasting became a household medium, at first on the AM band and later on FM. It is generally believed that radio in America has gone through three developmental stages—the "pioneer" period from the 1890s through the mid-1920s, the "golden age" of network programs in the 1930s and 1940s, and the "television age" which began in the late 1940s and is still in progress. It went through a period of early technological and commercial development, then through a boom period of unstable and rapid growth, and finally achieved a stable place in the structure of American business and culture.

The early development of the radio in the United States belongs to the decade of the 1920s, when it was a boom industry in a boom decade. Radio first burst upon the nation when it transmitted（传播） the results of the Harding election in 1920. In its first phase, the programs were broadcast as a public service without advertising sponsorship and with an eye mainly to profits for the equipment companies from the sale of sets. In the next phase, the late 1920s and early 1930s, advertising came to stay as the principal source of revenue, and the same centralizing force which operated in the other media brought the big broadcasting chains into radio. By 1934, when the Federal Communications Commission was established, the three big features of broadcasting—private enterprise, advertising sponsorship, and public regulation within broad limits—had become accepted.

During the Great Depression and throughout World War II, radio industry grew rapidly.

Franklin Roosevelt's famous "fireside chats" reassured anxious Americans during the Depression, CBS reporters and anchors, for example, told audiences different stories and impressions about the Vietnamese and the War. Voice of America is the most famous radio station for dissemination (散布) of information and propaganda(宣传) to foreign countries. It was originally established in 1942 to broadcast war information and now it comes under the leadership of the American International Communication Bureau. It sends news to the whole world in over 40 languages 24 hours a day.

Later, concerned that the medium would be wasted and fearful that a foreign company would control the vital resource, the U.S. government forced the combatants(竞争对手)to merge. Consequently, **American Marconi**[1], General Electric, **American Telephone & Telegraph**[2], and **Westinghouse**[3]—each in control of a vital piece of technology—joined to create the Radio Corporation of America (RCA). RCA was a government-sanctioned monopoly, but its creation avoided direct government control of the new medium.

Soon, such big networks as the National Broadcasting Company (NBC), the Columbia Broadcasting System (CBS), and the American Broadcasting Company (ABC) were founded respectively in the first half of the 20th century, setting the fundamental basis of broadcasting in the United States: (a) radio broadcasters were private, commercially owned enterprises; (b) governmental regulation was based on the public interest; (c) stations were licensed to serve specific localities, but national networks programmed the most lucrative(有利可图的) hours with the largest audiences; (d) entertainment and information were the basic broadcast content; and (e) advertising formed the basis of financial support for broadcasting.

Radio in Nowadays

However, just when radio was enjoying its heyday, television arrived. Network affiliation (附属机构) dropped from 97% in 1945 to 50% by the mid-1950s, as stations "went local" in the face of television's national dominance. By the same token, national radio advertising income dipped to $35 million in 1960, the year that television found its way into 90% of U.S. homes.

National Public Radio (NPR) was created in February 1970 to provide leadership in national newsgathering and production and to act as a permanent nationwide interconnection of noncommercial stations. NPR launched a tremendously successful Application Program Interface (API), and apps utilizing this API to access content have been developed for the IPhone and Android. And NPR podcasts are being downloaded more than 15 million times a month.

By offering FM, AM, and non-commercial programs, the radio industry has been able to attract a large population as its loyal audiences. According to the statistics in 2015, there are 13,012 radio stations operating in the United States today: 4,727 commercial AM stations; 6,015 commercial FM stations; and 2,234 non-commercial FM stations. In an average week, more than 200 million people, 95% of all Americans aged 12 and above, will listen to the radio. The majority of Americans, 60%, get their first news of the day from radio, and the large majority of all listening, 83%, occurs on cars on the road.

Notes

1. American Marconi 美国无线电报公司：马可尼公司始创于19世纪80年代，曾是世界上发展最快的通讯及IT公司之一，其创始人古列尔莫·马可尼曾完成了第一次横跨大西洋的无线电波传送、第一次SOS紧急信号的使用和第一次公共无线电广播。过去几十年里，马可尼在世界电信设备行业中占有重要席位，目前仍是英国最大的通信和IT设备提供商。

2. American Telephone & Telegraph 美国电话电报公司：AT&T公司是一家美国电信公司，是美国第二大移动运营商，创建于1877年，曾长期垄断美国长途和本地电话市场。AT&T在近120年中，曾经过多次分拆和重组。目前，AT&T是美国最大的本地和长途电话公司，总部曾经位于得克萨斯州圣安东尼奥，2008年搬到了得州北部大城市达拉斯。

3. Westinghouse 美国西屋电气公司：是世界著名的美国电工设备制造企业。世界500强企业，每年营业额超过百亿美元，广泛活跃在能源、交通、通信、军事、航天、环境健康管理领域。全世界五大洲数以亿计的家庭，商用建筑，政府部门都在使用Westinghouse的产品和服务。该公司于1886年1月8日，由乔治·威斯汀豪斯在美国宾夕法尼亚州创立。公司总部设在宾夕法尼亚州匹兹堡市。1889年时曾改名西屋电工制造公司（Westinghouse Electric Manufacturing Company），1945年10月改用现名。

Unit 3 Television

The story of electronic television begins in 1923, when Vladimir Zworykin, a Russian immigrant working for Westinghouse Corporation, developed the first practical electronic tube for a television camera. Zworykin developed the kinescope（电视显像管）, or picture tube. In 1928, General Electric began experimenting telecasting. NBC followed with experimenting telecasting in 1930, and by 1939, New York was offering regularly scheduled programs. However, it was not until 1939, New York World's fair that a large number of Americans saw television demonstrated for the first time. Television's breakthrough year was 1948, the year the CBS and NBC radio networks turned their attention toward it.

In the fall of 1948, the FCC (the Federal Communications Commission), recognizing that this new medium was going to grow rapidly, placed a freeze on TV-station authorizations, restricting the number to 124. During the freeze, which lasted until 1952, the FCC developed a comprehensive plan to allocate television frequencies to all parts of the United States. A microwave relay system was developed that allowed for the first coast-to-coast network broadcasts in 1951.

After the freeze was lifted, television expanded even more rapidly. NBC and CBS were far along in their efforts to shift their interests from radio to television. A third network—DuMont—was struggling to compete. ABC merged with Paramount Theaters and followed the other three networks into television. Later, DuMont was unable to compete with the three former radio networks and went out of business in 1955. In 1986, the Fox Broadcasting Company launched a challenge to the three big networks. Thanks to the success of the shows like The Simpsons, and the rights to show National Football League (NFL) games, Fox has established itself as a major player in broadcast television.

While TV primarily serves as a medium of entertainment, it also has a big role to play as a news broadcasting agency. Networks began experimenting with news at locally owned stations as early as January 1940. But, early-day television news could not begin to compare with radio news. Radio could go to the scene of the event and broadcast live. TV news, due to technical limitations, required motion-picture cameras, and the film had to be processed after it was shot. Some early network newscasts relied on motion-picture newsreel(新闻影片) photographers to provide footage, but often this material was not available until several days after the event. In the meantime, the network often used still photos, which the newscasters held up in front of them. However, by the 1960s, portable cameras and video tape recorders had made television a much more credible news medium because views saw pictures of the news events on the day they occurred. Eventually, TV provided more people with their news than newspapers and radio combined.

While an important role that TV programming has played is to shape and reflect the cultural changes that have been occurring in American society. For instance, when the Civil Rights Movement called for equality for all Americans gain momentum in the 1960s, TV started reflecting these changes. By the same token, during the Feminist Movement, women issues found their way into the TV program. More importantly, as a response to demands for racial and sexual equality as well as an effort to enlighten the general public, networks have employed more and more women in a variety of jobs in mass communication industry. One specific event that can show the power of media is the role that American media played during the Vietnam War. Journalists and TV reporters went to Vietnam and told the true stories about the war by displaying many lives yet terrifying pictures of the victims of the war.

Famous Television Systems

In December 1975, Home Box Office (HBO), an all-movie channel owned by Time Inc., became the first programmer to distribute its signal via satellite. The same technology allowed the founding of the Cable News Network (CNN) in 1980, which became the world's first 24-hour all-news channel. By early 1993, MTV, the leading American rock music TV network, had an audience of 46 million in the United States and 32 other countries. The four major television broadcasters in the U.S. are the National Broadcasting Company (NBC), Columbia Broadcasting System (CBS), the American Broadcasting Company (ABC) and the Fox Broadcasting Company (FOX). Other cable networks include USA Network (general entertainment), ESPN and Versus (sports) and the Disney Channel (family), etc.

In the United States, there is no government-owned television network. There are commercial television and public television. The worst to be said of commercial television is that it too often purveys (传播) programs of impoverished quality, matter that is sought, found, budgeted and produced in the hope that it will attract large numbers. A PBS station brochure on How Program Underwriting Works boasted that "commercial broadcasters count household tuned in. Public broadcasters count people turned on". Many adults are annoyed by the simplicity and triteness (陈腐) of most TV shows, they call the TV set the "idiot box" or the "boob tube".

"Public" television stations offer a wide variety of high-quality entertainment and information without the annoying interruptions of commercials. Funds to operate public TV come from donations by individuals and industries and, to a small degree from the government. Public television has been highly praised for imaginative appealing shows which help children learn basic reading concepts, valuable psychological insights, English and Spanish, and intelligent discussions of national problems often take up the evening hours on public TV. Also offered are college courses which gave academic credit to enrolled listeners. The Mobil Corporation, one of the PBS flock of angels, received seventy-five thousand letters in a single season, all praising Masterpiece Theater. Masterpiece Theatre is a drama anthology (选集) television series produced by WGBH Boston, a non-commercial educational PBS member television station.

Across the Charles in Boston, WGBH has developed the Teacher's Domain, a free collection of more than 2,000 digital resources covering diverse content for students and teachers. 2009 was the 40th anniversary of Sesame Street, just a few month later, PBS launched the PBS KIDS pre-school video player—with more than 87 million streams of educational content being delivered in just the first month. But it faces challenges, one of which is the *Copyright Act*. Congress passed special copyright exemptions for public broadcasting in the 20th century. "But these provisions no longer fulfill their original purpose. For example, current licensing practices inhibit public broadcasters from producing and distributing the highest quality digital programming. These exemptions should be updated to facilitate (促进) the distribution of the highest quality programming on 21st century digital platforms." Eugene J. Huang, an FCC officer said.

DirecTV[1] and Dish Network are the major satellite television providers, with 20 and 14 million customers respectively as of February 2014. Meanwhile, the major cable television providers are Comcast with 22 million customers, Time Warner Cable with 11 million, and Cox Communications, Charter Communications, AT&T U-Verse and Verizon FiOS (光纤上网) with 5 to 6 million each. At the same time, American entertainment is being absorbed increasingly by conglomerates. Not only are the imprimaturs of powerful companies visible on public and commercial TV, they are also big on the big screen. Paramount Pictures is a Gulf and Western company; Universal, an MCA company; Warner Brothers, a Warner communications company; 20th Century-Fox is controlled by an oil man; CBS for a time owned **the New York Yankees**[2]. All of the prime-time television networks are owned by major American corporations, including such corporate conglomerates as General Electric (owner of NBC) and Disney (owner of ABC). The

Turner broadcasting/CNN network was also purchased by a major corporation, Time Warner. Later, Time Warner was acquired by American Online (AOL), a merger that combined the world's then-largest media company with the world's then-largest online company. Fox Television has always been a part of Rupert Murdoch's publishing and Media Empire. In addition to taking part in mergers and acquisitions, many of these companies have formed partnerships with computer software makers, such as Microsoft, for joint electronic publishing ventures. "Twenty years ago, thirty corporations controlled 90 percent of the media. Today, it is a grand total of six mega-corporations—Rupert Murdoch's News Corporation, Disney, Viacom, Time Warner, CBS and Comcast. Besides accumulating their own profits, the media are daily trumpets for the rest of the corporate world's advertising."

The huge companies are linked to each other, owning parts of each other and engaging in ventures with each other. These arrangements reduce their competition, lower their risks, increase their profits, and at the same time erect high barriers for any upstarts that try to challenge their dominance.

Notes

1. DirecTV 直播卫星电视: DirecTV 是自美国加州 El Segundo 市开始推行的直播卫星(Direct Broadcast Satellite; DBS)服务,此服务发送数位卫星电视及音效到美国居家。DirecTV 由 DirecTV Group 所拥有,并由 News Corporation(新闻集团)下的 Fox Entertainment Group(福克斯娱乐集团)所辖控。

2. the New York Yankees 纽约扬基队:曾在 43 次美国职业棒球大联盟联赛的"世界大赛"中赢得 27 次冠军(紧跟其后的分别为圣路易红雀队与奥克兰运动家队的 9 次冠军)。纽约扬基队也是在所有的球队中,唯一每个守备位置皆有球员获选登录棒球名人堂中的球队。

Unit 4 Internet and Regulations

The Internet dates from 1960s, when it began life in the military and academic communities in the U.S. But the technological breakthrough that made Internet accessible to most people occurred in 1991 when the arrival of the World Wide Web.

For at least 10 years, every politician has felt the necessity of having a Web site. On the national level, political Web sites were created for the two major-party candidates for president for the first time in 1996. Since then, even the lowliest(地位低的)local politician feels obligated to have a Web site that is updated at least on occasion. Political candidates have used the Internet to raise tens of millions of dollars. Howard Dean did so in significant way during the Democratic primaries in the last presidential election cycle.

The word blog comes from Web log, a regular updating of one's ideas at a specific Web site. Not all of the millions of blogs posted daily are political in nature, but many are and they can have a dramatic influence on events, giving rise to the term blogosphere（博客圈）politics.

Blogs are clearly threatening the mainstream media. They can be highly specialized, highly political, and highly entertaining. And they are cheap. Once blogs—written words—became well established, it was only a matter of time before they could end up as spoken words. Enter **Podcasting**[1], so called because the first Internet-communicated spoken blogs were blogs downloaded onto Apple's iPods. Podcasts, though, can be heard on one's computer or downloaded onto any portable listening device. Podcasting can also include videos. Basically anyone who has an idea can easily create a podcast and make it available for downloading. Although politicians have been slower to adopt this form of communication, many now are using podcasts to keep in touch with their constituents.

Most recently, the internet in the U.S. has been trumpeted（宣扬）as the newest and best tool for increased democratic involvement and participation. Presidential candidate Ross Perot used the promise of an "electronic town hall" as a centerpiece of his 1992 campaign. Vice President Al Gore conducted history's first interactive, computer network conference on January 13th, 1994. In 2008, Barack Obama utilized the Internet to the fullest extent to date for his presidential campaign, making the virtual technology an effective tool to inform voters, to rally people behind him and to get young people interested in politics.

FCC released study of broadband adoption and use in American shows that 55% of broadband users also use social networking sites. Focusing on individuals aged 18 to 29, this number skyrockets to 85%. FCC has integrated the use of twitter, Facebook, idea scale and other tools into the fabric of the agency. In addition, the CDC's（Centers for Disease Control）use of social media has been instrumental in enabling them to get reliable information about the H1N1 virus to the public quickly. Between April and December of 2009, the CDC had more than 2.6 million downloads of H1N1 podcasts, more than 3 million views of H1N1-related YouTube videos, and more than 37 million views of H1N1-related media feeds.

The United States has one of the freest presses in the world. Nonetheless, regulation of the media does exist, particularly of the electronic media. Through the FCC, which regulates communications by radio, television, wire, and cable, the number of radio stations has been controlled for many years, even though technologically we could have many more radio stations than now exist.

Many FCC rules have dealt with ownership of news media, such as how many stations a network can own. In the past, the FCC auctioned off hundreds of radio frequencies, allowing the expansion of cellular telephone applications. In 1966, Congress passed legislation that had far-reaching（影响深远的）implications for the communication industry—the *Telecommunications Act*. The act ended the rule that kept telephone companies from entering the cable business and other communications markets, set aside a portion of the nation's airwaves for digital television broadcasts. Although the frequencies were valued at $70 billion, the act handed them to the broadcasters free of charge. If citizens had been aware of this legislation, they might have demanded that Congress, rather than handing the broadcasters a windfall(意外的收获), charge market value for the frequencies and use the $70 billion to support popular governmental programs. What this means is that a single corporation—whether **Time Warner**[2] or Disney—can offer long-distance and local telephone services, cable television, satellite television, Internet services, and, of course, libraries of films and entertainment. The act opened the door to competition and led to more options for consumers, who can choose among multiple competitors for all of these services delivered to the home. At the same time, it launched a race among competing companies to control media ownership.

The FCC promulgates rules on what media conglomerates can own. One measure of a conglomerate's impact is "audience reach", or the percentage of the national viewing public that has access to the conglomerate's outlets. The FCC places an upper limit on audience reach, known as the "audience-reach cap". A few years ago, the FCC raise the national audience-reach cap from 35 percent to 45 percent and also allowed a corporation to own a newspaper and television station in the same market. Congress rebelled against this new rule, however, pushed the national audience-reach cap back below 40 percent. Nevertheless, a corporation can still own up to three TV stations in its largest market. The reality today is that there are only a few independent news operations left in the entire company. FCC published a National Broadband Plan in March 2010, one of the goals of the plan as described on Broadband.gov is that at least 100 million U.S. homes should have affordable access to actual download speeds of at least 100 megabits per second and actual upload speeds of at least 50 megabits per second by the year 2020, and the United States should lead the world in mobile innovation, with the fastest and most extensive wireless networks of any nation.

Notes

1. Podcasting 播客: 英文全称"Personal Optional Digital Casting",中文译为"播客"。这是一种让用户自由地在互联网上发布文件,并允许用户下载文件的技术和理念,是一种全新的广播形式。"Podcasting"源于苹果公司的"iPod",兼具"broadcasting"(广播)和"webcasting"(网络广播)之意。

2.Time Warner 时代华纳 :2000—2003 年称为美国在线时代华纳,是美国一家跨国媒体企业,成立于 1990 年,总部位于纽约。其事业版图横跨出版、电影与电视产业,包括时代杂志、体育画报、财富杂志、生活杂志、特纳电视网、CNN、HBO、DC 漫画公司、华纳兄弟等具有全球影响力的媒体皆为旗下事业。

References

[1] JERVIS R. Consumers wary of comcast, time warner cable merger[EB/OL]. USA Today, 2014-02-13[2016-02-13].http://www.usatoday.com/story/money/business/2014/02/13/comcast-twc-merger-consumers/5457885/.

[2] U.S. FEDERAL COMMUNICATIONS COMMISSION. National Broadband Plan[EB/

OL]. 2013-09-1[2016-02-13]. https://www.fcc.gov/general/national-broadband-plan.

[3] LUEDTKE L. Making America the society and culture of the United States [M]. New Haven: Yale University Press, 1987.

[4] 江涛 . Listen to speeches in Massachusetts Institute of Technology [M]. 北京：石油工业出版社 , 2013.

[5] 周静琼 . 当代美国概况 [M]. 上海：上海外语教育出版社 , 2003.

[6] 王俊生 , 刘沛富 . 最新英美概况 [M]. 北京：外语教学与研究出版社 , 2007.

[7] 王恩铭 . 美国社会文化 [M]. 北京：北京大学出版社 , 2010.

Chapter Fifteen

American Values

As the 21st century begins, the United States probably has a greater diversity of racial, ethnic, cultural, and religious groups than any other nation on earth. From the beginning of the history of the United States, there has been diversity—Native Americans throughout the North American continent, Spanish settlers in the Southwest and in Florida, French missionaries (传教士) and fur traders along the Mississippi River, black slaves brought from African countries, Dutch settlers in New York, Germans in Pennsylvania, and, of course the British colonists, whose culture eventually provided the language and the foundation for the political and economic systems that developed in the United States.

Most early Americans recognized this diversity, or pluralism (多元化), as a fact of life. The large variety of ethnic, cultural, and religious groups meant that accepting diversity was the only practical choice, even if some people were not enthusiastic about it. However, in time, many Americans came to see strength in their country's diversity. Today, there is more recognition of the value of cultural pluralism than at any other time in the history of the United States.

When we examine the system of basic values that emerged in the late 1700s and began to define the American character, we must remember this context of cultural pluralism. How could a nation of such enormous diversity produce a recognizable national identity?

Historically, the United States has been viewed as "the land of opportunity", attracting immigrants from all over the world. The opportunities they believed they would find in America and the experiences they actually had when they arrived nurtured this set of values. In this chapter, we will examine six basic values that have become "traditional" American values. Three represent traditional reasons why immigrants have been drawn to America: the chance for individual freedom, equality of opportunity, and material wealth. In order to achieve these benefits, however, there were prices to be paid: self-reliance, competition, and hard work. In time, these prices themselves became a part of the traditional value system.

Individual Freedom and Self-Reliance (自立)

The earliest settlers came to the North American continent to establish colonies that were free from the controls that existed in European societies. They wanted to escape the controls placed on their lives by kings and governments, priests and churches, noblemen and aristocrats (贵族). To a great extent, they succeeded in 1776. The British colonial settlers declared their independence from England and established a new nation, the United States of America. In so doing, they overthrew the king of England and declared that the power to govern would lie in the hands of the people. They were now free from the power of the kings. In 1789, when they wrote **American Constitution**[1] for their new nation, they separated church and state so that there would never be a government-supported church. This greatly limited the power of the church. Also, in writing the Constitution, they expressly forbade titles of nobility to ensure that an aristocratic society would not develop. There would be no ruling class of nobility in the new nation. The historic decisions made by those first settlers have had a profound effect on the shaping of the American character. By limiting the power of the government and the churches and eliminating a formal aristocracy, they created a climate of freedom where the emphasis was on the individual. The United States came to be associated in their minds with the concept of individual freedom. This is probably the most basic of all the American values. Scholars and outside observers often call this value individualism, but many Americans use the word freedom. Perhaps the word freedom is one of the most respected popular words in the United States today.

By freedom, Americans mean the desire and the ability of all individuals to control their own destiny without outside interference from the government, a ruling noble class, the church, or any other organized authority. The desire to be free of controls was a basic value of the new nation in 1776, and it has continued to attract immigrants to this country.

There is, however, a price to be paid for this individual freedom: self-reliance. Individuals must learn to rely on themselves or risk losing freedom. This means achieving both financial and emotional independence from their parents as early as possible, usually by age 18 or 21. It means that Americans believe they should take care of themselves, solve their own problems, and "stand on their own two feet".

This strong belief in self-reliance continues today as a traditional basic American value. It is perhaps one of the most difficult aspects of the American character to understand, but it is profoundly important. Most Americans believe that they must be self-reliant in order to keep their freedom. If they rely too much on the support of their families or the government or any organization, they may lose some of their freedom to do what they want.

If people are dependent, they risk losing freedom as well as the respect of their peers. Even if they are not truly self-reliant, most Americans believe they must at least appear to be so. In order to be in the mainstream of American life—to have power and/or respect—individuals must be seen as self-reliant. Although receiving financial support from charity, family, or the government is allowed, it is never admired. Many people believe that such individuals are setting a bad example, which may weaken the American character as a whole. The sight of beggars on city streets and the plight of the homeless may inspire sympathy but also concern. Although Americans provide a lot of financial support to people in need through charities or government programs, they expect that help to be short-lived. Eventually, people should take care of themselves.

Equality of Opportunity and Competition

The second important reason why immigrants have traditionally been drawn to the United States is the belief that everyone has a chance to succeed here. Generations of immigrants, from the earliest settlers to the present day, have come to the United States with this expectation. They have felt that because individuals are free from excessive political, religious, and social controls, they have a better chance for personal success. Of particular importance is the lack of a hereditary (世袭的) aristocracy.

Because titles of nobility were forbidden in the Constitution, no formal class system developed in the United States. In the early years of American history, many immigrants chose to leave the older European societies because they believed that they had a better chance to succeed in America. In "the old country", their place in life was determined largely by the social class into which they were born. They knew that in America they would not have to live among noble families who possessed great power and wealth inherited and accumulated over hundreds of years.

The hopes and dreams of many of these early immigrants were fulfilled in their new country. The lower social class into which many were born did not prevent them from trying to rise to a higher social position. Many found that they did indeed have a better chance to succeed in the United States than in the old country. Because millions of these immigrants succeeded, Americans came to believe in equality of opportunity.

It is important to understand what most Americans mean when they say they believe in equality of opportunity. They do not mean that everyone is—or should be—equal. However, they do mean that each individual should have an equal chance for success. Americans see much of life as a race for success. For them, equality means that everyone should have an equal chance to enter the race and win. In other words, equality of opportunity may be thought of as an ethical rule. It helps ensure that the race for success is a fair one and that a person does not win just because he or she was born into a wealthy family, or lose because of race or religion. This American concept of "fair play" is an important aspect of the belief in equality of opportunity. President Abraham Lincoln expressed this belief in the 1860s when he said:

We... wish to allow the humblest man an equal chance to get rich with everybody else. When one starts poor, as most do in the race of life, free society is such that he knows he can better his condition; he knows that there is no fixed condition of labor for his whole life.

There is, however, a price to be paid for this equality of opportunity: competition. If much of life is seen as a race, then a person must run the race in order to succeed; a person must compete with others. If every person has an equal chance to succeed in the United States, then it is every person's duty to try. Americans match their energy and intelligence against that of others in a competitive contest for success. People who like to compete and are more successful than others are honored by being called winners. On the other hand, those who do not like to compete and are not successful when they try are often dishonored by being called losers. This is especially true for American men, and it is becoming truer and truer for women.

The pressures of competition in the life of an American begin in childhood and continue until retirement from work. Learning to compete successfully is part of growing up in the United States, and competition is encouraged by strong programs of competitive sports provided by the public schools and community groups.

The pressure to compete causes Americans to be energetic, but it also places, a constant emotional strain on them. When they retire (traditionally at age 65), they are at last free from the pressures of competition. But then a new problem arises. They may feel useless and unwanted in a society that gives so much prestige to those who compete well. This is one reason why senior people in the United States do not have as much honor and respect as they have in other, less competitive societies. In fact, any group of people who do not compete successfully—for whatever reason—do not fit into the mainstream of American life as well as those who do compete.

Material Wealth and Hard Work

The third reason why immigrants have traditionally come to the United States is to have a better life—that is, to raise their standard of living. For the vast majority of the immigrants who came here, it was probably the most compelling reason for leaving their homeland. Because of its incredibly abundant natural resources, the United States appeared to be a "land of plenty" where millions could come to seek their fortunes. Of course, most immigrants did not "get rich overnight", and many of them suffered terribly, but the majority of them were eventually able to improve upon their former standard of living. Even if they were not able to achieve the economic success they wanted, they could be fairly certain that their children would have the opportunity for a better life. The phrase "going from rags to riches" became a slogan for the great **American Dream**[2]. Because of the vast riches of the North American continent, the dream came true for many of the immigrants. They achieved material success; they became very attached to material things. Material wealth became a value to the American people.

Placing a high value on material possessions is called materialism, but this is a word that most Americans find offensive. To say that a person is materialistic is an insult. To an American, this means that this person values material possessions above all else. Americans do not like to be called materialistic because they feel that this unfairly accuses them of loving only material things and of having no religious values. In fact, most Americans do have other values and ideals. Nevertheless, acquiring and maintaining a large number of material possessions are of great importance to most Americans. Why is this so?

Probably the main reason is that material wealth has traditionally been a widely accepted measure of social status in the United States. Because Americans rejected the European system of hereditary aristocracy and titles of nobility, they had to find a substitute for judging social status. The quality and quantity of an individual's material possessions became an accepted measure of success and social status.

Americans have paid a price, however, for their material wealth: hard work. The North American continent was rich in natural resources when the first settlers arrived, but all these resources were undeveloped. Only by hard work could these natural resources be converted into material possessions, allowing a more comfortable standard of living. Hard work has been both necessary and rewarding for most Americans throughout their history. Because of this, they came to see material possessions as the natural reward for their hard work. In some ways, material possessions were seen not only as tangible evidence of people's work but also of their abilities. In the late 1700s, **James Madison**[3], the father of the American Constitution, stated that the difference in material possessions reflected a difference in personal abilities.

As the United States has shifted from an industry-based economy to one that is service or information-based, there has been a decline in high-paying jobs for factory workers. It is now much more difficult for the average worker to go "from rags to riches" in the United States, and many wonder what has happened to the traditional "American Dream". As the United States competes in a global economy, many workers are losing their old jobs and finding that they and their family members must now work longer hours for less money and fewer benefits. Faced with a decline in their standard of living, these people no longer believe that hard work necessarily brings great material rewards.

Most Americans, however, still believe in the value of hard work. They believe that people should hold jobs and not live off welfare payments from the government. In the 1990s, the welfare system came under attack. In a time when many people were working harder than ever "to make ends meet"（保持收支平衡）there was enormous resentment against groups such as "welfare mothers", young women who do not marry or hold a job but have children and are supported by payments from the government.

In understanding the relationship between what Americans believe and how they live, it is important to distinguish between idealism and reality. American values such as equality of opportunity and self-reliance are ideals that may not necessarily describe the reality of American life. Equality of opportunity, for example, is an ideal that is not always put into practice. In reality, some people have a better chance for success than others. Those who are born into rich families have more opportunities than those who are born into poorer families. Inheriting money does give a person a decided advantage（明显的优势）. Many black Americans have fewer opportunities than the average white American, and many women have fewer opportunities than men, in spite of laws designed to promote equality of opportunity for all individuals. And many immigrants today have fewer opportunities than those who came before them, when there were more high-paying factory jobs, and the economy was growing more rapidly.

The fact that American ideals are only partly carried out in real life does not diminish their importance. Many Americans still believe in them and are strongly affected by them in their everyday lives. It is easier to understand what Americans are thinking and feeling if we can understand what these basic traditional American values are and how they have influenced almost every facet of life in the United States.

The Challenge to American Values

Surely, Americans had experienced a number of things which had caused them to be more doubtful about the strength of their nation and its basic values. A popular President, **John F. Kennedy**[4], had been assassinated（暗杀）in 1963. After his death, the nation under President Johnson vastly increased the number of American troops in the Southeast Asian country of Vietnam. Johnson did this in order to prevent the Vietnamese communists from taking control of the country. He believed that communism would spread throughout Southeast Asia if it succeeded in Vietnam. By 1966, the struggle in Vietnam had become a major American war. Most Americans agreed with the action. But even so, there was stronger opposition to the **Vietnam War**[5] than to any previous American war in the twentieth century. Most of the opponents of the war attacked it as immoral. They believed it was immoral for the United States to try to determine the future of a distant country by means of war. Many opponents of the Vietnam War also attacked the nation's basic values as corrupt. Some of the harshest criticism of the United States and its values by American citizens was heard during this period of protest against the war.

While most Americans strongly rejected this harsh criticism of their nation's values, some observers believe that the anti-war movement made many Americans who supported the war more doubtful about their beliefs. An even greater blow to the majority who supported the war was the fact that the United States failed in its objective.

The result of the Vietnam War was discouraging to all Americans. The opponents of the war continued to feel that the nation had done something terribly immoral. The people who had supported the war were discouraged by its outcome. Most Americans had been brought up believing that the United States had never lost a war. Now it seemed that for the first time, this had happened. Was the nation losing its strength? If it was, was this because it was losing faith in its basic values? These were the kinds of troubling questions Vietnam raised in the minds of many Americans.

Before the Vietnam War was ended, **the Watergate Scandals**[6] involving the next President, Richard Nixon, dealt a second major blow to the confidence Americans had in their nation and its values. Because the President of the United States is supposed to be an outstanding example of the nation's values, the scandals tended to weaken the faith of many Americans in these values. President Nixon was forced to resign from office in 1974. Three aspects of the affair made it the most serious scandal in American history. First, illegal sabotage（蓄意毁坏）and espionage（间谍活动）activities on a large scale were carried out by agents and associates of the President against his leading political opponents in the United States. Men paid by President Nixon's reelection committee were arrested for breaking into the national headquarters of the opposition Democratic party (in the Watergate building) in order to place illegal listening devices on the telephones and to photograph party documents. Second, the President used all the powers of his office to keep law enforcement officials from finding out the truth about these activities. Third, he repeatedly lied to the American people, claiming to be innocent of all wrongdoing even after the American ceased to believe him.

Before the Watergate scandal, American Presidents, even unpopular ones, were thought to be basically honest, law-abiding men. President Nixon's conduct in office weakened the faith and respect Americans held for their presidents. Faith in American values was also weakened because of the belief that the President is the nation's first citizen and the most important defender of its values. "If you can't trust the President, who can you trust?" was the question on the minds of many.

The failure of the Vietnam War effort and the resignation of President Nixon in disgrace didn't destroy the faith of Americans in their values, but the faith seems to have been weakened by these events. After Vietnam War and Watergate scandal, a third development appeared which threatened to weaken the faith even further. This was the possibility that for the first time since the Great Depression of the 1930s the standard of living of the American people might decline significantly. The material abundance of the United States has served as a kind of sustaining food which has kept American values alive and strong. Americans have considered their high standard of living a reward for practicing their basic beliefs in individual freedom competition, and other values. The possibility of a significant decline in living standards during the 1980s and beyond, therefore, could present a danger to the continuing strength of these values.

In the late 1970s Americans became aware that the era of cheap and abundant energy was ending. In the 1980s Americans also began to discover that the nation's water supplies were declining at a rapid rate and that the amount of land available for farming was also, declining as more and more farmland was changed into business and residential neighborhoods. These and other facts pointed to a decline in the foundations of material abundance that the United States had enjoyed throughout its history.

Political events such as Vietnam War and Watergate scandal, and probably even more important, the fear that the nation's material abundance may be declining, seem to have made Americans less optimistic about the future of their country.

A Return to the Past

Faced with rapid change and the fear and uncertainty that go with it, individuals as well as nations sometimes seek to return to the ways of the past as a solution. In the early 1980s the idea of returning to the ways of the past had a strong appeal to many Americans who increasingly viewed their past as being better than their future. Until the 1970s Americans generally believed that the present was a better time for their country than the past and that the future would be better than the present; by 1978, however, public opinion polls showed that many Americans had come to believe that just the opposite was true: the past had been better for the country than the present, and the present was better than the future would be.

The popular appeal of returning to the ways of the past as a solution to the problems of the

1980s was demonstrated when Ronald Reagan was elected President of the United States in 1980: Time magazine chose President Reagan as its "man of the year" and said of him: "intellectually, emotionally, Reagan lives in the past."

One of President Reagan's basic beliefs is that the United States should return as much as possible to its pre-1930 ways. In those times business institutions were strong and government institutions were weak.

Regan believes that the American values of individual freedom and competition are strengthened by business and weakened by government. Therefore, his programs as President have been designed to greatly strengthen business and reduce the size and power of the national government. By moving in this way toward the practices of the past, President Reagan believed that the standard of living of Americans would begin to improve once more in the 1980s as it had done throughout most of the nation's history.

The Need for New National Values

A number of leaders in politics, education, and the professions take a different approach than does President Reagan. They believe that the nation must adopt new values to go along with the old values and that it must be prepared to make some changes in the old values when necessary.

What new values should be adopted? This is a very difficult question to answer. However, it became clear in the 1970s that there was no longer an abundance of cheap energy and that shortages of other essential resources such as water were becoming more serious. These facts suggested to many Americans that a greater value be placed on the conservation of natural resources, that is, that Americans should save more of these resources by learning to use less and waste less.

Conservation has never been a strong American value. Because of the vast resources and space of North-America, Americans came to believe that, abundance was endless. In such an environment, there seemed to be little need for conservation of resources. After World War II Americans believed that their modern technology could work wonders and provide a never-ending increase in their standard of living. It is not surprising, therefore, that in the United States before the 1980s conservation had little importance compared with such other values as freedom, equality of opportunity, hard work, and the accumulation of material wealth.

There is some evidence that the experience of greater shortages of energy during the 1970s caused Americans to place more emphasis on conservation. For example, a poll taken at the end of the decade showed that 66 percent of Americans agreed with the statement: "I'm not that unhappy about the possibility of shortages because I know it will encourage me to use everything efficiently and not wastefully."

Although Americans may agree with statements supporting the value of conservation, most of them are not yet applying these beliefs in their day-to-day actions. Belief in conservation, therefore, is still weak compared with other American beliefs. It can become stronger only as

Americans see the need for it more and more clearly. Conservation may well be a new value which needs to be added to the old basic values in order to help the United States deal with its future problems.

A second belief which has never been strong among the American people is a belief in the value of cooperation on a national scale to achieve some important national objectives. The American idea of the national good has never been based on national cooperation but rather on the freedom of the individual. Americans, therefore, tend to think of the national good in terms of maintaining those conditions that provide the greatest freedom for the individual. They believe that a nation of free individuals will be naturally strong and prosperous. Planned efforts at national cooperation, therefore, are not needed. More importantly, planned efforts at national cooperation would mean increasing the powers of the national government, which would endanger the freedom of the individual.

The American value of competition also hinders（阻碍）the development of a spirit of national cooperation.

This ideal often encourages Americans to work against each other. Even though competitive activity is supposed to be conducted according to fair rules, it does not encourage a spirit of cooperation. Rather, it sometimes encourages a spirit of mutual suspicion of the motives of others. A certain degree of trust in the motives of others is necessary for the success of efforts in national cooperation.

In time of war Americans have temporarily put aside their dislike of planned national cooperation. They have been willing to cooperate and make personal sacrifices under the direction of the national government to bring the war to a satisfactory conclusion. In peacetime, however, planned national cooperation is strongly resisted as a threat to individual freedom.

The almost unique American historical experience gives people a deeper understanding of this attitude: Almost every nation in the world has had, or still has the experience of being ruled by kings, emperors, dictators, or a hereditary（遗传的）class of aristocrats（贵族）. Such rulers are not elected by the free votes of the people and they have the power to say what the national good is and to force their people to cooperate if they cannot persuade them to do so. Out of these experiences there have developed traditions and habits of cooperation, sometimes for good purposes and sometimes for evil purposes.

Americans have never had the experience of being forced to cooperate on a national scale by non-elected rulers. For a time, they were the colonists of Great Britain and were legally bound to obey rulers in England whom they did not elect, but the British government allowed the colonists a great deal of freedom and self-government by the standards of the day. Still the American colonists were not long in demanding more freedom and self-government, and finally declaring their independence in 1776. From the time of their independence, Americans have freely elected their rulers. The experience of being compelled to cooperate by unelected national leaders is completely foreign to their experience. They are fearful that any scheme of national cooperation in peacetime will weaken or destroy their freedoms.

Americans have always viewed cooperation as important in small groups such as the family, the neighborhood, or the church. But on the large national scale where government becomes involved, it is seen as coercive（强制的）and destructive rather than voluntary and constructive. Americans tend to associate the greatness of their nation far more with such values as individual freedom, equality of opportunity, hard work, and competition than with national cooperation.

Yet the demands of the 1980s may compel Americans to place a greater value on national cooperation. It may well be that some of the problems facing them, such as scarcity of resources and the dangers of air and water pollution, cannot be solved without a greater degree of national cooperation. If Americans choose to give more emphasis to national cooperation, they will probably be very cautious about it. In order to protect their freedoms, they will move slowly in a step-by-step, problem-by-problem fashion, rather than accept a sweeping new plan involving dramatic change. Because of their tradition of self-government, they will probably insist on a good deal of public discussion before any single step toward national cooperation is taken.

Some observers believe that this slow, cautious approach may be too weak and too timid to meet the challenges of the future. Americans, however, believe that sudden revolutionary changes made in the name of the national good usually result in dictatorships in which freedom is lost and problems remain unsolved.

In the 21st century Americans may have arrived at a critical point in their nation's history, where major dangers must be faced and major choices must be made. On the one hand, they will wish to avoid the risk of making too many changes in the basic values which have inspired them in the past. On the other hand, they must avoid what may be the greater risk of refusing to change their values at all, even though conditions are changing rapidly all around them. The events of the past several decades have brought the American people and their basic values to a crossroad in their history. The new century will determine where they will go from there.

Notes

1. American Constitution 美国宪法：美国的根本大法，奠定了美国政治制度的法律基础。根据这部宪法，美国成为一个由各个拥有主权的州所组成的联邦国家。从此联邦体制取代了基于邦联条例而存在较为松散的邦联体制。1789年，美国宪法正式生效。美国宪法规定实行资产阶级性质的联邦制，肯定了以立法、行政、司法三权分立，相互制衡为原则的资产阶级总统制民主共和政体。美国宪法是世界上首部成文宪法，该宪法为日后许多国家成文宪法的制定提供了成功的典范。

2. American Dream 美国梦：源于英国对北美大陆的殖民时期，发展于19世纪，是一种相信只要经过努力不懈的奋斗便能在美国获致更好生活的信仰，亦即人们必须通过自己的工作勤奋、勇气、创意和决心迈向富裕，而非依赖于特定的社会阶级和他人的援助。通常这代表了人们在经济上的成功或是企业家的精神。许多欧洲移民都是抱持着美国梦的理想前往美国的。

3. James Madison 詹姆士·麦迪逊：詹姆士·麦迪逊（1751 年 3 月 16 日—1836 年 6 月 28 日），美国第四任总统（1809—1817）。他与约翰·杰伊及亚历山大·汉密尔顿共同编写《联邦党人文集》，亦被一些人视为“美国宪法之父”。他也是一名共济会成员。曾担任州众议员（1776 年）、州参议员（1784—1786）、大陆会议代表（1780—1783）、联邦众议员（1789—1797）和国务卿（1801—1809）。他还是制宪会议的主要人物、北部联邦党人文件的起草人之一、民主共和党的组织者。

4. John F. Kennedy 约翰·费茨杰拉德·肯尼迪：约翰·费茨杰拉德·肯尼迪（1917 年 5 月 29 日—1963 年 11 月 22 日），通常被称作约翰·F. 肯尼迪（John F. Kennedy）、JFK 或杰克·肯尼迪（Jack Kennedy），美国第 35 任总统，美国著名的肯尼迪家族成员，他的执政时间从 1961 年 1 月 20 日开始到 1963 年 11 月 22 日在达拉斯遇刺身亡为止。肯尼迪在 1942 年曾是一名海军中尉，在 1946—1960 年期间曾先后任众议员和参议员，并于 1960 年当选为美国总统。他以 43 岁的年纪当选总统，为美国截至 2017 年第二年轻的总统，也是美国历史上迄今唯一信奉罗马天主教的总统和唯一获得普利策奖的总统。

5. Vietnam War 越南战争：简称“越战”，是美国等资本主义阵营国家支持的南越（越南共和国）对抗苏联等社会主义阵营国家支持的北越（越南共产党）和“越南南方民族解放阵线”（越南民主共和国）的一场战争。其发生在冷战时期的越南（主战场）、老挝、柬埔寨。越战是二战以后美国参战人数最多、影响最重大的战争，最后美国在越南战争中失败。越南战争是冷战下的一次实战，希望统一越南的越南反政府武装越南南方民族解放阵线在越南民主共和国主席胡志明的支持下，推翻越南共和国总统吴庭艳的政府。美国则出兵帮助越南共和国。最后美国因为国内的反战浪潮，逐渐将美国国防军撤出越南。越南人民军和越南南方民族解放阵线最终推翻了越南共和国，统一了越南全国。

6. Watergate Scandals 水门事件：又称“水门丑闻”，是美国历史上最不光彩的政治丑闻事件之一，其对美国本国历史以及整个国际新闻界都有着长远的影响。在 1972 年的总统大选中，为了取得民主党内部竞选策略的情报，1972 年 6 月 17 日，以美国共和党尼克松竞选班子的首席安全问题顾问詹姆斯·麦科德（James W. McCord Jr.）为首的 5 人闯入位于华盛顿水门大厦的民主党全国委员会办公室，在安装窃听器并偷拍有关文件时，当场被捕。由于此事，尼克松于 1974 年 8 月 8 日宣布将于次日辞职，从而成为美国历史上首位辞职的总统。

References

[1] 王恩铭 . 美国社会文化 [M]. 北京：北京大学出版社 , 2010.

[2] 王恩铭 . 英语国家概况 [M]. 上海：上海外语教育出版社 , 2008.

[3] 常俊跃 , 李莉莉 , 赵永青 . 美国社会与文化 [M]. 北京：北京大学出版社 , 2009.

[4] 周静琼 . 当代美国概况 [M]. 上海：上海外语教育出版社 , 2003.

[5] 刘茜 . 轻松走遍美国 [M]. 北京：中国宇航出版社 , 2010.

[6] 张浩 . 一本书玩转北美 [M]. 北京：经济科学出版社 , 2013.

[7] 张浩 , 黄一飞 . 一本书读懂美国文化 [M]. 北京：中国时代经济出版社 , 2012.

[8] 肖冉等 . 边品美国文化边学英语 (基础篇) [M]. 北京：中国水利水电出版社 , 2009.

[9] 田耀 . 美国文化点滴 [M]. 天津：天津大学出版社 , 2009.

[10] 王晓红 . 美国社会与文化 [M]. 北京：世界图书出版公司 , 2010.
[11] 丁建军 . 英语国家概况 [M]. 西安：西安交通大学出版社 , 2010.
[12] 朱永涛 , 王立礼 . 英语国家社会与文化入门 [M]. 北京：高等教育出版社 , 2005.
[13] 梅仁毅 . 美国研究读本（第一辑）[M]. 北京：外语教学与研究出版社 , 2002.

Chapter Sixteen

The Great West

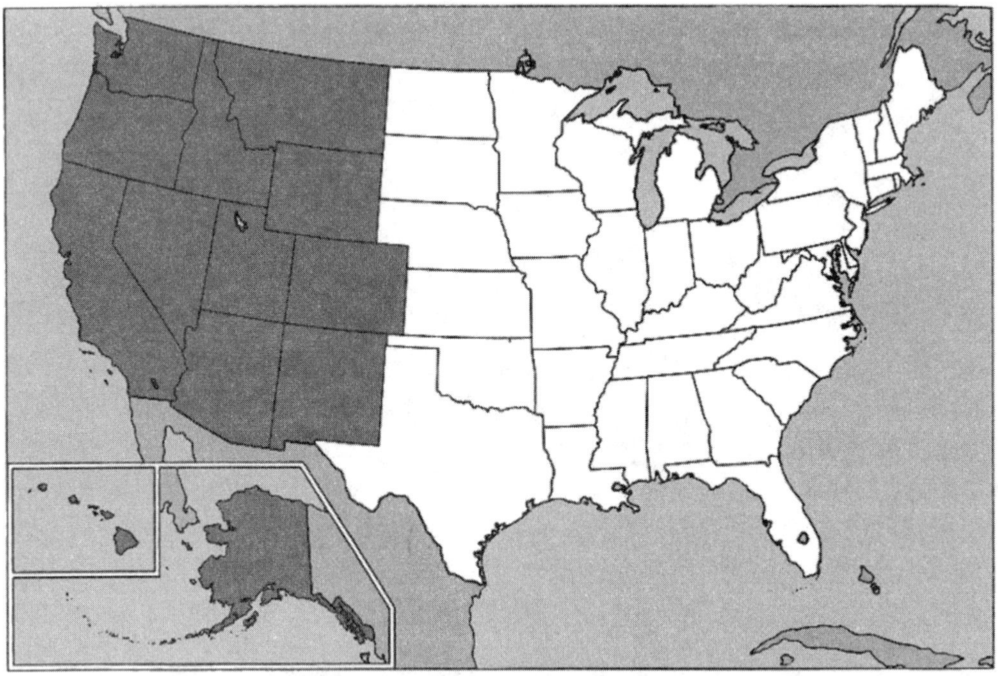

Thirteen States of American West

(Alaska, Arizona, California, Colorado, Hawaii, Idaho, Montana, Nevada, New Mexico, Oregon, Utah, Washington and Wyoming)

Unit 1 General History

As defined by the Census Bureau (人口调查), the western United States included 13 states: Alaska, Arizona, California, Colorado, Hawaii, Idaho, Montana, Nevada, New Mexico, Oregon, Utah, Washington and Wyoming. The western of the United States—commonly referred to as the American West or simply **the West**[1]—traditionally refers to the region comprising the westernmost states of the United States. Because the United States expanded westward after its founding the meaning of the West has evolved over time.

At the very beginning, the frontier (边疆) referred to the Atlantic coast, which bore a strong relationship with Europe. With the process of moving westward, the frontier shared more and more features of America. However, the frontier was a changing area, which had several natural boundaries in different time periods. Generally speaking, in the 17th century, the frontier referred to the "fall line", and the tidewater region became the settled area; and **the Alleghany Mountains**[2] marked the frontier of the 18th century; when time came to the first quarter of the 19th century, **the Mississippi River**[3] became the new frontier; and the Missouri that of the middle of this century; and until the time of **Frederick Jackson Turner**[4], the frontier again referred to **the Rock Mountains**[5] and the arid tract. Nowadays, as we know, the state of Alaska is called the "last frontier". That is to say, there is not frontier any longer in America. While this great expansion was originated from a large-scale westward immigration movement which was the so-called **"Westward Movement**[6]**".**

Westward Movement referred to the colonization and expansion from east to west in the United States from the Independence War till the end of 19th century, with the immigration and western development. And it can be divided into three phases. Firstly, from the late 18th century to the early 19th century it opened up the Ohio, Kentucky and Tennessee areas. The second phase began in 1815, the immigrants moved towards two directions: one part opened up the north region of the Ohio River, and the other part went into the plain areas between Southern Georgia and Louisiana. The third phase began in the mid-19th century, immigrants continued to move westward to the direction of the Pacific coast. Until 1890, the Westward Movement formally ended. Fundamentally speaking, the Westward Movement was a pioneering undertaking based on capitalism to explore the vast western areas. It enlarged American manufacturing bases and markets, greatly enhanced the development of American industry and agriculture, making America from a small country to a great and proud nation. This long-term movement with such a large scale was unparalleled even in world history. The influence it has made in American history was far-reaching, comprehensive and strategic.

Notes

1. the West 美国西部：泛指美国西部各州。由于美国自建国以来疆域多次向西扩展，因此美国西部的定义也随着时代而变化。一般多以密西西比河作为美国东西部的分界线。如果采用广义的定义，美国西部占去了美国一半以上的领土。美国西部包括了自路易西安纳购地中获得的土地、1818年自英国获得的土地、得克萨斯加入美国时的土地、1846年自英国获得的土地、1848年墨西哥割让予美国的土地及盖兹登购地中获得的土地。

2. the Alleghany Mountains 阿勒格尼山：北美洲阿巴拉契亚山系西北部的分支。延伸至美国宾夕法尼亚州、马里兰州、弗吉尼亚州和西弗吉尼亚州境内。东侧隔大谷地与蓝岭山脉相平行。连续不断的山峰海拔1,000米左右，峻拔的东斜面称为阿勒格尼峰，陡落于大谷地中。是大西洋水系和墨西哥湾水系的分水岭，开拓初期是向西移民的障碍。

3. Mississippi River 密西西比河：世界第四长河，全长6 020千米，其长度仅次于非洲的尼罗河、南美洲的亚马逊河和中国的长江，是北美洲流程最长、流域面积最广、水量最大的河流。位于北美洲中南部，注入墨西哥湾。流域各州包括明尼苏达州、威斯康星州、艾奥瓦州、伊利诺伊州、密苏里州、肯塔基州、田纳西州、阿肯色州、密西西比州、路易斯安那州等

10个。

4. Frederick Jackson Turner 弗雷德里克·杰克逊·特纳：弗雷德里克·杰克逊·特纳（1861年11月14日—1932年3月14日），19世纪末20世纪初美国历史学家。1893年在芝加哥美国历史协会年会上他宣读《边疆在美国历史上的重要性》一文，奠定其在美国史学界的地位，该理论被称为“边疆理论”。该学说对美国的史学研究产生重大影响，并由此形成一个颇具影响、并在美国史学界占据统治地位40年之久的“边疆学派”。

5. the Rocky Mountains 落基山脉：占北美大陆西部主要地形区大高原体系的大部地区。整体而言，落基山系所包含的各条山脉从亚伯达省北部和不列颠哥伦比亚省向南延伸，经美国西部至墨西哥边境，全长约4 800千米。落基山区景色奇特优美，有落基山、黄石、大蒂顿、冰川等国家公园以及月火山口、恐龙、大沙丘、甘尼森河布莱克峡谷等游览胜地。

6. Westward Movement 西进运动：西进运动是指美国东部居民向西部地区迁移和进行开发的群众性运动，始于18世纪末，终于19世纪末20世纪初。运动大大促进了美国经济的发展，但是，随着西进运动的进行，大批印第安人遭到屠杀，幸存者被强行赶到更为荒凉的“保留地”。印第安人被迫迁徙之路也被称为印第安人的“血泪之路”。

Unit 2 Important Fields of the Western Development

The western part of the United States has made great progress in the development of the 19th century, which mainly focused on the field of land policy, transportation revolution and immigrants.

Essentially the development of the western region promoted agricultural growth in the United States, formed the distinctively specialized economic zone, made the United States realize the agricultural mechanization, improved the process of agricultural modernization, and established the status of the United States to become one world-leading economic power. Basically, the land policy was the core of American agricultural development. As is well-known, American westward expansion started with **the Louisiana Purchase**[1] of 1803 from France. Shortly after its independence, the United States quickly took the path of large-scale territorial expansion. Until the 1840s-1850s, American territory has expanded from the Mississippi River to the Pacific seacoast.

To explore and consolidate the western frontier as well as solving the problem of governmental deficit, the federal government consequently promulgated three land acts. **The Land Law of 1784**[2] was drafted by Jefferson, it stipulated that the western land belonged to all the citizens of the United States, and the land was divided into 16 regions, when its population reached the number of that of the minimum state among the original 13 states, this region could possess equal status with the eastern states as a new state. This law was later modified to become the main contents of **the Northwest Land Ordinance of 1787**[3] and this law put up with the idea to build larger states in acreage but smaller amount in population (not less than three states, but not more than five states). *The Land Ordinance of 1787* determined the principle that state-owned land was sold to immigrants. According to the regulation of the law, the public land would be partitioned to the auction sale, the minimum land was 640 acres (about 388 acres), the lowest land price was $1 per acre, and all fees were paid once. Such land-selling policies in bulk encouraged people to possess, use and develop the land, attracted capitals of the east and Europe flowing into the west, and set off a wave of migration to the west. However, the truly significant impact on the development of the western region of the United States was **the Homestead Act of 1862**[4]. The law regulated, any American citizens who reached the age of 21, or as long as those who applied for citizenship and at the same time one had never fought against U.S. citizens could pay $10, one could register to receive 160 acres of the land, later after five years farming of the registered land, one would own it as one's own possessions. After implementing *the Homestead Act of 1862*, agricultural was in prosperity, and about more than 300 new farms were built. From the Civil War to the end of the 19th century, the arable (耕地) land area was doubled, the farmer's productivity increased by 50% on average. The flexible land policy set by the federal government, to a certain extent, met the needs of the immigrants for vast land, formed an army of self-raised funds of the land reclamation, the Westward Movement truly became a mass movement. Under the influence of this policy, a large number of peasants flocked to the west, promoting the development of the western land. Although in fact, the land promised by the government was not as fertile as they had expected, "the US government land policies were inadequately formulated to provide the homesteaders any assurance of a decent livelihood on the land".

As an integral part in the field of social production, the construction of transportation industry, lag or advance, would hinder or promote the economic development. In order to strengthen the building of the western traffic facilities, the U.S. government took many measures. Scholars called it "the transportation revolution", which focused on the construction of roads, canals, steamboats, railways and other aspects. The transportation revolution began with the large-scale construction of highways. Started in 1811, the building of the Cumberland Street was one of the most famous roads at that time, becoming a main road linking the east and the west. In 1807, **Fulton**[5] built "Claremont Steamboat", composing a new chapter of the transportation revolution. The invention of the steamboat was a great event in the 19th century of American transportation, it marked that the transportation industry has entered a "**Steamboat Era**"[6], when "steam power captured the American imagination and transformed the landscape". At the same time, the digging of the canal also caused great change of transportation, especially the successful construction of the **Erie Canal**[7] in 1825. As a result, the United States transportation entered into the "canal era". In the 19th century, however, the biggest change of American transportation history was the construction of the railway. Steamboat adoption and the digging of the canal were greatly limited by geographical factors, by contrast, railways had more advantages, which could wear mountain ridges and direct to the hinterlands in high speed with heavy loads. Therefore, the emergence of the railways could combine inland transport and water transport, truly completed transportation system, and fundamentally changed the transportation conditions of a country. Therefore, railways connecting the east and west were the most effective and powerful transport facilities, without being limited by regions. After the Civil War, it came to the climax of railway construction. In 1869, the first transcontinental railroad—**the Pacific Railroad**[8] was constructed in the North American continent, opening to San Francisco and getting behind in Omaha; hence the "Canal Era" has gone. Since then, the Santa Fe railway opened in 1881, Northern Pacific railway in 1883, the South Pacific and the great Northern railway in 1893. "Scholars of US expansionism often viewed the Pacific railroad as a consequence of **Manifest Destiny**[9]." Actually, the construction of railways has played an important role in the rise of urban railway towns, which drove the economic development of the towns along the railway, especially the agricultural trade economy. In addition, the emergence of the "animal kingdom" also greatly benefited from this. The transportation infrastructure construction and development provided great convenience for the Westward Movement of that time, connected the developed regions and underdeveloped regions, broke the isolated state of the west, and accelerated the speed and efficiency of the western social economic life, which was beneficial to the professional development of regional economy and the commercialization of the whole national economy.

With the progress of the Westward Movement, the United States appeared a continuous mass movement of immigration to the western regions, including three main waves. First immigration boom appeared between the late 18th century and the early 19th century, at that time because the U.S. government promulgated a series of land laws and bought the Louisiana area from France, immigrants felt that the colonizing activities would have a certain guarantee and then they decided to flood to the west, expanding the Ohio, Kentucky, Tennessee and other regions, which laid a foundation for later growing Mid-western bread basket. The second migration climax occurred since 1815, two groups of immigrants moved toward two directions. One group came from the coastal strip and German immigrants, they together migrated toward the great lakes region, gradually expanded the northern part of the Ohio River, established the grain production and the chip industry bases. The other group of immigrants was from the Southeast, they entered the plains which were close to **the Gulf of Mexico**[10] between Southern Georgia and Louisiana. At first, in this region, there was a string of small farmers and small producers developing the fertile land, and then gradually they established big plantations which mainly engaged in the production and sales of cotton, thereby this expanded the Southern slavery economy. The third immigration boom was accompanied by American territorial expansion and merger in the middle of the 19th century. At that time, the territorial expansion in the United States continued to push forward in the direction of two: **the Annexation of Texas**[11] of 1845 and taking half of Mexican territory in **the Mexican-American War**[12] of 1848 in the Southwest; in the Northwest, after a long negotiation with Britain, till 1846 the US got large areas of land in Oregon. Finally, the expansion of the two directions met in California, completing the whole great western occupation. At the same time, due to the discovery of gold in California, it caused mining gold waves of immigrants pouring into the west. Later, some immigrants of **the Gold Rush**[13] turned to farming or open a shop, becoming permanent residents of California; Others from California came to the Northwest to explore mineral deposits. During 1850s—1860s, a lot of small farmers began to work on grain production and the western regions of the Rocky Mountains were divided into some States and territory, those former camps of mineral deposits exploitation became permanent residential areas.

Through the research of the land policy, transportation revolution and immigrants of the 19th century in the process of western development, it is obvious to see the crucial role that the west has played in the rise of the U.S. economy. The flexible land policy attracted a large number of migrants at home and abroad to the western construction; the transportation revolution injected fresh vigor to western development; immigrants not only enriched the labor market, but also brought the advanced technology and experience, which accelerated the urbanization of the west. Such a systematic and accomplished engineering set a good example for many less developed areas to follow.

Notes

1. the Louisiana Purchase 路易斯安那购地案：美国于 1803 年以大约每英亩三美分向法国购买超过 529 911 680 英亩（2 144 476 平方千米）土地的交易案，该交易的总价为 1 500 万美元或相当于 8 000 万法郎（如以国内生产总值相对比例计算，此数在 2004 年相当 4 178 亿美元）。法国路易斯安纳属地的版图超出今日美国路易斯安纳州的实际范围很多；购地所涉土地面积是今日美国国土的 22.3%，与当时美国原有国土面积大致相当。

2. The Land Law of 1784 1784 年颁布的土地法令：1780 年 10 月 10 日，美国国会通过了一项法令，规定为了美国的利益，为了在美国西部土地上建立新的州，授予政府出售和赠送西北部国有土地的权力。1784 年，美国的退伍军人（包括华盛顿在内）、金融家及许多其他阶层的人士都在呼吁联邦国会采取实际步骤来分配西部的国有土地。美国国会于 1784 年春天任命了由杰佛逊领导的委员会来研究解决这个问题的对策，并于 1785 年 5 月 7 日向国会提交了由杰佛逊亲笔起草的报告。这个报告虽然未被国会所接受，但却成了 1785 年土地法令的基础。

3. the Northwest Land Ordinance of 1787 1787 年的《西北条例》：正式规定了西部由领地到州转变的法律程序和条件。条例强调西部“将永远是美利坚合众国联邦的一个部分”，领地或州的政体必须是“共和制”，在西部领地内“不得有奴隶或强迫劳动”，必须保证领地居民的民权和自由。1787 年《西北条例》具有重要意义，是西部地方政权组织形式的纲领性文件。1787 年《西北条例》体现了美国人民追求民主和自由、独立和平等的理念，其核心精神被融入 1787 年宪法中，成为指导整个国家政治生活的至高无上的原则。1787 年《西北条例》和 1787 年联邦宪法的重要意义在于它给予西部同东部平等的政治地位，在西部实行民主共和政体。

4. the Homestead Act of 1862《1862 年宅地法》：由美国总统林肯颁布，旨在无偿分配美国西部的国有土地给广大移民的法令。美国独立后，联邦政府对西部土地实行国有化，并决定按地段分块出售，以增加政府的收入，偿还国债和满足土地投机者的要求。

5. Fulton 富尔顿：富尔顿（1765—1815），美国著名工程师。在一次社交场合，富尔顿结识了蒸汽机发明家瓦特，他们成为莫逆之交。1807年，他利用英国机器制成了世界上第一个蒸汽机轮船“克莱蒙脱号”，是世界上轮船的首创者。他为世界人类航海事业的发展做出了卓越的贡献。

6. Steamboat Era（蒸）汽船时代：1807年8月，”克莱蒙特”，它的平均时速达到5.6千米，从此揭开了蒸轮船时代的帷幕。富尔顿取得了在哈德逊河上航行的独占权，并开办了船运公司。富尔顿的成功很快引来无数的效法者。在5年以内，美国和欧洲的内陆河流中已经有50多艘蒸汽轮船投入了营业性航运。自从富尔顿成功地发明了蒸汽轮船之后，这种高耸着烟囱，冒着浓浓的黑烟，两只巨大的明轮哗哗作响的轮船，开始一艘接一艘地航行在美国的内河上并从美国传到了欧洲。在此后一个多世界的时间里，世界的许多河流上都跑着这种明轮船。明轮船的出现在人类船舶制造业的发展史上揭开了崭新的一页。尽管这种以蒸汽机为动力，靠明轮推进的轮船，在今天看来过于愚笨，还有许多致命的缺点，但它在当时所发挥出来的巨大航运作用，是无法被抹杀的。

7. the Erie Canal 伊利运河：一条位于美国纽约州的运河，连接哈德逊河与伊利湖，将五大湖与大西洋水域连接起来，现在属于纽约州运河系统。伊利运河最初是在1699年被提出兴建的提案，但是一直到1798年才由尼亚加拉运河公司开始准备兴建。运河的第一段在1819年完工，整段运河则在1825年10月26日开放通行。伊利运河的全长为584千米（363英里），整条运河的河堤为12米（39英尺）宽、1.2米（4英尺）深。整条运河总共有83个水闸，每个水闸有27米乘4.5米（90英尺乘15英尺），最高可以行驶排水量68公吨（75吨）的平底驳船。伊利运河是第一条提供美国东海岸与西部内陆的快速运输工具，这比当时最常用的以动物拉动的拖车还快许多。伊利运河不只加快运输的速度，也将沿岸地区与内陆地区的运输成本减少了95%。快捷的运河交通使得纽约州西部更便于到达，因此也造成中西部的人口快速成长。

8. the Pacific Railroad 太平洋铁路：第一条横贯北美大陆的铁路，被英国BBC评为自工业革命以来世界七大工业奇迹之一。 太平洋铁路为美国的经济发展做出了巨大的贡献，从一定意义上说，正是这条铁路成就了现代美国。它全长3 000多千米，穿越了整个北美大陆，是世界上第一条跨洲铁路，这条在美国人心目中被看成是奇迹的铁路，在当时的条件下，建设过程极其艰难。其中成千上万的中国劳工应召参加了最艰巨的中央太平洋铁路的建设。在工程中，他们以中国人特有的吃苦耐劳精神和出众的聪明才智，为筑路发挥了关键性作用，做出了决定性的贡献。他们还付出了惨重的代价，大量华工在高强度、高风险劳动中死亡。然而令人愤慨的是，中国劳工在当时受到了酬金微薄、种族歧视和排华浪潮等不公正待遇。

9. Manifest Destiny 天定命运论：19世纪40年代美国产生的一种扩张主义思潮。这一词语首先由一位名叫奥沙利文的记者提出。按字面意义理解，即美国人是上帝的选民，起对新大陆的统治和主宰是天意的安排，种族优越论和扩张是其思想核心。它迎合了当时美国国内进行领土扩张的需要，为美国兼并得克萨斯等地提供了借口和理论依据。这一说法成为早期美国的主流思想，迄今仍影响着美国外交政策的走向。

10. the Gulf of Mexico 墨西哥湾：因濒临墨西哥，而得名墨西哥湾。位于北美洲大陆东南沿海水域，部分为陆地环绕。墨西哥湾是北美洲南部大西洋的一个海湾，以佛罗里达半

岛 - 古巴 - 尤卡坦半岛一线与外海分割。北为美国，南、西为墨西哥，东经佛罗里达海峡与大西洋相连，经尤卡坦海峡与加勒比海相接，是著名的墨西哥湾洋流的起点。墨西哥湾面积约 154 万平方千米，东西最长处长约 1 600 多千米，南北最宽处宽约 1 300 千米，平均深度 1 512 米，最深处超过 5 200 米。

11. the Annexation of Texas 得克萨斯兼并：得克萨斯州原属于墨西哥的领土。1821 年，得克萨斯是西班牙殖民地的一部分；墨西哥独立后，得克萨斯成为墨西哥的一部分。1836 年，得克萨斯正式宣布独立，建立了得克萨斯共和国；且请求加入美国联邦。而美国碍于当时国内奴隶制问题及避免与墨西哥交战多次拒绝了得克萨斯的申请，后因问题的解决接受了得克萨斯的申请。1845 年，得克萨斯加入美国成为美国第 28 个州。

12. the Mexican-American War 美墨战争：美国与墨西哥之间于 1846 年至 1848 年爆发的一场战争。战争后墨西哥丧失了大半国土，元气大伤，美国通过这场规模不算很大的战争夺取了 230 万平方千米的土地，一跃成为地跨大西洋和太平洋的大国，世界罕见，从此获得在美洲的主宰地位。美墨战争的爆发原因是墨西哥与得克萨斯共和国之间未解决的边境问题以及美国的扩张主义。美墨战争的结果使美国获得了西南部广阔肥沃的土地和丰富的资源，推动了西进运动的发展，有利于经济大国的布局，并加快了工业化的进程。美墨战争对美国国内政治特别是围绕奴隶制的争论产生重大的影响。美墨战争后，在这场奴隶制限制反限制的斗争激化情况下，终于导致了美国南北战争的爆发。

13. the Gold Rush 淘金热：由于西进运动的发展引发的人口迁移为开端。在人口第三次大规模的浪潮来临之际，美国移民萨特在加利福尼亚的萨克拉门托附近发现了金矿，并有冒险商人、操纵者、土地投机家布兰那使金矿发现的消息扩大到全世界。西进运动的发展首先是由于布兰那在加利福尼亚的企业中首次与顾客用金沙交换商品并从中捕获商机开始的，由于他的宣传在一定程度上产生了经济效应。更为重要的是美国政府的支持和引导。美国政府支持西部牛仔向西部披荆斩棘，并在淘金热兴起前后准备正式兼并加利福尼亚，即便在加利福尼亚商品匮乏之时也设法调剂和统筹商品货源。成千上万的淘金者使加利福尼亚人口猛增。并且许多新近出现的城镇很快成为国际性的城市。

Unit 3 The Positive and Negative Significance of the Western Development

Every coin has two sides, so does the Westward Movement. It brought the United States benefits as well as losses.

On one hand, the Westward Movement of the United States was under the background of a free market economy and territorial expansion. It completed the political and economic integration between the eastern and western regions, promoted the development of the capitalist industrialization, contributed to the modern agricultural revolution, industrial revolution and revolution of knowledge. What's more, it cultivated the pioneering spirit of the American people especially that of not afraid of arduousness and sacrifice, high-spirited, new cowboy spirit that constantly looking for new land and wealth. The frontier spirit in the western development later became part of American's national spirits which are optimistic, brave, and adventurous and so on. In a word, through the Westward Movement in the United States, the progress made in modernized agriculture, animal husbandry and industry has a decisive influence in pushing the United States to become the world's leading economic power.

On the other hand, in the process of US western development, because of the lack of the sense of resources protection and coupled with the federal government's indifference in the bourgeoisies'（中产阶级的） plundering（掠夺）nature, the scale of ecological destruction was not only serious but also the duration was long, making the forest resources, soil resources, biological resources suffer an unprecedented havoc（浩劫）. The most prominent example was the bison（野牛）, which was the lifeline and material basis for the survival of the Indians. According to the record, when **Christopher Columbus**[1] arrived in America, there lived about 60 million bison in America, but till the 19th century, bison were in extinction. In addition, the combination of cheat and kill policy taken by the white towards the Indians drove the Indians to its narrow **Reservation**[2] step by step, which was a historical tragedy and also a stain that can never be rinsed in American history, and also that's why the history of the United States was called the Indians' trails of tears.

In conclusion, bursts of florid rhetoric accompanied territorial growth, and American used the slogan "Manifest Destiny" to justify and account for it. By the 1840s, absorption of the Louisiana Territory, rapid population growth, and advances in transportation, communication, and industry bolstered a sense of national superiority. American western development with the long history of 200 years has played a huge role in advancing the agriculture, industry, and technology modernization, enhancing the comprehensive national strength, speeding up the upgrading of industrial structure, development at home and abroad market, improving the international competitiveness and realizing economic revitalization and development of the United States. All in all, it can be said that without the west development, there will not be today's America, and without western development, there will not be America's today as well.

Notes

1. Christopher Columbus 克里斯托弗·哥伦布：克里斯托弗·哥伦布（1451年10月—1506年5月20日），意大利的探险家、殖民者、航海家。生于意大利热那亚，卒于西班牙巴里亚多利德。先后移居葡萄牙和西班牙。相信大地球形说，认为从欧洲西航可达东方的印度和中国。在西班牙国王的支持下，先后四次出海远航发现了美洲大陆，他也因此成为名垂青史的航海家。

2. Reservation 保留地：保留地是指政府为印第安人保留的地方，是由土著北美部落管理的地区，由美国内政部印第安事务局负责。因为土著北美部落有有限的国家主权，保留地内的法律不同于周围地区。这些法律可能会允许赌场以吸引游客。根据美国官方解释：保留地是一度遍及大陆的印第安土地的最后残余部分。保留地已经成为印第安人永久可靠地基地，他们可以闯荡白人居住的世界，还可以随时回到保留地的家，这里是他们避风的港湾。如今在美国、加拿大、哥伦比亚等都有印第安人保留地，美国政府和各个印第安部落政府都认为保留地是保存印第安传统的一种方法。

References

[1] FRANCVIGLI V R, BRYAN J L J. "Are we chimerical in this opinion?" visions of a Pacific railroad and westward expansion [M]. California: Pacific Historical Review, 2002.

[2] HAROLD L D. Thomas Jefferson: westward the course of empire [M]. Washington: Journal of the Early Republic, 1999.

[3] JEFFERY N, FREDERICK H, WINKLER D. The American people: creating a nation and a society [M]. Kansas: Library of Congress Cataloging-in-Publication Data, 2000.

[4] KRALL L. US land policy and the commoditization of arid land (1862-1920) [M]. New York: Journal of Economic Issues, 2001.

[5] 葛承群 . 美国西部开发的基本经验及借鉴 [J]. 比较与借鉴，2000(7)：78-80.

[6] 刘宜照、张翔 . 浅析美国西进运动产生的历史背景 [J]. 牡丹江师范学院学报（哲社版），2011(2)：37-39.

[7] 田耀 . 美国文化点滴 [M]. 天津：天津大学出版社，2009.

[8] 王储、蒋涛 . 美国西部开发史研究综述 [J]. 河西学院学报，2012(6)：17-18.

[9] 王丽娜 . 西进运动对美国农业现代化的影响 [J]. 绵阳师范学院学报，2011(9)：28-29.

[10] 张兹署 . 美国西进运动与特纳边疆学说评介 [J]. 高校社科信息，2003(4)：40.

Chapter Seventeen

Native Americans

Unit 1 Ancient Indians

Thousands of years before the European exploratory voyages in the 1490s, the history of humankind in the North America began. Thus, American history can begin with some basic questions: who were the first habitants of the Americas? Where did they come from? What were they like? How had the societies' forms changed over the millennia that preceded European arrival? Can their history be reconstructed from the mists of prehistoric time?

Migration to the Americas

Nearly every Native American society has its own story about its origins in the Americas. However, paleoanthropologists(古人类学家), scientists, who study ancient peoples, generally agree that the Americas were nomadic (流浪的)bands from Siberia, hunting big-game animals such as bison, caribou, and reindeer. These sojourners (旅居者)from Asia began to migrate across a land bridge connecting northeastern Asia with Alaska. Geologists believe that this land bridge, perhaps 600 miles wide, existed most recently between 25,000 and 14,000 years ago, when massive glaciers locked up much of the earth's moisture and left part of **Bering Sea**[1] floor exposed. Ice-free passage through Canada areas possible only briefly at the beginning and end of this period, however, at other times melting glaciers flooded the land bridge and blocked foot traffic to Alaska. The main migration apparently occurred between 11,000 and 14,000 years ago, although possibly much earlier. Some new archaeological finds suggest multiple migrations, both by sea and land, from several regions of Asia and between from Europe.

Population Density

The population figure for Native Americans in 1492 is a hypothetical and forever elusive number. Since early estimates were made after European-spawned diseases and warfare had had an impact on native peoples, and since they were regional and unscientific at best, modern scholars have had to devise their own system of calculation. Yet, the methods have produced enormous discrepancies, from a native population of 15 million for the entire continent to as high as 60 million. Although the figure is perhaps moot(无实际意义的) in terms of the number of Indian tribes and lifeways, it has great significance with regard to the degree of European impact.

Religion

The religious beliefs, rituals and myths of the aboriginal (土著人的) America seem to arise from the diffusion and cross-fertilization of two distinct cultural traditions: the Northern Hunting tradition and the Southern Agrarian tradition.

Indians were traditionally a holistic and reverent people, viewing themselves as extensions of animate and inanimate nature. Religion and ritual were a function of all activity: the food quest and other survival-related work, technology, social and political organization, warfare, and art. Religion and magic were fused with practical science. Myth was a way of understanding reality. Religion played a prominent role in the interpretation of the universe and in the adaptation of human activity to the patterns of nature.

In addition to this holism (整体论), other generalizations can be made with regard to Indian religion. Part of the special intimate relationship with nature involved a sense of kinship (亲属关系) with natural world and the attribution of innate souls and human properties to plants, animals, inanimate objects, and natural phenomena. Indian religion generally also involved the belief that the universe is suffered with preternatural (不可思议的) forces and powerful spirits. Other traits characteristic of most traditional Indian cultures were a richness of myths and legends, ceremonies and sacred objects; the quest for visions and the use of psychotropic plants to facilitate those visions; music and dance as part of ritual; the notion of sacrificed to fain the favor of the gods or spirits.

Apart from these shared traits, however, Indian religion presents a wondrous variety of beliefs, sacraments, and systems. Different tribes or related groups of peoples had different views of the supernatural world, with varying types of deities and spirits.

In the conquest of aboriginal America, European civilization waged ideological as well as military and economic warfare against the integrity of Native American culture. The European powers that colonized North America sent forth not only armies and traders but also missionaries to convert the Indians from so-called pagan (异教徒) and primitive ways to Christian religion and Western customs. The resulting effect of Christian missionaries on tribal culture has been as profound in its way as the Indian wars, the fur trade, and European diseases.

Notes

1. Bering Sea 白令海: 是太平洋沿岸最北的边缘海，介于(66° 31′ N, 51° 22′ N) 之间，海区呈三角形。北以白令海峡与北冰洋相通，南隔阿留申群岛与太平洋相联。位于太平洋最北端的水域。它将亚洲大陆(西伯利亚东北部) 与北美洲大陆(阿拉斯加) 分隔开。白令海是以丹麦航海探险家 V. 白令的名字命名的，白令海一名最早出现于 1778 年。在 1724—1749 年的北方大考察时，他于 1725—1728 年在俄国服役，在俄国彼得大帝的授命下，两次来到这个海区，探测亚洲和美洲是否在此相连。1778 年，英国库克探险队的队员福斯到此海考察，并正式以“白令海”一词命名此海。

Unit 2 Indians History

Indians in the Colonial Period

The postcolonial history of North American Indian is to an unfortunate extent a chronicle of hostilities. There were clashes between two cultures—Indian and European, with some Indian nations aligning（使结盟）themselves against other nations.

The Indian's response to the Europeans entering to their domain for the first time was varied. Some people avoided all contact; some were open to interaction and trade; some saw the visitors as gods; some regarded them as invading armies. During Christopher Columbus's voyage in 1492, Columbus and his Spanish crew were welcomed and aided by Indians. During the second voyage to the Americas in November 1493, Columbus found that the fort had been burned to the ground and his 43 men killed by Indian warriors. He learned that the Spanish had repeatedly abused the native people. In March 1495, the Spanish launched a concerted military campaign against them. It was at this time that Columbus turned to enslaving the Indians.

With the increasing European settlement in North America came growing conflict. Every region saw hostilities between the first citizens and newcomers. Every foreign nation was faced with Native resistance.

One of the important wars between the Indians and the Europeans is **the French and Indian Wars**[1]**.** These wars in North America represent just one of many fronts in the European clash for World Empire. In any case, these conflicts might just as well as be viewed as one long war broken up by periods of truce. And French and Indian War, the American phase of a worldwide nine-year war（1754—1763）fought between France and Great Britain. The French and Indian War began over the specific issue of whether the upper Ohio River valley was a part of the British Empire, and therefore open for trade and settlement by Virginians and Pennsylvanians, or part of the French Empire. The first four years saw nothing but severe reverses for the British regulars and American colonials, primarily because of superior French land forces in the New World. Lack of colonial assistance to the war effort compounded British problems. By the end of 1757, however, the course of the war began to be altered.

In 1758 and 1759, aided by effective blockades off the coast of France as well as in the Gulf of St. Lawrence, the British won important victories at Louisburg, Fort Frontenac, Fort Carillon（later Ticonderoga）, and Crown Point, and at Fort Duquesne（now Pittsburgh）and Fort Niagara. The climax came with the British victory on the Plains of Abraham（September 13th, 1759）, where Quebec was forced to surrender and where both commanders, James Wolfe and the marquis de Montcalm, were fatally wounded. A year later Montreal and the whole of New France had fallen.

By **the Treaty of Paris**[2]（February 10th, 1763）, France ceded（割让）its territory on mainland

North America east of the Mississippi River (including Canada) to Great Britain, and Spain ceded Florida to Britain but in return received the Louisiana Territory and New Orleans from the French. Ironically, Britain's problems arising from victory, such as war debts and the administration and settlement of an expanded colonial empire, contained the very seeds of the conflict that would lead to **the American Revolution**[3] during the following decade.

As for the Indians and their involvement in the French and Indian Wars, in the board historical sense they can be regarded as pawns (喻人质) in the long world power struggle. But during the many conflicts, they were often willing players, choosing sides based on what they considered their best interests in protecting their territories, maintaining trade, or settling old inter-tribal scores. Moreover, they often fought on one side or another for what was offered to them—bounties for scalps, regular pay and rations, firearms and blankets.

Indians in the American Revolution

By the time of the revolution, the major coastal tribes had been decimated (大批杀害) by warfare and disease, their villages displaced by white settlement. Powerful tribes, however, still dominated the interior between the Appalachians and the Mississippi River. In the south, five tribes dominated the interior.

When the Revolutionary War began, British and American officials urged the Native Americans, to maintain neutral. However, the Native Americans were too important militarily for either side to ignore. By the spring of 1776, both were seeking Native American alliances. Recognizing their stake in the conflict, the Native Americans made different options.

In the *Treaty of Paris* of 1783, which officially ended the American Revolution, the British made for many tribes who had supported their effort. The people of the new nation thought of Indians as enemies. As it is, for their efforts in the Revolution, Native Americans suffered many casualties (伤亡人数), experienced the devastation (毁坏) of villages and crops, lost much of their land in cessions, ended the unity of one of the oldest surviving Indian confederacies (联盟)—**the Iroquois League**[4].

During the immediate postwar years, Congress operated as if the Native Americans of interior were "conquered" peoples—allies of England who had lost the war were now under U.S. Control. Such claims were grounded in notions if the Native American's social and cultural inferiority (劣势). Even the most sympathetic whites believed that Native Americans must forgo their tribal ways before they could coexist with white society. Most whites simply argued that the Native Americans must be driven out of white settlers' way.

For a few years, the conquest strategy seemed to work. During the mid-1780s, Congress imposed land treaties on the interior tribes, they lost their land. And they struggled against disease and poverty, their traditional lifeways gone, their self-confidence broken.

The revolution left behind a legacy of bitterness: among Native Americans because they had suffered defeat and among faced growing tide of white settlement, among white Americans because the Native Americans had sided with England and thus threatened the Revolution's success. Such bitterness would trouble Native American—white relations for years to come.

Indians in the Early Republic

Indian-white relations took a dramatic turn in the early years of the nineteenth century. In 1790, vast areas of trans-Appalachia (横贯阿巴拉契亚) were still controlled by Native American tribes. North of the Ohio River, the Shawnee, Delaware, and Miami formed a western confederacy capable of mustering (集合) several thousand warriors. South of the river lived totally nearly 60,000 people. By 1830, however, the balance of power throughout trans-Appalachia had shifted decisively as white settlers, many of them bringing their black slaves with them south of Ohio River, streamed into the region.

In response, tribal groups devised various strategies of resistance. Less dramatic but no less important, the social and cultural separation of Indians and Americans sharpened during these years. As late as the 1780s, Indians still walked the streets of New York and Philadelphia, while countless Indians and white Americans interacted as Native Americans were confined on reservations or forced to move farther west.

Indian Policy

During the years from 1790 to 1830, the federal government established policies that would govern Indian-white relations through much of the nineteenth century. Intended in part to promote the assimilation (同化) of Native Americans into white society, the policies actually speeded the transfer of Indian land to white settlers and set the stage for later, more dramatic program of Indian removal.

With the government's initial "conquest" theory rendered obsolete by the Indians' refusal to be regarded as conquered people, U.S. officials shifted course by recognizing Indian rights to the land they inhabited and declaring that all future land transfers would come through treaty agreements. A goal of federal Indian policy was to "civilize" and "Christianize" Native Americans, and then assimilated (同化) them into white society. With the government blessing, **Moravians**[5] (摩拉维亚教徒), **Baptists**[6] (浸礼会教友), and other religious groups sent scores of missionaries to live among the Indians, preach the Gospel, and teach whites ways. Although white assimilationists cared deeply about the physical and spiritual fate of Native American people, they showed little sympathy for Indian culture, for they demanded that Native Americans give up their language, religion, and extended family arrangements and adopt the ways of white society. Assimilation or removals were the stark (明显地) alternatives posed by even the most benevolent whites.

In the early nineteenth century, the vast lands of the five "civilized nations" of the Southeast (the Cherokee, Choctaw, Chickasaw, Seminole, and Creek) had been seriously eroded (侵蚀) by land-hungry whites supported by military campaigns led by professional Native American fighters such as Jackson. The Creek lost 22 million acres in Georgia and Alabama after Jackson defeated them at Horseshoe Bend in 1814. Land cessions to the government and private sales accounted for even bigger losses: Cherokee holdings of more than 50 million acres 20 years later.

A Supreme Court decision in 1823 declaring that Native Americans could occupy but not hold title to land in the United States bolstered（支撑）the trend. Seeing that their survival was threatened, Native American nations acted. By 1825, the Creek, Cherokee, and Chickasaw restricted land sales to government agents. Native American determination to resist whites confronted white resolve to gain tribal lands for cotton.

In 1830, **President Andrew Jackson**[7] signed the *Indian Removal Act* to relocate to a designated eastern tribes Indian Territory east of the Mississippi River—a swift and final solution, it was thought, to the persistent tension between Indians and land land-hungry non-Indians. Thus began a decade of torment and tragedy for the tribes of the Southeast. Many Southeast Indian tribes, especially the Cherokee, had adapted to the ways of the Euro-American culture around them, educating themselves, establishing an efficient agriculture-based economy, and finding a new, vital cultural mix of tradition and progress. Working within the American legal system, a faction（派系）of the tribe under John Ross resisted the *Removal Act* in the courts, finally winning their case before the Supreme Court. However, their efforts were to no avail（效用）. Andrew Jackson ignored the decision and ordered the army to evict the tribe anyway, along with the Choctaw, Creek, Chickasaw, and Seminole, from their ancestral lands.

The Choctaw were the first to go. Conditions were miserable. Because of the inadequate federal funds for the removal, there were shortages of food, blankets, wagons and horses. Roadside merchants charged exorbitant（极高的）prices for supplies. Bandits（土匪）preyed upon the weak and exhausted migrants. Disease ran rampant（蔓延的）. At least a quarter of the Choctaw migrants died before even reaching the Indian Territory. And many more died afterword, as they struggled to build new lives in the rugged terrain, with meager supplies and surrounded by the hostile western Indians.

The other tribes also endured maltreatment, hardship, and death in similar ordeals（严峻的考验）of forced exodus（离去）. The most famous removal of all is that of the **Cherokee**[8]. The fact that their great suffering followed a successful legal battle led by Chief John Ross to save their lands, with Chief Justice John Marshall in favor of Cherokee sovereignty, makes their story more poignant. After the futile legal attempt, the state of Georgia, with President Jackson's blessing, ruthlessly began liquidating（变卖）Indian lands for paltry prices and promises of land in the West. Cherokee homes and possessions were plundered by opportunistic whites. The Cherokee migration of 1838—came to be called the "Trail of Tears". The name now stands for the forced removal and suffering of the various Southeast tribes, and by extension, the forced relocation of the Old Northwest and all other displaced Indians.

Strategies of Survival

Faced with the loss of land and tribal autonomy, Native Americans devised various. Lake led his people through a religious renewal and cultural revitalization. Far to the south, the Cherokee followed a different path of accommodation. As the nineteenth century began, the Cherokee still controlled millions of acres in Tennessee, Georgia, and the western Carolinas. Their land base, however, was shrinking.

Notes

1. the French and Indian Wars 法国—印第安人战争：或魁北克所称的征服战争，是1754—1763年间英国和法国在北美的一场战争。1756年，战争扩大至世界范围，成为七年战争的一部分，加拿大英语区和欧洲使用“七年战争北美战场”称呼此战。印地安人在这场战争中与法国结盟，攻打英国。1760年英国攻陷蒙特利尔，战事结束。1763年2月10日英法等参战国缔结巴黎条约，西班牙割让佛罗里达给英国，法国割让密西西比河以东法属路易斯安那给西班牙作为补偿。这场战争是法国在北美势力的转折点，并确认了英国在北美东半部的控制地位。

2. the Treaty of Paris 巴黎条约：1763年2月10日英国、葡萄牙同法国、西班牙为结束七年战争而缔结。英国为一方，法国、西班牙为另一方（后葡萄牙加入）在巴黎签订《巴黎条约》。条约规定，在美洲，法国将加拿大、布雷顿角岛、密西西比河以东的全部土地（新奥尔良除外）让给英国，西班牙将佛罗里达让给英国，从法国手中得到路易斯安那、新奥尔良和部分金钱补偿。该条约的签订打击了法国在海外的势力，标志着英国海上霸权的确立。

3. the American Revolution 美国革命：指在18世纪后半叶导致了北美洲十三个州的殖民地脱离大英帝国并且创建了美利坚合众国的一连串事件与思想。美国独立战争（1775—1783）是革命的其中一部分，然而革命在莱克星顿与康考德打响的第一发子弹之前就已经开始了，并且在英国于约克镇投降之后还持续下去。普遍而言，历史学家认为革命大约起源于法印战争（1754—1763）的时候，然后结束于1789年乔治·华盛顿当选为美国第一任总统。

4. the Iroquois League 易洛魁联盟：又称“易洛魁”，是一群居住于今日美国纽约上州、宾州、俄亥俄州和加拿大魁北克的印第安人，在16世纪末，由五大部族莫霍克人、奥奈达人、奥农达加人、瑟内萨人和卡尤加人在纽约地区北部组成联盟，塔斯卡洛拉族人于后来加入成为第六个部族。易洛魁联盟是美国东北部和加拿大东部最强大的原住民势力。这个同盟在17世纪末达到巅峰。他们缔造了很多成就，包括建立彼此制衡的政治体系，这也可能就是美国建国者民主思想的渊源。易洛魁同盟法律的中央思想是，彼此永不互相争战。而在对抗敌人时，他们的联合政治及军事力量往往所向披靡。

5. Moravians 摩拉维亚教徒：摩拉维亚教会是遍布全球的基督新教徒团契。该教派诞生于摩拉维亚，是第一个积极参与传教活动的新教团体。成员认为《圣经》是他们信仰与实践的唯一标准，并且特别强调基督徒在日常生活中的行为。摩拉维亚教会在组织上分为几大自治的区域，由主教担任属灵领袖，处理少量的行政事务。1735年，摩拉维亚传教士抵达乔治亚州，不久后定居宾夕法尼亚州，并在那里建立了伯利恒和拿撒勒两座城市。现在，美国有两个摩拉维亚团体。

6. Baptists 浸礼会教友：浸礼宗，又称“浸信会”，是17世纪从英国清教徒独立派中分离出来的一个主要宗派，因其施洗方式为全身浸入水中而得名。此宗派的特点是反对婴儿受洗，坚持成年人始能接受浸礼；实行公理制教会制度。浸礼宗于17世纪30年代随清教徒移民传入北美，主要是特救浸礼派。18世纪后，此派开始了联合运动，由于南、北方对奴隶制的态度不同而走向分裂。1845年美国南方各州建立了“南方浸信会”。1907年北方各教会联合建立了“北方浸礼会”。随着美国内战的结束和解放宣言的公布，各浸礼会加强了在黑人中布道传教，建立黑人教堂与教会，培训黑人牧师。在美国黑人民权运动的推动下，该教会号召坚决消除教会内存在的种族隔离现象，所有教会及其神职对一切种族开放；并要求信徒遵从1964年的民权法案。在国际关系方面，该教会呼吁帮助发展中国家，救济南非种族隔离制度的受害者。

7. President Andrew Jackson 安德鲁·杰克逊总统：安德鲁·杰克逊（1767年3月15日—1845年6月8日）是美国第7任总统（1828—1836）。首任佛罗里达州州长、新奥尔良之役战争英雄、民主党创建者之一，杰克逊式民主因他而得名。在美国政治史上，19世纪二三十年代的第二党体系以他为极端的象征。时至今日，安德鲁·杰克逊总统在职期间是最受人争议者，或为其印地安人相关政策。杰克逊为印地安人排除政策之倡议者，他于1830年签署印地安人排除法案，成为一项法律。与公众的误解相反的是，该项排除法案并未下令遣走任何印地安人，而是授权总统与印地安部落洽商购地条款，即以东部的部落所有地，交换当时已有州界以外之西部遥远国土。杰克逊执政期间，向西迁移了超过45 000名的印地安人。搬迁的进程普受美国人欢迎，却使印地安人各族受苦，甚至死亡。杰克逊当时因在这些事件之角色而遭非议，批评逐年增长。罗伯特·雷米尼称这段搬迁印地安人的时期为“美国历史中最令人不快的一章”。

8. Cherokee 切诺基人：切诺基人是原本生活在美国东南部的一个大部族，使用易洛魁语。他们发源于五大湖地区，在16世纪以前向南迁徙到了南卡罗来纳和佐治亚一带。他们是最早接受西方文化的部族之一，思想较为开放，科技也比其他很多部落发达。切诺基人有自己的医学，他们善于使用一些草药来治疗一些病症。独立战争中，切诺基人偏向英国人。他们一度出兵袭击美军，但是被击败。因为隔阂相对较少，美国独立后，切诺基人很快就变成了公民。然而在19世纪30年代，他们还是受到了印第安人驱逐运动的波及，被美军强行驱离了世代繁衍的美国东南部。他们和附近的赛米诺人、克里克人、奇克索人和乔克托人一起被驱赶到了密西西比河，随后又进一步被撵进了遥远的俄克拉荷马。在迁徙过程中，大量的切诺基人死亡，因此这一路迁徙被叫做“眼泪之路”。

Unit 3 Contemporary Indians

Native Americans likewise remained outsiders in the postwar years. As power lines reached their reservations and they partook of the consumer culture, old patterns inevitably changed. Reservation life lost its cohesiveness（内聚性）, and alcohol became a major problem. With good jobs unavailable on the reservations, more and more Indians gravitated to the cities. But they often had difficulty adjusting to urban life and frequently faced hostility from white Americans.

Urban Indians

It is estimated that one-third to one-half of the Native American population in the United States now live in the cities. From 1900 to 1940, the percentage of the urban Indian population fluctuated within the range of 1-10 percent. Urbanization began to accelerate during World War II, however, when great numbers of Indians jointed the armed services or worked at off-reservation wartime jobs, breaking traditional ties. With the federal government's termination and relocation policies of the 1950s and 1960s, migration toward the cities continued at a fast rate. In fact, at an every 10-year census from 1940 to 1970, the urban percentage almost doubled, from seven to 13 to 28 to 45 percent, before slowing; the percentage stood at about 65 percent (as of 1990 census). Some Native Americans have made the move as a result of own in search of government-sponsored consulting and training, and others have moved on their economic opportunity.

But few in both groups have been able to break out of the cycle of poverty, unemployment, and societal (社会的) discrimination or indifference. The newfound cultural isolation (文化隔离) of the cities has led many to opt for the poverty of the reservations. Those who do stay in urban centers fall into at least three recognizable patterns: first, skilled laborers, often living on the edges of cities in Indian enclaves; second, those remaining oriented to their home reservations or communities journeying back and forth depending on seasonal jobs; and third, an Indian middle class interspersed (散置) in non-Indian cultural and political affairs and, like the others, can be called bicultural (二元文化的).

Because of difficult social conditions and detachment from direct tribal affiliations, the urban setting has fostered, especially in the 1960s and 1970s, but with a carryover to present times, a new brand of Indian social and political activity urban centers with programs and services designed to ease the transition to city life and encourage a sense of "Indianness" and belonging, as well as political groups. Another outcome of Indian urbanization has been a certain amount of "brain drain" (人才流失) on the reservations, with many of the more successful and upwardly mobile individuals siphoned off. However, the growth of Indian gaming since the late 1980s, with increasing job opportunities, has led to the return to reservations of a number of urbanized tribal members. The greatest concentration of urban Indians is found in the Los Angeles—Long Beach area of California.

Nonreservation Rural Indians

In the discussion of contemporary Native Americans, quite often a third category Native Americans is overlooked—those Indians living in cohesive rural communities without federal or state acknowledgment or trust status. As is the case with some urban Indian communities, many of those groups are just culturally and politically integrated and organized as the legally defined tribes.

Nonreservation Indian communities evolved out of three differing sets of circumstances. In the East, where the majority of such groups exist, the fact that many Indian people were defeated and displaced long before American independence meant a minimum of reservations. In the West, **the federal allotment polity**[1] beginning in the 1887 meant the breakup of many reservations, as did termination 60 years later. Many of those groups have sought federal acknowledgment in order to protect their culture and resources.

Indian Social Conditions

The U.S. Indian population has been growing since its low point of less than 250,000 at the start of the 20th century. According to the 1990 census, there are almost two million Native Americans. In analyzing the results of any census, the systems of collection and classification have to be taken into consideration, with a plus or minus margin assumed. In recent census, the method of self-identification is employed, along with the gathering of tribal lists; respondents are asked to enumerate（列举）the ethnic groups with which they identify, leading to the inclusion of a certain number of people of mixed ancestry and the exclusion of others. The large increase in the Native American population from 827,108 in 1970 to 1,418,195 in 1980 to 1,967,367 in 1990 is attributed to better census-taking methods and greater Indian cultural identification, in addition to a climbing birth rate.

Despite the fact of a growing population, a positive sign for the future, Indian social conditions on and off reservations remain problematic. Naive Americans as an ethnic group, on a national average, have consistently ranked among the highest percentages with regard to the following: short lifespan; high infant mortality rate; high suicide rate; low per capita income; poor housing; and inadequate health care, with extensive diabetes, tuberculosis, high blood pressure, respiratory disease, and alcoholism. Many factors account for these conditions: unproductive land; lack of education; a cycle of poverty difficult to escape; and cultural dislocation and depression caused from an existence as a conquered culture.

Red Power

In essence **Red Power**[2] is a form of Pan-Indianism committed to radical action. The first broad-based and enduring Indian organization with political change as its purpose was founded soon after World War II. About 25,000 Indians had served in the armed services and on returning to civilian life were unwilling to accept the Indian stereotype. They were largely instrumental（有帮助的）in founding the National Congress of American Indians（美国印第安人的全国代表大会）in 1944, an organization designed to speak for Indians. The activities of the organization include aiding local groups in taking effective stands, pooling useful information, and lobbying for Indian causes.

Notes

1. the federal allotment polity 联邦分配政策：指《道斯法案》，又称《道斯法令》《道斯土

地分配法》，1887 年 2 月 8 日美国国会为同化印第安人而通过的土地法令。因马萨诸塞州国会参议员 H.L. 道斯为提案人而得名。此法授权总统解散印第安人保留地，废除原保留地内实行的部落土地所有制，将土地直接分配给居住在保留地内外的印第安人。部落土地所有制的废除使印第安社会解体，部落权威遭受沉重打击。原保留地中的大部分土地通过拍卖，转入白人之手。这项试图使印第安人融入美国社会的法令实施后，对务农毫无准备的印第安人在取得土地后不久便因受骗等各种原因失去土地，生活日趋恶化。富兰克林 · D. 罗斯福“新政”时，美国国会通过 1934 年《印第安人改革法》，废除了将印第安人土地分成小块进行分配的做法。

2. Red Power 红种人权力：随着印第安人族裔意识的形成和逐渐增强，土著美国人采取了各种方式抵制殖民者和美国政府对其生活、文化、政府以及资源的控制，掀起了一系列的抗争和社会运动。19 世纪初随着美国西进运动迅速开展，印第安人中间激起第一场民族主义运动，即特库姆赛领导的泛印第安人主义运动。但是，面对美国军队的进攻和屠杀，运动最终一蹶不振。19 世纪 60 到 70 年代，美国的各个族裔、阶级和性别群体都在黑人民权运动下发起了轰轰烈烈的社会运动。许多印第安人也积极行动起来，将印第安人的问题融入轰轰烈烈的社会运动大潮中，“红种人权力”运动由此产生。

Unit 4　Civilizations of Ancient Indians

General Development of Civilizations

The necessary ingredients had been developed: the use of fire, technology, agriculture, religion, houses, and villages. Now civilizations would occur: large centralized populations, even cities; complex social and religious organizations; and highly refined arts and crafts.

Most full-fledged（成熟的）civilizations would arise where agriculture had first appeared: Mesoamerica（中美洲）and the Andes region（安第斯山脉地区）of south America. To the north in the American Southwest, other civilizations would flower on a smaller scale but with many of the same cultural elements. And while all this occurred, other peoples—beyond the villages and planted fields—would wander as always, hunting and gathering.

Regional Northern American Cultures

By about 1200 B.C.E., in the Southwestern region of North America, **the Anasazi society**[1] developed planned villages composed of large, terraced, multistoried buildings, each with many rooms and often constructed on defensive sites that would afford the protection from their northern enemies. By the time the Spanish arrived in the 1540s, the indigenous（土生土长的）people were using irrigation canals, dams, and hillside terracing to water their arid maize fields. In its agricultural techniques, skill in ceramics, use of woven textiles for clothing, and village life, their society resembled that of present communities in many parts of Europe and Asia.

Far to the north, on the Pacific coast of the Northwest, native Tlingit, Kwakiutl, Salish, and

Haida people lived in villages of several hundred, drawing their sustenance(营养) from salmon and other spawning fish and living in plank houses displaying elaborately carved red cedar(铅笔柏) pillars and guarded by gigantic totem poles(图腾柱) depicting animals with supernatural power.

Far to the east, Native American societies have been traced as far back as about 9000 B.C.E. From the Great Plains of the midcontinent to the Atlantic tidewater region, a variety of tribes came to be loosely associated in four main language groups: Algonquian, Iroquoians, Muskhogean, and Siouan. Like other tribal societies, they had been transformed by the agricultural revolution, gradually adopting semifixed settlements and developing trading networks that linked societies occupying a vast region.

Art and Technology

There are many varying artistic and technological traditions at both regional and tribal levels. Art for Native Americans was not an entity itself, but an integral part of other activities, whether in the decoration and creation of objects with strictly practical purposes, such as hunting and fishing equipment, or in the making of objects for the ceremonial cannot even be made, because the Indians considered their essential to their survival.

Bone, Horn, Antler, and Tusk Work

Native Americans used the bones, horns, antlers(鹿角) and tusks(獠牙) of the land and sea mammals and other creatures in numerous functions, in particular for pointed implements, such as spear, harpoon(鱼叉), arrow, dart(飞镖), and club points, as well as fishhooks, needles, pins, weaving tools, knives, scrapers, and chisels(凿子).

Shellwork

Seashells (and fresh water shells), with a variety of practical and decorative applications, spread all over the continent as trade items, Indians utilized them as blades, bowels and spoons, and in the making of jewelry as beads, pendants, earrings, gorgets(饰领), plus decoration on clothing.

Games and Toys

Indian games were remarkably similar throughout North America, indicating intertribal influence. There were two basic kinds: games of chance and gambling, and games of skill and dexterity(灵巧). Games of chance included dice, marked sticks, guessing games, and hand games. Athletic game included archer(射箭), spear throwing, racing, juggling lacrosse(曲棍球). Indians also made a variety of toys for their children out of the materials at hand.

Painting, Dyeing, and Engraving

Native Americans added design to their crafts through painting, dyeing, and engraving. They extracted their paints from a variety and of raw materials. Paints were applied with fingers, sticks, and brushes or sprayed from the mouth, and ears often held in the shells. Body paints and tattoos also were used for systematic purposes; i.e., to indicate social position or an intent to make war. Indians also frequently engraved wood, bark, stones, bones, etc. Different forms of expression came to be highly developed in different parts of the continent.

There are many other kinds of arts, such as basketry, textiles, woodwork, stonework, pottery.

Notes

1. the Anasazi society 阿纳萨齐社会：公元200—1450年，阿那萨齐人居住在北美洲西南部的一片崎岖的高原台地上，气候和地理条件都极端恶劣。最早的阿那萨齐人在公元200年左右发展出其代表性的文化特征。早期阿那萨齐人居住在坑道里房屋中，因他们编织的器皿质地精美，故而被称为编筐人。后来，他们发明了陶器制造术，并迁到地上生活。他们的后代发明了多层石屋群和崖屋。这些发明在今天成为他们建筑技术的纪念碑。公元1000—1300年间，该文化达到顶峰。绘制单调的陶器被复杂的艺术品所取代。接着，可能由于很多种原因—如气候变化、环境恶化或者可能有的社会摩擦，阿那萨齐人的世界渐渐缩小。人们遗弃了祖先居住的地方，迁往其他地区。但是随着欧洲殖民的开始，阿纳萨齐人的文化便遭遇了欧罗巴文化的侵袭。

References

[1] DOBYNS F H. Native American historical demography [M]. Bloomington and London: Indiana University Press, 1976.

[2] KEITH I. Encyclopedia of Indians of the Americas (vol. 1) [M]. New York: Scholarly Press Inc., 1974.

[3] Nash B G. The American people: creating a nation and society [M]. 7th ed. New York: Pearson, 2010.

[4] OSWALT H W. This land was theirs: a study of north American Indians (third edition) [M]. New York: John Wiley & Sons Press, 1978.

[5] WALDMAN C. Atlas of the north American Indian revised edition [M]. New York: Facts On File, 2000.

Chapter Eighteen

American Sports and Entertainment

Unit 1 Sports

Sports play an important role in American society. Most social scientists believe that the sports that are organized by a society generally reflect the basic values of that society and attempt to strengthen them in the minds and emotions of its people. This is certainly true in the United States, where the four most popular sports are American football, basketball, baseball, and ice hockey. Sports are seen by Americans as an inspiring example of equality of opportunity in action. In sports, people of different races and economic backgrounds get an equal chance to excel. To Americans, success in sports represents the faith that individuals and teams have an equal opportunity to win, but that hard work and merit lifts some above others. Teams and heroes in each sport become mythical, legendary, and historic. Sports have contributed to racial and social integration and over history have been "social glue"(社会凝聚力) bonding the country together.

American Football

Football, also known as gridiron or American football outside the U.S. and Canada, attracts more television viewers than baseball, due to football's significantly shorter schedule (although baseball attracts significantly more ticket sales) and is considered the most popular sport in the United States by some.

It was evolved from various types of **rugby**[1] played in English-speaking countries. Originally, it was a pretty rough sport, with many injuries and even deaths. In 1905 and 1906, President Theodore Roosevelt urged to reform the rules and made the sport safer. People who come from other countries often have the impression that American football is a dangerous and aggressive sport, something of a carryover from the Roman "lions vs. the sacrificial humans" who fought to death in the arenas of Roman rule. In fact, all of the types of football have a taint of aggression and competition in them, but American football players do have protective pads and equipment including helmets, face guards, teeth pads, shoulder pads, rib pads, and hip pads as well as cleated shoes(足球鞋) to give better traction on grass or artificial turf. Most American football teams now have excellent physical training and trainers, and usually a team doctor on hand for every game.

The **National Football League (NFL)**[2] is the preeminent professional league in the United States. Through expansion teams and the landmark merger with the American Football League in 1970, the NFL has reached its current mark of 32 franchises divided into two conferences. After a 16-game regular season, each conference sends six teams to the play offs, which eventually culminate in the league's championship game, the **Super Bowl**[3]. Super Bowl Sunday is the biggest annual sporting event held in the United States. The Super Bowl itself is always among the highest-rated programs annually in the Nielsen ratings and worldwide.

Additional millions also watch college football throughout the autumn months, and some communities, particularly in rural areas, place great emphasis on their local high school team. The popularity of college and high school football in areas such as the Southern United States and the Great Plains stems largely from the fact that these areas generally do not possess markets large enough for a professional team. Nonetheless, college football has a rich history in the United States, predating even the NFL, and fans and alumni are generally very passionate about their teams.

As a spectator sport, football is extremely popular, especially among men. Women sometimes call themselves "football widows"（足球寡妇）because during the football season their boyfriends or husbands are either at the stadium or glued to the TV set. Both college football and professional football attract huge audiences. At the end of the college football season, the best teams compete in Bowl games. The day's festivities are colorful and exciting, involving parades with floats and marching bands. Bowl games attract huge crowds and big TV audiences. The professional football season ends with the Super Bowls, the game between the country's top two teams. More than 130 million people worldwide watch it on TV. It is the most watched TV show in the world. Because of this huge audience, advertisers pay about $ 2 million for a 30-second advertisement.

Baseball

Baseball is the oldest of these traditionally American team sports and is considered the national sport of the US. It is basically a summer game, adapted by the Americans from the English game of cricket. This is a much cruder and simpler game than cricket, and resembles the game called rounders often played by children elsewhere.

Baseball pits one man with a bat in his hand against a team of men ready to put him out. It represents the individual in competition against other men in one-on-one situations where no one can interfere to help the player succeed or fail. The game is highly-nuanced and every play has a winner and a loser. The man who "wins" hits the home run（本垒打）, strikes out the batter（击球手）, steals second base, or makes the game-winning catch near the wall in left field; the loser swings and misses, fails to catch the ball, shows bad judgment by throwing the wrong pitch or being caught off base. One team wins and one team loses, but the credit is given to a "hero" and failure is blamed on a "goat". The size of the player is irrelevant but the skill of the player is all important. Time is not a factor and game length depends on how long it takes to play nine innings, as measured by the success or failure of individuals to get base hits or to make outs. Baseball is orderly and appeals to the American legal sense as an umpire rules on every single action of the game. Baseball is played on grass and the generally slow speed of the action reflects the preindustrial pace of life and offers a respite from the hurried world of urban living.

The professional baseball dates from 1869 and had no close rivals in popularity until the 1960s. Also unlike the professional levels of the other popular spectator sports in the U.S., **Major League Baseball**[4] teams play almost every day from April to October. Like football, baseball enjoys immense popularity among Americans, particularly among men. Professional baseball teams have enthusiastic following, and important baseball games arouse great interest among American sports fans, being followed on television all across the nation. Like football, baseball is also a large-scale commercial enterprise in the United States, bringing huge financial rewards to players and management. More than any other American sport, baseball lends itself to legend. The statistical records give each game a mythic dimension as the hits, runs, errors, and strikeouts are carved into money and the record books.

The most popular baseball league in the U.S. is Major League Baseball. Due to its 162-game schedule, it attracts more ticket sales than any other sport in the United States, and is considered the second most popular professional sport. Teams play almost every day from April to October. The World Series is the championship series of Major League Baseball, the culmination of the sport's postseason（季后赛）each October. It is played between the winner of each of the two leagues, the American League and the National League and the winner is determined through a best-of-seven playoff. Notable American baseball players in history include Ted Williams, Babe Ruth, Mark McGwire, Sandy Koufax, Willies Mays, Joe Dimaggio, Stan Musial, Lou Gehrig, Nolan Ryan, Hank Aaron, Mike Schmidt and Jackie Robinson, who was instrumental in dissolving the color line and allowing African-Americans and Latin Americans into the white major leagues. Today, some of the notable American players include, Alex Rodriguez, Joe Mauer, Josh Hamilton and Randy Johnson.

Major League Baseball and the variant, **Softball**[5], are also popular participatory sports in the U.S. However, unlike American football, baseball is also popular in many other countries, notably Japan, South Korea and Latin American countries such as the Dominican Republic, Cuba, Puerto Rico, Mexico, and Venezuela. These countries are represented well in Major League Baseball today by players such as Hideki Matsui, Ichiro Suzuki, Alvert Pujol, David Ortiz, Ivan Rodrigues and Johan Santana.

Basketball

Basketball, invented in 1891 by Canadian-born physical education teacher James Naismith in Springfield, Massachusetts, is the second most popular sport behind football. However, in regards to professional sports, basketball, or the NBA, is ranked third in popularity behind the NFL and MLB. The **National Basketball Association**[6], more popularly known as the NBA, is the world's premier men's professional basketball league and one of the major professional sports leagues of North America. It contains 29 teams in the U.S. and 1 in Canada that play an 82-game season from November to April. After the regular season, eight teams from each conference compete in the playoffs for the Larry O'Brien Championship Trophy (拉里·奥布莱恩冠军奖杯). The American Basketball Association, active from 1967 until 1976, when it merged with the NBA, was the last major competitor of the NBA. Notable NBA players in history include Kareem Abdul-Jabbar, Larry Bird, Wilt Chamberlain, Michael Jordan, Magic Johnson, Bob Cousy, Pete Maravich, Oscar Robertson, Bill Russell, John Stockton, and Jerry West, whose silhouette is featured on the NBA's logo. Notable players in the NBA today include Kobe Bryant, Tim Duncan, Kevin Garnett, LeBron James, David Lee, M and Shaquille O'Neal.

With 17 NBA All-Star selections, an NBA MVP, five NBA championships with the Lakers, two Olympic gold medals and a relentless work ethic, Kobe Bryant is one of the greatest players in the history of basketball. Kobe entered the NBA directly from high school. He was drafted out of high school by the Charlotte Hornets with the 13th overall pick in 1996 but was traded to the Lakers. He has played for the Lakers his entire career, winning five NBA championships.

Bryant is a 15-time member of the All-NBA Team, and 12-time member of the All-Defensive team. He has led the league in scoring twice, and he ranks third on both the league's all-time regular season scoring and all-time postseason scoring lists. He's the only player to spend 20 consecutive seasons with the same team. On November 29th, 2015, Bryant announced via a letter poem on The Players' Tribune that he will be retiring at the end of the season. On April 13th, 2016, Bryant played his final NBA game against the Utah Jazz, scoring a season-high 60 points, including outscoring the entire Jazz team 23–21 in the fourth quarter, in the Lakers' 101–96 victory.

In the past decade, an increasing number of players born outside the United States have signed with NBA teams, sparking league interest in different parts of the world. Among the notable foreign-born players in the NBA today are two-time MVP Steve Nash (a South Africa-born Canadian), Peja Stojakovic (Serbia), Andrei Kirilenko (Russia), Andrea Bargnani (Italy), Yao Ming (China), Tony Parker (France), Gasol brothers Pau and Marc (Spain), Mau Ginobili (Argentina), and Dirk Nowitzki (Germany), who was the first European player to win the NBA **Most Valuable Player Award**[7]. Notable retired foreign-born players include Hakeem Olajuwon (Nigeria), who has won an MVP award, two Defensive Player of the Year awards, and two Finals MVP awards, and Dikembe Mutumbo (DR Congo), who has won four Defensive Player (防守球员) of the Year awards.

Since the 1992 Summer Olympics, NBA players have represented the United States in international competition and won several important tournaments. The Dream Team was the unofficial nickname of the United States men's basketball team that won the gold medal at the 1992 Olympics.

Like American football, basketball at both the college and high school levels is quite popular throughout the country. Every March, a 65-team, six-round, single-elimination tournament（淘汰赛）determines the national champions of college basketball. Most U.S. states also crown state champions among their high schools. More Americans play basketball than any other team sports, according to the National Sporting Goods Association. **Netball**[8], a derivative of basketball invented in the United States and usually played by women, is popular in Australia, New Zealand, Sri Lanka, the United Kingdom, and the West Indies.

Ice Hockey

Until the mid-1980s it was usually accepted that ice hockey was derived from English field hockey and Indian **Lacrosse**[9] and was spread throughout Canada by British soldiers in the mid-1800s. Research then turned up a mention of a hockey very similar to hokey, played in the early 1800s in Nova Scotia by the Indians, it appeared to have been mainly influenced by the Irish game of hurling; it included the use of a stick and a square wooden block instead of a ball. It was most likely that this game then spread throughout Canada via Scottish and Irish immigrants and the British army. The players adopted elements of field hockey, such as the "bully", later the face-off, and "shinning", hitting your opponent to the shins with the stick or playing with the stick on one "shin" or side, this later evolved into an informal ice game later known as shinny. The name hockey—as the organized game came to be known—has been attributed to the French word hoquet, shepherd's stick. Rules were set by students at McGill University in Montreal, Canada, in 1879, and several amateur clubs and leagues were established in Canada by the late 1880's. The game is believed to have been first played in the United States in 1893. By the beginning of the twentieth century the sport had spread to the UK and other parts of Europe. The modern game developed in Canada, and is now very popular in the USA and Eastern Europe.

The **National Hockey League (NHL)**[10] is the most important league in the world. It comprises teams from the USA and Canada, but for many years almost all NHL players were Canadians. The winning team of this competition is awarded the **Stanley Cup**[11] trophy. Ice Hockey was added to the Olympic Games in 1920, being one of the most popular events at the Winter Olympics.

Ice hockey is another popular sport in the United States. The game is most popular in regions of the country with a cold winter climate, namely New England and the Midwest. However, since the 1990s, hockey has become increasingly popular in the Sun Belt due to the expansion of the National Hockey League（NHL）. The NHL is the major professional hockey league in North America, with 24 U.S.-based teams and six Canadian-based teams competing for the Stanley Cup. Other professional leagues in the U.S include the **American Hockey League**[12] and the **ECHL (East Coast Hockey League)**[13]. Additionally, nine U.S.-based teams compete in the three member leagues of the Canadian Hockey League.

USA Hockey is the official governing body for amateur hockey in the U.S. The United States

Hockey Hall of Fame is located in Eveleth, Minnesota.

Although hockey does not enjoy the same popularity as football, baseball and basketball in the U.S., one of the nation's greatest ever sporting moments came during the 1980 Lake Placid Olympics when the U.S. hockey team beat the Soviet Union 4-3 in the first game of the medal round before going on to beat Finland to claim the gold medal. The game has since been called the "Miracle on Ice".

Historically, the vast majority of NHL players had come from Canada, and almost all of the non-Canadians in the league were Americans. This began to change in the 1970s with an increase in the number of American-trained players and an influx of players from Europe, mostly from Sweden and Finland. Today, a slight majority of NHL players are Canadian, slightly more than 20% are Americans, and almost all of the remainder are European-trained. Notable NHL players in history include Wayne Gretzky, Eddie Shore, Stan Mikita, Guy Lafleur, Steve Staios, Martin Brodeur, Jarome Iginla, Joe Thornton, Chris Pronger, and Patrick Kane.

Americans are avid sports fans. Not only is track and field popular, but Americans support racing of all sorts: horses, dogs, automobiles, and bicycles. Court games such as tennis, racket ball, and volleyball have their supporters and other field games such as field hockey, lacrosse, and particularly soccer, gain new spectators daily. The intensely individual sports of golf and bowling have many amateur participants, and sponsored matches are watched by many on television. Professional wrestling is now a branch of the entertainment business, but collegiate wrestling is a serious sort, and boxing, both amateur and professional, has a large number of followers, nourished unfortunately by the urge to wager money.

Notes

1. Rugby 英式橄榄球：原名“拉格比足球”，简称“拉格比”。橄榄球的中文译名因其使用的椭圆形（橄榄形）用球而得名。美式橄榄球（American football）源自英式橄榄球，为北美四大职业体育之首。传入美国后规则改变，改为采取攻防线进行回合制争球、没有跑位限制，并且可以向前抛掷传球，这运动的目的是要把球推进到对手的端区得分，得分方法有多种，包括持球越过底线，抛球到在底线后的队友，或把直放在地上的球踢过两支门柱中间射门。比赛时间完时得分较多的一队胜出。美式橄榄球是一种对抗性很强的接触性体育运动，由于球赛中往往会与对方球员有强烈的身体冲撞，因此球员需穿戴头盔和护具出场。

2. National Football League（NFL）美国国家橄榄球联盟：简称“NFL”（美球），是世界最大的职业美式橄榄球联盟，也是世界最具商业价值的体育联盟。大部分的美国大城市，除了第二大城加州洛杉矶及得州圣安东尼奥，都设有一支球队。

3. Super Bowl 超级碗：职业美式橄榄球在20世纪60年代中期成长快速，超越棒球成为美国最具观赏的运动。1960年美国美式橄榄球联盟（American Football League，AFL）成立。1970年，与美国国家橄榄球联盟的赛季合并，即“职业美式橄榄球世界冠军”（World Championship of Professional Football），在合并之后改名成超级碗，转为NFL的冠军赛。

4. Major League Baseball 美国职棒大联盟：简称MLB，是美国最著名的职业棒球联赛。

1903 年由国家联盟和美国联盟共同成立。是美国四大职业体育联盟之一。前身是国家协会（National Association）成立于 1871 年，5 年后由现今的国家联盟接手。

5. Softball 垒球：诞生于 19 世纪 80 年代的美国芝加哥，与棒球相似，球更大，更软，技术难度、运动剧烈程度低于棒球，后成为女子项目。这项运动很快发展起来，现在全世界有 2,000 万人进行这项体育运动。

6. National Basketball Association 全美篮球协会：简称 NBA，成立于 1946 年。NBA 有东西两个联盟，每个联盟里分别有 3 个赛区，每个赛区中有 5 支球队，一共是 30 支球队。夏休之后，NBA 队伍在 10 月份开始组织训练。NBA 常规赛开始于 11 月的第一个星期，进行 82 场比赛。季后赛在 4 月底开始，每个赛区派出 8 支球队参赛。前 4 位种子席位由 3 个分赛区的冠军和常规赛成绩最好的一支球队获得，后 4 位种子席位根据常规赛成绩排名确定。

7. Most Valuable Player Award NBA **最有价值球员：**简称 MVP，是由美国国家篮球协会颁发给每年表现最优秀的球员的奖项。首次颁奖在 1955—1956 赛季举行。该奖项的奖杯是为纪念 NBA 首任主席莫里斯·波杜夫（Maurice Podoloff）而命名的。他从 1946 年到 1963 年为止，为 NBA 服务了 18 年。

8. Netball 篮网球：又称为投球、英式篮球、无板篮球，是一种发源自篮球的团队球类运动，一般被视为系以女性为主的运动项目，运动发源于 19 世纪 90 年代的英格兰，随后成为英联邦国家中一项非常流行的女性体育活动。

9. Lacrosse 袋棍球：又称长曲棍球。是一种使用顶端具有网状袋子的长棍作为持球工具的团队球类运动。起源于北美印第安人部落，原本不限人数，双方最多可达各 1 000 余人。移民至此的法国人发现后，加以改良并制订规则，因而形成今日的状态。现主要盛行于北美地区和英国等地。

10. National Hockey League（NHL）美国国家冰球联盟：由北美冰球队伍所组成的职业运动联盟，是全世界最高层级的职业冰球比赛，为北美四大职业运动之一。队伍共分成东、西两个大区，每个大区各分为三个分区，每年东西两区的冠军会在联盟总决赛中争夺斯坦利杯。

11. Stanley Cup 斯坦利杯：是加拿大国家冰球联盟的最高奖项，在每个赛季后颁给联盟的冠军队伍。斯坦利杯是由加拿大总督法德克·斯坦利捐赠，为了纪念其为冰球运动的贡献，以他的名字命名。

12. American Hockey League 美国冰球联盟：简称 AHL，是北美的一个职业冰球联盟。全部 AHL 的 29 支队伍都和 NHL 的 30 支球队有着密切的合作。AHL 即为 NHL 联盟的小联盟，有着相当高的比赛水平，比赛激烈程度并不亚于 NHL 联赛。联盟办事处设在斯普林菲尔德，马萨诸塞州。每年季后赛冠军授予以 NHL 第一任总裁弗兰克·考尔德（1917 至 1943 年）命名的考尔德杯。

13. ECHL（East Coast Hockey League）东海岸冰球联盟：目前有 25 支球队，是 NHL 下属联盟，其规模仅次于美国冰球联盟。

Unit 2 Entertainment

Although politics, economy, education, religion, and law form a sizable staple of their lives, the vast majority of Americans, like people in any other country in the world, spend most of their non-work time and energy on leisure activities, which can take a variety of forms, from watching television to go fishing, from go malling to travelling.

Popular Outdoor Activities

What do people want in outdoor recreation? They seek a variety of experiences. They may want to escape from routines and pressures, but usually they get away together in groups. They want an experience based on the natural environment, but that environment may range from the primitive to the highly developed. They want a break, seeking settings where they can take risks and "be themselves."

1.Fishing

Americans are enthusiastic about both fresh and saltwater fishing. One main reason of fishing is readily accessible: it can be carried on in many different settings—in local streams, ponds, and lakes, along ocean beaches, or from private or commercial fishing raft（木筏）.

As a form of outdoor recreation, fishing varies greatly, often according to geographical or climate-based factors. For example, through much of the American Midwest, ice fishing on frozen lakes represents a legendary part of the region's culture.

At another level, growing numbers of fishermen and women enjoy their hobby at private trout- or bass-fishing preserves, paying fees for boat rentals and trophy fish based on a per-pound charge.

Another example of fishing's popularity may be found in cable television fishing shows or huge bass-fishing（钓鲈鱼）competitions held today around America. Major tournaments sponsored by organizations like the Bass Anglers Sportsman Society offers prizes amounting to hundreds of thousands of dollars.

2.Jogging

The latest polls have demonstrated that jogging remains a constant favorite leisure activity for many Americans. The running revolution that erupted in the 1970s today has slowed to a walk as bad-kneed baby boomers have settled into middle age. But a great number of Americans still lace up their Nikes to jog along streets and school tracks, and not all are student athletes, cutting class for an afternoon jaunt.

In America, joggers tend to live in areas where they can run year-round, either outdoors in Sunbelt communities—like Houston or San Diego—or in the nation's big cities, where abundant health clubs（健身俱乐部）offer indoor tracks（室内运动）. The highest proportions are college-educated singles in their 20s and 30s who hold well-paying jobs in business, finance, or entertainment services.

Although jogging does not carry the same implication of high status as sailing or skiing, both defined as high-status sports that require a great deal of expensive equipment or an expensive setting or both, joggers are more likely to play upper-middle-class sports like tennis and racquetball（美式壁球）. They seldom pursue such proletariat activities as bowling and billiards either. Indeed, when they're not jogging after work, joggers are a fairly civilized lot, enjoying jazz, theater, and gourmet cooking（美食烹饪）.

While jogging critics may think that all that roadwork is excessive if not downright obsessive, joggers counter that they run to maintain their equilibrium. Have you ever imagined that joggers in America are heavy consumers of **Ben & Jerry's and Häagen-Dazs**[1]? This reflects their ethic: work hard, run hard, and eat guilty-free.

Vocation

For many Americans, leisure life would never be complete if vacations are not included. As far as school children are concerned, there are always winter and summer vacations to look forward to. Since there are no national or even state-wide dates for school vacations, each school district sets its own. Generally, "school is out" is from around the first week in July until the last week in August. As for adult Americans, the average employee usually has three or four weeks of paid vacation（带薪休假）time during the year, though it may vary from one occupation or company to another. Some American families simply spend their vacations at home, that is, time is used to work around the house. They do so for domestic or health reasons, or simply because they want or need to avoid extra expenses. Others might own or rent a cottage near a lake or in the mountains where the whole family can spend a cool summer together. Locations where swimming, fishing, and other water activities are available are especially popular, and the number of vacationers there is always high. However, for a great many Americans, vacations are the time for them to take to the road and see the country. The widely available and inexpensive camp grounds throughout the nation give American families the chance to travel on an affordable budget. Many county, state and national parks have well-equipped camping facilities, and every year millions of Americans visit these parks. In the minds of most Americans, **Walt Disney World**[2], **Yellowstone National Park**[3], **the Grand Canyon**[4], **Niagara Falls**[5], and **Las Vegas**[6] always remain high on their tourist destination list. Of course, for those who can afford it, international travel to Europe, Asia, and the Caribbean beaches never fails to lose its attraction, for such expeditions can provide the opportunity for them to meet new people, make new friends, and share new experiences with them.

Indoor Leisure Activities

1.Go Malling

Shopping continues to be the most popular trip activity for U.S. adults. About 91 million people included shopping as an activity on a trip in 2000. The most popular place to shop is malls, which attracted 62% of shoppers in 2000. It makes sense that urban critics predict that the urban center in the U.S. for the 21st century is the Regional Mall.

The Mall of America may well be called the "avant guard" of shopping malls in America. Located in Bloomington, Minnesota, outside of Minneapolis, the 4.2 million square foot mall is expected to draw more visitors than Walt Disney World or the Grand Canyon. During the first three months of its opening in 1992 nearly a million people a week visited the mall. The mall is very large. It has four department stores, about 360 specialty stores, more than 40 restaurants, all of which are grouped around a seven acre glass roofed courtyard containing an amusement park with 22 rides, two theaters, and many smaller attractions. The stores in the mall close at 10 P.M. and the nightclubs there stay open until 1 A.M. The average visitor to a regional mall spends three hours there, but more than four hours in the Mall of America.

The Friday after the American holiday of Thanksgiving is called Black Friday. Black Friday is considered the official start of Christmas shopping season. It occurs after Thanksgiving, which falls on the fourth Thursday of November. Black Friday is known as the busiest and the most popular shopping day of the year. On that day, retailers slash prices to get consumers to buy. It is also the time when many Americans start their Christmas shopping. This day is a shopper's dream and shoppers will be lining up in front of the doors to be one of the first to walk into the shop and get a big discount. Electronics like flat screen TVs are usually the first items to go.

2.Electronic Entertainment

Without question, the most significant influence on the use of leisure has so far been television and the varied forms of electronic entertainment that followed it. TV set in 98% of American households, and many have two or three. About 82% of American homes have a videocassette recorder (VCR), which is capable of recording and playing back TV shows or movies.

By far, the most popular leisure-time activity is watching television in America. There is at least one What's on TV? Afternoon programming consists mostly of game shows, talk shows, and never-ending dramas commonly called soap operas. For children, daytime TV offers clever programs that educate while entertaining. There are also a lot of cartoons. At dinner time, news is broadcast. Evening entertainment consists mostly of situation comedies (sitcoms) which portray some aspects of life (families, singles, seniors, and so on) in a humorous way. There are also movies, adventure shows, dramas, and various weekly shows with the same cast of characters and general theme but a different story each week. The most popular shows include American Idol, Ellen Show, Survivor, NFL Monday Night Football, Friends, Prison Break, Gossip Girl, Sex and the City, and The Big Bang Theory, and so on.

For those who want more TV than the free stations provide, cable TV is available in most parts of the country. To receive cable TV, one must pay a monthly subscription free. Wires are attached to the TV set to enable the subscriber to receive the cable broadcasts. Cable channels tend to specialize in one type of program. There are station for news, sports, movies, music video, business, health, history, and arts.

The popularity of home computers and "surfing the net"— seeing what is on the Internet and the World Wide Web — has brought a whole new world of leisure activities to Americans. Through the Internet, people can explore personal, business, or leisure interests and make friends around the world by "surfing" through a limitless variety of sources. What's more, people can meet electronically while maintaining their anonymity.

To tweet or not to tweet, that is the question. There's no denying that Twitter is a social networking phenomenon in America. Despite the fact that it was originally meant to help teens keep track of each other, it has grown up considerably over the past year. In fact, the vast majority of the network's users are adults, not kids. Only 11% of Twitter's users are between the ages of 11 and 17. Twitter has become much more than just another way to find out if your friend is at the coffee shop or if **Ashton Kutcher**[7] is vacationing in the Caribbean.

So why do the adult interest? Although Twitter has a 140-character limit on posts, it is not about just sending mundane messages. **CNN**[8] acquired a ton of followers themselves and they add up to over 2.8 million people receiving their breaking news. There's big business to be found on Twitter. More and more companies are jumping on the bandwagon to offer links to websites, coupons, information on new products, sale announcements, and more. Twitter（推特，微博）is even becoming a great place to find a job. Companies that are looking for social-media savvy employees have decided that the best way to find them is to go to the source. As job boards become more saturated, hiring professionals are finding more of what they want on Twitter, and at a cheaper cost than advertising on the regular boards.

There are few options out there that allow people to make a brief, instant connection with potentially 19.2 million people in such an easy, cheap and fun way. Whether they are job hunting, researching a product, or just keeping up with their favorite sports team, Twitter has an application to help them achieve their goals for both business and leisure.

Other activities Americans are most likely to do as indoor pastimes include dining out, entertaining friends or relatives at home, reading books, barbecuing, playing cards, attending music performances, and going to bars or night clubs.

Notes

1. Ben & Jerry's and Häagen-Dazs 两种美国知名冰淇淋品牌: BEN & JERRY'S 是由两位童年玩伴 Ben Cohen 和 Jerry Greenfield 创办的，以口感香醇和口味新奇闻名。哈根达斯是风靡全球的冰淇淋品牌，1921 年由鲁本・马特斯（Reuben Mattus）研制成功，于 1962 在美国纽约布朗克斯命名并上市。

2. Walt Disney World 沃尔特・迪斯尼世界: 1955 年，富裕想象力和创造精神的美国动画片先驱沃尔特・迪斯尼在加利福尼亚州创办了第一座现代化的游乐园，取名迪斯尼乐园，是世界上第一个现代意义上的主题公园。

3. Yellowstone National Park 黄石国家公园: 美国最大、最著名、建立最早的国家公园，以流经其中的黄石河命名，内有森林、瀑布、山谷幽潭、间歇泉等各色景色，其中最著名的间歇泉是“老忠实泉”（Old Faithful），因其有规律的喷发而得此名。

4. The Grand Canyon 大峡谷：美国亚利桑那州西北部科罗拉多河的峡谷，由一系列错综复杂的山峡和深谷组成，岩壁陡峭，断层清晰可见。整个地貌十分奇特壮观，为世界罕见的自然奇观，其中最为壮观的一段自 1908 年被规划为“大峡谷国家公园”。

5. Niagara Falls 尼亚加拉瀑布：位于加拿大和美国交界的尼亚加拉河中段，号称世界七大奇景之一，与南美的伊瓜苏瀑布及非洲的维多利亚瀑布合称世界三大瀑布。它以磅礴的气势、丰沛而浩瀚的水汽，震撼了所有游人。从伊利湖滚滚而来的尼亚加拉河水流经此地，突然垂直跌落 51 米，巨大的水流以银河倾倒之势冲下断崖，声及数里之外，场面震人心魄，形成了气势磅礴的大瀑布。

6. Las Vegas 拉斯维加斯：美国最大的赌城和娱乐城。这座城市以赌博业为中心的庞大的旅游、购物、度假产业而著名，是世界知名的度假胜地之一。它是位于内华达州南部的一座沙漠城，由洛杉矶沿着 15 号洲际公路，往北直行，便可抵达这座身处于内华达沙漠中的不夜城。1905 年，拉斯维加斯建市。20 世纪 30 年代，内华达州决定使赌博成为合法的事业，市区的赌场纷纷成立，查尔斯顿娱乐区和死谷国家博览馆就很具代表性。拉斯维加斯的“赌场”之名就此传开。

7. Ashton Kutcher 阿什顿库彻：美国著名演员，曾在《乔布斯》里出演史蒂夫·乔布斯一角。此外，库彻还是硅谷著名天使投资人，除了 Skype，库彻的投资还包括了：社交应用 Foursquare、社交杂志应用 Flipboard、社交应用 Path 等。

8. CNN 美国有线电视新闻网：英文全称“Cable News Network”，是美国的有线电视频道，由特纳广播公司（TBS）董事长特德·特纳于 1980 年 6 月创办，通过卫星向有线电视网和卫星电视用户提供全天候的新闻节目，总部设在美国佐治亚州的亚特兰大，目前为时代华纳所有。它是第一个全天候 24 小时的新闻频道，任何突发的新闻，都会率先做现场报道。

References

[1] HUFFMAN M F, HUFFMAN D M. Inside U.S. culture and life[M]. Beijing: Foreign Language Teaching and Research Press, 2009.

[2] 王恩铭 . 美国社会文化 [M]. 北京：北京大学出版社 , 2010.

[3] 王恩铭 . 英语国家概况 [M]. 上海：上海外语教育出版社 , 2008.

[4] 常俊跃，李莉莉，赵永青 . 美国社会与文化 [M]. 北京：北京大学出版社 , 2009.

[5] 周静琼 . 当代美国概况 [M]. 上海：上海外语教育出版社 , 2003.

[6] 刘茜 . 轻松走遍美国 [M]. 北京：中国宇航出版社 , 2010.

[7] 张浩 . 一本书玩转北美 [M]. 北京：经济科学出版社 , 2013.

[8] 张浩 , 黄一飞 . 一本书读懂美国文化 [M]. 北京：中国时代经济出版社 , 2012.

[9] 肖冉 , 等 . 边品美国文化边学英语 (基础篇) [M]. 北京：中国水利水电出版社 , 2009.

[10] 田耀 . 美国文化点滴 [M]. 天津：天津大学出版社 , 2009.

[11] 王晓红 . 美国社会与文化 [M]. 北京：世界图书出版公司 , 2010.

[12] 丁建军 . 英语国家概况 [M]. 西安：西安交通大学出版社 , 2010.

[13] 朱永涛,王立礼 . 英语国家社会与文化入门 [M]. 北京:高等教育出版社 , 2005.
[14] 玛丽安娜 · 卡尼 · 戴特斯曼,乔安 · 克兰德尔,爱德华 · N. 卡尼 . 美国文化背景 [M]. 北京:世界图书出版公司 , 2002.
[15] 王俊生,刘沛富 . 最新英美概况 [M]. 北京:外语教学与研究出版社 , 2012.

Chapter Nineteen

American Gay Culture

Homosexuality has been a common but special social feature of human culture since earliest history. As a sexual orientation, homosexuality refers to "an enduring pattern of or disposition to experience sexual, affection, or romantic attractions primarily to" people of the same sex; it also refers to an individual's sense of personal and social identity based on those attractions, behaviors expressing them, and membership in a community of others who share them. Gay culture, in its widest definition, simply means how gay people live their lives: how their gay identity forms, how they live their lives, how they create extended-family and social networks, how they regard themselves in relation to heterosexual society, how they express themselves artistically. Since the gay community is composed of women and men with a wide range of other identities racial, national, class, ethnic, religious its boundaries are open-ended.

Unit 1 History of Homosexuality in the United States

A long history of invisibility and suffering highlighted the distinctive subculture of homosexual. Shouldering both internal and external burden and oppression, a considerable portion of this community underwent excessive discrimination and possessed inferior social status. Because of the unfriendly attitude towards homosexuality, the American **Gay Rights Movement**[1] went through a difficult historical path for American homosexuals fighting for legal rights.

Early Oppressed and Persecuted Years

From the early colonial time, because of historical, cultural, ethnical, religious reasons, condition of American homosexuals was extremely strenuous and arduous. Since homosexuals were also the pious of believer of God, they tried to hide their special orientation from being condemned as sinful and immoral people. In this way, they feel normal as other believers of God and it made them avoid condemnation and exclusion from the public.

Besides spiritual and religious torture in their mind, a huge psychological burden of a medical diagnosis placed on American homosexuals— "gender inversion" or "sexual psychopaths". More seriously, they were enlisted as one of mental diseases by psychiatrists. Under the oppression from external environment, coming out of closet was tantamount to being deprived of virtually all that they once possessed. In addition to the general perception of homosexual minority as sinful and pathological, authority and mass media applied various channels to deteriorate the already negative stereotype by way of publicity and dissemination.

Since they were relatively isolated and marginalized, they endured both surrounding oppression and further inward confusion. Shrouded by qualm and trepidation penetrating the entire society, a portion of homosexual was perplexed with their self-identity and self-consciousness. They passively accepted and were settled with social intolerance and discrimination, unenthusiastic about transforming or improving their status quo and disinclined to pitch in with other radicals who strived for equality and fairness in initial time. They were accustomed to being outsiders and were used to be invisible. American homosexuals in this period were living under three pressures—the religious sinner, the mental disorder and immoral criminal. They chose to be silent and oppressed because they were not normal human beings and they deserved to be punished. In the following decades, intensive persecution and suppression led to the awakening of self-awareness and group identity of American homosexuals.

After the World War II, with economy prospering, technology advancing, and urbanizing speeding up, living an affluent and abundant life, American people started to develop new interests for their leisure time. Those with homosexual inclinations found one another at that time that they found the freedom to express themselves without ever-present familial and religious disapproval. During this time, there was a large growth in the number of American homosexuals. Gradually, saloon and bar became the appropriate places for homosexuals to meet each other and enjoy the time. In these relatively safe places, sense of homosexual identity and their self-awareness were aroused and fostered. They aimed to develop their specific "homo-language" to communicate in a secret way.

In such ever-changing circumstances, several homosexual organizations sprang up in succession, including **Mattachine Society**[2] and the **Daughters of Bilitis**[3]. The members of Mattachine Society summoned homosexual together and arranged activities fighting for their civil rights. There was a news blackout on the information regarding homosexuality; no press releases were accepted by any newspapers, magazines, or radio stations. The Mattachine Society was forced to circulate information solely through postings and flyers distributed in areas where homosexuals usually congregated. Nevertheless, the event drew tremendous and quiet support, and membership in the Mattachine Society grew by several thousands in succeeding weeks. The Daughters of Bilitis was established for the lesbians to express their political thoughts. It published its own magazine Leader, for lesbians to realize their homosexual identity.

In the 1950s, fears generated by Joseph McCarthy's campaign regarded "homosexual" as an equivalence of "Communist". In 1953, under President Eisenhower, homosexuality became by executive order a necessary and sufficient reason in itself to fire any federal employee from his or her job. Most defense industries and others with government contracts followed suit, and the U.S. Postal Service aided these industries by putting tracers on suspected homosexuals' mail in order to gather enough evidence for dismissal and possibly arrest. This crazy oppression was commented by American scholar Andrew as a repression "equal to other persecution movement in

American history, such as the Slaughter of American Indians, or racial discriminations".

The Rise of National Protests

The homosexual history stretched long pre- and post- sixties in the United States, and a strong sense of self-identity and self-emancipation was established. It was this period of time which witnessed their principal and paramount endeavor to gain recognition and inalienable rights.

The 1960s of America is a time uprising and protest, which composed the unprecedented **Counter Culture Movement**[4] and Civil Rights Movement resonating with the mainstream of time. The members of gay community in New York had suffered considerable discrimination and were inspired by the Civil Rights Movement which was winning new rights for women and other minorities. They were also influenced by the counter culture which was encouraging more open attitudes toward sex, new lifestyle and belief. With tension and collision roaring up around, a restless mood gradually built up within the homosexual community. They had many of the same complaints that blacks and women and students did. Social causes were all around them roaring through the culture like prairie fires. American homosexuals learned the rebellious spirit and fighting strategy from the Counter Culture Movement, and applied them in their Gay Rights Movements.

In the 1970s, American homosexuals aimed at achieving normalization of homosexuality and fighting for legal rights. On June 27th, 1969, Stonewall riots took place in a gay bar named the Stonewall Inn which was a place gay and lesbians usually went to. Police in New York and other cities would regularly raid bars and other places where gay people gathered and arrested the people there. This time, however, the people in the Stonewall Inn resisted the police and other people joined the crowd outside the bar in protest of against the police actions. As people who had been arrested were brought out of the bar, the police and the crowd outside turned violent and the police were unable to control the situation. In the following four days, thousands of American homosexuals gathered in city squares, protesting against the injustice and discrimination. Later, more than 4 million homosexuals from all over the country participated in the demonstration, fighting for their "equality, freedom and human rights".

The Stonewall Riots[5] was the watershed in the history, igniting wide-scope Gay Liberation Movement and stimulating the establishment of various homophile organizations, including Gay Liberation Front, Gay Activists Alliance, and so forth. Following the Stonewall Riots gay support groups were organized in New York and other places to fight openly for gay rights. A year later, the first gay pride parade was held in New York and Los Angeles. One result of these early public actions in New York and elsewhere was that for the first time, large numbers of Americans began to consider the rights of gay people.

In December 1973, the Gay Rights Movement achieved a major victory when American Psychological Association excluded homosexuality as a mental disorder and posed the gesture to support homosexual civil rights, which was one of the most profound and pivotal achievements in the history of homosexual emancipation. Such decision not only changed the abnormal status of homosexuality, but also changed people's attitudes and misunderstandings. As years passed, ordinary American citizens and famous artists, musicians, actors, politicians, TV personalities and religious leaders openly stated that they were lesbian, gay, bisexual or transgender. This was called "coming out of closet" because closets are closed place in which you cannot see. As increasing numbers of gays and lesbians became more open about their sexual preferences, Americans were forced to openly discuss gay issues in families, in schools, in media, in the government, in churches and elsewhere. Since the 1970s, American homosexuals were on the way to gain formal citizenship and civil rights confidently.

Peaceful Time after 1980s until Present

In the 1980 election, leaders of the Religious Right were squarely behind Ronald Reagan. As gay right is one of the issues galvanizing the Religious Right, democratic leaders can't afford to lose by supporting gay rights. They delivered a speech in the party platform: "All groups must be protected from discrimination based on race, color, religion, national origin, language, age, sex or sexual orientation." Three years later, Gary Hart became the first major-party presidential candidate to address an **LGBT**[6] organization.

Through the 1980s, gay rights became a big issue of discussion for a second time in America when the gay male community was decimated by the AIDS epidemic. As the disease spread among the community of gay men, anti-gay groups used this to become more active and open in their activities against gay people. Many gay men died from the disease, but the disease and the attacks against gay people caused them to become better organized, more open and stronger. As many as one million gay rights supporters joined the marches on Washington in 1987 and again in 1993.

In the last decade of the 20th century, an actress named Ellen DeGeneres came out on national television in April 1997, presaging a new era of gay celebrity power and media visibility. Among the most vocal activists, celebrity performers, both gay and heterosexual, called for tolerance and equal rights. As a result of hard work by countless organizations and individuals, gay and lesbian couples gained new legal rights in the 21st century.

Present-day Battles over Gay Marriage

The 1990s has witnessed ups and downs of homosexuals in fighting for their right to marriage. Homosexual marriages were faced with all kinds of objections. As America is a religious country, it is widely accepted that God created man and woman in his image and that in the complementarily of the sexes, they are called to reflect the inner unity of the Creator. Many people believed that marriages only refers exclusively to the relationship between man and woman, so almost all the states in America refused to give license to same-sex marriage. Same-sex marriage activists scored their first major victory in 1993, in the Hawaii case of Baehr v. Lewin. Nina Baehr sued the state of Hawaii, alleging that the state's refusal to issue her and her same-sex partner a marriage license amounted to illegal discrimination. The Hawaii Supreme Court declared that, barring a "compelling state interest", the State of Hawaii could not bar same-sex couples from marrying without violating its own equal protection statutes. The Hawaii state legislature soon amended the constitution to overrule the Court. This backlash stimulated the national debate over same-sex marriage—and the pandering efforts of many state legislatures to ban it. Even in 1996, President Bill Clinton ratified the passage of the anti-gay **Defense of Marriage Act**[7]**.** This law will prevent states from being forced by the Full Faith and Credit Clause to recognize same-sex marriages as the union of one man and one woman. DOMA aimed to prevent any future hypothetical same-sex married couples from receiving federal benefits.

Things began to improve since California established a statewide domestic partnerships registry available to same-sex couples. In 1999, three same-sex couples sued the State of Vermont for denying them the right to marry—and, in a mirror of the 1993 Hawaii decision, the state's highest court agreed. In 2000, rather than amending the constitution, Vermont established civil unions—a separate but equal alternative to marriage that would grant same-sex couples the same rights available to married couples. Several states had established that same-sex couples could achieve some basic partnership rights through the separate-but-equal standards of domestic partnership and civil unions. Massachusetts became the first state to perform same-sex marriages in 2003. With the end of state sodomy laws, gay Americans were finally free from criminal classification. On May 9th, 2012, Barack Obama became the first sitting U.S. President to publicly declare support for the legalization of same-sex marriage. On November 6th, 2012, Maine, Maryland, and Washington became the first states to legalize same-sex marriage through popular vote. As of June 13th, 2014, nineteen states and the District of Columbia, routinely issue same-sex marriage licenses. Utah, Oklahoma, Virginia, Michigan, Idaho, Arkansas, Texas and Wisconsin are awaiting appellate court decisions after lower courts ruled in favor of allowing such licenses.

Notes

1. Gay Rights Movement 同性恋权利运动：或称“同志运动”，是指一批松散结合的公民权利团体、人权团体、支持团体与政治行动者，追求来自社会对于非异性恋（如：同性恋与双性恋等）与跨性别的接受、包容与平等。尽管这个运动通常被称为同性恋权利运动，但运动成员也会争取其他不一定会被定义为“同性恋”的人的权利。他们的观点对某些人来说具有争议性，而同性恋权利运动受到的反对有来自于包括个人以及宗教与政治团体。可是，社会上也有团体反对性倾向条例，认为这等条例会导致逆向歧视。

2. Mattachine Society 玛特欣协会：1951年，由Harry Hay、Chuck Rowland和Robert Hull创建。它是最早的同性恋组织之一，致力于保护和改善同性恋者的权利。

3. Daughters of Bilitis 比利蒂斯女儿：1955年成立于旧金山的“比利蒂斯女儿”（The Daughters of Bilitis，DOB）是一个服务于女同性恋者的讨论和社交团体。它的创立者戴尔·

马丁和菲利斯·莱昂以及其他三对伴侣在最初讨论建立一个安全的场所以取代酒吧聚会时，并不知道"玛特欣协会"的存在。很快，她们发现了"玛特欣协会"，这两个组织便开始经常共同活动，但仍是两个独立的组织。

4. Counter Culture Movement 美国的反主流文化运动：主要指对美国主流文化的反叛与背离，其主体是青年，又称"青年文化运动"。指同美国的传统的政治制度、意识形态（包括文化、道德、宗教、伦理观念）相对立而言的一种文化形式，是在反主流社会文化的共同目标下，由各种力量组成的联合势力。其共同点是对传统文化采取不妥协主义。美国加利福尼亚州立大学的历史学教授 Theodore Roszak 将"反文化"归结为 20 世纪 60 年代发生在美国社会政治、文化领域的一切青年人抗议运动，"既包括校园民主运动、妇女解放运动、黑人民权运动、反战和平运动、环境保护运动、同性恋者权利运动等方面的政治'革命'，也包括摇滚乐、性解放、吸毒、嬉皮文化及神秘主义和自我主义的复兴等方面的文化'革命'"。反文化运动所到之处，以强调工作、清醒、俭省、节欲为人生态度的美国新教伦理和清教精神都受到了强烈的冲击和批判。他们试图通过各种反叛活动表达对主流文化、现存制度的不满，对妇女、少数民族处境的同情，以及对和平生活的向往。

5. Stonewall Riots 石墙事件：在同性恋维权的历史上是一个标志性的事件，它引发了美国同性恋群体维权的行动，并扩展到世界范围内。一个强大的同性恋维权组织"同性恋解放阵线"成立。石墙骚乱是指发生在纽约的一次同性恋者和警察间的一系列暴力冲突。这次骚乱开始于 1969 年 6 月 27 日星期五，在石墙旅馆外，格林威治村的同性恋住所。"石墙"，被认为是美国乃至世界现代同性恋权利运动的起点。它是第一次有同性恋者拒绝警方的逮捕。在石墙骚乱以前，警方对同性恋酒吧和夜总会的搜捕行动是城市同性恋者生活的一部分。警方通常会登记出席的人的姓名以便用于报纸的刊登，然后把尽量多的同性恋者押上警车。接吻、牵手，甚至在同性恋酒吧出现都是被逮捕的理由。

6. LGBT: 是女同性恋者（Lesbians）、男同性恋者（Gays）、双性恋者（Bisexuals）与跨性别者（Transgender）的英文首字母缩略词。1990 年代，由于"同性恋社群"一词无法完整体现相关群体，"LGBT"一词便应运而生并逐渐普及。在现代用语中，"LGBT"一词十分重视性倾向与性别认同文化多样性，除了狭义的指同性恋、双性恋或跨性别族群，也可广泛代表所有非异性恋者。

7. Defense of Marriage Act《婚姻保护法案》: 简称"DOMA"，由美国前总统比尔·克林顿于 1996 年签署，界定婚姻为一男一女。法案第三节界定婚姻为一男一女的结合，条文使得同性恋伴侣无法如异性恋夫妻一样，享有税务、保险、继承、移民等权利。国会的 535 名议员中，只有 81 名对提案表示反对。2013 年 3 月 27 日，这个法案经由最高法院审核，法官将决定该法案是否遵循美国的国家精神，即崇尚自由、平等以及最最重要的——公正的精神，并依此断定它是否符合宪法。当地时间 2013 年 6 月 26 日，依据美国宪法第五修正案以 5:4 的比率裁定捍卫婚姻法案第三章违宪。

Unit 2 Homosexuality in Art

One of the ways that gay culture in its broadest sense—how gay people live their lives—

clearly manifests itself to mainstream culture is through the production of art, especially in literature and film.

Homosexual Characters in Theatre *Angels in America*[1]

As one of the most outstanding playwrights of contemporary American literature, Tony Kushner enjoys a great reputation in American theatre. *Angels in America*: A Gay Fantasia on National Themes is not only a gay play, but also his masterpiece which touches upon various social problems, including religious belief, moral crisis, and AIDS pandemic. In *Angels in America*, Kushner illustrates his thought on the construction of the contemporary utopia. He observes people's pursuit of life and sexuality, whether heterosexual or homosexual love, combining the traditional values such as kindness, tolerance and responsibility, constitutes a great power in solving social problems and reconstructuring an ideal society. Angels in America is almost the first homosexual play which described homosexual characters and is depicted from an entirely homosexual perspective. Set in New York City in 1985, *Angels in America* focuses on the stories of two troubled couples, one gay, and one straight: "word processor" Louis Ironson and his lover Prior Walter, and Mormon lawyer Joe Pitt and his wife Harper. The characters' pursuit of homosexual love, responsibility and life is elaborated in the Angles in America. In the pursuit of homosexual love, Louis and Prior are faced with the deadly disease AIDS. Though they have undergone series of twist and turns, Louis eventually comes back to his former AIDS lover. The return symbolizes certain sense of humanity and love. Joe, after abandoning his valium-addicted（安定药上瘾）wife, gradually realizes he is unable to abandon his commitment to his conventional family responsibility. By the end of the play, Joe's return to Harpers indicates the reenactment of responsibility. Another character Roy Cohn, a notorious figure, the power obsessed lawyer, remains in the closet until he dies of AIDS. By the end of the play, he transforms into living "Issac" and gives his blessing to Joe as a patriarchal character. The AIDS patient, Prior Walter's rejected of the role of prophet and quested for more life, forecasting the positive prospect of existence of homosexuality.

By presenting a world inside the homosexuality, it seems that what Kushner wants to convey is that homosexuality bears more pressure from the AIDS, conventional morality and heavy family restrictions. In a larger sense, Kushner's Angels in America subverts the traditional view of homosexuality. To some extent, Angels denied the opposition of homosexuality and heterosexuality. Their pursuit of love, responsibility and life are essential three aspects of humanity thus the Angels brings the ultimate message that what the homosexuals are pursuing are identical to what straight people are pursuing. Moreover, Angels also suggests a more accepted attitude toward homosexuality. Homosexuality ought not to be regarded as something awkward and anomaly. On the contrary, people ought to provide more tolerance to the individuals with same sex orientation. *Angels in America* is considered to be an appeal for equal status and respect for homosexual individuals.

Homosexuality in the Film *Brokeback Mountain*[2]

Brokeback Mountain (2005) is a moderm homosexual movie based on the short story by Annie Proulx and directed by Ang Lee, *Brokeback Mountain* situated a love story between two closeted cowboys at the heart of American mythology. It won **Academy Award**[3] for Best Directing and Best Adapted Screenplay.

Ennis Del Mar and Jack Twist signed up to herd sheep for the summer. According to the situation, one of them must illegally pitch a tent near the sheep at night to watch for wolves ,while the other maintains the base camp at the base of the mountain. The two men discovered a quiet affection for each other to spend the lonely time in Brokeback Mountain. Incredibly, their silent relationship transforms into a physical one. At the end of the summer, the two go back to their winter lives. Ennis marries his fiancee Alma Jack heads out on the places where he meets Lureen and soon goes to work for her father in Texas. Several years when the two men meet each other again, they immediately embrace with great passion. They spend a few weeks a year on Brokeback Mountain living a carefree life. The two men have been on a secret affair for 20 years, despite of their family. Gradually, tragedy strikes when their wives found out that their husbands are gay. Ennis and Jack can't maintain such deviant relationship as before. Jack wants them to get divorced and tend a ranch together, but Ennis is too afraid of the burden and discrimination brought by homophobia society. Finally they decided to depart. Several days later, a postcard Ennis sends to Jack is returned stamped "Deceased". In a telephone conversation, Lureen tells Ennis that Jack died when a tire he was changing exploded.

This movie implies that the homosexual lifestyle is a doomed tragedy in the real Society. Its tragedy lies in their lifestyle conflicts with the morally—accepted lifestyle in the heterosexual families. Besides, there are many other homosexual movies produced by Hollywood. It is said that 2006 was known as "The Year of the Homosexual" in Hollywood.

The evolution of gay culture in America was shaped by resistance to the mainstream society's repression. It was from the Stonewall Riots that American homosexuals turned to the trajectory of improving their situation and legalizing their rights. American Gay Rights Movement experienced from repression to active fight, from direct action to peaceful dialogue. At different stages of the Gay Rights Movement, homosexual pioneers insisted on battling against discrimination and persecution, in search of their homosexual identity and legal rights. With the scientific development, more scholars have tried their best to make comprehensive explanation about homosexuality in scientific way, putting forward the gene theory, hormonal theory and acquired theory. From the 1970s till today, social tolerance and acceptance have been dramatically improved.

In 1973 by the **American Psychiatric Association**[4] (APA) removed homosexuality from the list of disorders contained in the **Diagnostic and Statistical Manual of Mental Disorders**[5] (DSM). Most people gradually know the facts about homosexual orientation, and there is no relation between different sexual orientation and mental health. Despite of few hostile attitudes towards homosexuality, there is a growing trend that American public advocate equal status and civil rights for them as other American citizens. The issues of gay marriage, gays in the military, gays in church, gays in art and gays adopting and raising children are hot issues for American politicians. As of June, 2014, same-sex marriage is allowed in 15 states in the United States. The development of homosexual rights has entered a new stage, showing a bright future for the American gay culture.

Notes

1.*Angels in America*《天使在美国》: 由美国剧作家托尼·库士纳创作的一部共两部分的戏剧，后来又被改编为电视连续短剧和歌剧。故事发生于20世纪80年代中期的纽约，犹太人路易·爱恩森与同性恋爱人普莱尔·沃尔特住在一起。但普莱尔后来发现自己患有艾滋病，臭名昭著的麦卡锡主义者罗依·康为他提供了一份十分有前途的工作。路易十分后悔抛弃了爱人，时刻受到良心的折磨；乔的妈妈汉娜(Hannah)得知儿子是同性恋后搬到纽约，原来冷战时期因为罗依·康的幕后操纵而被美国司法处以极刑的共产党人艾瑟尔·罗森堡也化为鬼魂来报复他。全剧充满了黑色幽默与悲剧色彩，对白极为出色，在一些需要特殊效果衬托的地方展现出很浓的戏剧风格。大多数演员都一人分饰几角，比如扮演普莱尔的护士的演员，也同时扮演美国天使。剧中对圣经和美国政治、经济、文化、种族、环境现象有非常多的引用，也有发生在南极和天堂的戏份，也涉及了旧金山的大地震与纽约中央公园中的毕士大(Bethesda)天使像。

2.*Brokeback Mountain*《断背山》: 一部2005年的美国爱情、剧情片，改编自安妮·普露所著的同名短篇小说《断背山》，由华人导演李安执导，好莱坞著名影星杰克·吉伦哈尔、希斯·莱杰、米歇尔·威廉姆斯和安妮·海瑟薇倾情出演。影片讲述了1963年至1981年的美国怀俄明州，两个男人之间情与爱的复杂关系。该片在威尼斯电影节夺得金狮奖，在第78届奥斯卡金像奖中获得八项提名，并夺得了最佳导演、最佳改编剧本与最佳电影配乐三项大奖。《断背山》在商业上也获得了巨大成功，在史上爱情、剧情片中票房排名第八(1.78亿美元)。该片上映时形成一阵席卷全球的文化现象，对学术、时装和乡村音乐等不同文化领域产生广泛影响，在社会上也掀起对同性之爱的大讨论。该片也获得了各大影评人和媒体的一致好评。

3. Academy Award 奥斯卡金像奖： 也称"奥斯卡奖"，原名"学院奖"，正式名称是"电影艺术与科学学院奖"，设立于1927年，每年一次在美国洛杉矶举行。该奖是由美国电影艺术与科学学院颁发，旨在鼓励优秀电影的创作与发展的奖项，半个多世纪来一直享有盛誉。第86届奥斯卡颁奖典礼于2014年3月2日(周日)举行。

4. American Psychiatric Association 美国精神医学学会： 美国精神科医生的专业组织，在行内具有全球性的影响力。现有约38 000名会员，大部分在美国。其出版刊物除包括学术期刊以及小册子以外，最为人熟悉的就是《精神疾病诊断与统计手册》，简称"DSM"。这本手册是美国主要诊断精神疾病的重要标准，亦是全世界许多国家在诊断精神疾病上的重要参考。

5. Diagnostic and Statistical Manual of Mental Disorders 精神疾病诊断与统计手册： 简称"DSM"，由美国精神医学学会（American Psychiatric Association, APA）出版，是一本在美国与其他国家中最常使用来诊断精神疾病的指导手册。

References

[1] ANDREW K. Why gay legal history matters[J]. Harvard Law Review, 2000 (113):2040-2041.

[2] BARON M. Genetic linkage and male homosexual orientation[J]. BMJ, 1993,8(7): 337–338.

[3] BASWELL J. Christianity, social tolerance, and homosexuality [M]. Chicago: University of Chicago Press, 1980.

[4] BULLOUGH V L. Sexual variance in society and history[M]. New York: Wiley, 1976.

[5] CLENDILEN D, ADAM N. Out of good: the struggle to build a gay rights movement in America[M]. New York: Simon & Schuster, 1999.

[6] FRISCH M, HVIID A. Childhood family correlates of heterosexual and homosexual marriages: a national cohort study of two million Danes[J]. Arch Sex Behav, 2006(5): 533–47.

[7] HENDIN H. Homosexuality: the psychosocial dimension[J]. Journal of American Academy of Psychoanalysis, 1978(6): 479–96.

[8] ISAY R A. Becoming gay: the journey to self-acceptance[M]. New York: Pantheon, 1996.

[9] KALLMAN F. J. Comparative twin study on the genetic aspects of male homosexuality[J]. Journal of Nervous and Mental Disorders, 1952(115):283.

[10] LEKUS I. The Long Sixties[J]. OAH Magzine of History, 2006 (202) : 32-38.

[11] LUNG F W, SHU B C. Father-son attachment and sexual partner orientation in Taiwan[J]. Comprehensive Psychiatry, 2007, 48 (1): 20–26.

[12] ROSE R M, POE R O. Androgen Response to Stress[J]. Psychosomatic Medicine.,1969 (31): 418.

[13] STRASSER M. Legally: same-sex marriage and the constitution[M]. Ithaca: Cornell University Press, 1997.

Chapter Twenty

American Holidays

Americans celebrate a variety of holidays throughout the year. They can be religious, secular（俗界的）, international, or uniquely American. America, a nation of immigration, is blessed with a rich and diverse ethnic heritage. Therefore, almost all the holidays within the country were brought here by immigrants from their own mother countries. And the traditions and customs are variations of those back in their old homes except some American-born ones'. In the next four units, there will be an extensive introduction to these holidays.

Unit 1 Federal Holidays

In the Unites States, a federal holiday refers to an authorized holiday recognized by US Federal government. On a US federal holiday, non-essential federal government offices are closed, and every federal employee is paid for the holiday. Of course, the US Federal government can only recognize federal holidays that pertain（有关）to its own employees. There are eleven such holidays: ten annual one and a quadrennial one.

New Year's Day

New Year's Day is observed on January 1st in America, but Americans usually begin their celebrations on the night of December 31st, which is called New Year's Eve（除夕夜）. They celebrate the New Year's Day in many different ways. One of the most prominent celebrations in America is the "ball drop" held in New York City's Time Square, which has been held since 1907. **The Time Square Ball**[1] Drop is one of the best-known New Year's celebrations internationally. It is attended by at least 1 million spectators yearly and enjoys a national television audience across New Year's Eve specials on several of the United States' major broadcast television networks, along with coverage on several major cable networks.

On this day, people also visit relatives and friends, attend church services, enjoy a traditional family meal, or watch New Year's parades on television. Two of the most famous parades are **the Mummers Parade**[2] in Philadelphia, Pennsylvania, and **the Rose Parade**[3] in Pasadena, California. Americans also watch football games on television on New Year's Day. In the Unites States, January 1st is the traditional date for many post-season college football games. For those who have been busy at work or school, New Year's may be a day of rest. They spend the time thinking about, and preparing for the demands of the New Year.

Martin Luther King, Jr. Day

Martin Luther King, Jr. Day is officially called Birthday of Martin Luther King, Jr., an American federal holiday in honor of Martin Luther King, Jr.'s birthday. It is observed on the third Monday of January each year, which is around the time of King's birthday, January 15st. King was the leader of African-American Civil Rights Movements, who was best known for using nonviolent methods to protest racial discrimination. The proposal for a federal holiday in King's honor began soon after his assassination in 1968. However, the idea of Martin Luther King, Jr. Day as a holiday was opposed by many states at first. After years of struggle, President Ronald Reagan finally signed the holiday into law in 1983. At first, some states resisted observing the holiday, giving it alternatives or combining it with other holidays. It was officially observed in all 50 states for the first time in 2000. On Martin Luther King, Jr. Day, people hold memorials for King; students will attend public service.

Presidents' Day

Presidents' Day is a United States federal holiday observed on the third Monday of February every year. Before Presidents' Day became a federal holiday, Americans used to celebrate President Lincoln's Birthday on February 12th and Washington's on February 22nd. In 1971, Presidents' Day was set on the third Monday in February by **the Uniform Monday Act**[4] to honor all American Presidents, not just George Washington and Abram Lincoln, though their birthdays are definitely the origin of this holiday. On this day, many stores, especially car dealers, hold sales; more and more businesses are staying open; many colleges and universities hold regular classes and operations; but some schools often close for the entire week as a "mid-winter recess"(冬季休会). Although the use of Presidents' Day is predominant(占主导地位的), Presidents Day is also considered correct.

Memorial Day

Memorial Day is a federal holiday in the United States for commemorating the soldiers who died in the military service. It is celebrated every year on the last Monday of May, which usually symbolizes the start of the summer vacation. During this day, many parades will be held in large or small cities all over the country; the flag of the United States will be lowered to the half-staff position until noon; people also go to church, sweep the tombs and pay silent tribute, etc. But **the Indianapolis 500**[5], an auto race which has been held every year since 1911, might be the most special and longest-standing tradition on this day. This event will be given a live broadcast to 184 countries.

Independence Day

Independence Day, well-known as the Fourth of July, is the National Day of the United

States. It is a federal holiday commemorating the adoption of the Declaration of the Independence on July 4st, 1776 when the United States officially declared independence from the Great Britain (America did not achieve independence until 1783). It's been the most important patriotic holiday ever in American history. Traditionally, the celebrations involved the parades with marching bands, patriotic speeches, guns and fireworks and so on. Today, the use of fireworks and firearms has been forbidden by local ordinances. The army marks the occasion by firing a 13-gun salute every year. Other celebrations include picnics, concerts barbecues, baseball games, carnivals and races, etc. All non-essential federal institutions are closed on this day.

Labor Day

In America, Labor Day is observed annually on the first Monday of September. It is a celebration of the American labor movement, in honor of the nation's working people. The origin of this holiday is associated with a man named Peter J. McGuire who proposed to the Labor Union of New York the first Monday of September as the Labor Day in 1882. It was first established as a federal holiday in the year of 1894. On Labor Day, parades are held and speeches are made by imminent figures. Labor Day usually marks the symbolic end of a long summer and the return to school. It is also retail sale day during which those who work in retail sector not only work, but work longer hours. It also marks the beginning of the NFL (National Football League) and college school teams.

Columbus Day

Columbus Day is celebrated on the second Monday in October in the United States. It commemorates the day when Italian navigator Christopher Columbus landed in the New World. It first became a federal holiday in the United States in 1937, though people have celebrated Columbus's voyage since colonial period. Columbus Day might be the most controversial holiday in America. The observance of Columbus Day varies in different parts of the Unites States, ranging from large-scale parades to complete non-observance. Some are even opposed to the celebrations of Columbus Day.

Veterans Day

Veterans Day is a federal holiday in honor of people who have served in the U.S. Armed Forces. It is celebrated on November 11th every year. However, if the date happens to be on a Saturday or Sunday, the adjacent(临近的) Friday or Sunday will be designated for holiday leave. In 1954, Veterans Day, replacing **the Armistice Day**[6], became a federal holiday. On Veterans Day, many American workers and students have a day off; non-essential federal government offices are closed; many fast food and restaurant chains offer free meals for Veterans.

Inauguration Day (美国总统就职日)

Inauguration Day happens in the US once every four years on January 20th (21st if the 20th is a Sunday). The original date for inauguration was on March 4th and it was changed to January 20th later by the *Twentieth Amendment to the United States Constitution*. It occurs in the year after presidential elections have been held. On this day, the President-elect and vice president-elect in the previous year swear into office. The Oath of Office (宣誓就职) is the main focus of the day, and the only activity required by law. It is usually followed by a parade along the Pennsylvania Avenue. Since Inauguration Day is not a public holiday, many people still have to work as usual. Many schools, stores and other organizations are open in most parts of the United States. It is a federal holiday for some federal employees who work in the District of Columbia or the surrounding areas.

Thanksgiving Day

Thanksgiving Day is observed on the fourth Thursday in November every year. Thanksgiving today is, in every sense, a national annual holiday on which Americans of all faiths and backgrounds join in to express their thanks for the year's bounty and reverently ask for continued blessings. The first American Thanksgiving Day was held in Plymouth, Massachusetts in 1621, jointly celebrated by Puritans and Indians. Modern Thanksgiving was fixed on the fourth Thursday in November in the year of 1941 by President Franklin D. Roosevelt. Thanksgiving is a family day, so most Americans will go home to reunite with their families. Many traditions of modern American Thanksgiving could be traced back to the first Thanksgiving celebration. On this day, Americans will have big dinners, which usually consist of roast turkey, corn, pumpkin pie and cranberry sauce, with their family. Today, for many Americans, Thanksgiving is a four-day holiday so many Americans choose to take a trip. Thanksgiving is one of the few truly secular holidays on American calendar.

Christmas Day

Christmas Day is a federal holiday celebrated on December 25th. It is a Christian holiday commemorating the birth of Jesus Christ. It is the most festive (喜庆的) holiday of the whole year in the United States. In America, most of the Christmas traditions practiced now are the variations of those brought here by European immigrants, such as decorating houses and yards with lights, putting up Christmas trees, exchanging gifts, sending greeting cards. On Christmas Day, Americans go to church; after service, they will enjoy a traditional Christmas meal, including ham or turkey, nuts and sweet potatoes, etc. Students have a two-week vacation, starting shortly before Christmas and ending soon after the New Year's. Many families choose to go for a travel during the holiday.

Notes

1. the Time Square Ball 时代广场球：1904 年 12 月，在《纽约时报》的努力下，人们第一次在时报广场上举办了庆元旦狂欢活动。从 1907 年起，热力四射的狂欢活动又增加了“坠球”仪式。每年迎新之夜，伴随着新年钟声的敲响，高高悬挂的巨型水晶彩球从广场一幢大厦落下，五彩烟花霎那间划破宁静的夜空。当晚，有大批民众来到时报广场前来观看水晶球坠落，也有全球多家电视台转播的传统节目庆典，将节日的喜庆气氛传遍世界每一个角落。

2. the Mummers Parade 化妆游行：每年美国宾夕法尼亚州费城举行的新年游行活动。正式开始于 1901 年的新年大游行传统，是北欧、英国和非洲裔美国人的传统的混合。

3. the Rose Parade 玫瑰游行：加利福尼亚帕帕萨迪纳市每年 1 月 1 日举行的大型新年庆祝活动。起源于 1890 年，至今已举办了 127 届。当天，会有来自全美乃至全世界各地的玫瑰花与各种花装饰的大型花车、乐队以及游行队伍。

4. the Uniform Monday Act 美国统一假期法案：是美国国会 1968 年签署 1971 年 1 月 1 日生效的法案。此法案修正美国法典中关于美国节日的部分条款，对美国的节日有了比较规范的规定。它确定了阵亡将士纪念日、美国劳动节、哥伦布日等节日的庆祝日期。

5. the Indianapolis 500 印第安纳波利斯 500 英里比赛：每年在美国印第安纳波利斯赛车场举行的赛车比赛。1911 年以来，与摩纳哥大奖赛和勒芒 24 小时耐力赛并称为最重要的三大汽车赛。此赛事每年在阵亡将士纪念周周末举行。

6. Armistice Day 休战纪念日：为纪念 1918 年签订第一次世界大战停战协议而设立的纪念日，美国原先于 11 月 11 日庆祝休战纪念日。1954 年以后，与“退伍军人纪念日”合在一起纪念。

Unit 2 National Holidays

Precisely speaking, the United States of America doesn't have national holidays. By "national" holiday here, it is referred to as those holidays established by law and observed nationwide, but people won't take the day off.

Earth Day

Earth Day[1] is a holiday observed on April 22nd held to demonstrate support for environmental protection. It was first celebrated in 1970 in the United States and now it is a global holiday celebrated by more than 192 countries. On Earth Day, activities will be held to improve ecology, protect life on earth, and care about pollution of the soil, air and water.

Mother's Day

Mother's Day in the United States is an official holiday observed on the second Monday of May in honor of mothers and motherhood(母亲身份). It was proposed by **Anna Javis**[2], whose mother had founded work clubs for women in West Virginia, to establish Mother's Day as a national holiday. In 1914, President Woodrow Wilson made it official. On this holiday, mothers will be honored with flowers, usually carnations, greeting cards, candy or a special cake, etc.

Flag Day

In the United States, **Flag Day**[3] is an annual event observed on the June 14th. It is a holiday honoring the adoption of the American flag the Stars and Stripes by **Second Continental Congress**[4] in 1777. It first became an official holiday in the year of 1916 issued by the President Woodrow Wilson. It was not until the August 1949 that it became a national holiday with the passage of the National Flag Day. On the Flag Day, American President will issue a proclamation（宣言书）urging U.S. citizens to fly the American flag. It is also a time for parents to educate their children.

Father's Day

In the United States, Father's Day is celebrated on the third Sunday in June in honor of fathers and fatherhood. It is a complement（补充）to Mother's Day. Unlike Mother's Day, which was established as a national holiday shortly after it was proposed, Father's Day was not established as a national holiday until 1972, several decades after it was first proposed in 1910. On Father's Day, children give presents to their father or invite him to a good restaurant to make him feel special.

Notes

1. Earth Day 世界地球日：即每年的 4 月 22 日，它是一项世界性的环境保护活动。2009 年第 63 届联合国大会决议将每年的 4 月 22 日定为“世界地球日”。该最初在 1970 年的美国由盖洛德 • 尼尔森和丹尼斯 • 海斯发起，随后影响越来越大。活动宗旨在唤起人类爱护地球、保护家园的意识，促进资源开发与环境保护的协调发展，进而改善地球的整体环境。

2. Anna Javis 安娜 • 贾维斯：1907 年，贾维斯写信给西弗吉尼亚州格拉夫顿的安德鲁斯循道圣公会教堂，请求为她已逝世两周年的母亲做特别追思礼拜。她母亲生前为这一教堂的星期日学校服务了 20 多年。1908 年，教堂宣布贾维斯母亲忌日——5 月的第二个星期日为母亲节。贾维斯组织了一个母亲节委员会，开始大规模宣传，呼吁将母亲节定为法定假日。1910 年，西弗吉尼亚州成为美国第一个庆祝母亲节的州。1914 年，美国时任总统伍德罗 • 威尔逊签署命令，正式将每年 5 月的第二个星期日在全美范围内定为母亲节。

3. Flag Day 国旗日：国旗日是纪念美国大陆会议 1777 年 6 月 14 日通过了美国第一面正式国旗。目前，每逢是日，到处可见美国国旗迎风飘扬，全国各地都要举行纪念活动，以示对国旗的敬意。

4. Second Continental Congress 第二届大陆会议：大陆会议是 1774 年至 1789 年英属北美十三个殖民地以及后来美利坚合众国的立法机构，共举办了两届。1774 年 9 月 5 日到 10 月 26 日，在费城召开了殖民地联合会议，史称“第一届大陆会议”。 1775 年 5 月 10 日，第二届大陆会议在费城召开。与会议通过并且发布了《独立宣言》，正式宣布北美 13 个殖民地断绝与英国的隶属关系，成立“美利坚合众国”。

Unit 3　Religious Holidays

In America, some religious holidays are usually celebrated just by some specific ethnic groups, like Easter by Christians, Rosh Hashanah by Jews and Ramadan by Muslims.

Easter

Easter[1] is now a Christian holiday celebrating the Resurrection of Jesus Christ（耶稣基督复活）. However, the festival of Easter stretches back to pre-Christian times. In civil calendar, Easter is not a fixed holiday, which is established as the first Sunday after the full moon following the March equinox（昼夜平分点）. Some customs related to Easter are Easter parades, Easter egg decoration, egg hunting and Easter Bunny. And children will be given baskets of candy on this day.

Rosh Hashanah(哈桑纳节或犹太新年)

Rosh Hashanah is the Jewish New Year, which is usually celebrated in the early autumn of the Northern Hemisphere. It is a two-day celebration beginning on the first day of the **Tishrei**[2] , which most people believe the anniversary of the creation of Adam and Eve. Most typical customs on this day include sounding the shofar（羊角号）and eating some symbolic food such as apples dipped in honey, hoping a “sweet new year”.

Ramadan (斋月)

Ramadan is an Islamic holiday observed in the ninth month of the Islamic calendar. It is a one-month fasting（禁食的）for adult Muslims, except those who are ill, traveling, and pregnant and so on. For Muslims fasting is an activity of many rewards, and the rewards multiply on Ramadan. Some other typical activities are offering prayers and recitation of **Quran**[3]. Most Muslims do charity on Ramadan, which is a very important event for Islam.

Notes

1. Easter 复活节：纪念耶稣基督复活的节日，西方信基督教的国家都过这个节。在西方教会传统里，春分之后第一次满月之后的第一个星期日即为复活节。东方教会则规定，如果满月恰逢星期日，则复活节再推迟一周。因此，节期大致在 3 月 22 日至 4 月 25 日之间。复活节是最古老最有意义的基督教节日之一，庆祝的是基督的复活，世界各地的基督徒每年都要举行庆祝。复活节还象征重生和希望。

2. Tishrei 希伯来历：又称为“犹太历”，是以色列国目前使用的古老历法，是一种阴阳合历。每月以月相为准，和伊斯兰历一样，以新月初升为一月的开始，但设置闰月，使每年和太阳周期一致。以每年秋分后的第一个新月为一年的开始，设置闰月和中国农历一样，每11年4闰，但闰月统一放到闰年的第六个月之后。纪年以《圣经》中的上帝开始创造世界的第一个星期日为开始，犹太教徒认为是在公元前3760年，所以2004年9月27日为希伯来历5765年的开始。全世界的犹太教徒都依据希伯来历计算犹太教的节日。

3. Quran《古兰经》：伊斯兰教一部节文精确而详明的经典。伊斯兰教相信《古兰经》的原文在世界未创造之先早已存在天国，后由加百列天使启示穆罕默德才传至世间。穆罕默德从第一次得到启示（穆罕默德被安拉委为先知）到逝世的二十二年两个月又二十二天中，神的"圣言"逐章逐节不断地赐下来，由他口传给门徒。

Unit 4 Other Important Holidays

Although these are not official holidays, they are very popular among Americans.

Valentine's Day

Valentine's Day is also known as Saint Valentine's Day, a holiday observed on February 14th each year honoring the romantic love between lovers. It is believed that this holiday is in honor of Saint Valentine of Rome who was imprisoned for performing the marriage ceremonies for soldiers forbidden to marry. During his imprisonment, he fell in love with the jailer's daughter and cured her blindness. Before his execution, he signed "from your Valentine" in his last massage to her as a farewell. That's how the name came into being. Some of the popular Valentine's Day gifts are candy, chocolates, dinner, flowers and jewelry.

April Fools' Day

April Fools' Day, sometimes also April Fool's Day, is celebrated on the first day of April every year. Although it is not a holiday in its own right, it is a notable day celebrated in many countries on April 1st. It is also very popular among the Americans. On this day, people play practical jokes（恶作剧）on each other. April fools refer to the jokes and their victims.

Halloween

Halloween is celebrated on October 31st as both a secular and religious holiday. It is a holiday dedicated to the dead. Its origin is believed to be of pagan tradition, although many believe the Christian celebration came first. The story is about an Irishman name Jack who was sent to hell because of his stinginess with money. However, he was again kicked out of hell because he played tricks on the Devil. So he was made to walk on the earth forever. Many Halloween traditions come from a mixture of Christian and pagan traditions. Some of the typical Halloween activities include trick-or-treating, attending the costume parties, carving pumpkins into **Jack-o'-lanterns**[1] and telling scary stories, etc. On Halloween, children may choose to collect for charity.

Notes

1. Jack-o'-lantern 杰克南瓜灯：通常以甜菜或南瓜雕成一个有盖子和洞的灯笼，洞的图案通常是像怪物般的脸，在万圣节的时候放进点燃的蜡烛，吓走游魂。传说一个名叫杰克的人非常吝啬，因而死后不能进入天堂，而且因取笑恶魔也不能进入地狱，只能提着灯笼四处游荡，直到审判日那天。

References

[1] 朱岩岩，王泉 . 每天读点世界文化——这里是美国 [M]. 北京：中国水利水电出版社，2012.
[2] 陈宏俊，李险峰 . 英美文化体验 [M]. 北京：中国人民大学出版社 , 2008.
[3] 王晓红 . 美国社会与文化 [M]. 西安：世界图书出版社 , 2010.
[4] 王俊生，刘沛富 . 最新英美概况 . 北京：外语教学与研究出版社，2012.

Chapter Twenty-one

American Music

Unit 1 American Music Genres

Early African-American Music

1.Work Song

When the African slaves were transported to America, they were allowed to take the instruments, drums mostly, with them. Slaveholders, however, discovered that African slaves could use drums to communicate among themselves and by the 1700s, drums had been banned on many plantations. To ease the stress the hard work brought, the slaves often sang. A common feature of African American work songs was the call-and-response(前后呼应)format, where a leader would sing a verse and the others would respond to that.

The subject of the work songs varied according to the work the slaves were doing. Corn was a very common subject of work songs on a typical plantation because the crop was the main component of most Africans' diet. They would often sing about it regardless of whether it was being harvested.

2.The Negro Spiritual

One of the most widespread of early musical forms among southern blacks was the spiritual (黑人灵歌). Spirituals are generally Christian songs that were created by African slaves in the United States. Spirituals were originally an oral tradition that imparted Christian values while also describing the hardships of slavery. After their arrival at the New Land, slaves were forbidden from speaking their native languages, and were generally converted(皈依)to Christianity. Spirituals were a distinctly African American response to American conditions. It was neither black versions of white hymns(圣歌) nor transformations of songs from Africa, They expressed the longing of slaves for spiritual and bodily freedom, for safety from harm and evil, and for relief from the hardships of slavery.

3.Minstrel[1]

The Minstrel Show[1] began in the 1830s. White performers would blacken their faces with burnt cork or greasepaint(化妆用的油彩), dress up as plantation slaves, and then perform songs and skits that mocked African Americans. Thomas D Rice was one of the most popular minstrel show entertainers during that time. He is considered the "father of American minstrelsy".

On one hand, the Minstrel Show had strong racist aspects; on the other, it afforded white Americans a singular and broad awareness of what somc whites considered significant aspects of black culture in America. The Minstrel Show reached its zenith（顶峰）between 1850 and 1870, and then gradually disappeared from professional theaters.

Early Popular Music in America

1.March

A march is a piece of music with a strong regular rhythm which in origin was expressly written for marching to and most frequently performed by a military band. The March music era existed from 1850s to 1940s. Earlier marches tended to be part of a symphony or a movement in a suite. March music was originally used to play while the troops marched to battle, and that the reason why March music is a military's music. While the tradition of soldiers playing music marching into battle had ended soon after the American Civil War, military bands continued to perform marches during related ceremonies and other events. This actually became a whole new tradition of playing marched as a source of entertainment.

2.Ragtime[2]

Ragtime originated from African American music in the late 19th century. Ragtime became the first nationally popular form of American music in 1899, when **Scott Joplin**[3]'s "Maple Leaf Rag"(《枫树叶拉格泰姆》) enjoyed unprecedented success, selling over a million sheet-music copies. By the beginning of the 20th century, Ragtime music became widely popular throughout North America.

3.The Blues[4]

The Blues is perhaps the simplest American musical form and yet also the most versatile. Along with jazz, Blues takes its shape and style in the process of performance, and for this reason it possesses a high degree of flexibility. Although certain musical and lyrical elements of the Blues can be traced back to West Africa, the Blues, like the spiritual, is a product of slavery. No one can say for sure when and where the blues originated.

The Blues emerged towards the end of the 19th century. This early style of Blues was known as country blues（乡村布鲁斯）and was usually a solo singer accompanied on guitar or piano.

Until the end of the 19th century, America was largely a rural community. In the early twentieth century large numbers of people started to move to industrial cities. After the Civil War and emancipation of slaves the Blues spread, together with the people who sang and played it. Many former slaves moved from the southern states to northern cities such as Chicago and Detroit, where the Blues became hugely popular.

Different styles of blues emerged, known collectively as city Blues（城市布鲁斯）or urban Blues. During the 1940s and 1950s city Blues was very popular in black clubs and bars. Some of these Blues styles were jazz influenced and many had amplified bands.

4.The Rise of Jazz

Jazz, which has been called "America's classical music", is perhaps the most creative and complex music the nation has produced. Although no one can say for sure where the origins of jazz lie, it combines the musical traditions of black New Orleans with the creative flexibility of the Blues.

Three cities had great importance on the development of jazz: jazz originated from African American communities of New Orleans in the United States during the late 19th and early 20th centuries. Due to social changes in the country, many jazz musicians and musician industries moved to Chicago at the beginning of the 20th century, which made jazz flourished in the city. This period was usually called "Jazz Age" in American history. At the beginning of 1930s, New York City began to lead the development of jazz after the Great Depression, and brought jazz to a new era.

As jazz spread around the world, it was affected by different national, reginal and local musical cultures, which gave rise to many distinctive styles. Well-known styles include cool jazz（冷爵士）、hard bop（硬波普）、the Third Stream（"第三潮流"爵士）and free jazz（自由爵士）.

Modern Popular Music in America

1.Country Music[5]

American country music, also known as country western music, has a very long history. It originated in the Southern United States in the 1920s. Country music uses simple music and words to express everyday feelings such as loneliness, love, and sadness. That is to say, country music describes life. It is believed that country music, comes from two kinds of music. One is the traditional music of the people in the Appalachian Mountains in the eastern United States. The other is traditional cowboy music from the west. The singers usually play guitars, and in the 1920s they started using electric guitars. At first city people said country music was low class. It was popular mostly in the South. But during World War II, thousands of Southerners went to the Northeast and Midwest to work in the factories. They took their music with them. Soldiers from the rest of the country went to army camps in the South. They learned country music. Slowly it became popular all over the country.

The most successful country-music singer now in America is Taylor Swift. She is known for narrative songs about her personal experiences. As a songwriter, she has been honored by the Nashville Songwriters Association（纳什维尔作曲家协会）and the Songwriters Hall of Fame（创作人名人堂）. Swift's other achievements include ten Grammy Awards（格莱美奖）, one Emmy Award（艾美奖）, twenty two Billboard Music Awards（公告牌音乐奖）, eleven Country Music Association Awards（乡村音乐协会奖）, eight Academy of Country Music Awards（乡村音乐学院奖）, and one Brit Award（全英音乐奖）. She is one of the best-selling artists of all time.

2.Rock and Roll[6]

Originating in the United States during the late 1940s and early 1950s, Rock and Roll, is characterized by electronically amplified instrumentation, a heavily accented beat, and relatively simple phrase structure and youth-oriented lyrics. It's a form of popular music arising from and incorporating a variety of musical styles, especially rhythm and blues, country music and gospel.

Rock and roll influenced people's lifestyles, fashion, attitudes, and language. Many early rock and roll songs dealt with issues of cars, school, dating, and clothing. The lyrics of rock and roll songs described events and conflicts that most listeners could relate to through personal experience. Topics such as sex that had generally been considered taboo began to appear in rock and roll lyrics. This new music tried to break boundaries and express emotions that people were actually feeling but had not talked about. An awakening began to take place in American youth culture.

Well-known rock and roll singer include **Elvis Presley**[7]（猫王）, **Madonna Ciccone**[8] and **Michael Jackson**[9].

3.Disco

Disco is a kind of dance music containing elements of funk, soul, pop, and salsa. It achieved popularity during the mid-1970s to the early 1980s. The term is derived from discothèque, which means "library of phonograph records" in French, but it was subsequently used as a term for nightclubs in Paris Disco can be seen as a reaction against both the domination of rock music and the stigmatization（责难）of dance music by the counterculture during this period. It was popular with both men and women, from many different backgrounds.

4.Punk[10]

Punk, or punk rock, is a rock music genre that developed between 1974 and 1976 in the United States. It is characterized by harsh lyrics attacking conventional society and popular culture, and often expressing alienation（疏离）and anger. Punk rock goes against stereotyping（刻板印象）, which would be the conventional society and popular.

5.Reggae[11]

Reggae is a kind of popular music that is originally from Jamaica and that combines native styles with elements of rock and soul music. The subject of Reggae usually relates news, social gossip, and political comment. Reggae incorporates some of the musical elements of rhythm and blues, jazz, **mento**[12]（门特）, African music, as well as other genres.

6.Soul[13]

Soul refers to the music that originated in black American gospel singing, is closely related to rhythm and blues, and is characterized by intensity of feeling and earthiness（质朴）. Catchy（容易记住的）rhythms stressed by handclaps and plastic body moves, are an important feature. Other characteristics are a call and response between the soloist and the chorus, and an especially tense vocal sound.

7.Rap[14]

Rap is the most complex and influential form of hip-hop culture, combining elements of the African American musical tradition（blues, jazz, and soul）with Caribbean music and dance-hall reggae. Rap's subject matter varies. Many rappers tell tragic tales of decaying neighborhoods, vicious(恶意的)murders, and police brutality. Others celebrate black history, black families, and black communities, or they brag of their successes in the bedroom, on the streets, and in the record studio.

Notes

1. the Minstrel Show 化妆黑人游唱剧：出现于19世纪二三十年代，这种游唱剧是由白人喜剧演员用软木塞烧成的炭把脸涂黑，称为"黑脸歌手"(Negro Minstrelsy)，他们装扮成黑人，专门表演黑人、模仿黑人生活、演唱带黑人味的歌曲。

2. Ragtime 拉格泰姆音乐：一种美国流行音乐。它把非洲音乐节奏的基本元素引入流行音乐，为爵士乐的兴起创造了条件。拉格泰姆主要由钢琴弹奏，钢琴家用左手弹出稳定均匀的重音节奏，用右手弹出切分音旋律，对通常情况下的弱拍加以强调。这种夹杂着弱拍节奏、切分音不断进行的音乐情绪热烈，很有感染力。

3. Scott Joplin 斯考特·乔普林：斯考特·乔普林(1869—1917)是美国拉格泰姆音乐家中最著名的一位，被称为"拉格泰姆之王"。1899年乔普林出版了乐曲《枫树叶拉格泰姆》，深受大众欢迎，他本人也因此名声大振。

4. the Blues 蓝调：为爵士、摇滚及福音歌曲(Gospel)的老祖宗，原本只是美国早期黑奴抒发心情时所吟唱的12小节曲式，演唱或演奏时大量蓝调音的应用，使得音乐上充满了压抑及不和谐的感觉，这种音乐听起来十分忧郁。但就是这么一股"反骨"气息，使得它后来在叛逆的摇滚乐中发扬光大。蓝调以歌曲直接陈述内心想法的表现方式，与当时白人社会的音乐截然不同。

5. country music 乡村音乐：一种具有美国民族特色的流行音乐，于20世纪20年代兴起于美国南部，其根源来自英国民谣，是美国白人民族音乐代表。乡村音乐的特点是曲调简单，节奏平稳，带有叙事性，具有较浓的乡土气息，亲切热情而不失流行元素。多为歌谣体、二部曲式或三部曲式。

6. Rock and Roll 摇滚乐：兴起于20世纪50年代中期，主要受到节奏布鲁斯、乡村音乐和叮砰巷音乐的影响发展而来。早期摇滚乐很多都是黑人节奏布鲁斯的翻唱版，因而节奏布鲁斯是其主要根基。摇滚乐分支众多，形态复杂，主要风格有：民谣摇滚、艺术摇滚、迷幻摇滚、乡村摇滚、重金属、朋克等，代表人物有：埃尔维斯·普莱斯利(猫王)、鲍勃·迪伦、披头士乐队、滚石乐队等，是20世纪美国大众音乐走向成熟的重要标志。

7. Elvis Presley 埃尔维斯·普莱斯利：埃尔维斯·普莱斯利(1935—1977)，是20世纪50年代最有名的摇滚乐歌手，是他把摇滚乐推广到整个社会，人们称他为"摇滚乐之王"，绰号"猫王"。

8. Madonna 麦当娜·西科尼：1958年8月16日出生于美国密歇根州底特律，美国女歌手、演员。1983年，麦当娜出版了首张以她名字命名的专辑*Madonna*。1984年，麦当娜的第二张专辑*Like a Virgin*发行，随后开始了她的第一次巡回演出。1991年1月，麦当娜在第18届全美音乐奖中，以一曲*VOGUE*赢得最受欢迎舞曲奖。1997年，麦当娜因出演《贝隆夫人》获得金球奖最佳音乐剧女演员奖。2003年4月，麦当娜推出*American Life*，9月出版童话《英国玫瑰》，11 月出版第二部童话《皮伯迪先生的苹果》。2008 年 3 月，麦当娜入选美国“摇滚名人堂”。2012 年 1 月，麦当娜凭借 *W.E* 获得第 69 届金球奖最佳电影原创歌曲奖。

9. Michael Jackson 迈克尔 · 杰克逊：1958 年 8 月 29 日在美国印第安纳州加里市出生，美国歌手、词曲创作人、舞蹈家、表演家、慈善家、音乐家、人道主义者、和平主义者、慈善机构创办人。杰克逊一生中两次入选摇滚名人堂，获得了 13 个格莱美奖和 26 个全美音乐奖。在他单飞生涯中，他拥有 13 支美国冠军单曲。2000 年吉尼斯世界纪录大全里认证他资助过 39 个慈善机构。

10. punk 朋客摇滚乐：最原始的摇滚乐。由一个简单悦耳的主旋律和三个和弦组成。其变化在于朋克摇滚将过去的旧式摇滚演奏得更快速更激昂。朋克摇滚是起源于 1974—1976 年的美国、英国、澳洲，是摇滚乐的分支音乐类型，有“反社会原则”的特色。伦敦的性手枪（Sex Pistols）、冲击合唱团；纽约的雷蒙斯合唱团（Ramones）被视为朋克摇滚的先锋。

11. Reggae 雷鬼音乐：一种由斯卡（Ska）和洛克斯代迪（Rock Steady）音乐演变而来的牙买加流行音乐，也译“雷吉”。事实上，很难在洛克斯代迪和雷鬼音乐之间划出明确的界限。只是后者较前者更为细腻，更多地使用电声乐器和更加国际化。如果说斯卡音乐还只是在美国流行音乐的影响下产生的一种拉美流行音乐的话，那么雷鬼则已发展成为欧美摇滚乐主流中的一种重要的载体了。

12. mento 门特：牙买加当地的传统民间音乐，由四方巡游的教士运用吉他、土制手鼓和钢片琴，即兴创作的一些讽刺性的小调。

13. soul 灵歌：北美黑人的宗教礼拜歌曲。内容大多反映黑人遭受残酷奴役、痛苦无告、只好把希望寄托在宗教上的悲惨处境。用英语演唱，其旋律朴素，多数为五声大调式（如《溜回去》《没有人知道我的痛苦》《下来，可爱的马车》）或七声小调式（如《去吧、摩西》《钉十字架》），富于切分节奏，和声近似美国基督教会的赞美诗。由于经常即兴演唱，几乎没有定谱可以遵循。南北战争后，由于菲斯克大学黑人歌唱团等黑人歌手的传播，作为美国最有代表性的黑人民歌而闻名于世，并成为爵士音乐的重要素材。北美白人演唱的民间赞美诗，亦称灵歌。

14. Rap 说唱乐：曾经是 20 世纪 90 年代初风靡欧美的一种音乐流派。那时的说唱乐在 MC.Hammer、Vanillalce 等艺人的大力推广下，加上 MTV 的推波助澜，一时间风光无限。但随后由于 Grunge、Britpop 等音乐的崛起，Rap 被打入冷宫，也曾有人预言 Rap 将会就此消亡。但是 Rap 在新世纪再度成了乐坛的热门。

Unit 2 Music Awards and Festivals in America

Grammy Awards[1]

The Grammy Awards recognizes the yearly achievements of the music industry. The awards are presented by the National Academy of Recording Arts and Sciences (NARAS) and feature performances by the year's most prominent musicians. Award winners are chosen by voting members of the Academy. For most awards, members are only permitted to vote in their areas of expertise.

First awarded in 1959, the awards aimed to recognize artists who may never earn a star on Hollywood Boulevard. The four most popular Award categories include Album of the Year, Record of the Year, Song of the Year and Best New Artist. In total, there are more than 80 different categories, in which an artist may receive one or more awards. This event is usually held in late January or early February every year.

American Music Awards[2]

The American Music Awards (AMAs) is an annual American music awards show. The awards are determined by a poll of the public and fans, who can vote through the AMAs website. And that is the reason that AMAs are considered as the business indicators of the mainstream music. The hosts are usually famous singers or actors. The AMAs have held in November since 2003 to nominate the works released between December 1st of the previous year and September 1st of the current year. The record for most American Music Awards won is held by Michael Jackson, who has won 26 awards.

Billboard Music Awards[3]

The Billboard Music Award is an honor given by Billboard, a publication and music popularity chart covering the music business. The Billboard Music Awards show had been held annually since 1989 in December until it went dormant in 2006. The awards returned in 2011 and are held annually in May. Current award categories include Top Artist, Top Billboard 200 Album, Top Hot 100 Song and Top New Artist.

MTV Video Music Awards[4]

The MTV Video Music Awards (VMA) is an annual award show that seeks to honor achievements in the music video industry. Conceptualized(概念化) by MTV, the show has been hosted by MTV since its inception in 1984. The ceremony is usually televised live from either a venue in Los Angeles or New York, however the event has also been held in Miami and Las Vegas. Current award categories include Video of the Year, Best Male Video, Best Female Video and the Michael Jackson Video Vanguard Award for lifetime achievement. Although the nomination and award selection process has not been made transparent by MTV, viewers and fans are encouraged to vote for their favorite nominees within each category. Once announced, the winner of each category is rewarded with a symbolic VMA moon man trophy. The VMA awards are not held on a specific calendar day but rather on a Sunday in late August or early September as decided by MTV.

Country Music Association Awards[5]

The Country Music Association Awards（CMAs）, presented annually in October or November, are considered the most prestigious awards in the country-music industry. Voting is limited to current CMA members, who select winners in a two-round balloting（投票）process. Current award categories include Entertainer, Male Vocalist, Female Vocalist, New Artist, Vocal Group, Vocal Duo, Single, Album, Song, Musical Event, and Musician.

South by Southwest Music Festival[6]

The South by Southwest Music Festival is one of the largest and most influential global music events of the year, taking place every March in Austin, Texas—the Live Music Capital of the World. The music event has grown from 700 registrants in 1987 to over 28,000 registrants.

South by Southwest Music Festival is one of the three components of the South by Southwest（SXSW）, with the other two components SXSW film and SXSW interactive.

Bonnaroo

The Bonnaroo Music Festival（波纳若音乐节）is held in Manchester, Tennessee at the beginning of the summer season each year. Hosting over 125 bands and comedy acts over four days, the Bonnaroo Music Festival is one of the country's largest music and arts gatherings. The music festival invites fans to set up camp on a large farm south of Nashville, Tennessee for four days of live music, dancing, food, entertainment and networking.

The first Bonnaroo Music Festival was held in 2002 to showcase the talents of emerging and popular artists, performers and comedians. Since then, the festival has grown to become one of the largest music and camping events in the country and is the only round-the-clock music festival in the United States. In 2008, Rolling Stone magazine called the Bonnaroo Music Festival "the ultimate over-the-top summer festival".

Summerfest

Summerfest is "The World's Largest Music Festival", which was certified by the Guinness World Records in 1999. Each year Summerfest attracts 800,000 to 1,000,000 people to come to Milwaukee, Wisconsin, where the festival is held. The festival lasts for 11 days, and it is made up of 11 stages with performances from over 700 bands, and since the mid-1970s the festival has run from late June through early July, usually including the 4th of July, the National Day.

Lollapalooza(拉帕鲁扎音乐)

Lollapalooza is one festival featuring alternative rock, hip hop, and punk rock bands, dance and comedy performances, and craft booths. It has also provided a platform for non-profit and political groups. Lollapalooza has featured a diverse range of bands and has helped expose and popularize alternative groups.

Since its inception, Lollapalooza has its great success and decline, revival and rebirth. It has debut outside of the United State, and begun its international expansion since 2011, with a branch of festivals staged in countries like Chile, Brazil, Argentina, and Germany.

Notes

1. Grammy Awards 格莱美奖：简称"Grammys"，美国录音界与世界音乐界最重要的音乐奖项之一，由国家录音艺术与科学学院（National Academy of Recording Arts and Sciences, NARAS）颁发。学院由录音业的专业人士所组成，目的在于奖励过去一年中业界出色的成就。格莱美奖是美国四个主要音乐奖之一（另三个为公告牌音乐奖、全美音乐奖和摇滚名人堂收录典礼）。格莱美奖每年 2 月颁发。

2. American Music Awards 全美音乐奖：简称"AMA"，它是美国最富盛名的音乐颁奖礼之一，由迪克・克拉克创办于 1973 年，与格莱美奖、公告牌音乐奖一起被称为美国三大颁奖礼。由于它的评审方式的特殊性，它被认为是最能代表主流音乐的商业指标。

3. Billboard Music Awards 公告牌音乐奖：简称"BMA"，是由美国知名音乐杂志《公告牌》主办的音乐奖。其中最重要的排行榜为公告牌单曲榜（Billboard Hot 100）（单曲排行）与 Billboard 200（专辑排行）。在 2007 年停办，于 2011 年 5 月恢复重办。

4. MTV Video Music Awards 音乐录影带大奖：简称"VMA" 也称"MTV 音乐电视大奖"。音乐录影带大奖是美国的音乐奖项之一，创办于 1984 年夏末，其目的是表彰那些最受人喜爱的 MV。举办过 VMA 的地点包括纽约，洛杉矶，迈阿密和拉斯维加斯。VMA 于每年的 7 月 1 日开始资格审查，8 月末到 9 月中旬之间颁奖，而奖杯是宇航员在月球上的雕像。

5. Country Music Association Awards 美国乡村音乐协会奖：由美国乡村和西部音乐学院于 1964 年在洛杉矶创办，其宗旨是在美国西部地区推广乡村音乐。1965 年颁发了第一届乡村音乐协会奖。乡村音乐协会奖是美国乡村音乐界的风向标，能够获奖的乡村音乐人都是在过去的一年里在乡村音乐方面取得不俗成绩的艺人，他们的作品可以代表和引领美国乡村音乐的潮流走向。乡村音乐学院奖奖项有：年度艺人、年度歌曲、年度单曲录音、年度专辑、最佳男歌手、最佳女歌手、最佳二重唱、最佳组合、最佳新人、年度音乐录音带、年度音乐事件、年代艺人。

6. South by Southwest Music Festival 美国南部及西南音乐节："SXSW" 是英文（西南边的南边，这是得州的地理位置）的简写。这是一个每年都在美国得克萨斯州（Texas）举办的可能是世界上规模最大的音乐盛典。每年都有来自世界各地的上千万的音乐人，乐队报名参加。所有大小唱片公司及媒体都会派代表到场，在一千多场演出之间奔波。很多还没有被签约的乐队，也希望能借他们在这里演出，吸引媒体、唱片公司的注意力。

Unit 3 Music Education in America

Music has been taught to students in the United States for a long time. Music education can actually be traced back to the colonial era, when the European immigrants settled down on the new land and brought the European music tradition with them.

In 1717, the first American singing school（歌咏学校）was found in Boston, Massachusetts. In the following two decades of the century, more singing schools, formal or informal, were founded in the cities. The singing schools mainly focused on helping students develop skills in reading music and singing in religious celebrations, for the Puritans in New England praised God through the singing of psalms（赞美诗）.

Public education in the United States first offered music as part of the curriculum in Boston in the 1830s. With the help of **Lowell Mason**[1], a singing teacher and the founder of **Boston Academy of Music**[2]（波士顿音乐学院）**,** the Boston School Committee ultimately pushed for music to be included as part of the syllabus（教学大纲）. In the years that followed, music education became part of the school curriculum for all ages of students, and the city of Boston became the prime example of music education nationwide.

By the early 1900s, colleges that offered degrees spanning four years included music in their programs. The **Oberlin Conservatory**[3] in Ohio was the first to offer a full Bachelor's degree in Music Education. Aside from the Music Education Degree, many notable events that would firmly plant music in the educational system of the United States also happened during this time.

Music Education in the United States took a big turn with the creation of the Music Supervisors National Conference, which was officially established in 1910 at Cincinnati, Ohio. The Music Supervisor's National Conference was started to promote the study and teaching of music. And the name was changed to Music Educators National Conference（MENC）. The purpose of MENC was for mutual helpfulness and the promotion of good music through the instrumentality（部门，机构）of the public schools, although MENC does not define "good music". During World War I MENC promoted community singing and patriotic music and advocated "music for every child" for a democratic society. With the World War II MENC promoted "American Unity through Music", trained community song leaders, and again pursued patriotic motives of music for a democratic society. In the following decades, through 1960s to the beginning of 1990s, MENC kept contributing to the development of music education through symposiums and publications.

The rise of music taught in high schools also encouraged students to create marching bands and school orchestras or other musical groups. One of the most valuable progressions was made when a teacher, **Frances Elliott Clark**[4], won the approval to use phonographs and music libraries in schools. Music appreciation became popular with the use of phonograph records, radio programs and young people's concerts by symphony orchestras（交响乐团）. Many universities and colleges also started to offer endowments, grants and scholarships to promising music students.

During the second half of 20th century, several symposiums（讨论会）were organized through the decades to discuss the methodology（方法论）and effectiveness of how music was taught. The federal government played a large role in funding music education projects included the Yale Seminar(耶鲁研讨班) on Music Education and the Juilliard Repertory Project(茱莉亚音乐文库计划).

Yale Seminar was one of the first conferences on arts education that were funded by the federal government. It took place at Yale University, June 17th-28th, 1963. Musicians, musicologists (音乐学家)and music teachers from different places to the conference to consider the problems music education was facing and to propose possible solutions. The Seminar held that students in America had been underestimated under the existing curriculum in the schools, due to the lack of creativity and artistic values of the curricula. To solve those problems, Juilliard School of Music (茱莉亚音乐学院)applied for a grant from the U.S. Office of Education to develop a large body of authentic(真正的)and meaningful music materials to argument and enrich the repertory available to music teachers in the early grades. The grant was approved and the Project was established in July 1964, with Giannini as director. The purpose of the Project was to collect music of high quality. The repertory was compiled by three groups: musicologists, music educators, and public elementary school music teachers.

Following Yale Seminar, organized and sponsored by MENC, the Tanglewood Symposium (坦格伍德研讨会) was held in 1967 in Tanglewood, Massachusetts. The purpose was to define the role of music education in contemporary American society and to make recommendations to improve the effectiveness of music instruction. At the Symposium, music educators agreed to statements promoting music of all styles and cultures, the use of technology, solutions to problems of the inner city, and programs to prepare teachers to teach courses in the humanities and related arts. Tanglewood Symposium was the largest-scale academic conference in the history of American music education.

In 2007, the second Tanglewood Symposium was held at Boston University to examine the progress of music education over the last forty years. During this symposium, a declaration was drafted to detail priorities in music education for the next four decades. Music educators from around the world were present to chime in on the value of music and how it is taught to students.

Modern music education in America has matured both in curriculum and teaching methods. Elementary schools in the United States typically offer music classes several times a week, with classes ranging from thirty to forty-five minutes in length. Beginning in about fourth grade, performance opportunities are often provided in the form of choirs or orchestral (especially wind) bands. Music is generally optional in high school in the United States, and may or may not be required in middle or junior high school. Concert bands and marching bands are also commonly offered, as are choirs and theatrical performances that often include music.

Notes

1. Lowell Mason 洛厄尔·梅森: 洛厄尔·梅森(1792—1872),美国音乐教育家、作曲家,1832年创办了"波士顿音乐学院"。后为波士顿公立学校编审音乐教材并出版音乐杂志。以音乐教育家的身份来说,梅森是美国近代音乐发展史上最重要的人物,被称为美国学校音乐教育之父。1855 年纽约大学赠他"荣誉音乐博士"学位，为接受美国大学授予是项学位的第一人。

2. Boston Academy of Music 波士顿音乐学院：于 1867 年建校，自建校之日起，波士顿音乐学校的天份、聪明、创造性与整个波士顿城市、整个地区、乃至整个国家共成长、共繁荣。如今，那里已经成为一个为国家甚至世界培养演员、艺术家、音乐家、教育家的摇篮。她已经发展成熟，并不断吐故纳新，为学生的未来发展鞠躬尽瘁，她成为了一颗明珠。波士顿音乐学院（波士顿）因提供综合性学习环境而闻名，可授予硕士学位和学士学位。学士学位课程主要有：应用课程、铜管乐器、室内乐和协作、谱曲、指挥、合奏、通俗音乐、吉他、竖琴、音乐的历史、音乐理论、敲打乐器、声音和歌剧、木管乐器、琴、营养学、芭蕾学技巧、演艺实习等。硕士学位课程：应用课程、铜管乐器、室内乐和协作、谱曲、剧本、剧院曲目、文化前景及剧院、表演、爵士、芭蕾、敲打乐器、声音和歌剧等。

3. Oberlin Conservatory 欧柏林音乐学院：欧柏林音乐学院位于美国俄亥俄州，是美国最古老的坚持运作的音乐学院。欧柏林也是唯一一所音乐与文理学院紧密结合的大学。每年有 500 多场音乐会，其交响乐团也享誉全美。欧柏林的座右铭是"Learning and Labor"，体现了欧柏林将学习与现实结合的灵活教育。欧柏林的口号则是"We are Oberlin, fearless（我们欧柏林，勇往无惧）"，是美国第一所授予音乐教育学士学位的院校。

4. Frances Elliott Clark 弗朗西丝·埃利奥特·拉克：弗朗西丝·埃利奥特·拉克（1860—1958）是美国最早倡导"音乐欣赏"的教育者之一。

References

[1] BRYAN K M. Survey of American music[M]. 2nd ed. Purina: Kendall Hunt Pub Co, 2005.

[2] MARK M, GARY C. A history of American music education[M]. Lanham: Rowman & Littlefield Education, 2007.

[3] KINGMAN D. American music: a panorama[M]. San Francisco: Wadsworth Publishing, 1990.

[4] PELLS R H. Modernist America: art, music, movies and the globalization of American culture[M]. New Haven: Yale University Press, 2012.

[5] The history of African American music[EB/OL]. African-American Years: Chronologies of American History and Experience，2013.[2016-05-22] . http://www.encyclopedia.com.

[6] 何平 . 走进美国音乐：一个美国音乐文化的历史透析 [M]. 广州：华南理工大学出版社，2008.

[7] 邵怀宇 . 美国好莱坞与现代音乐 [M]. 北京：北京大学出版社，2001.

[8] 杨会军 . 列国志 (美国)[M]，北京：社会科学文献出版社，2015.

[9] 周静琼 . 当代美国概况 [M]. 上海：上海外语教育出版社，2003.

[10] 伯克霍尔德 . 美洲各国的音乐及其历史的叙述 [J]. 中央音乐学院学报 , 2011(3)：119-121.

[11] 王媛媛 . 美国音乐教育发展简介和几点启示 [J]. 科教文汇，2006(4)：78-80.

Chapter Twenty-two

American Car Culture

America is a country on wheels. American culture of the 20th century is almost unthinkable without the car. Its impact has been of truly seismic proportions. The automobiles' impact on American life is everywhere, for the car is much more than a means for traveling from one place to another. They are an important part of American society and culture. They influence where Americans live and how they live. American society and culture have been changed by the car culture. What cars gave Americans is the ability to travel as fast and as far as trains but with the freedom to go wherever and whenever they want.

Unit 1 The Development of the Car Culture

Early Years

The American car culture began to develop rapidly when **Henry Ford**[1] started to sell a car called the Ford Model T in 1908. The Model T was inexpensive, rugged and reliable. Before this, automobiles were considered fussy toys for the rich and famous for their cost and impracticality made them inaccessible for the average citizens. With the Model T, Americans who had previously been unable to afford a car were for the first time able to buy one.

The Great Depression and Wartime: 1929 to 1950

At the start of the Great Depression, auto production was at an all-time high. In 1929, the year of the stock market crash, the auto industry was still primarily made up of many small companies. By the end of the Great Depression, one-half to one-third of these companies had failed or were taken over by competitors. In the US, the "**Big Three**[2]", General Motors, Ford, and Chrysler, emerged as a formidable force in the auto industry and enjoyed significant advantages over the smaller independent auto companies due to their financial strength, which gave them a big edge in marketing, production, and technological innovation.

World War II brought a period of great economic growth to the auto industry and the world. Car companies produced vehicles for the military, and this production gave rise to the reintroduction of technologies like headlights and front-wheel drive. World War II somehow forced the growth of this industry.

Automobiles Take Over: 1950 to 1980

Development of the freeway system began in the 1920s, but freeway development really took off during the 1950s. After WW Ⅱ, a massive plan was launched to build a system of interstate highways in the United States. Americans call these interstate highway "freeway" because they are free to drive on. Americans instantly fell in love with their highways, and these highways helped the car culture grow. Individuals began to see the automobiles as an extension of themselves. The American interstate highway system is now the largest in the world.

The **Oil Shock**[3] of the 1970s also briefly influences the auto industry. Small fuel-efficient cars from foreign automobiles took a sharply higher share of the U.S. auto sales market. For a time, car makers worked to improve the fuel efficiency of their vehicles. The customers also began to take the car's fuel efficiency as a considering point when they purchase a car. However, when fuel became affordable again, consumer priorities shifted back towards powerful comfortable vehicles that could seat several passengers.

Recent Years: 1980 to Present Day

During the last few decades, safety has become a major priority for auto manufactures and car consumers. Development like air bags, antilock brakes, and seat belt pretensions have made cars safer than ever. Additionally, large recalls from a number of manufactures placed greater public emphasis on safety. By the mid-1980s, oil prices had fallen sharply, helping lead to the revitalization of the American auto industry. During the 1990s and early 2000s, vehicles were large and powerful. Consumers wanted cars that could transport large amount of cargo and many passengers. In recent years, historically high fuel prices have caused consumers to change their priorities, and fuel-efficient vehicles are powerful.

With the increased emphasis on fuel economy, many car companies began to produce alternative fuel vehicles. Options range from hybrids like the **TOYOTA**[4] Prius to plug-in vehicles and cars that burn bio-diesel or natural gas.

Notes

1. Henry Ford 亨利·福特： 亨利·福特（1863 年 7 月 30 日—1947 年 4 月 8 日），美国汽车工程师与企业家，福特汽车公司的建立者。他也是世界上第一位使用流水线大批量生产汽车的人。他的生产方式使汽车成为一种大众产品，它不但革命了工业生产方式，而且对现代社会和文化起了巨大的影响。美国学者麦克·哈特所著的《影响人类历史进程的 100 名人排行榜》一书中，亨利·福特是唯一上榜的企业家。

2. Big Three 美国汽车业三巨头： 指福特汽车公司（Ford），通用汽车公司（GM）和克莱斯勒汽车公司（Chrysler）。

3. Oil Shock 石油危机： 又称"Oil Crisis"，为世界经济或各国经济受到石油价格的变化，所产生的经济危机。1960 年 12 月石油输出国组织（OPEC）成立，主要成员包括伊朗、伊拉克、科威特、沙特阿拉伯和南美洲的委内瑞拉等国，而石油输出国组织也成为世界上控制石油价格的关键组织。迄今被公认的三次石油危机，分别发生在1973年、1979年和1990年。

4. TOYOTA 日本丰田汽车公司： 世界十大汽车工业公司之一，日本最大的汽车公司，创立于1933年，现在已发展成为以汽车生产为主，业务涉及机械、电子、金融等行业的庞大工业集团。丰田公司早期以制造纺织机械为主，创始人丰田喜一郎1933年在纺织机械制作所设立汽车部，从而开始了丰田汽车公司制造汽车的历史。1935年，丰田AI型汽车试制成功，第二年即正式成立汽车工业公司。但在整个20世纪30年代和40年代该公司发展缓慢，只是到了二战之后，丰田汽车公司才加快了发展步伐。它们通过引进欧美技术，在美国的汽车技术专家和管理专家的指导下，很快掌握了先进的汽车生产和管理技术，并根据日本民族的特点，创造了著名的丰田生产管理模式，并不断加以完善提高，大大提高了工厂生产效率和产品。汽车在本世纪60年代末即大量涌入北美市场。1972年，该公司累计生产汽车1 000万辆。

Unit 2 Culture Icons Generating with Cars' Development

Suburbanization

Suburbanization can be linked to a number of different factors, but the development of cars would definitely be the most important one. With inexpensive cars and the gasoline and free highways after World War Ⅱ, Americans began to move out of cities with lower quality of life caused by industry, and live in the suburbs which were being built outside the major cities. In the suburbs they could have their own detached houses with yards, gardens and garages for their cars instead of living in apartments in the cities and taking public transportation or walking. In a process called "White Flight", white people who had sufficient money left cities for the new white suburbs while poorer minorities and immigrants were left in the increasingly crowded, polluted and decaying center of cities.

People living in the suburbs are called "suburbanites". They drive their cars every day. Cars take them to work, to school, to church, for shopping and for entertainment. Suburbs have huge shopping centers with vast parking areas that draw people out from the cities to do their shopping. Americans love the freedom that their cars give them. They can live in the quiet countryside or in suburban areas, drive to work and go wherever and whenever they want in their cars.

The Drive-ins

A wide of variety of drive-in and drive-through businesses were developed to serve people in their cars in America. The drive-ins became popular places where young people could have something to eat and hang out with their friends.

Drive-in restaurants, where customers park their cars, order their food from inside their cars, and then eat their food in their cars, were very common in the United States.

A **drive-in theater**[1], on the other hand, usually consist a large outdoor movie screen, a projection booth, a concession stand and a large parking area for automobiles. Within this enclosed area, customers can view movies from the privacy and comfort of their cars. Drive-in theaters were quite popular for a time, but are very rare now. One of the largest drive-in theaters was in Copiague, Long Island, New York. Covering over 29 acres, it could park 2,500 vehicles. It had a full-service restaurant with seating on the roof, and a trolley system to take children and adults to a playground and a large indoor theater for bad weather or for those who wanted to watch in air-conditioned comfort.

There are also many types of drive-through services in America where one can pull up their car to a window, conduct their business, and then drive away. It is quite common to find banks, coffee shops and restaurants that offer drive-through services. In Las Vegas, there is even a drive-through wedding chapel where couples can get married in their car.

The Motels

A motor hotel, or motel for short (also known as motor inn, motor court, motor lodge, tourist lodge, cottage court, auto camps, or tourist home), is a hotel designed for motorists, and usually has a parking area for motor vehicles. As the provincial highways and the United States highway system began to develop in the 1920s, long-distance road journeys became more common, and the need for inexpensive, easily accessible overnight accommodation sited close to the main routes led to the growth of the motel concept. Motels peaked in popularity in the 1960s with rising car travel, only to decline in response to competition from the newer chain hotels which became commonplace at highway interchanges as traffic was bypassed onto newly constructed freeways.

The Auto-heroes on the Screen

Cars began to pervade American culture, not only on the streets and in local drive-ins, but in entertainment as well. In movies, the cars were often a combination of character and car.

In 2001, Universal Pictures released ***Fast & Furious***[2]. It was a movie full of car-racing, car stunts and of course different famous brand cars. The hot music, hip clothes and flashy cars gave the film a uniquely broad appeal. After the first success, five more *Fast & Furious* series of movies were released one by one in the following years. Each of them got high reputation from all over the world. Everyone could appreciate the high-performance automobiles, even if you were not a car enthusiast. *Fast & Furious* series of films sparked a whole new generation of auto enthusiasts anxious to put their tuning skills to the test.

Transformers[3] was the only film that sets the cars as the main characters through the film history. The prototypes of these transformers were all best-selling cars in USA. For example, Barricade's prototype was Ford Mustang, which was such a popular car that many American boys' dream was to own one Ford Mustang. Some prototypes also revealed the development of cars.

The prototype of Bumblebee was Chevrolet Camano Z28 at first, which was released by GM in 1974. It was old-fashioned, shabby and the hero didn't like it. Afterwards, the car scanned other Chevrolet and turned into a concept car of **Chevrolet**[4] released in 2010. Another Chevrolet in this movie was the prototype of Jolt, which was Chevrolet volt, a hybrid-electric car. Due to the oil price and environment situation, the motor companies are engaged in developing new clean energy powered cars, and Chevrolet volt is a good example.

School Bus

Due to the huge amount of cars in America, traffic safety becomes a major priority to Americans, which could be seen from their school bus. Since the first development of consistent school bus standards in 1939, many of the ensuing changes to school buses over the past 75 years have been safely related, particularly in response to more stringent regulations adopted by state and federal governments.

Yellow School Bus. Yellow was adopted as a standard color of American school bus decades ago. The color which became known as "school bus yellow" was selected because black lettering on that specific hue was easiest to see in the semi-darkness of early morning and late afternoon.

Traffic Priority. All the U.S. States have some sort of school bus traffic stop laws requiring motorists to stop for school buses while children are loading and unloading.

Safety Devices. In addition to the entry door, all school buses have at least one emergency exit door in the rear of the bus. Some states as well as some school districts and bus operators also call for stroke lights on the roof of the bus.

Notes

1.Drive-in theater 汽车电影院：一般建在一大块空地上，竖起一个巨大的屏幕，来看电影的人只要把车头对着屏幕停下，通过特制的高保真电影声响装置，则可以十分清晰地听到电影配音及音乐，在车中欣赏电影。在汽车电影院附近，一般设有咖啡馆，可以买了咖啡坐在车中边看边喝。目前全美已有 4 000 多家这样的汽车电影院。

2.*Fast & Furious*《速度与激情》: 以赛车为主题的系列电影。其片名恰如其分的点出了这类电影的两大元素：以各种名牌跑车狂飙于公路的激情，还有体验着超过 200km/h 的极限速度。《速度与激情》系列电影从 2001 年第一集诞生至今，培养了一大批陪伴剧中各位主角亡命狂奔十年之久的狂热粉丝。2009 年上映的《速度与激情 4》更是在全球席卷了 3.5 亿美元票房。导演林诣彬也凭借该系列的热卖成为好莱坞的新锐华裔导演；截至 2013 年底，已更新至第 6 部。

3.*Transformers*《变形金刚》: 一部基于"变形金刚"玩具产品改编的 2007 年美国科幻动作片。这部集合了计算机动画和真人演出的电影由迈克尔·贝执导，斯蒂芬·斯皮尔伯格出任执行制片人，是《变形金刚》系列真人电影的开山之作。希亚·拉博夫在片中扮演一个名叫萨姆·维特维奇（Sam Witwicky）的少年，因机缘巧合而卷入了英勇的汽车人和邪恶的霸天虎之间的战争，后两者是两派来自同一个外星球但相互对立的机械生命体，可以变形成人类生活中常见的机械。霸天虎一欲夺得火种源，这种东西拥有赋予机器生命的力量，而且变形金刚也正是由火种源所创，霸天虎希望可以将其用来在地球上建立一个机器军团，而汽车人则要想方设法阻止对方。

4.Chevrolet 雪佛兰：美国通用汽车公司（General Motors，GM）旗下的一个汽车品牌，1911 年 11 月 3 日创立，创始人为威廉・杜兰特（William C. Durant）和路易斯・雪佛兰（Louis Chevrolet）。雪佛兰也被称为 Chevy，1918 年被通用汽车并购，现在为通用汽车旗下最为国际化和大众化的品牌。雪佛兰的车型品种非常广泛，从小型轿车到大型四门轿车，从厢式车到大型皮卡，甚至从越野车到跑车，雪佛兰几乎生产消费者所需要的任何一种车型。

Unit 3 Laws and Regulations on Automobiles

Concerning the roadway safety, the environmental issues, and car consumers' rights, the American government and Congress have drafted and passed many traffic and safety laws and regulations to ensure the citizens' safety on the road, relative acts to reduce the pollution to the environment, and recall system and lemon laws to guarantee the consumers' right.

Traffic and Safety Laws and Regulations

Traffic crashes are the number-one killer of American under the age of 34, and a staggering 42,000 deaths are recorded each year on U.S. highways. Considering the high risks that driving may take to people, American federal and state government enacted laws and strict standards about automobiles in efforts to keep roadways safer.

National Traffic and Motor Vehicle Safety Act

The *National Traffic and Motor Vehicle Safety Act* were enacted in the United States in 1966 to empower the federal government to set and administer new safety standards for motor vehicles and road traffic safety. The Act was one of a number of initiatives by the government in response to increasing number of cars and associated fatalities and injuries on the road following a period when the number of people killed on the road had increased 6-fold and the number of vehicles was up 11-fold since 1925. The reduction of the rate of death attributable to motor-vehicle crashed in the United States represents the successful public health response to a great technologic advance of the 20th century—the motorization of America.

Federal Motor Vehicle Safety Standards

Federal Motor Vehicle Safety Standards[1]（FMVSS）are U.S. federal regulations specifying design, construction, performance, and durability requirements for motor vehicles and regulated safety-related components, systems, and design features. FMVSS, which embodies three categories: crash avoidance, crash worthiness, and post-crash survivability, are developed and enforced by the National Highway Traffic Safety Administration（**NHTSA**[2]）pursuant to statutory authorization in the form of the *National Traffic and Motor Vehicle Safety Act* of 1966.

SAFETEA

The *Safe, Accountable, Flexible, and Efficient Transportation Equity Act*: A Legacy for Users (SAFETEA-LU) was a funding and authorization bill that governed United States federal surface transportation spending. It was signed into law by President George W. Bush on August 10th, 2005, and expired on September 30th, 2009.

The $286.4 billion measure contained a host of provisions and earmarks intended to improve and maintain the surface transportation infrastructure in the United States, including the interstate highway system, transit systems around the country, bicycling and pedestrian facilities, and freight rail operations. Congress renewed its funding formulas ten times after its expiration date, until replacing the bill with *Moving Ahead for Progress in the 21st Century Act* in 2012.

Environmental Policy

With the rapid development of American economy, environment problems were coming along with the blooming industry and were getting worse and worse, which lead to people's great concerns on this issue. Motor vehicles contribute a great deal to air pollution. Harmful chemicals such as nitrogen oxide, hydrocarbons, carbon monoxide and sulfur dioxide are released from motor vehicles. Some of these also react with sunlight to produce photochemical. These harmful substances change the climate, alter ocean PH and include toxins that may cause cancers, birth defects or respiratory illness. Thus, a series of acts had been enacted since the 1950s.

The Air Pollution Control Act of 1955[3] was the first United States Clean Air Act enacted by Congress to address the national environmental problem of air pollution on July 14th, 1955. This Act was the culmination of much research done on fuel emissions by the federal government in the 1930s and 1940s. A replacement, the *United States Clean Air Act of 1963*, was enacted to substitute the *Air Pollution Control Act of 1955*. A decade later, the *Motor Vehicle Air Pollution Control Act* was enacted to focus more specifically on automotive emission standards.

The *Motor Vehicle Air Pollution Control Act* is a 1965 amendment to the *U.S. Clean Air Act of 1963*. The amendment set the first federal vehicle emissions standards, beginning with the 1968 models. These standards were reductions from the 1963 emissions: 72% reduction for hydrocarbons, 56% reduction for crankcase hydrocarbons. The impact the regulatory standards will have on air quality in the future, as well as the potential characteristics of the vehicle fleet can be analyzed with the use of roadway air dispersion models.

Automobiles also play a great role in environment pollution as a main source of noise pollution. In 1972, the Congress enacted the **Noise Control Act**[4] which is a statute initiating a federal program of regulating noise pollution with the intent of protecting human health and minimizing annoyance of noise to the general public. The Act established mechanisms of setting emission standards for virtually every source of noise, including motor vehicles, aircraft, certain types of heating, ventilation, and air-conditioning equipment and major appliances.

Recall System

An automobile recall is a way for a manufacturer to tell you that there could be something about your car or truck that presents a risk of injury or property damage. American automobile recall system was initiated during the 1960s when safety issues led to striker government regulation of the auto industry, and its establishment spurred in part by **Ralph Nader**[5] and his book: *Unsafe at Any Speed: The Designed-in Dangers of the American Automobiles*. Under his influence and the social pressure, Congress passed the *National Traffic and Motor Vehicle Safety Act*, which authorized the U.S. Department of Transportation's National Highway Traffic Safety Administration (NHTSA) to set national safety standards and to order an auto manufacturer to repair safety-related defects at no cost to the consumer. Even if the fix is something as minor as a missing washer or a faulty electrical connection, the manufacturer stands to lose millions of dollars in the process. How much it may cost depends on the number of cars and trucks affected by the recall, the cost of the replacement parts and the time it takes a technician to make the repair. Since the enforcement of recall regulations, 211.5 billion cars and over 24 million tires have been recalled. In most of these recalling cases, manufacturers recalled the defected cars; while in the other cases, the consumers must defense themselves through NHYTSA or the court.

Automobile Warranties and Lemon Laws

Lemon Laws are American state laws that provide a remedy for purchasers of cars and other consumer goods in order to compensate for products that repeatedly fail to meet standards of quality and performance. Although there may be defective products of all sorts ranging from small electrical appliances to huge pieces of machinery, and there is even a "puppy lemon law", the term "lemon" is generally thought of as applying to defective vehicles such as automobile trucks, SUVs, and motorcycles. These vehicles and other goods are called "lemons".

The federal Lemon Law was enacted in 1975 and protects citizens of all states. State Lemon Laws vary by state and may not necessarily cover used or leased cars, and other goods. The rights offered to consumers by Lemon Laws may exceed the warranties expressed in purchase contracts.

Lemon law[6] is the common nickname for those laws, but each state has different names for the laws and acts. The Lemon Law of New York State was enacted in 1983. By 1990, 12 big car manufacturers had refunded 100 million dollars to the car purchasers who bought their new cars in this state. During the same period, the amount of the refund that the "Big Three" paid to the consumers was up to 1 billion dollars. The Lemon Laws not only guarantee the consumers' warranty rights but also lead the automobile industry to develop in a healthy competitive way.

Notes

1. Federal Motor Vehicle Safety Standards 美国联邦机动车安全标准：简称“FMVSS”，由美国运输部国家公路交通安全管理局制定，为汽车安全认证的法规依据。

2. NHTSA 美国高速公路安全管理局：美国高速公路安全管理局是美国政府部门汽车安全的最高主管机关。作为美国政府部门车辆安全监管的权威性机构，承担着确保各类车辆必须符合机动车安全法规要求的重要职责。NHTSA 主要是通过测定模拟人所承受的全面双向（正面和侧面）撞击，进行车辆安全性五颗星级的评定。

3. Air Pollution Control Act of 1955《大气污染控制法》：是美国国会在 1955 年颁布的旨在解决国家环境污染控制问题，是美国第一部清洁空气法案，后被 1963 年《清洁空气法》取代。

4. Noise Control Act《噪声控制法》：1972 年在美国国会通过，该法案将“改善环境使所有美国人从危害他们健康和福利的噪声中解脱出来”作为一项国家政策。这项法律在联邦和州、地方政府之间分配权利，联邦的首要职责是噪声源排放控制，州和其他行政部门保留对噪声源的使用和环境允许噪声水平进行控制的权利。

5. Ralph Nader 拉尔夫·纳德：美国律师，百万富翁，公民活动家，现代消费者权益之父，曾催生汽车召回制度，曾五次参加美国总统竞选，最成功的是 2000 年搅局，使得艾伯特·戈尔败于小布什。

6. Lemon law 柠檬法：一种美国的消费者保护法，主要是在保障汽车买主的权益。柠檬法的名称起源于美国经济学家乔治·阿克罗夫（George A. Akerlof）所发表的一篇经济学论文，因为这缘故，对于出厂后有瑕疵问题的汽车，通常也会称呼其为柠檬车（Lemon Car）或直接就称为柠檬。

Unit 4 The Green Vehicle and Obama's Clean Energy Strategy

Energy supply security and global warming continue to challenge all countries around the world in terms of global economy and planet environment. Renewable energy technologies are being explored to meet the challenges of energy security and climate change, as well as to boost regional economic development. Automobiles emissions are estimated to increase by 84% to 2030. Key technologies such as hydrogen fuel cells, electric cars and biofuels are expected to contribute to emission reduction in the long run. In recent years, hydrogen electric and hybrid cars have been developed and demonstrated in global automotive exhibitions. Major car manufacturers are seeking leadership in future green vehicle markets.

The government and Congress have made great efforts to stimulate the development of green vehicles and efficient transportation by drafting bills and standards. When President Obama took office, both GM and Chrysler teetered on the brink of bankruptcy. Despite some public and congressional opposition, the president provided loans to the automobiles to prevent their collapse and provide them with time to restructure on the condition that the companies had to develop aggressive plans to return to viability by investing in energy-efficient cars. Both companies agreed to move towards a more fuel-efficient fleet.

On his seventh day in office, President Obama launched the development of the first improved fuel economy standards in 20 years. His administration, supported by 13 major auto companies, the United Auto Workers, the State of California, and environmentalists, promulgated rules to double automobile fuel economy by 2025 while slash carbon pollution by 6 billion tons. The modern standards will save drivers $8,200 in lower gasoline purchases over the life of their 2025 vehicle, and will reduce oil consumption by 2.2 million barrels per day.

In February 17th, 2009, President Barack Obama signed ***American Recovery and Reinvestment Act***[1] of 2009, commonly referred to as the stimulus or *The Recovery Act*. It was an economic stimulus package enacted by the 111th United States Congress in February 2009. The approximate cost of the package was estimated to be $787 billion at the time of passage, later revised to $831 billion between 2009 and 2019. Large amount of the investment was put into energy efficiency and renewable energy research.

Another bill passed by Obama administration was the American ***Clean Energy and Security Act of* 2009**[2] (ACESA), which was an energy bill that would have established a variant of an emissions trading plan. The bill was approved by the House of Representatives on June 26th, 2009 but was defeated in the Senate. This bill subsidizes new clean energy technologies and energy efficiency, including renewable energy sources and energy ($90 billion in new subsidies by 2015), carbon capture and sequestration ($60 billion), electric and other advanced technology vehicles ($20 billion), and basic scientific research and development ($20 billion).

Americans love cars. They have always cherished personal freedom and mobility, rugged individualism and masculine force. The automobile traveled faster than the speed of reason; it promised to make everyone a pathfinder to a better life. It was the vehicle of personal democracy, acting as a social leveling force, granting more and more people a wide range of personal choices—where to travel, where to work and live, where to seek personal pleasure and social recreation. Unquestionably, the automobile was one of the most significant technologies in twentieth-century American life, for the car has so thoroughly shaped the country's history, economy, environment, law system, and culture. And in the future, the exploration of clean energy will definitely be an important part not only in American automobile industry but in the whole world.

Notes

1. *American Recovery and Reinvestment Act*《美国复兴与再投资法案》: 由美国总统奥巴马于2009年签署生效，通过高达7 870亿美元的政府投资来振兴美国经济。这其中有大量资金被投入到清洁能源以及可再生能源的研究与开发当中。

2. *Clean Energy and Security Act of 2009* 2009年《美国清洁能源及安全法案》: 2009年6月26日在美国众议院获得通过。这是美国颁布的第一部关于温室气体减排的法案。《法案》的主要目的是减少对外能源依赖、减少温室气体排放、刺激美国经济复苏。该法案主要包括了清洁能源、提高能源效率、减缓全球变暖及向清洁能源经济转型等四方面主要内容。

References

[1] WEISS D J. President Obama's clean energy progress: how the top 10 energy priorities fared during his first term[EB/OL]. [2016-05-22].http://www.americanprogress.org/wp-content/uploads/2013/01/ObamaFirstTermEnergy1.pdf.

[2] LUTZ R C. On the road to nowhere? California's car culture [J]. California History, 2000: 50-55.

[3] ZHANG FANGZHU, PHILIP COOKE. The green vehicle trend: electric, plug-in hybrid or hydrogen fuel cell? [EB/OL]. [2016-05-22].http://www.dime-eu.org/files/active/0/Cooke-09-Fang-Green-vehicle-Review.pdf.

[4] WIKIPEDIA. American Recovery and Reinvestment Act of 2009 [EB/OL]. [2016-05-22]. http://en.wikipedia.org/wiki/American_Recovery_and_Reinvestment_Act_of_2009.

[5] 李蘅 . 轮子上的美国汽车文化 [J]. 中国机电日报 , 2002(12): 50-52.

[6] 孙龙林 . 浅析能源政策下的美国汽车工业 [J]. 汽车工业研究 , 2011(10):45-48.

[7] 余卓,于善虎. 美国汽车产品市场准入制度 [J]. 广东交通职业技术学院学报 ,2010(6)23-25.